BROADMAN COMMENTS 1996-97

52 Ready-To-Teach Bible Study Lessons

BROADMAN COMMENTS 1996-97

52 Ready-To-Teach Bible Study Lessons

ROBERT J. DEAN
J. B. FOWLER, JR.
JAMES E. TAULMAN

Based on the International Sunday School Lessons

Each Plan Includes These Sections: Studying the Bible · Applying the Bible · Teaching the Bible

Nashville, Tennessee

4217-41
ISBN: 0-8054-1741-9

Dewey Decimal Classification:
Subject Heading: SUNDAY SCHOOL LESSONS—COMMENTARIES

ISSN: 0068-2721

POSTMASTER: Send address change to *Broadman Comments,*
Customer Service Center, 127 Ninth Avenue, North
Nashville, Tennessee 37234

Library of Congress Catalog Card Number: 45-437
Printed in the United States of America

WRITERS

STUDYING THE BIBLE

Robert J. Dean continues the theological traditions of *Broadman Comments* while adding his own fresh insights. Dean is retired from the Baptist Sunday School Board, and is a Th.D. graduate of New Orleans Seminary

APPLYING THE LESSON

J. B. Fowler, Jr. is a freelance writer from San Antonio, Texas. He was formerly editor of *Baptist New Mexican* of the New Mexico Baptist Convention.

TEACHING THE CLASS

James E. Taulman is a freelance writer in Nashville, Tennessee. Prior to that, Taulman was an editor of adult Sunday school materials for the Baptist Sunday School Board.

ABBREVIATIONS AND TRANSLATIONS

Scripture passages are from the authorized King James Version of the Bible. Other translations used:

Contents

FIRST QUARTER
God's People Face Judgment

SECOND QUARTER
New Testament Personalities

THIRD QUARTER
Hope for the Future (1 and 2 Thessalonians, Revelation)

FOURTH QUARTER
Guidance for Ministry

A Call to Faithfulness

Alternative lesson for January 19th

God's People Face Judgment

INTRODUCTION

This quarter's studies deal with the period from the fall of Samaria in 722 B.C. to the fall of Jerusalem in 587 B.C. During this period several efforts were made by kings and prophets to reform God's people and avert tragedy. This series of lessons explores the meaning of sin, judgment, repentance, and grace.

Unit I, "Responses to Wrong," tells of the reforms of Kings Hezekiah and Josiah. God called Jeremiah as a prophet to proclaim God's word of judgment on the sins of Judah. Habakkuk wrestled with dilemmas of injustice, but he committed himself to continue to rejoice in the Lord no matter what happened.

Unit II, "Judah's Internal Decay," draws on the prophecies of Jeremiah and Ezekiel to define the nature of Judah's sins. Jeremiah exposed the insincerity of his people's faith and their self-deception about security and peace. Ezekiel condemned rebellion and predicted disaster, but he held out hope for individuals who chose to obey God.

Unit III, "The Fall of Jerusalem," deals with Ezekiel's prediction of the fall, with the account in 2 Kings of the fall, and with reactions to this terrible event. The Book of Lamentations gives a vivid description of the fall of the city and the personal anguish that resulted. Ezekiel held out hope of eventual renewal through the grace and power of God.

September

1

1996

Holding Fast to the Lord

Background Passage: 2 Kings 18–20
Focal Passages: 2 Kings 18:1–8; 20:16–21

The reign of Hezekiah (hez ih KIGH uh) is treated at great length because he was a good king who trusted in the Lord and also because of his association with Isaiah. (Most of 2 Kings 18–20 is also found in Isaiah 37–39.) Generally speaking, Hezekiah and Isaiah shared the same spirit of trust in the Lord. On a few occasions, Isaiah was forced to condemn Hezekiah; however, these were the exception rather than the rule. The emphasis in the Bible passage is on Hezekiah's trust in holding fast to the Lord.

Study Aim: *To identify evidences of Hezekiah's trust in holding fast to the Lord*

STUDYING THE BIBLE

OUTLINE AND SUMMARY

I. Hezekiah and His Reforms (2 Kings 18:1–8)
1. Good King Hezekiah (18:1–3)
2. Hezekiah's reforms (18:4)
3. Hezekiah's trust in the Lord (18:5–8)
II. The Assyrian Threat (2 Kings 18:9–37)
1. The fall of Israel (18:9–12)
2. Tribute to Assyria (18:13–16)
3. Jerusalem threatened (18:17–37)
III. Jerusalem Delivered (2 Kings 19:1–37)
1. Isaiah's reassurance to Hezekiah (19:1–7)
2. Hezekiah's prayer (19:8–19)
3. Isaiah's prophecy and its fulfillment (19:20–37)
IV. Hezekiah's Illness and Healing (2 Kings 20:1–11)
V. Hezekiah and the Envoys from Babylon (2 Kings 20:12–19)
1. Revealing Judah's treasures (20:12–15)
2. Prophecy of captivity in Babylon (20:16–18)
3. Hezekiah's response (20:19)
VI. Hezekiah's Achievements (2 Kings 20:20–21)

Hezekiah was a good king (18:1–3) who sought to destroy idolatry (18:4). His steadfast trust in the Lord resulted in the Lord's blessings (18:5–8). During Hezekiah's reign, the Assyrians (uh SIRH ih uns) defeated the Northern Kingdom (18:9–12). When the Assyrians captured some cities in Judah, Hezekiah paid tribute to them (18:13–16). The Assyrian army threatened to capture Jerusalem (18:17–37). When Hezekiah appealed to Isaiah, the prophet reassured him (19:1–7). After the Assyrians continued to send their threats, Hezekiah prayed for deliverance (19:8–19). Isaiah's prophecy of deliverance came to pass (19:20–27). When Hezekiah was deathly ill, God responded to his prayers by lengthening his life (20:1–11). After Hezekiah showed Judah's treasures to envoys from Babylon (BAB ih lahn; 20:12–15), Isaiah predicted Judah's Babylonian captivity (20:16–18). Hezekiah declared that God's ways are good (20:19). Among Hezekiah's accomplishments was a water system for Jerusalem (20:20–21).

I. Hezekiah and His Reforms (2 Kings 18:1–8)

1. Good King Hezekiah (18:1–3)

1 Now it came to pass in the third year of Hoshea [hoh SHE uh] son of Elah [EE luh] king of Israel, that Hezekiah the son of Ahaz [AY haz] king of Judah began to reign.

2 Twenty and five years old was he when he began to reign; and he reigned twenty and nine years in Jerusalem. His mother's name also was Abi [AY bigh], the daughter of Zechariah [zak uh RIGH uh].

3 And he did that which was right in the sight of the LORD, according to all that David his father did.

Hezekiah began to reign over Judah during the final years of their sister kingdom to the north (2 Kings 17). The most notable fact about Hezekiah was that he did what was right in the sight of the Lord. This was in striking contrast to most of Judah's kings. For example, Ahaz, Hezekiah's father, "did not *that which* was right in the sight of the LORD his God" (2 Kings 16:2).

How do we explain an evil father having a good son? Perhaps Hezekiah had a godly mother. All we know of her is her name, but she may have been a person of faith. Isaiah had begun his ministry as Ahaz began his sixteen-year reign (Isa. 1:1; 6:1; 2 Kings 16:2). Thus Isaiah was around when Hezekiah was growing up.

Everyone is exposed to good and bad influences, and each person decides which influence to follow. Hezekiah decided not to follow the example of his father but to listen to people like Isaiah. Sadly, Hezekiah's own son Manasseh (muh NASS uh) rejected the example of his father and the words of Isaiah (2 Kings 21:1–18).

2. Hezekiah's reforms (18:4)

4 He removed the high places, and brake the images, and cut down the groves, and brake in pieces the brasen serpent that Moses had made: for unto those days the children of Israel did burn incense to it: and he called it Nehushtan [nih HUHSH tan].

Judah had adopted the practices of pagan people. "High places" were Canaanite (KAY nuhn ight) shrines to Baal (BAY uhl; 2 Kings 16:4). The word "groves" is literally "Asherah" (ASH uh ruh), the female consort of Baal. This shows that Hezekiah attacked the remnants of Baal worship. He also set out to destroy other expressions of pagan worship.

Verse 4 reveals a striking example of the people's bent toward idolatry. They were even worshiping the brazen serpent that the Lord had used in the wilderness as a sign of divine deliverance (see Num. 21:4–9; John 3:14–15).

3. Hezekiah's trust in the Lord (18:5–8)

5 He trusted in the LORD God of Israel; so that after him was none like him among all the kings of Judah, nor any that were before him.

6 For he clave to the LORD, and departed not from following him, but kept his commandments, which the LORD commanded Moses.

7 And the LORD was with him; and he prospered whithersoever he went forth: and he rebelled against the king of Assyria, and served him not.

8 He smote the Philistines [fih LISS teens], even unto Gaza [GAH zuh], and the borders thereof, from the tower of the watchmen to the fenced city.

Verse 5 uses the usual Hebrew word for "trust" to describe Hezekiah's uncommon reliance on God. At least, such trust was uncommon among the kings of Judah. The word "clave" in verse 6 is the same word used in Genesis 2:24 for the oneness of a husband and wife. Hezekiah held fast to the Lord and joined himself together with the Lord. Verse 6 also stresses that Hezekiah's trust in God was expressed in obedience to the commands of God.

Verse 7 adds that "the LORD was with him." This closeness was the result of trusting in, cleaving to, and obeying the Lord. The evidence of the Lord's abiding presence was the success of Hezekiah in achieving his objectives. Specifically, the king of tiny Judah found the courage to stand against the power of the mighty Assyrian king. Hezekiah's armies also prevailed in battles with their longtime enemies, the Philistines.

II. The Assyrian Threat (2 Kings 18:9–37)

1. The fall of Israel (18:9–12)

During Hezekiah's reign, the Northern Kingdom was overrun by the Assyrians. The survivors were carried away and transplanted in other lands (see 2 Kings 17).

2. Tribute to Assyria (18:13–16)

After destroying Israel, the Assyrians swarmed into Judah. After the Assyrians captured outlying cities, Hezekiah sent gold and silver as tribute to the Assyrian king.

3. Jerusalem threatened (18:17–37)

The king of Assyria sent messengers to insist that Hezekiah surrender. The messengers warned against relying on Egypt for help. The messengers spoke loudly enough to be heard by defenders on the walls of Jerusalem. The Assyrians warned the Judeans that they would suffer and die if they allowed their king and their God to deceive them into resisting the might of Assyria.

III. Jerusalem Delivered (2 Kings 19:1–37)

1. Isaiah's reassurance to Hezekiah (19:1–7)

Hezekiah sent messengers to Isaiah. The prophet told Hezekiah's officials not to be afraid of the Assyrians because God would send them back to their country.

2. Hezekiah's prayer (19:8–19)

After the Assyrians sent another threatening message, the Judean king spread it before the Lord and prayed for deliverance.

3. Isaiah's prophecy and its fulfillment (19:20–37)

The Lord's response was to send a message through Isaiah to Hezekiah. God was in control of events, including the boastful Assyrians. God promised that the land that was now threatened with war and famine would bloom and bear fruit. As for the king of Assyria, he would not shoot an arrow against the city that God defended. Thousands of the Assyrians died in their camp, and the king returned home, where he was assassinated.

IV. Hezekiah's Illness and Healing (2 Kings 20:1–11)

When Hezekiah became ill, Isaiah told him that he would die. Hezekiah prayed earnestly that he might live. Isaiah returned to assure the king that God had added fifteen years to his life.

V. Hezekiah and the Envoys from Babylon (2 Kings 20:12–19)

1. Revealing Judah's treasures (20:12–15)

When envoys from Babylon arrived in Jerusalem, Hezekiah welcomed them and showed them Judah's storehouses of treasures. When Isaiah quizzed Hezekiah about the visitors and Hezekiah's actions, the king related what he had done.

2. Prophecy of captivity in Babylon (20:16–18)

> 16 And Isaiah said unto Hezekiah, Hear the word of the LORD.
>
> 17 Behold, the days come, that all that is in thine house, and that which thy fathers have laid up in store unto this day, shall be carried into Babylon: nothing shall be left, saith the LORD.
>
> 18 And of thy sons that shall issue from thee, which thou shalt beget, shall they take away; and they shall be eunuchs in the palace of the king of Babylon.

After Hezekiah had shown the treasures to the Babylonians, Isaiah predicted that the time would come when Babylonians would seize all Judah's treasures. Isaiah also predicted that Hezekiah's royal descendants would be taken to Babylon and become eunuchs in the palace of the king of Babylon. The Hebrew word "eunuch" sometimes referred to a literal eunuch; at other times, the word was used of a government official (Gen. 37:36; 39:1).

Assyria was the dominant power in the time of Hezekiah and Isaiah. Isaiah, however, warned that when Babylon became the dominant power, the Babylonians would defeat Judah. Many years after the time of Isaiah. Babylon defeated Judah and carried her king and treasures away (2 Kings 24:8–16).

3. Hezekiah's response (20:19)

> 19 Then said Hezekiah unto Isaiah, Good is the word of the Lord which thou hast spoken. And he said, Is it not good, if peace and truth be in my days?

There are two ways of understanding Hezekiah's words. According to the first view, he was unconcerned about what later generations would endure—as long as he personally would not have to endure it. According to the second view, verse 19 expresses trust that God's ways have a good purpose and gratitude that Hezekiah's own generation would know peace and security.

VI. Hezekiah's Achievements (2 Kings 20:20–21)

20 And the rest of the acts of Hezekiah, and all his might, and how he made a pool, and a conduit, and brought water into the city, are they not written in the book of the chronicles of the kings of Judah?

21 And Hezekiah slept with his fathers: and Manasseh his son reigned in his stead.

Among Hezekiah's other achievements was the construction of a water system for Jerusalem. This and other deeds of Hezekiah are recorded in 2 Chronicles 29–32.

APPLYING THE BIBLE

1. Trust anyone under thirty? Several years ago, an internationally read magazine printed an article asking the question, "Can you trust anyone under thirty?" The article set me to thinking: John Keats wrote "Ode to a Grecian Urn" and "Endymion" before he died at 26; William Cullen Bryant, the father of American poetry, wrote "Thanatopsis" when he was about twenty; Thomas Jefferson was less than thirty when the Senate had to suspend its rules so he could be seated and was only thirty-four when he wrote the "Declaration of Independence."

Patriot Nathan Hale was only twenty-one when he cried, "All I regret is that I have but one life to give for my country." The Pilgrim fathers averaged only twenty-six years of age. Joan of Arc led France to victory when she was just sixteen. Johannes Brahms was only twenty when he composed piano pieces that are still being played today.

Hezekiah was only twenty-five when he ascended the throne of Judah, "and he did that which was right in the sight of the LORD" (v. 3).

2. In spite of. Many people have accomplished much in spite of difficulties. In spite of having only a year of formal schooling, Abraham Lincoln became president of the United States and freed four million black slaves with his Emancipation Proclamation. In spite of suffering twelve years in Bedford, England's jail, John Bunyan used his time well in writing *The Pilgrim's Progress*. In spite of a drunken father and deafness that set in at twenty-eight, so that by fifty-nine he could communicate only by writing, Beethoven composed enduring masterpieces. In spite of having only three months of formal education and near deafness, Thomas A. Edison patented more inventions than any other person in history.

And in spite of idolatry and turmoil within Judah and crises outside of Judah, Hezekiah stood by his convictions "and clave to the LORD, and departed not from following him" (18:6). He is a good example of one who served God faithfully and is listed in the genealogy of Jesus (Matt. 1:9–10 "Ezekias"). He left a good example for us to emulate.

3. Touching others.

My life shall touch a dozen lives
Before the day is done;
Leave countless marks for good or ill,
Ere sets the evening sun.
So this the wish I always wish,
The prayer I ever pray;
Lord, may my life help other lives
It touches by the way.
—Anonymous

4. We are witnesses for good or evil. We probably don't understand the scope of our influence as Christians for good or evil. People are watching us and listening to us all the time and our behavior points them to Christ or away from Him.

An incident in the life of the late President Theodore Roosevelt illustrates this. On an extended vacation one summer, Roosevelt met an unusual man everyone called "Uncle Joe." As Roosevelt was leaving after a pleasant hour of visiting with Uncle Joe, the old man said, "Mr. President, we have a lovely little church here in our village; but I haven't seen you in our services any Sunday you have been here. I know you are a Christian gentleman, and your coming would mean so much to our people."

Roosevelt said he felt thoroughly chastised and humbled and promised he would be there the following Sunday, and he never missed another Sunday service when he was there on vacation. Later, Roosevelt confessed he was ashamed of himself before his Heavenly Father for being such a poor witness for Him.

Hezekiah ruled Judah for twenty-five years; and, although he was far from perfect, he strove to serve God faithfully and honor Him daily (vv. 5–7).

5. A man sent from God. John Wesley, the founder of Methodism, once preached the gospel among the miners of Cornwall, England. Many people and villages were transformed.

A stranger visiting the Cornwall district once asked about the picture of Wesley he saw hanging in so many homes, and he was told: "There was a man sent from God whose name was John."

Hezekiah was a man sent from God who made a mighty impact on Judah and her surrounding neighbors in a most critical period of Judah's history. God used Hezekiah mightily. In doing God's will faithfully we, too, will make a contribution to the lives of others that will live on long after we are gone.

TEACHING THE BIBLE

- *Main Idea:* God supports those who trust Him and hold fast to Him.
- *Suggested Teaching Aim:* To encourage adults to trust God and to hold fast to Him.

A TEACHING OUTLINE

1. Introduce the Bible study by sharing an illustration.
2. Enlist members to help you in summarizing and presenting the material.
3. Use lecture and group discussion to search for biblical truth.
4. Use brainstorming to help members apply the Scripture to their lives.

Introduce the Bible Study

Use the illustration "In spite of" from "Applying the Bible" to introduce the Bible study.

Search for Biblical Truth

IN ADVANCE, prepare a lesson outline poster like the one on page 2 and display it on the focal wall. Also enlist one or more members to summarize the following segments: 2 Kings 18:9–37; 2 Kings 19:1–37; and 2 Kings 20:1–11. Give the member(s) the material from "Studying the Bible." Call on them at the appropriate time.

Since the background passage covers so much material, enlist two readers to read alternately the eleven statements of the summary to introduce the lesson at this point.

Call for a volunteer to read 2 Kings 18:13. Using the *Holman Bible Dictionary* or another Bible dictionary, give a brief summary of Hezekiah's life. Point out that Hezekiah and Isaiah lived at approximately the same time.

Ask a volunteer to read 18:4 and let members list Hezekiah's reforms. Explain "high places," "images," "groves," and "brasen serpent." (See "Studying the Bible" for help.)

Ask a volunteer to read 18:5–8. Ask: What successes did Hezekiah have? (Prospered, rebelled against Assyria, defeated Philistines.) What in these verses indicates why he could do this? (He trusted, clave to, departed not from, kept commandments of, the Lord).

DISCUSS: What would you have to do to trust, cleave to, depart not from, and keep the commandments of the Lord? How would this change the way you live? Would the United States experience the same benefits Israel did if their leaders responded to the Lord the same as Hezekiah? Why?

Call on the enlisted member(s) to summarize 2 Kings 18:9–20:15.

Ask a volunteer to read 20:16–18. Set the context for these verses by explaining Hezekiah's foolish response to the Babylonians. Point out the approximate date of Hezekiah's reign (716–687 B.C.) and that although Jerusalem did not fall until a hundred years after his death, Isaiah's prophecy was fulfilled.

Call for a volunteer to read 20:19. Ask members what they think Hezekiah's response meant. Use "Studying the Bible" to explain two possible meanings.

Call for a volunteer to read 20:20–21. If you have access to the *Holman Bible Dictionary*, show the photograph of the tunnel Hezekiah constructed to bring water into the city from the Gihon (GIGH hahn) Spring outside the city. Point out that the reference to the "book of the chronicles of the kings of Judah" refers to 2 Chronicles 29–32.

Give the Truth a Personal Focus

Ask: Do you believe that God still blesses those who trust in Him? How? Why?

Ask members to suggest steps they can take to increase their trust in the Lord. List these on a chalkboard or a large sheet of paper.

Suggest members select one of these ways and commit themselves to trust God in this area. Close in a prayer of commitment.

September

8

1996

Obeying God's Commands

Basic Passage: 2 Kings 22:1–23:20

Focal Passage: 2 Kings 23:1–8*a*

Hezekiah (hez ih KIGH uh) and Josiah (joh SIGH uh) were Judah's two best kings. Hezekiah is remembered for holding fast to the Lord when Assyria threatened to overrun Judah. Josiah is remembered for a religious revival inspired by a new awareness of God's Word. Two wicked kings—Manasseh (muh NASS uh) and Amon (AY mahn)—reigned between Hezekiah and Josiah (see 2 Kings 21). Their evil policies had polluted the temple and almost destroyed the worship of the Lord. Josiah tried to undo their evil and to restore Judah to obedience to God's commands.

Study Aim: *To recognize Josiah's role in seeking to lead Judah to obey God's commands*

STUDYING THE BIBLE

OUTLINE AND SUMMARY

I. King Josiah (2 Kings 22:1–2)

II. The Book of the Law (2 Kings 22:3–20)

1. **Repair of the temple (22:3–7)**
2. **Discovery of the book of the Law (22:8–10)**
3. **Josiah's initial response (22:11–13)**
4. **Huldah's prophecy (22:14–20)**

III. Josiah's Religious Revival (2 Kings 23:1–20)

1. **Public reading of the book of the covenant (23:1–2)**
2. **Renewing the covenant (23:3)**
3. **Purification of religious life (23:4–20)**

King Josiah did what was right in the sight of the Lord (22:1–2). He ordered extensive repairs to the temple (22:3–7). The book of the Law was found in the temple and read to the king (22:8–10). Josiah was deeply disturbed because he realized that God's wrath was directed against the sins of Judah (22:11–13). The prophetess Huldah (HUHL duh) confirmed that God would punish Judah, but she commended Josiah (22:14–20). Josiah read the book to the people (23:1–2) and led them to renew their covenant with God (23:3). Then Josiah launched a vigorous campaign to root out all vestiges of past idolatry (23:4–20).

I. King Josiah (2 Kings 22:1–2)

Josiah's father Amon died young (2 Kings 21:19–26); therefore, Josiah was only eight years old when he became king. Like Hezekiah, Josiah proved to be a worthy descendant of their forefather David (compare verse 2 with 2 Kings 18:3).

II. The Book of the Law (2 Kings 22:3–20)

1. Repair of the temple (22:3–7)

The temple had been desecrated by Manasseh during his long reign of fifty-five years (2 Kings 21:4–5,7). Josiah sent his scribe Shaphan (SHAY fan) to Hilkiah (hil KIGH uh) the high priest with a message about the temple. Josiah authorized extensive repairs to be made in the temple. Workmen were to be hired and the work done so thoroughly and honestly that no financial accounting would be needed.

2. Discovery of the book of the Law (22:8–10)

Shaphan reported to Hilkiah that he had found the book of the Law in the house of the Lord. Shaphan reported to Josiah on the progress of the project to repair the temple, including the finding of a book. Shaphan read the book to Josiah.

3. Josiah's initial response (22:11–13)

When Josiah heard the reading of the book of the Law, he tore his clothes in grief and conviction. He dispatched Hilkiah, Shaphan, and others to inquire of the Lord about the plight of Judah. The king felt that God's wrath was directed against Judah for their failure to obey the commands of God in the book.

4. Huldah's prophecy (22:14–20)

The king's delegation consulted Huldah, a prophetess, about the situation; and she delivered God's message. The Lord said that the sins of Judah had become so great that His wrath against Jerusalem could not be quenched. The Lord commended Josiah because he had humbled himself.

III. Josiah's Religious Revival (2 Kings 23:1–20)

1. Public reading of the book of the covenant (23:1–2)

> 1 And the king sent, and they gathered unto him all the elders of Judah and of Jerusalem.
>
> 2 And the king went up into the house of the LORD, and all the men of Judah and all the inhabitants of Jerusalem with him, and the priests, and the prophets, and all the people, both small and great: and he read in their ears all the words of the book of the covenant which was found in the house of the LORD.

When we read the account of 2 Kings 22–23, we wonder: "What exactly was the book that was found? How could it have been lost?" The book is described as "the book of the law" (22:8,11) and "the book of the covenant" (23:2). Although 2 Kings never tells us exactly what it was, we assume it was all or part of the first five books of the Bible.

Many Bible scholars think that the book—or actually, scroll—was from Deuteronomy. Three factors support this view. First, Josiah's words in 2 Kings 22:13 and Huldah's words in 2 Kings 22:19 sound like the curses against disobedience in Deuteronomy 28. Second, the words of covenant renewal in 2 Kings 23:3 ("with all their heart and all their soul") sound like Deuteronomy 6:5. Third, the attacks on idolatry and the positive aspects of Josiah's revival have parallels in Deuteronomy.

How could such a valuable document have become lost? Keep in mind that this was centuries before printing was invented. Scrolls were copied by hand. Thus there were fewer copies than in the age of printing. We should not overlook the influence of Manasseh's fifty-five-year reign, during which the evil king did everything possible to stamp out worship of the Lord and to replace it with various forms of idolatry. During those years, many believers were killed (2 Kings 21:16). Apparently, copies of the Law were either destroyed or hidden during those dark years.

Josiah's first action, therefore, was to summon all the people to the temple to hear the king read from the newly found book of the covenant. Verse 2 elaborates on the groups who came to hear the reading. The congregation included not only the prophets and priests but also the inhabitants of Judah and of Jerusalem. The prominent citizens were there, but so were the common people.

Verse 2 is very much like what happened after the people returned from Babylonian (bab uh LOH nih un) exile; and Ezra read "the book of the law of Moses" to men, women, and children (Neh. 8:1–3). We know from the New Testament that synagogue services included the reading of the Scriptures (Luke 4:16–20; Acts 13:15). We also know that the great revivals of Christian history have included the public reading of the Word of God.

2. Renewing the covenant (23:3)

> 3 And the king stood by a pillar, and made a covenant before the LORD, to walk after the LORD, and to keep his commandments and his testimonies and his statutes with all their heart and all their soul, to perform the words of this covenant that were written in this book. And all the people stood to the covenant.

The reading of the book of the covenant was followed by a ceremony in which Josiah led the people in renewing the covenant. The reading of the book had shown them the distinctive covenant that God had made with the descendants of Israel. The people of Israel were called to a distinctive faith in the one true God and to a distinctive way of life involving obedience to His commands. The renewal ceremony emphasized the obligation of the people to walk in the Lord's way by obeying all His commands with all their heart and soul.

No generation of Israelites could afford to take the covenant for granted. Each generation had to commit themselves anew to the covenant. Often the same generation had to renew their covenant relationship and obligations. Indeed the Book of Deuteronomy tells how Moses led the second generation out of Egypt to renew the covenant that God had made with their parents at Mount Sinai (SIGH nay ih).

Under the new covenant, each person must accept or reject God's covenant. Our response involves trust and obedience. Because the heart of this covenant is a personal relationship with God, such a relationship must be expressed daily and renewed continually.

3. Purification of religious life (23:4–20)

> 4 And the king commanded Hilkiah the high priest, and the priests of the second order, and the keepers of the door, to bring

forth out of the temple of the LORD all the vessels that were made for Baal, and for the grove, and for all the host of heaven: and he burned them without Jerusalem in the fields of Kidron [KID ruhn] and carried the ashes of them unto Bethel.

5 And he put down the idolatrous priests, whom the kings of Judah had ordained to burn incense in the high places in the cities of Judah, and in the places round about Jerusalem; them also that burned incense unto Baal, to the sun, and to the moon, and to the planets, and to all the host of heaven.

6 And he brought out the grove from the house of the LORD, without Jerusalem, unto the brook Kidron, and burned it at the brook Kidron, and stamped it small to powder, and cast the powder thereof upon the graves of the children of the people.

7 And he brake down the houses of the sodomites, that were by the house of the LORD, where the women wove hangings for the grove.

8 And he brought all the priests out of the cities of Judah, and defiled the high places where the priests had burned incense, from Geba [GHEE buh] to Beersheba [Bee ehr SHE buh].

These verses reveal the terrible extent of the idolatry that afflicted Judah and the zeal of Josiah in trying to destroy it. Much of the idolatry had to do with Baal worship. The word "grove" is literally "Asherah" (ASH uh ruh), the name of the female god of Baal religion. The word is sometimes translated "Ashtaroth" (ASH tuh rahth; Judg. 2:13; 1 Sam. 7:3–4). She was often worshiped as an image. Baal worship was a fertility religion that involved male and female prostitutes as an integral part of the religion.

Another form of idolatry involved worship of the sun, moon, and stars. Whereas Baal worship had its roots in Sidon (SIGH duhn) and Canaan (KAY nuhn), the worship of the heavenly host came from Assyria (uh SIRH ih uh) and Babylonia (bab uh LOH nih uh). When Manasseh built altars for such, he showed his subjection to Assyria. By the time of Josiah, the power of Assyria was waning; and the zealous young king could assert his independence by destroying the altars of Assyrian worship.

The idols were not only found in the local shrines ("high places") scattered throughout the land, but had taken over the temple itself. Josiah removed the altars of Baal worship and Assyrian worship from both the temple and the high places. He deposed the priests who had served at these pagan altars. He burned the image of Asherah at Kidron, pounded it to powder, and further defiled it by sprinkling the powder on graves—which the people considered unclean. Josiah destroyed the houses of the male prostitutes of Baal, which adjoined the temple. Josiah defiled all the high places where idolatry had been practiced.

Josiah zealously set out to destroy all the idols and to defile all the pagan places of worship in Judah and Israel. This included the valley where child sacrifice had been practiced (v. 10). He removed horses and chariots used in sun worship (v. 11). He destroyed idols set up by previous kings, including some that went back to the time of Solomon (vv. 12–14). Josiah also defiled the altar at Bethel, which had led to the doom of the Northern Kingdom (vv. 15–18). He destroyed the high places in Israel and killed the priests who had served there (vv. 19–20).

APPLYING THE BIBLE

1. Early commitment to Christ. One day in a seminary evangelism class, Professor Ray Summers asked all those who had accepted Christ before they were ten to raise their hands. By far the majority of those in the very large class raised their hands. Summers then stated that he and his wife prayed daily that their children would receive Christ as their Savior at the first recognition of their sin and guilt, not spending even one day in rebellion against God. What a prayer for parents to pray and what a marvelous ideal! But, unfortunately, the majority of parents today do not recognize their own need of Jesus let alone that of their children. To be sure, the children must be dealt with cautiously, but Solomon's admonition is still the best advice that can be given on behalf of an early commitment to Jesus: "Remember now thy Creator in the days of thy youth, while the evil days come not, nor the years draw nigh, when thou shalt say, I have no pleasure in them" (Eccles. 12:1).

"Good King Josiah" was one of those who sought the Lord early. Crowned king at the age of eight (2 Kings 22:1), he "began to seek after the God of David" in the eighth year of his reign (2 Chron. 34:3).

2. The lost Bible. The late Baptist historian Dr. Robert A. Baker in his book *A Summary of Christian History* writes: "Pope Innocent III (1198–1216) denounced the translation of the Scriptures to the language of the people, and the possession of Scriptures in the vernacular tongue was looked on as heresy."[1] But the word of God cannot be bound! Through the work of immortal, sacrificial believers such as Wycliffe, Tyndale, Luther, and others, the Bibles began to be put in the hands of Europeans all across the continent; and reformation resulted!

The same thing happened in the eighteenth year of Josiah's reign when a "book of the law" was found while repairs were being made on the temple (2 Kings 23:1). Scholars believe the lost book contained portions of Deuteronomy that called Israel to exclusive loyalty to Jehovah. Again, as the Scriptures were read, reformation resulted (23:1–25).

What do you suppose a diligent daily reading of God's Word could mean to our homes and nation today?

3. One who suffered to put the Scriptures in the hands of common people. We take our Bible for granted. It's easy to own a Bible, and we do not suffer for having one. Yet it was not always so. Many believers, whose crime was nothing more than loving the Word of God, were persecuted by the Roman Catholic Church. One of them was William Tyndale.

Born in England in 1494, Tyndale was one of the leaders of the Protestant Reformation. Determined to give the Bible to the people, he was forced into exile in 1535. With a bounty on his head, he taught himself Hebrew and worked six days a week from dawn to dusk for eleven years translating the Scriptures. Finally, the work was completed and Tyndale's finished Bible was smuggled into England. Tyndale was caught in 1536, and Henry VIII condemned him to be hanged. Before Tyndale went to the gallows, he prayed: "Lord, open the eyes of the king of England."

God answered his prayer, and in 1539 King Henry sent a royal decree encouraging all printers and publishers to publish the Scriptures for "the free and liberal use of the Bible in our native tongue."

Like Josiah of old, Tyndale was faithful to the Word of God. Pick up your Bible and look at it. Remember that Josiah, Tyndale, and others have given it to you at great cost. Then ask yourself: "How can I do less than love it and follow it?"

4. Keeping the Commandments. An early-day preacher was once confronted by one of the sophisticated ladies of his congregation, so it is told, who rebuked him for introducing new "rituals" into their worship service.

"And what new ritual is that?" asked the pastor. "Oh, I hear that you are now reading the Ten Commandments in the service," sniffed the parishioner.

"Is that all you heard?" asked the preacher. "But you need to understand that we have added a ritual that goes even further than that," replied the pastor. "I am telling our people that we ought to live by those Commandments."

When the lost book of the Law was discovered, Josiah not only read the Scriptures to the people but told them they must keep them.

The Ten Commandments are not ten suggestions. God still commands us to live by them in our lost, pagan world today.

TEACHING THE BIBLE

➧ *Main Idea:* God calls on us to remove idolatrous practices from our communities.

➧ *Suggested Teaching Aim:* To encourage members to take a positive role in helping to eliminate those things that are displeasing to God in their community.

A TEACHING OUTLINE

1. Use a collection of objects to introduce the lesson.

2. Use charts, lecture, and group discussion to study the Bible.

3. Use brainstorming to apply the Bible to life.

Introduce the Bible Study

Collect several objects, pictures, or relics that could be worshiped or are worshiped by certain religions. Include items that your class could worship (job, family, money, and so forth). Ask members which of these they worship. Point out that at times even good things (job, family) can become idols. Suggest that today's lesson will encourage them to take a positive role in helping to eliminate those things that are displeasing to God in their community.

Search for Biblical Truth

Enlist a member to present a monologue in which the person describes the events in the introduction and points I and II. If you choose not to do this, summarize these events in a brief lecture.

Ask a volunteer to read 2 Kings 23:1–2 and explain Josiah's actions. Explain that many Bible scholars suggest three reasons why they believe the scroll was Deuteronomy. On a chalkboard or a large sheet of paper, make the following chart:

	2 Kings	Deuteronomy
1.	22:13, 19	28:15–68
2.	23:3	6:5
3.	23:4, 6, 7, 14	7:5; 12:3; 16:21

Ask half of the class to look at the references in 2 Kings and the other half to look at the references in Deuteronomy. Point out that the references in number 3 refer only to the abolition of the groves or Asherim.

Using "Studying the Bible," explain how such an important document could have been lost. Call on a volunteer to read 23:3 and point out the people's renewal of the covenant.

DISCUSS: What value do periodic covenant-renewal services such as revivals have for believers? How can we keep our covenant with God and not let it get broken? What role does the Bible play in helping us eliminate idolatrous practices from our lives?

Ask members silently to read 23:4–8 and, based on what the people destroyed, list what kinds of idolatrous worship the people engaged in. (We can assume that because Josiah destroyed the groves or Asherah [or Asherim (plural)] they worshiped Asherah.) List these on a chalkboard or a large sheet of paper in one column. Then opposite each idolatrous action, list what Josiah and his reformation did to this practice. Some practices/actions are given below, but your members may find others:

Idolatrous Practice	Josiah's Actions
Worshiped Asherah	Destroyed her images
Worshiped sun, moon, and stars	Destroyed images
Worshiped golden calf at Bethel	Defiled image by scattering ashes
Idolatrous priests burned incense	Removed priests
Worshiped Asherah in temple	Burned image in Kidron
Used male prostitutes	Destroyed prostitutes' house
Worshiped at high places	Defiled high places

Give the Truth a Personal Focus

Ask members to list some idolatrous practices they find in their lives and in their community. Write these on a chalkboard or a large sheet of paper.

Ask: What can we do to eliminate idolatrous practices in our lives? What can we do to lead out in eliminating idolatrous practices in our community?

Encourage members to choose both personal and community projects and set some goals that will help them reach these. Suggest that faithfulness to Bible study will help them as it did Josiah.

---

1. Robert A. Baker, *A Summary of Christian History,* rev. ed. by John M. Landers (Nashville: Broadman & Holman, 1994), 184.

September
15
1996

Hearing God's Call

Basic Passage: Jeremiah 1

Focal Passages: Jeremiah 1:4–10,14–17

Jeremiah was the key prophet of God during the final years of Judah. For over four decades, he spoke God's word concerning the coming fall of Jerusalem. However, as his messages of judgment were being fulfilled, he became a prophet of hope—a hope that looked beyond the exile. The Book of Jeremiah begins with the account of God's call to Jeremiah and of Jeremiah's response.

Study Aim: *To describe God's call to Jeremiah and his response*

STUDYING THE BIBLE

OUTLINE AND SUMMARY

I. Introduction to the Book of Jeremiah (Jer. 1:1–3)

II. God's Call to Jeremiah (Jer. 1:4–19)

1. **Set apart to be a prophet (vv. 4–5)**
2. **Jeremiah's sense of inadequacy (v. 6)**
3. **Equipped and commissioned (vv. 7–10)**
4. **Vision of an almond branch (vv. 11–12)**
5. **Vision of a boiling pot (vv. 13–16)**
6. **Challenged and reassured (vv. 17–19)**

The word of the Lord came to Jeremiah (vv. 1–3). God set him apart to be a prophet before he was born (vv. 4–5). Jeremiah said that he was too young to speak for God (v. 6). God touched his mouth and commanded him to speak His word (vv. 7–10). Jeremiah saw an almond branch, reminding him that God was watching over His word (vv. 11–12). Jeremiah saw a boiling pot, representing the coming of invaders (vv. 13–16). God challenged Jeremiah to speak without fear because God would be with him (vv. 17–19).

I. Introduction to the Book of Jeremiah (Jer. 1:1–3)

Jeremiah was the son of a priest. He grew up in Anathoth (AN uh thawth), in the portion of the land where Benjamin's descendants settled years before. The word of God came to him in the thirteenth year of Josiah (joh SIGH uh) or 627 B.C. His prophetic ministry continued until the eleventh year of Zedekiah (zed uh KIGH uh) or 586 B.C., when Jerusalem was captured.

II. God's Call to Jeremiah (Jer. 1:4–19)

1. Set apart to be a prophet (vv. 4–5)

4 Then the word of the LORD came unto me, saying,

5 Before I formed thee in the belly I knew thee; and before thou camest forth out of the womb I sanctified thee, and I ordained thee a prophet unto the nations.

Verse 4 uses terms that are found throughout the Book of Jeremiah. Over and over, Jeremiah testified, "The word of the LORD came unto me." Jeremiah did not decide on his own to be a prophet, nor did he make up his own messages. From his initial call until his final prophecy, Jeremiah was someone to whom God's word came and who in turn declared that word to others. At the beginning of his written prophecies, the prophet told how he came to be a man controlled by the word of the Lord.

Actually, the beginning was well before the time when Jeremiah first heard God's call. God's call was the expression of a purpose that extended back before Jeremiah was born. The word "formed" was used in Genesis 2:7 to describe God's creation of Adam from the dust of the earth. Jeremiah 1:5 uses the same word to describe what takes place within a mother's womb as a new life is created by the hand of God.

God not only "formed" Jeremiah within his mother's womb; the Lord "knew" him. The word denotes personal knowledge. God did not first notice Jeremiah after he was born and showed distinctive personal traits. God created him and knew him from before he was born. Jeremiah's awareness of this divine purpose for his life helped him persevere through the difficult years of his ministry. Jeremiah realized that God had been at work to endow and shape him for the task to which God called him.

In addition to "formed" and "knew," verse 5 uses two other words to describe God's call of Jeremiah. The word "sanctified" literally means to be set apart. God had set him apart to be a special person with a special mission from God. He was consecrated to be a holy person with a holy mission.

The word "appointed" carries the idea of being "given." The Lord had given Jeremiah as a prophet to the nations. Although his message focused on Judah, Jeremiah's word from God often included other nations. Neither Judah nor the nations recognized Jeremiah as a gift of God to them.

2. Jeremiah's sense of inadequacy (v. 6)

> 6 Then said I, Ah, Lord GOD! behold, I cannot speak: for I am a child.

The word "child" generally was used to refer to a young, unmarried man. Thus Jeremiah was not what we would call a child, but a single young adult, perhaps even a teenager. Unlike our society, where younger people often have great influence, the world of Jeremiah listened primarily to the words of married people of more maturity. Older people were considered to be especially wise. Thus Jeremiah responded to God's call by noting that he lacked the maturity to speak in such a way that people would pay attention.

The part of Jeremiah's response about his inability to speak sounds like what Moses said when the Lord called him. Moses protested, "O my Lord, I am not eloquent, . . . but I am slow of speech, and of a slow tongue" (Exod. 4:10). Moses based his inadequacy on being unable to speak eloquently. Jeremiah based his inadequacy on his youth.

When we compare verse 6 to Isaiah 6:8, we see that Jeremiah was not an eager volunteer like Isaiah. On the other hand, Jeremiah's words do not reflect an unwillingness to answer God's call. They do reveal a deep sense of personal inadequacy for the task. Verse 6 also is the first of many candid prayers of Jeremiah. The Book of Jeremiah contains many dialogues between God and Jeremiah. Both Jeremiah and God spoke to each other with total honesty.

3. Equipped and commissioned (vv. 7–10)

> 7 But the LORD said unto me, Say not, I am a child: for thou shalt go to all that I shall send thee, and whatsoever I command thee thou shalt speak.
>
> 8 Be not afraid of their faces: for I am with thee to deliver thee, saith the LORD.
>
> 9 Then the LORD put forth his hand, and touched my mouth. And the LORD said unto me, Behold, I have put my words in thy mouth.
>
> 10 See, I have this day set thee over the nations and over the kingdoms, to root out, and to pull down, and to destroy, and to throw down, to build, and to plant.

God told Jeremiah not to see his youth as a reason not to obey. Instead, Jeremiah was to go to those to whom God sent him and to speak what God told him to speak. Jeremiah was not to be worried with how people might respond to his words; instead he was to obey God and leave the outcome in the hands of God.

What God told Jeremiah to do was easier said than done. How was the young man to be able to speak to his sinful generation? God told him not to fear the menacing looks and threatening words of people. Where was he to find his courage? The Lord promised to be with him. "Fear not: for I am with thee" (Isa. 43:5) is a recurring theme in the Bible. The assurance of the abiding presence of God is the antidote for the many fears that rise up before us and within us.

One sign of the Lord's presence with Jeremiah was that the Lord put His words into the prophet's mouth. As a sign of this, the Lord touched the prophet's mouth with His hand. The Lord sent an angel to touch the lips of Isaiah for cleansing (Isa. 6:5–7). This prepared Isaiah to hear and respond to God's call. In Jeremiah's case, God touched his lips to reassure the young man that God would use him to speak His words. Thus Jeremiah did not need to worry about his youth and inexperience as a speaker. God would be with him and would speak through him.

God was going to endow the young prophet with authority over nations and kingdoms. He would be God's representative to people of power and position. His task was described in six symbolic words; four of them negative and two positive. Most of Jeremiah's ministry was pronouncing judgment on evil. This is depicted as rooting out, pulling down, destroying, and throwing down. Jeremiah did not choose such a ministry. He was chosen for it by God because the times required it. As judgment began to fall, God began to give more hopeful messages to the prophet.

This is depicted as building and planting.

4. Vision of an almond branch (vv. 11–12)

God called Jeremiah's attention to an almond branch. The almond tree was among the first plants to awake from winter. The Lord told Jeremiah that He was awake and watching over His word to perform it.

5. Vision of a boiling pot (vv. 13–16)

Then God called Jeremiah's attention to a boiling pot that faced from the north and thus was prepared to overflow toward the south (v. 13).

> 14 Then the LORD said unto me, Out of the north an evil shall break forth upon all the inhabitants of the land.
>
> 15 For, lo, I will call all the families of the kingdoms of the north, saith the LORD; and they shall come, and they shall set every one his throne at the entering of the gates of Jerusalem, and against all the walls thereof round about, and against the cities of Judah.
>
> 16 And I will utter my judgments against them touching all their wickedness, who have forsaken me, and have burned incense unto other gods, and worshipped the works of their own hands.

The boiling pot was a sign that enemies from the North would bring judgment on Jerusalem and the cities of Judah. Jeremiah often warned of invaders from the North. This sign, which came as part of Jeremiah's call, did not identify the invaders by name.

Jeremiah's call came at about the time that the Assyrian (uh SIHR ih uhn) Empire crumbled. A number of powers were vying to become the next superpower. Eventually Babylonia (bab uh LOH nih uh) came out on top. Later in Jeremiah's ministry, he identified the Babylonians as the instruments of divine judgment on Judah.

The Bible accurately represents the events of history when they intersected events in God's plan of redemption. The Bible interprets history from this perspective: God is the sovereign Lord of all nations. He moves in the affairs of history to accomplish His divine purpose. One example of this was God's use of the Babylonians to punish the people of Judah for their persistent idolatry. The Babylonians were not aware that they were instruments in the hands of God, but they were nonetheless.

6. Challenged and reassured (vv. 17–19)

> 17 Thou therefore gird up thy loins, and arise, and speak unto them all that I command thee: be not dismayed at their faces, lest I confound thee before them.

The men of Jeremiah's day wore long robes. When they prepared to work or run, they gathered up the robes about their waists and tied them. This is the image behind the frequent use in the Bible of the words "gird up thy loins." People today sometimes say, "Roll up your sleeves." Both expressions mean the same thing: get ready for vigorous exercise or hard work.

The word "arise" was a call to get up and begin the task. God had called, equipped, and commissioned Jeremiah. Now was the time for him to begin to do what God had called him to do.

The last part of verse 17 expands on the words "be not afraid of their faces" in verse 8. This warning against fear implies that Jeremiah would face many scary situations and people.

Verses 18–19 spell this out more clearly. Everyone in Judah was going to oppose him. This included kings, princes, priests, and all the people. Later chapters record their ridicule, threats, and persecution of Jeremiah. He would face more than enough to strike terror into the heart of a young man listening to God's call. God did not hide this from Jeremiah. Instead God warned him ahead of time. However, God repeated the gist of verse 8.

First of all, Jeremiah was not to be frightened or dismayed by the angry faces and threatening words and actions of those to whom he spoke. God warned the prophet that if he gave way to fear, God would let him reap the consequences of his fear. However, God said that there was no need to fear. God promised, "I am with thee, saith the LORD, to deliver thee" (v. 19).

APPLYING THE BIBLE

1. Jeremiah was the foremost man in the seventh century B.C., so says Old Testament scholar John R. Sampey. Jeremiah was called to be a prophet to Judah in the thirteenth year of the reign of Judah's great king Josiah (1:2).

2. God's knowledge of and call to Jeremiah before he was born. One of the strongest, clearest verses in the Old Testament that ought to empower believers in their relentless opposition to the hideous sin of abortion appears in vv. 4–5 of our lesson today. Read it carefully.

Will the abortionists be held innocent on Judgment Day who have mutilated and murdered those "formed," "known," "sanctified," and "ordained" by God before they were born?

3. A common problem. Fear is a problem to us all—even to Jeremiah (v. 6). When God called Jeremiah to his prophetic office, he shrank back in fear from the responsibility.

An ancient Arabian legend tells of two travelers meeting outside a city. One was a hideous-looking creature who, when asked by the other traveler his name and where he was going, replied: "My name is Pestilence, and I am going into the city to take five thousand lives."

Sometime later, the two met again and the traveler said to Pestilence, "You lied to me, for you took fifty thousand lives."

"No," Pestilence said, "I lied not to you. I took only five thousand lives; the rest died from fear of me!"

Courage is not the absence of fear; rather, it is going on to do one's duty in spite of fear. And Jeremiah must be credited with a great deal of courage to assume the mantle of leadership that cost him so much.

What is your greatest fear? Tell it to Jesus, for He is good for even that!

4. Again' it! Calvin Coolidge was a shy, silent man who had little to say. He served as our president in the mid-1920s. Years ago, the story goes, a man met Coolidge on his way home from church. "Where you been, Cal?" he asked, and Coolidge replied, "Church." "What did the preacher preach on, Cal?" the neighbor asked. "Sin," Coolidge replied. "And what did he say about it?" the neighbor asked. "Said he was again' it!" and Coolidge walked on.

Jeremiah let the people of Judah know that God was against their sin. The task of every preacher is to let people know that God hates their sins but loves them with an everlasting love.

5. "You have been warned." The noted British minister William Barclay, whose books line the studies of thousands of preachers today, tells about a stretch of road under repair in the north of England. Warning signs were posted on the dangerous, steep road with a sharp bend. The last sign read, "You have been warned!"

Judah had been warned by the prophets, including Jeremiah, that her sins were going to cost her everything; but rather than heeding the warnings, the nation plunged on into chaos.

Warning people and pleading for them to repent were the first message Jesus preached. They are the preacher's primary message needed in our wicked world today.

6. The prophet's work can be disappointing. It is told that Billy Graham was once flying on a crowded plane when a drunken man got up, walked back to Graham, stuck out his hand and said: "Put'er there, Billy. I'm really glad to see you. You have no idea how much your sermons have helped me!"

The preacher's work is often discouraging. We don't see the results we would like to see. Jeremiah faithfully declared God's word to the people of Judah, but they would have none of it. The hardness of their hearts cost them dearly when they were carried off into the Babylonian exile.

Jeremiah's life seems like a complete failure, but not so. Anyone who stands against sin and for righteousness is always an immense success.

TEACHING THE BIBLE

- *Main Idea:* God calls people to serve Him in difficult days.
- *Suggested Teaching Aim:* To encourage adults to respond to God's call.

A TEACHING OUTLINE

1. *Use an illustration to introduce the Bible study.*
2. *Use lecture and group discussion to guide the Bible study.*
3. *Use questions to apply the Bible.*

Introduce the Bible Study

Use "The prophet's work can be disappointing" from "Applying the Bible" to introduce the lesson.

Search for Biblical Truth

IN ADVANCE, prepare a poster with the outline of the background passage on it and place paper strips over each point. Prepare a lecture covering the material in "Studying the Bible."

Uncover "I. Introduction to the Book of Jeremiah (Jer. 1:1–3)."

IN ADVANCE, enlist a member to prepare a brief report on Jeremiah based on the *Holman Bible Dictionary* or summarize the material in "Studying the Bible" under this point.

Uncover "II. God's Call to Jeremiah (Jer. 1:4–19)" and "1. Set apart to be a prophet (1:4–5)." Explain the following: "The Word of the LORD came unto me" (1:4), "formed," "knew," "sanctified," and "appointed" (1:5).

DISCUSS: What does God's knowledge of Jeremiah before birth say about God's concern for all people? What purpose did Jeremiah's awareness of God's divine purpose have?

Uncover "2. Jeremiah's sense of inadequacy (1:6)." Explain the meaning of the word "child" (1:6). Compare and contrast the call of Jeremiah with the calls of Moses and Isaiah.

DISCUSS: Why does God call certain people to His ministry? Did Jeremiah have an opportunity to refuse? Do we?

Uncover "3. Equipped and commissioned (1:7–10)." Point out the twofold warning ("Say not" and "be not afraid") and the sixfold mission ("root," "pull," "destroy," "throw," "build," and "plant").

DISCUSS: Would we be more likely to listen to a young evangelist or an older one? How can we tell if God is speaking through either? How do you think Jeremiah felt about his ministry?

Uncover "4. Vision of an almond branch (1:11–12)," and relate the meaning based on the paragraph in "Studying the Bible."

Uncover "5. Vision of a boiling pot (1:13–16." Ask members to name some symbols the prophets used to get their message across. Point out that Jeremiah here used a pot sitting in a fire and filled with boiling water. The pot was tipped so that when the water started to boil, it spilled over. Explain the meaning of the symbol.

DISCUSS: Why does God allow evil people to defeat good people? What does this say about God's control of all the nations of the earth? Do you believe God is in control of all the nations of the earth today? Why?

Uncover the last point: "6. Challenged and reassured (1:17–19)." Explain "gird up thy loins." Point out the four instructions to Jeremiah in 1:17: "gird up," "arise," "speak," and "be not dismayed." Point out that it was now time for Jeremiah to get on with his task.

DISCUSS: Why does God call us to tasks in which people will oppose and ridicule us? What does God do to prepare us for our tasks?

Give the Truth a Personal Focus

Ask: Does God still call us today as He called Jeremiah? Has He called you to some task?

Remind members that God still calls people to difficult tasks. Ask members seriously to consider God's call for their lives. Pray that all will respond as God calls.

Proclaiming God's Word

September

22

1996

Basic Passage: Jeremiah 7

Focal Passage: Jeremiah 7:1–15

Jeremiah 7 records a memorable example of the prophet's proclamation of God's word. As we noted in studying Jeremiah's call, God called him to proclaim His word to people who responded by rejecting the word and persecuting the prophet. At times in his difficult ministry, Jeremiah tried to refrain from speaking God's word. However, Jeremiah testified that he had to proclaim God's word because it was like a fire in his bones (Jer. 20:9).

Study Aim: *To summarize the main points of Jeremiah's temple sermon*

STUDYING THE BIBLE

OUTLINE AND SUMMARY

I. Jeremiah's Temple Sermon (Jer. 7:1–15)

1. Setting and theme of the sermon (vv. 1–4)

2. What God expects (vv. 5–7)

3. Hypocritical worship and sinful living (vv. 8–11)

4. Sure judgment (vv. 12–15)

II. Jeremiah Told Not to Pray for the People (Jer. 7:16–20)

III. God Demands Obedience (Jer. 7:21–34)

1. God's command to Israel (vv. 21–23)

2. Israel's persistent disobedience (vv. 24–31)

3. Terrible judgment (vv. 32–34)

Speaking at the gate of the temple, Jeremiah spoke God's word, which called the people to change their ways and to cease chanting their false assurance about the temple (vv. 1–4). The Lord promised that if they changed their ways by practicing justice and ceasing idolatry, they would continue to dwell in the land (vv. 5–7). Unfortunately, the people broke God's commandments and went to the temple like a band of robbers retreating to the safety of their den (vv. 8–11). As God destroyed Shiloh (SHIGH loh) and Israel, so He would destroy Judah for their refusal to hear God's persistent call (vv. 12–15). The people had become so wicked that God forbade Jeremiah to pray for them (vv. 16–20). God's basic command to Israel had been to obey His voice (vv. 21–23), but Israel had continually disobeyed God (vv. 24–28). They had committed such abominations (vv. 29–31) that nothing remained but terrible judgment (vv. 32–34).

I. Jeremiah's Temple Sermon (Jer. 7:1–15)

1. Setting and theme of the sermon (vv. 1–4)

> 1 The word that came to Jeremiah from the LORD, saying,
> 2 Stand in the gate of the LORD's house, and proclaim there this word, and say, Hear the word of the LORD, all ye of Judah, that enter in at these gates to worship the LORD.

Jeremiah took his stand at one of the entrances to the temple. From this point, he was able to speak to the people in the outer court as they prepared to go through their acts of worship.

Most Bible students think that Jeremiah 26:1 gives the setting for Jeremiah's temple sermon. Josiah [joh SIGH uh] had tried to revive worship in the temple. Jeremiah had received his call a few years before Josiah began his reforms (Jer. 1:1; 2 Kings 22:3). Thus the prophet was aware of what Josiah tried to do. Jeremiah was already a prophet when Josiah was killed in battle, when Jehoahaz [jih HOH uh haz] reigned for three months, and when Jehoiakim [jih HOY uh kim] became king (2 Kings 23:29–37). Jeremiah 26:1 says that Jeremiah spoke in the temple at the beginning of the reign of Jehoiakim which was in 609 B.C.

> 3 Thus saith the LORD of hosts, the God of Israel, Amend your ways and your doings, and I will cause you to dwell in this place.
> 4 Trust ye not in lying words, saying, the temple of the LORD, The temple of the LORD, The temple of the LORD, are these.

The word "amend" means to do good. *Repentance* means turning from sin and with God's help beginning to do good. God promised the people of Judah that He would allow them to continue to dwell in the promised land if they amended their habits and actions.

The Lord warned them not to trust in lying words about the temple. The content of this false trust is described further in verse 9. Verse 4 says that the lie took the form of a chant that repeated "the temple of the LORD." They assumed that the temple was protection against whatever threatened them.

Jeremiah was by no means the only person in the land who professed to be a prophet of the Lord. The other "prophets" proclaimed a different message than Jeremiah. They preached peace and security for God's people. They based this on God's deliverance of Jerusalem from the Assyrians during the time of Isaiah and Hezekiah [hez ih KIGH uh] (see the lesson for September 1). Thus when Jeremiah warned of judgment on Judah and the destruction of the temple, the other prophets assured the people that God would never allow anything bad to happen to His people and to His holy house.

2. What God expects (vv. 5–7)

> 5 For if ye thoroughly amend your ways and your doings; if ye thoroughly execute judgment between a man and his neighbour;
> 6 If ye oppress not the stranger, the fatherless, and the widow, and shed not innocent blood in this place, neither walk after other gods to your hurt:
> 7 Then will I cause you to dwell in this place, in the land that I gave to your fathers, for ever and ever.

Verses 5–7 expand on the meaning of verse 3. In Hebrew, these are one long sentence with several "if" clauses, which lead up to a promise. If Israel met the conditions stated in the "if" clauses, God promised that they could continue to dwell in the land.

The "if" clauses in verses 5–6 further define what ways and doings needed to be amended. The last part of verse 5 shows that God expected His people to practice justice (the meaning of "judgment") in their dealings with other people.

The first part of verse 6 reflects special concern for foreigners, orphans, and widows. These groups were exploited by unscrupulous people and ignored by selfish people. The Law commanded the Israelites not to mistreat these dependent groups (Deut. 24:17–18). The prophets repeated this command: "Learn to do well, seek judgment, relieve the oppressed, judge the fatherless, plead for the widow" (Isa. 1:17).

The warning against shedding innocent blood in the temple included actual murders in the temple (such as the incident in 2 Chron. 24:20–21; Matt. 23:35 refers to this incident). These words also applied to those who came to the temple with hands stained by innocent blood (vv. 9–10; Isa. 1:15).

Verse 7 also contains a warning against the Israelites' besetting sin of idolatry, which they had sometimes practiced even in the temple (2 Kings 21:3–5).

3. Hypocritical worship and sinful living (vv. 8–11)

> 8 Behold, ye trust in lying words, that cannot profit.
>
> 9 Will ye steal, murder, and commit adultery, and swear falsely, and burn incense unto Baal, and walk after other gods whom ye know not;
>
> 10 And come and stand before me in this house, which is called by my name, and say, We are delivered to do all these abominations?
>
> 11 Is this house, which is called by my name, become a den of robbers in your eyes? Behold, even I have seen it, saith the LORD.

Verses 8–11 expand on the warning against false trust in the temple in verse 4. Both passages show that the people had put their trust in lying words about the temple. Two piercing questions in verses 9–11 reveal how they deceived themselves and perverted the purpose of the temple.

The first question in verses 9–10 shows what the lie was. They had convinced themselves that they could practice the worst of sins and still be safe—as long as they continued to go through the motions of worship in the temple. Their sins included breaking the Sixth (murder), Seventh (adultery), Eighth (stealing), and Ninth (false swearing) Commandments. They also broke the first two Commandments by their worship of other gods.

You can almost hear the shock and anger in the prophet's voice as he condemned this unbelievable hypocrisy. They committed these terrible sins. Then they came to the temple, which was supposed to represent the holy name of God. They said that their faithfulness in temple observances protected them from harm and thus freed them to continue their abominations!

The question in verse 11 asks if they were not thinking of the temple the same way that robbers thought of their den. A robbers' den was thought of as a safe place to stay between crimes.

4. Sure judgment (vv. 12–15)

> 12 But go ye now unto my place which was in Shiloh, where I set my name at the first, and see what I did to it for the wickedness of my people Israel.
>
> 13 And now, because ye have done all these works, saith the LORD, and I spake unto you, rising up early and speaking, but ye heard not; and I called you, but ye answered not;
>
> 14 Therefore will I do unto this house, which is called by my name, wherein ye trust, and unto the place which I gave to you and to your fathers, as I have done to Shiloh.
>
> 15 And I will cast you out of my sight, as I have cast out all your brethren, even the whole seed of Ephraim [EE frih uhm].

Shiloh had been an important place of worship during Israel's early history. Joshua chose Shiloh as the resting place for the tabernacle (Josh. 18:1). It was still there during the time of Eli (1 Sam. 1:3). Eli's two evil sons took the ark of the covenant from Shiloh when the Israelites fought the Philistines [fih LISS teens]. The people thought that the presence of the ark would ensure victory for them (1 Sam. 4:3). Instead, the ark was captured and the Israelites defeated (1 Sam. 4:11). Judging from Jeremiah's words, the place of worship at Shiloh was destroyed.

Speaking through Jeremiah, the Lord accused the Israelites of putting their trust in the temple in the same way their forefathers had trusted in the ark from Shiloh. God said that He would destroy the temple as surely as He had destroyed Shiloh when it became a place of hypocritical worship. Verse 13 describes the persistent but futile entreaties of the Lord to His people. They had refused His every plea. Nothing remained but destruction like that of Shiloh and of the Northern Kingdom (Ephraim).

II. Jeremiah Told Not to Pray for the People (Jer. 7:16–20)

God took the drastic step of ordering Jeremiah not to intercede anymore for Judah. Their sins had caused them to pass beyond the point of no return. Ahead lay sure judgment.

III. God Demands Obedience (Jer. 7:21–34)

1. God's command to Israel (vv. 21–23)

The Lord reminded the people that His basic command was not to offer burnt offerings, but to obey the Lord.

2. Israel's persistent disobedience (vv. 24–31)

The history of Israel had been a history of disobeying God. Since the deliverance from Egypt, God had sent prophets calling the people to repent and obey; but Israel had continually hardened their hearts. Judah should prepare for judgment because of such abominations as idol worship in the temple and child sacrifice.

3. Terrible judgment (vv. 32–34)

The valley where children had been sacrificed would become a place where evildoers would be slaughtered. All sounds of joy would disappear from the desolate land.

APPLYING THE BIBLE

1. Tall enough to reach heaven. A church elder once came to his bishop requesting that he send a preacher to serve among them. The bishop asked, "And how big a man do you want?" The elder replied: "We do not care about his size, but we want a preacher who is tall enough to reach heaven on his knees!"

Such a man was Jeremiah in Judah's most trying hours. Still the nation did not listen to him or heed his divine warnings.

2. Only outward obedience. A little boy who was standing in his chair at the dinner table was told by his mother to sit down. But he paid her no mind even as she insisted that he sit down. Finally, she plopped him down in the chair; and he blurted through tears, "I may be sitting down on the outside, but I'm standing on the inside!"

That was the same kind of disobedience that marked Judah. She involved herself in the outward adornments of serving God, but in her heart she rebelled against what God commanded her to be and do (vv. 8–12).

3. Friends of Jesus? Dr. R. A. Torrey (1856–1927) was a Congregationalist preacher, teacher, and evangelist who made a great impact for Christ. One evening Torrey was told that a minister's son was to be in the large meeting Torrey was conducting. Although the young man was a professing Christian, Torrey was told the young man's life gave little indication of it.

Meeting him at the door, Torrey asked, "Are you a friend of Jesus?" Quickly the young man replied, "I consider myself to be a friend of Jesus." To which Torrey replied: "Ye are my friends if you do whatsoever I command you." The young man's eyes fell and he replied, "If those are the conditions, I suppose I am not."

Loudly and frequently, in their temple worship, Judah claimed to be a friend of God, but her works denied her profession (vv. 1–11).

Are you a friend of Jesus?

4. Partial obedience. Adoniram Judson was a pioneer missionary to Burma. When Judson finished seminary, he was offered a call from a fashionable church in Boston to serve as assistant pastor. His future looked very bright, and his mother begged him to accept the call where he could be close to home and loved ones. But young Judson replied: "My work is not here. God is calling me beyond the seas. To stay here would be partial obedience, and I could not be happy with that."

Judah tried to practice partial obedience. She tried to serve both the Lord God and heathen gods (vv. 4, 6). But there is no partial obedience. It is either complete obedience or disobedience.

Would this not be a good time for us to evaluate our own lives?

5. Responsible to God. Senator Daniel Webster (1758–1843) was the best-known American orator of his day. While Webster was Secretary of State under President Fillmore, he attended a dinner with twenty gentlemen at the Aston House in New York. Unusually quiet, one man, in an attempt to draw Webster out, asked him what he considered to be the most important thought that ever occupied his mind. Pausing for several minutes, Webster replied: "The most important thought that ever occupied my mind was my individual responsibility to God." With that, he arose and left the room.

This thought ought to be always uppermost in our minds; but like the people of Judah, too often we live and act as though we are not responsible to God. In spite of Jeremiah's warnings and pleadings, Judah closed her eyes and ears and hardened her heart. In 587 B.C. the divine judgment fell upon her when she was carried away into Babylonian captivity, where she remained for seventy years.

TEACHING THE BIBLE

➧ *Main Idea:* God warns the people to trust Him, not their religion and institutions.

➧ *Suggested Teaching Aim:* To identify ways they trust the things of God instead of God Himself.

A TEACHING OUTLINE

1. *Use an illustration to introduce the Bible study.*
2. *Use a chart to guide the Bible study.*
3. *Use volunteer readers to read the Scripture.*
4. *Use an outside assignment to involve a member in the Bible study.*
5. *Use list-making to give the truth a personal focus.*

Introduce the Bible Study

Use "Friends of Jesus?" from "Applying the Bible" to introduce the lesson.

Search for Biblical Truth

Briefly present the seven summary statements in the "Outline and Summary." Point out where Jeremiah delivered his sermon (temple) and why (people trusted temple instead of God). Point out that this likely took place some time after Jehoiakim became king (609 B.C.).

IN ADVANCE, write *If* and *Then* on a chalkboard or a large sheet of paper. Call for a volunteer to read verses 3–7. Ask members to identify God's demands ("Amend") in verse 3 and the result if the people obeyed ("cause you to dwell"). Point out that the people believed that God would never allow anything bad to happen to His people and to His holy house.

Call for a volunteer to read verses 5–7. Ask the people to identify God's demands ("If") and the results ("Then"). Write these on the chart. Use "Studying the Bible" to explain the nature of God's demands. Point out the particular social nature of the demands: how they treated others reflected their relationship to God.

Call for a volunteer to read verse 8 and another to read verses 9–11. Point out that the two questions (vv. 9–10 and v. 11) explain what were the "lying words" to which Jeremiah referred in verse 8. Verses 9–10 show that they had convinced themselves that they could practice the worst of sins and still be safe—as long as they continued to go through the motions of worship in the temple.

Ask members to turn to Exodus 20:13–17 and determine which Commandments the people were breaking.

The second question is in verse 11 and it shows that the people's attitude toward the temple was nothing more than how robbers thought about their den. The people thought of the temple as a safe place to stay between crimes.

Call for a volunteer to read verses 12–15. Use "Studying the Bible" to explain the image of Shiloh. **IN ADVANCE,** enlist a member to prepare a report on Shiloh based on the *Holman Bible Dictionary.* Call for the report at this time. Use "Studying the Bible" to explain the image of Shiloh in Jeremiah.

Briefly summarize the rest of the background passage to conclude the lesson.

Give the Truth a Personal Focus

Ask: What do we trust today that might parallel the way Judah was trusting the temple to keep them safe? (Two examples would be our church membership and baptism.) List these on a chalkboard or a large sheet of paper.

After you have listed all of the members' suggestions, ask what we can expect to happen to us if we trust our religion and its institutions instead of trusting God. Challenge members to place their trust in God alone and to live for Him.

September

29

1996

Continuing to Trust

Basic Passage: Habakkuk 2–3

Focal Passages: Habakkuk 2:1–4; 3:17–19

Like Jeremiah, Habakkuk (huh BAK uhk) was a prophet during the last years of Judah. Also like Jeremiah, he engaged in a dialogue with God in which he expressed some hard questions. Both prophets were perplexed by what was going on around them. They expressed their perplexity to God. In this regard, they were like Job and the writer of Psalm 73. All these people engaged in dialogue with God about the injustices of life. Two facts show that all of these were people of faith: (1) Each expressed his questions to God Himself—a form of prayer. (2) Each continued to trust God even when many questions and problems continued.

Study Aim: *To identify evidences of Habakkuk's trust in the face of existing injustices and expected troubles*

STUDYING THE BIBLE

OUTLINE AND SUMMARY

I. Questions and Answers About Injustice (Hab. 2:1–20)

1. Patient amid perplexity (2:1)

2. God's revelation (2:2–3)

3. Fate of the righteous and the wicked (2:4–5)

4. Woes on the wicked (2:6–20)

II. Habakkuk's Prayer and Song (Hab. 3:1–19)

1. Prayer (3:1–2)

2. Revelation of God's awesome power (3:3–15)

3. Faith, hope, and joy (3:16–19)

After Habakkuk expressed concern about injustices, he waited patiently for God to answer (2:1). God told Habakkuk that His revelation would surely come, but that it might seem slow by human standards (2:2–3). God's basic answer was that His righteous and faithful people would live, but arrogant and greedy people would perish (2:4–5). A series of woes were pronounced on the latter group for their aggression, exploitation, cruelty, inhumanity, and idolatry (2:6–20). Habakkuk prayed that the Lord would be merciful and renew His works among His people (3:1–2). The prophet described how God's past mighty acts had delivered His people and crushed the wicked (3:3–15). Habakkuk expressed faith, hope, and joy as he awaited a time of troubles and divine deliverance (3:16–19).

I. Questions and Answers About Injustices (Hab. 2:1–20)

1. Patient amid perplexity (2:1)

1 I will stand upon my watch, and set me upon the tower, and will watch to see what he will say unto me, and what I shall answer when I am reproved.

Habakkuk 2–3 cannot be understood without being tied to chapter 1. Wicked people triumphed over the righteous, and God seemed deaf to the prophet's prayers about such injustices (1:1–4). God answered that He was sending the Chaldeans [kal DEE uhns], another name for the Babylonians (bab uh LOH nih uhns), to execute divine wrath (1:5–11). Habakkuk was even more perplexed by this revelation. He asked how a holy God could use wicked men to overcome others more righteous than they (1:12–17).

Verse 1 of chapter 2 expressed the prophet's determination to wait patiently until God revealed an answer to this dilemma. Habakkuk pictured himself as being like a watchman on the wall of a city. Ancient cities were protected by strong, high walls. A watchman was stationed on the wall to look for an approaching enemy (Ezek. 33:2–6). The prophets were often described as being like watchmen appointed by God to warn against the coming of divine judgment (Jer. 6:17; Ezek. 3:17; 33:7; Hos. 9:8). Habakkuk used the figure to describe the proverbial patience needed by a faithful watchman.

The final line in verse 1 is not easy to understand. The sentence sounds as if Habakkuk expected to be reproved. More likely, the meaning is that he was expecting God's answer to his complaint to prepare him to speak God's word to the people. What is clear is that Habakkuk expected God to provide an answer, and he was willing to wait patiently for God's answer.

2. God's revelation (2:2–3)

> 2 And the LORD answered me, and said, Write the vision, and make it plain upon tables, that he may run that readeth it.
>
> 3 For the vision is yet for an appointed time, but at the end it shall speak, and not lie: though it tarry, wait for it; because it will surely come, it will not tarry.

The word "vision" denotes the supernatural nature of God's revelation. Habakkuk was told to write or inscribe the words on tablets. The tablets could have been of stone, clay, or metal; but clay tablets were more common. When clay tablets hardened, they lasted a long time. Indeed, many ancient inscriptions have been preserved on clay tablets. Thus Habakkuk was to provide a lasting record.

He also was told to make the writing plain or clear. The writing should be clearly read by a runner, either a herald who ran with the message or a person hurrying by where the tablet was displayed.

The need for a lasting record implied that the fulfillment would be in the future. Verse 3 confirms this understanding. The fulfillment would seem to tarry from a human point of view, but it would not tarry forever. It would surely come because it was the word of God. It would come at the time appointed by God. Because God is not bound by human limitations of time, His appointed times often seem unreasonably long to impatient people (see 2 Pet. 3:3–12).

3. Fate of the righteous and the wicked (2:4–5)

> 4 Behold, his soul which is lifted up is not upright in him: but the just shall live by his faith.

Habakkuk 2:4 is the crux of God's revelation to the prophet about the injustices he described in 1:2–4,12–17. This is also the best-known verse in the Book of Habakkuk.

The first part of verse 4 introduced a revelation that took more shape in verses 5–20. The person whose soul is lifted up in him is an arrogant person. Such a person is the opposite of an upright person. Verse 5 describes arrogant people of insatiable greed. Part of God's revelation is that such people eventually will perish. They may appear to be riding high for a long time, but someday they will reap what they have sown (see Gal. 6:7).

The last part of verse 4 states the positive side of God's revelation. These few words describe the righteous and faithful people of God. God's promise is that they—in contrast to the wicked—shall live. The New Testament gives the full revelation of all that is involved in the words "shall live." Jesus described such life as abundant and eternal (John 3:16; 10:10).

Christians are familiar with the last part of Habakkuk 2:4 because Paul made this a key text for justification by faith (Rom. 1:17; Gal. 3:11). The main idea in the Old Testament word was faithfulness. Faith and faithfulness go together. Sometimes faith is stressed, at other times faithfulness; but in the long run, they go together. Paul emphasized the total reliance on God and not self for salvation, but he made clear that good works and the fruit of the Spirit go with such faith (Eph. 2:8–10; Gal. 5:23–24).

God was contrasting wicked and righteous (just) people in Habakkuk 2:4. Truly righteous people are people of total reliance on God who show their faith in God by their faithfulness to God. Habakkuk's own faith is clear in verses like 2:1 and 3:17–19. These passages also testify to his steadfastness.

4. Woes on the wicked (2:6–20)

A series of woes were pronounced on the wicked because of aggression (vv. 6–8), exploitation (vv. 9–11), cruelty (vv. 12–14), inhumanity (vv. 15–17), and idolatry (vv. 18–20). Because of their terrible sins, judgment was sure. This judgment would fall on the evildoers in Judah and also eventually on the wicked Chaldeans, whom God would first use to punish His people.

Hidden amid these words of judgment are two more positive and memorable verses: "For the earth shall be filled with the knowledge of the glory of the LORD, as the waters cover the sea" (v. 14); and "the LORD is in his holy temple: let all the earth keep silence before him" (v. 20).

II. Habakkuk's Prayer and Song (Hab. 3:1–19)

1. Prayer (3:1–2)

Habakkuk prayed that the Lord would show mercy to His people by reviving or renewing His work among them.

2. Revelation of God's awesome power (3:3–15)

God's awesome power had in the past been exercised for the deliverance of His people and the destruction of the wicked. The Exodus experience of Israel lies behind many of the graphic word pictures of divine power.

3. Faith, hope, and joy (3:16–19)

Fear and trembling were Habakkuk's first responses to this dazzling reminder of God's salvation and judgment. The last part of verse 16 shows that the prophet believed the terrible prophecy of the coming of the Babylonians as invaders of Judah (1:5–11). He also believed that at God's appointed time, the Babylonians would themselves be judged (2:5–20) and God's people would be delivered (3:3–15). Habakkuk also knew that, meanwhile, God's people must maintain their faith and faithfulness (2:4). Verses 17–19 show how he responded to these words from God.

> 17 Although the fig tree shall not blossom, neither shall fruit be in the vines; the labour of the olive shall fail, and the fields shall yield no meat; the flock shall be cut off from the fold, and there shall be no herd in the stalls:
>
> 18 Yet I will rejoice in the LORD, I will joy in the God of my salvation.
>
> 19 The LORD God is my strength, and he will make my feet like hinds' feet, and he will make me to walk upon mine high places. To the chief singer on my stringed instruments.

These verses rank among the most amazing expressions of faith in the Bible. At this point in his experience, Habakkuk had much in common with the New Testament teaching to rejoice in times of trouble. This teaching of Jesus (Matt. 5:11–12) was repeated by Paul (Rom. 5:3–4), Peter (1 Pet. 1:6), and James (James 1:2–3). In the same spirit, Habakkuk testified that he would continue to rejoice in the Lord although the worst happened.

Verse 17 describes some of the worst things imaginable in Habakkuk's day and time. People depended on fig trees, grape vines, olive trees, and the other crops for food, oil, and other staples. They also depended on their flocks of sheep and herds of cattle for wool, milk, and meat. Habakkuk knew that when ruthless invaders swept into Judah, all these things probably would be destroyed.

If such a time came, how would the prophet respond? The prophet used the words "rejoice" and "joy" to reinforce the commitment he was making. He testified that if the horrors of verse 17 happened, he would still rejoice in the Lord. How could he rejoice at such a time? He could rejoice because of his confident hope in God's promise that the final outcome would be judgment on sinners and salvation for the faithful righteous.

He also could rejoice because, even as he passed through the worst of times, the Lord God was his strength. Habakkuk even compared himself to the fleet-footed hind or deer. The deer were known not only for their swiftness but also for their surefootedness.

Habakkuk 3 was written like a psalm or song. It was to be set to music. The word "selah" scattered throughout verses 3–15 was a notation to musicians. Likewise, the final line of the book makes clear that the words were to be set to music and sung. The song's note of joyful hope and faith amid trouble has been the testimony of believers down through the centuries.

APPLYING THE BIBLE

1. Background. Old Testament scholar Clyde T. Francisco says that the time of Habakkuk's prophecy can be determined with considerable exactness. Assyria is off the scene and Chaldea (Babylon) is coming into power. "The time, therefore, must be after 612 B.C. Judah has not yet been invaded, so it must be before the first invasion [of Judah by Babylon] in 605 B.C. . . . After the death of [king] Josiah, the people reverted to the sins they were committing before his reforms."[1]

Judah, it appears, had learned nothing from the tragedy of the ten northern tribes. It is the nature of sin to blind sinners to its terrible power and consequences.

2. Why? Habakkuk was a different kind of prophet from those who had preceded him. They spoke for God to the people, but Habakkuk spoke to God for the people. The prophet addressed the inaction of God as the wicked prospered and the people of God languished. He asked God why and waited for God to answer. Yet his questions were not rebellious ones. [2]

When we get hurt, how often have we asked God why? Yet that is no sin!

3. Where is God when we need Him? An embittered soldier in Vietnam, who had seen his buddies killed said, "I'll tell you what is wrong with our world; your God has let us down!"

A university student whose life had been transparent, whose grades were high, and whose future seemed bright was engaged to marry a beautiful girl. On the way to his college commencement he was killed. The family asked bitterly, "Where was God when we needed Him?"

A young couple much in love were anticipating the birth of their first child, but the child was born terribly handicapped.

Where is God when we most need Him? Read Habakkuk's brief prophecy and note the questions he asked God. They were also the questions the people were asking. Like us, Habakkuk wondered why God seemed to be hiding when His presence and power were so much in need by Judah. Habakkuk learned that though God delays He is always dependable (3:16ff).

Hope on! Hope in the darkness! God is there too, but he walks among us on quiet feet.

4. Never Alone. The late Dr. Norman Vincent Peale tells about a woman who was trapped in an elevator between floors in a New York City skyscraper. When the building manager called her on the emergency telephone in the elevator, he asked her if she were alone. "Oh, no," the lady answered calmly. "I am not alone." When finally the elevator was repaired and the lady walked off, the manager looked at her in surprise and said, "But you said you were not alone."

"I was not alone," she replied. "God was with me."

Judah was rebellious, living in opposition to what God had told them to do. They had often been warned to repent and return to God. But their hearts were hard, and they continued in their rebellion. In spite of it all, God was still with them (3:18–19).

In all circumstances—good and bad—God is with the believer, but our sins and lack of faith hinder our fellowship with Him and dull the sense of His presence.

5. Holding on in hard times. Martha Berry founded the Berry School for needy children at Mount Berry, Georgia. A woman of great courage and faith; she was named one of the twelve outstanding women in America in a 1932 national poll.

Trying to get her fledgling school off the ground, she went to automobile magnate Henry Ford and asked for $1 million, but he gave her only a dime! She could have felt insulted but, instead, she determined not to let Ford's insensitivity defeat her. Using his dime, Berry bought a bag of peanuts and set her boys to planting them. The next season she planted more peanuts, bagged them and sold them at the nearby crossroads market.

She then wrote Mr. Ford: "Remember that dime? Well, sir, I invested it in peanuts and made enough money to buy a piano for my music students. How's that for dividends?"

Ford was so impressed with her courage and optimism that he invited her to Detroit, where he presented her with a gift of $1 million!"[3]

Habakkuk asked a good many questions about the conditions that prevailed in Judah. But his faith in God's love and power never waned. Habakkuk closes his book with a great exclamation of faith and joy (3:17–19).

As we face difficulties that try our faith, let us follow Habakkuk's example. Faith shines a light in the darkness and we move on (Rom. 8:28).

TEACHING THE BIBLE

- *Main Idea:* God calls His people to trust in the face of existing injustices and expected troubles.
- *Suggested Teaching Aim:* To identify elements that will help adults trust God in the face of injustice and trouble.

A TEACHING OUTLINE

1. Use an illustration to introduce the lesson.

2. Use a chart, brief lectures, and group discussion to search for biblical truth.

3. Use a paraphrase and/or hymn writing to interpret Scripture.

4. Use brainstorming to apply the Scripture to members' lives.

Introduce the Bible Study

Use "Where is God when we need Him?" to introduce the lesson.

Search for Biblical Truth

Briefly set the context of these verses by overviewing the summary in "Studying the Bible."

On a chalkboard or a large sheet of paper, write:

Habakkuk's Questioning and Faith	
Stand	("stand upon my watch")
Set	("me upon the tower")
Watch to see	("what he will say") ("what I will answer when reproved")

Call for a volunteer to read Habakkuk 2:1 and ask members to complete the above chart by adding the material in parentheses and explaining Habakkuk's questioning and faith.

Ask members to look at 2:2–3. Ask: Why do you think God wanted Habakkuk to write the message on tablets? (Let them respond. Consider this: it was going to be a while before the message was fulfilled and God wanted to be sure the message survived.)

DISCUSS: Why do you think God delays in executing His judgment on the wicked?

Read aloud 2:4. Ask members to look at Romans 1:7 and Galatians 3:11. Point out that the main idea of the Old Testament word for "faith" was "faithfulness." Because God's people were faithful to Him, they would live. The wicked would be destroyed. Use "Studying the Bible" to explain the New Testament use of this significant passage.

Briefly summarize the material in "Studying the Bible" for 2:6—3:16 so members will be able to understand the climax to the book.

DISCUSS: How can we develop the faith to be faithful to God in times of crisis? What does our faithfulness say about our faith in God?

Call for a volunteer to read 3:17–18. Call for this verse to be read in as many different translations as you have. Use the comments in "Studying the Bible" to point out the marvelous expression of faith voiced by Habakkuk. Distribute paper and pencils and ask members to paraphrase these verses. Encourage them to use modern events in their writing.

As an alternate activity, ask members either individually or as a group to paraphrase these words so they can be sung to an existing hymn tune (such as "All the Way My Savior Leads Me" or some other tune in the same meter.) Sing the hymn as a conclusion to the lesson.

Give the Truth a Personal Focus

Ask: What made Habakkuk so confident in his trust in God? Write members' comments on a chalkboard or a large sheet of paper.

Next ask them to evaluate their own lives to see which of these qualities they need to add so that they can develop a similar faith and faithfulness. Point out that we have the benefit of God's divine record of faithfulness to His people in the Bible and 2,500 years of history proving He does care for His people. In addition, we have the Holy Spirit to guide us and support us in our tasks.

If members wrote a hymn, read or sing it in closing. Close with a prayer, encouraging members to trust God in the face of injustice and trouble.

---

1. Clyde T. Francisco; *Introducing the Old Testament*, rev. ed. (Nashville: Broadman Press; 1977), 196.

2. Ibid.

3. Robert Hastings in *Proclaim* (January/February/March 1993): 28. From Margaret T. Applegarth, "Twelve Baskets Full," *Harper's* 1957, 124–25.

October

6

1996

A Vain Search

Basic Passage: Jeremiah 5
Focal Passage: Jeremiah 5:1–6

In ancient Greece, Diogenes went through the streets of Athens searching for a truthful man. In ancient Judah, Jeremiah went through the streets of Jerusalem searching for a man of justice and truth. Instead, the prophet found people whose lives were the opposite of what he sought. God used this experience to show Jeremiah why He intended to punish Judah.

Study Aim: *To describe the results of Jeremiah's search for a person of justice and truth*

STUDYING THE BIBLE

OUTLINE AND SUMMARY

I. The Search for a Person of Justice and Truth (Jer. 5:1–9)
- **1. Searching for one person of justice and truth (v. 1)**
- **2. False swearing (v. 2)**
- **3. Hardened hearts (v. 3)**
- **4. Rich and poor (vv. 4–5)**
- **5. Coming destruction (v. 6)**
- **6. Beyond pardon (vv. 7–9)**

II. Announcement of Divine Judgment (Jer. 5:10–19)
- **1. Judgment on complacent sinners (vv. 10–14)**
- **2. A nation from afar (vv. 15–17)**
- **3. A glimmer of hope (vv. 18–19)**

III. The Depth of Judah's Sin (Jer. 5:20–31)
- **1. Spiritual blindness and rebellion (vv. 20–25)**
- **2. Sins of the rich (vv. 26–29)**
- **3. Lying religious leaders and complacent people (vv. 30–31)**

God commanded Jeremiah to search Jerusalem for a man of justice and truth (v. 1). The people swore false oaths using God's name (v. 2). They hardened themselves against divine corrections (v. 3). Such rebellion was found even among those who had been taught the ways of God (vv. 4–5). Judgment would come like a wild animal pouncing on its prey (v. 6). Idolatrous and adulterous people were beyond pardon (vv. 7–9). Judgment was coming on a fruitless and faithless people who discounted the warnings of true prophets (vv. 10–14). A distant nation would be God's instrument of judgment (vv. 15–17). Some would survive to testify to the justice of divine judgment (vv. 18–19). Spiritually blind people were ungrateful and rebellious (vv. 20–24). The rich oppressed rather than helped the needy (vv. 25–29). The horrible truth was that lying, self-serving religious leaders led a complacent people toward a terrible end (vv. 30–31).

I. The Search for a Person of Justice and Truth (Jer. 5:1–9)

1. Searching for one person of justice and truth (v. 1)

> 1 Run ye to and fro through the streets of Jerusalem, and see now, and know, and seek in the broad places thereof, if ye can find a man, if there be any that executeth judgment, that seeketh the truth; and I will pardon it.

Since Anathoth (AN uh thawth), Jeremiah's hometown, was only a few miles from Jerusalem, Jeremiah no doubt had often walked through the streets of Jerusalem. That was before he became a prophet. Jeremiah 5:1 records a divine command about a special trip to Jerusalem.

This command seems to have come early in the prophet's career. God was laying the foundation for his lengthy ministry to Judah. From the time of his call, Jeremiah had known that his primary mission was to preach judgment to sinful Judah (see Jer. 1). God's command to search for a person of justice and truth was designed to help the young prophet better understand the depth and extent of the people's sins and the reasons for God's wrath against them.

The first part of verse 1 stresses the thoroughness of the search. The prophet was to run to and fro through the streets of the city. The words "see," "know," and "seek" underscore the diligence with which Jeremiah was to search. He was to go through the streets and alleys as well as into the open places, like the marketplaces and squares.

Two words describe the kind of person he was seeking. "Judgment" is the familiar Old Testament word for justice. It means to do right, especially in dealings with other people. It has a negative side and a positive side. On one hand, a just person does not oppress or take advantage of other people. On the other hand, a just person defends those who are mistreated and challenges the oppressors.

The word "truth" has the root meaning of "firmness." The word carries the ideas of steadfastness and stability. The word thus describes a person who is firm in their faith in God and in their faithfulness to God. This firmness shows itself in fidelity and integrity in relating to other people. The best uses of our word "integrity" capture much of the meaning of the word. A person of integrity is a person who remains true to themselves, their God, and others.

God told Jeremiah that the purpose of the search was that God might pardon Jerusalem. Jeremiah was familiar with the intercessory prayer of Abraham for Sodom (SAHD uhm) as recorded in Genesis 18:22–33. Abraham had asked if it was right to punish the righteous with the wicked. Based on that plea, he asked God to spare Sodom if a few righteous people were found. Abraham began by asking that the city be spared for the sake of fifty and finally asked that it be spared for the sake of as few as ten. God said that He would spare Sodom for the sake of ten righteous men, but there were not ten righteous people in Sodom. The implication of the last line of Jeremiah 5:1 is that God would spare Jerusalem if Jeremiah could find even one righteous person.

2. False swearing (v. 2)

> 2 And though they say, The LORD liveth; surely they swear falsely.

Verse 2 accuses the people of being the opposite of the kind of person for which Jeremiah was to search. When the people wanted to stress that they were speaking the truth, they often took an oath using the words "the Lord lives." In other words, they would use the name of the Lord in swearing that they spoke the truth.

Verse 2 says that even as they swore by God's name, they knew that they spoke lies. They piously used God's name, thus claiming to represent the God of truth and justice. They used this false piety to try to hide their lying. They lied while swearing by everything sacred and holy. This is such a heinous sin that two of the Ten Commandments forbid taking God's name in vain and bearing false witness (Exod. 20:7,16).

3. Hardened hearts (v. 3)

> 3 O LORD, are not thine eyes upon the truth? thou hast stricken them, but they have not grieved; thou hast consumed them, but they have refused to receive correction: they have made their faces harder than a rock; they have refused to repent.

God's judgments had already fallen on people who played false with the truth. These initial judgments were designed to discipline and correct. However, the people refused to accept correction for their sins. Instead, they hardened their hearts like a rock. They refused to repent.

4. Poor and rich (vv. 4–5)

> 4 Therefore I said, Surely these are poor; they are foolish: for they know not the way of the LORD, nor the judgment of their God.
>
> 5 I will get me unto the great men, and will speak unto them; for they have known the way of the LORD, and the judgment of their God: but these have altogether broken the yoke, and burst the bonds.

Verses 2–3 describe what Jeremiah found during the first round of his search for a man of justice and truth. Verse 4 shows how he tried to put the best face on what he had found. He said to himself that he must have seen only the kind of people who lacked the advantage of religious training and experience.

"The poor" is used in verse 4 to describe people whose lives consisted of such ceaseless drudgery that they had no time for seeking to understand God's commandments and promises. This verse cannot be used to justify neglecting God's Word. Sometimes the "poor" in the Old Testament described people of humble and genuine faith (see 1 Sam. 2:8; Ps. 40:17). Most often, "poor" refers to those whom others are to help (see Pss. 41:1; 82:3–4).

Jeremiah tested his conclusion that the people described in verses 2–3 might have disregarded God and His laws because they had never been taught any differently. He tested this theory by examining the lives of people who had been taught about God and His laws. When Jeremiah examined the lives of the "great men" of the city, he found no difference between them and those who knew little about God.

These "great men" had been trained in the religion of their fathers, yet they had rebelled against their God. They are pictured as being like oxen who broke their yoke and burst their bonds. These privileged people lacked moral restraint and lived in open defiance of God and His ways.

5. Coming destruction (v. 6)

> 6 Wherefore a lion out of the forest shall slay them, and a wolf of the evenings shall spoil them, a leopard shall watch over their cities: every one that goeth out thence shall be torn in pieces: because their transgressions are many, and their backslidings are increased.

Verse 6 describes the sure judgment coming on the people for their rejection of God. The people of that day either lived in walled cities or locked themselves at night behind strong doors. Outside were dangers from enemies and wild animals. Verse 6 uses three wild animals to depict their coming death. They would perish as if a lion from the forest or a wolf out of the darkness sprang on them. Judgment hovered over them like a leopard hungrily watching over their city, ready to pounce on anyone who ventured outside.

6. Beyond pardon (vv. 7–9)

Such people were beyond pardon. They had forsaken the Lord for other gods. The men trooped to houses of prostitution and lusted after their neighbors' wives.

II. Announcement of Divine Judgment (Jer. 5:10–19)

1. Judgment on complacent sinners (vv. 10–14)

God issued a command for the partial destruction of His fruitless and faithless people. In their complacency, the people said that God would never send judgment on them. They called prophets like Jeremiah "windbags." God warned that He would use the words like a wind to spread the fire of judgment among them.

2. A nation from afar (vv. 15–17)

The executioners of divine wrath on Judah would be people from a distant nation. The mighty men of that nation would destroy the cities, crops, and people of Judah.

3. A glimmer of hope (vv. 18–19)

Not all the people would be destroyed. Some would survive to explain the reason for the divine judgment that fell on Judah for forsaking their God.

III. The Depth of Judah's Sins (Jer. 5:20–31)

1. Spiritual blindness and rebellion (vv. 20–25)

The people were blind to the goodness that God had shown to them and their forefathers. Instead of being grateful to God for His goodness, they were ungrateful and rebellious.

2. Sins of the rich (vv. 26–29)

The rich were especially guilty. They trapped the poor like a fowler snares birds. Not only did they not defend the cause of the needy, but also they exploited the needy. Their wickedness knew no bounds. Nothing remained but destruction for such people.

3. Lying religious leaders and complacent people (vv. 30–31)

The moral and spiritual plight of Judah was appalling. Prophets spoke lies. Priests did as they pleased. Few protests were raised against these false religious leaders. This was because the people themselves loved to have things just as they were. The chapter closes with a haunting question, "What will you do when the end comes?" (v. 31, RSV).

APPLYING THE BIBLE

1. To find an honest man. Darrel Teel was an honest man according to an Associated Press account. Homeless, broke with only nine cents in his pocket, Teel found a bundle of $100 bills one Sunday night. He admitted that for a little while he was tempted to keep the unexpected windfall. "I carried them bills around for about twenty minutes," he told authorities. "I thought about buying myself a new suit and getting a haircut, but I just couldn't keep it." When asked why he turned the $29,200 in to the police, Teel confessed: "I was afraid of God." For his honesty the lady whose savings had been turned in to the police by the homeless Teel gave him a measly $200.

God tells Jeremiah to walk Jerusalem's wicked streets and see "if ye can find a man . . . that seeketh the truth" (v.1).

God sought an honest man then as he seeks honest men and women to serve him today. Our churches are full of well-dressed, prosperous people, but how many of them are truly honest? Ponder the question in light of Malachi 3:8–10!

2. The value our society puts on God. Several years ago, *The New York Times Magazine* set up at a large book fair with what they called a library for the model modern home. In the library were five hundred well-chosen books of classic literature. There were only three or four dealing with religion, but they were included only because they were literary classics.

What a commentary this is on the state of our homes and society today! No wonder crime runs rampant across our nation, and gangs kill the innocent with neither reason nor remorse. The average American knows little, if anything, about the Ten Commandments or the Word of God. Genuine righteousness plays virtually no part in the scheme of things in American life.

This was Judah's condition when Jeremiah spoke as God's prophet (vv. 1–9). Repeatedly, he warned of impending national disaster; but they were deaf to the divine warnings (vv. 3:6–7).

3. Are you for real? Anthony Henderson was eight years old when President George Bush visited Anthony's school. But Anthony was skeptical. "How do I know you are the real president?" Anthony asked. Mr. Bush pulled out his driver's license and said: "There it is. I am George Herbert Walker Bush." Then Bush pulled out his American

Express card and told Anthony to look at the name. "I can even give you a ride in my black limousine," Mr. Bush said, wanting to be sure Anthony was convinced.

The next edition of *USA Today* told the whole story. Anthony was sitting next to the president examining his credit card! [1]

We claim to be Christians, but how hard would we have to work to convince our neighbors and acquaintances that we are really what we profess to be?

The people of Jerusalem and Judah made loud claims to being the people of God, but their lives denied it (vv. 1–3).

4. Unforsaken sins. Unconfessed, unforsaken sin is the costliest thing imaginable for the believer.

In his book *Iron Shoes*, the late Dr. Roy Angell tells about a deacon who came to see Angell one day. The deacon confessed his lack of joy and that he could no longer pray. "The heavens seem as glass," he confided. "What is wrong with me?"

Angell told the deacon that there must be some pet sin to which he was clinging, but the deacon empathetically denied that was the problem. They knelt and prayed, but in a week the deacon was back asking the same question but denying any unconfessed sin in his life. Four times this process was repeated, and each time the deacon went away with a heavy heart and a lack of joy.

Angell moved to another pastorate, and two years rolled by. One day as he walked out of the church, he came face to face with the deacon. After an embrace and a warm greeting, the deacon confessed that he had traveled a long way to set things right.

"Pastor, I lied to you two years ago when I came to see you. I was doing something wrong, plenty wrong. It had built a barrier between God and me. I have confessed and forsaken it; now I ask you to forgive me," he said. The two knelt again and prayed and the man went on his way with peace and joy in his heart.

That's the answer to the believer's sin. We pay too great a price to hold on to things that displease God. That was Judah's answer, too; but Judah steadily refused to repent and return to God even though she had been repeatedly warned about the tragedy that lay ahead.

TEACHING THE BIBLE

- *Main Idea:* God demands that His people do justice and seek truth.
- *Suggested Teaching Aim:* To lead adults to identify ways they can do justice and seek truth.

A TEACHING OUTLINE

1. Use an illustration to introduce the Bible study.
2. Use assignments to involve two members in teaching the lesson.
3. Use a poster to help members search for biblical truth.
4. Use brainstorming to help members apply the Bible to their lives.

Introduce the Bible Study

Use "To find an honest man" in "Applying the Bible" to introduce the Bible study.

Search for Biblical Truth

To set the context of the lesson, read or briefly summarize the twelve sentences immediately following the printed outline. **IN ADVANCE,** enlist one or two members to prepare a two-minute word study of "justice" and "truth" by reading the articles on these words in the *Holman Bible Dictionary* or another Bible dictionary. **IN ADVANCE,** prepare the following chart on a large sheet of paper or a chalkboard. Leave space between each of the three subheadings to add information called for in the teaching plan.

The Person God Is Looking For
Will Do
What He Found
Our Response

Call for a volunteer to read Jeremiah 5:1. Ask: What two qualifications is God looking for in a person? (Does justice and seeks truth.) Write these on the poster. Call for the enlisted members to report on their word studies. Point out that if God can find just one person who will do these, He will not destroy the whole city of Jerusalem. Ask: What would persons of Jeremiah's day do if they did justice and sought truth?

DISCUSS: How can one person who does justice and seeks truth influence a whole city for good today?

Point out that instead of finding people who did justice and sought truth, God found people who disregarded these qualities. Ask members to look at 5:4 to identify one category of people Jeremiah went to first. (The poor.) Ask them to find in 5:5 the people Jeremiah went to next. (The people of power.) Write these on the chart.

Ask members to search 5:2–3 and identify some of the characteristics of the people in Jerusalem. (Swore falsely, refused to grieve for their sins, refused God's correction, hardened their hearts.) Write these on the chart under "The Poor."

Point out that Jeremiah went next to the people of power. Ask members to look at 5:5 and find what Jeremiah discovered about the "great men." (Broken the yoke, burst the bonds.) Write these under "The People of Power."

DISCUSS: What evidence do you see that both leaders and common people have ignored God in our society?

Give the Truth a Personal Focus

Ask: How are we different from the people of Jeremiah's day? What would Jeremiah find if he came to our city today? How can we do justice? (List members' responses on the chart under "Our Response.") What can we do to seek truth? (List responses on the chart.)

Encourage members to identify one activity they can do as a class to emphasize justice and truth and one step they can take in their personal lives. Develop plans as a class to accomplish the one activity you chose.

---

1. Rick Lance in *Proclaim* (April/May/June 1993): 27.

October

13

1996

False Hopes for Peace

Basic Passage: Jeremiah 28–29

Focal Passage: Jeremiah 28:5–14

Both were prophets. Both claimed to speak the word of the Lord. Both addressed the same issue. Both spoke with conviction. Yet they spoke contradictory messages. Such situations often happened during Old Testament times. Several passages tell how to distinguish true from false prophets (see Deut. 13:1–5; 18:14–22; Jer. 23:9–40). Several passages provide examples of confrontations between prophets with different messages. None is more dramatic than the clash between Jeremiah and Hananiah (han uh NIGH uh) in Jeremiah 28 (see also 1 Kings 22).

Study Aim: *To contrast Jeremiah and his message with Hananiah and his message*

STUDYING THE BIBLE

OUTLINE AND SUMMARY

I. Clash Between Two Prophets (Jer. 28:1–17)
- **1. Hananiah's optimistic prophecy (28:1–4)**
- **2. Jeremiah's initial response (28:5–6)**
- **3. History of true prophecy (28:7–9)**
- **4. Hananiah's symbolic action (28:10–11)**
- **5. The yoke of iron (28:12–14)**
- **6. Judgment on Hananiah (28:15–17)**

II. Jeremiah's Letters to the Exiles (Jer. 29:1–32)
- **1. The first letter (29:1–23)**
- **2. Letter about Jeremiah (29:24–28)**
- **3. Another letter from Jeremiah (29:29–32)**

Hananiah predicted that Judah would be delivered from the Babylonian yoke within two years (28:1–4). Jeremiah said "amen" to that (28:5–6). However, Jeremiah proposed that they apply the history and tests of true prophecy (28:7–9). Hananiah then broke the yoke from Jeremiah's neck (28:10–11). The Lord told Jeremiah to declare that the yoke of subjection to Babylon would become like an iron yoke (28:12–14). Jeremiah announced God's judgment on Hananiah (28:15–17). Jeremiah wrote the exiles in Babylon, warning them not to listen to the false assurances of those who promised speedy deliverance (29:1–23). One of the prophets in exile sent a letter advising that Jeremiah be treated as a crazy man (29:24–28). Jeremiah was told by God to write a letter announcing God's judgment on this false prophet (29:29–32).

I. Clash Between Two Prophets (Jer. 28:1–17)

1. Hananiah's optimistic prophecy (28:1–4)

Two other Bible passages provide essential information for studying Jeremiah 28. Second Kings 24:10–17 sheds light on the historical setting. The events of Jeremiah 28–29 took place after Judah's first defeat by Babylonia but before the final destruction of the nation (2 Kings 25). Nebuchadnezzar (neb u kad NEZZ ur) of Babylonia had carried King Jeconiah (jek oh NIGH uh) and many leading citizens to Babylon. He also had taken many of the temple treasures.

The immediate context for Jeremiah 28 is in chapter 27. Using prophetic symbolism, Jeremiah had put a wooden yoke around his neck. He declared that Judah and the other small nations should give up plans to rebel against Babylon. Such rebellion would prove futile and fatal because God had given Nebuchadnezzar authority to rule for the immediate future. Thus Judah's Zedekiah was warned to submit to the yoke of Babylonia. Jeremiah warned against prophets who assured the people that the temple vessels in Babylon would be returned. Jeremiah predicted that the vessels still in Jerusalem would be taken to Babylon.

Jeremiah 28:1–4 tells how another prophet challenged the unpopular prophecy of Jeremiah. Hananiah predicted that within two years the temple vessels would be returned to Jerusalem and King Jeconiah would be restored to Judah.

2. Jeremiah's initial response (28:5–6)

> 5 Then the prophet Jeremiah said unto the prophet Hananiah in the presence of the priests, and in the presence of all the people that stood in the house of the LORD.
>
> 6 Even the prophet Jeremiah said, Amen: the LORD do so: the LORD perform thy words which thou hast prophesied, to bring again the vessels of the LORD's house, and all that is carried away captive, from Babylon into this place.

Jeremiah said "amen" to Hananiah's prophecy and then expressed his sincere desire that the words of Hananiah might indeed be the words of the Lord. How can we explain such a positive response from Jeremiah to a prediction that contradicted his own prophecy?

We do not know Jeremiah's tone of voice. He may have spoken with a note of sarcasm in his voice because he knew these words did not come from the Lord. An earlier prophet, Micaiah [mich KAY uh], used this strategy when he was confronted with words of prophets who spoke words of false assurance (1 Kings 22:14–17).

Jeremiah may have spoken in complete sincerity. As a Judean, he was no less patriotic than his fellow countrymen. Thus he yearned that the prediction might be true. Perhaps he thought that Hananiah had indeed received a fresh word from the Lord. Jeremiah knew that God had at times relented from intended destruction. The Book of Jonah provides a striking example. But Jeremiah also knew that God relented when people repented, and he had seen no signs of such repentance in Judah.

3. History of true prophecy (28:7–9)

> 7 Nevertheless hear thou now this word that I speak in thine ears, and in the ears of all the people;
>
> 8 The prophets that have been before me and before thee of old prophesied both against many countries, and against great kingdoms, of war, and of evil, and of pestilence.

9 The prophet which prophesieth of peace, when the word of the prophet shall come to pass, then shall the prophet be known, that the LORD hath truly sent him.

Jeremiah reminded himself and his hearers of the history and tests of true prophecy. Jeremiah and Hananiah interpreted the same history differently. Hananiah claimed to stand in the line of prophets who promised divine deliverance to God's people.

Although Hananiah didn't refer directly to Isaiah, he and his fellow prophets built their approach on Isaiah's prophecy of Jerusalem's deliverance from the Assyrians (Isa. 37). These prophets claimed that Isaiah's words meant that God would never allow His nation and city to fall into the hands of a godless nation. Thus Hananiah saw himself as a new Isaiah predicting a dramatic deliverance of God's people and His holy city.

Jeremiah knew the history of Isaiah as well as Hananiah. He sincerely wished that deliverance could come to Jerusalem. However, Jeremiah recognized that Isaiah and the other past prophets had often been forced to predict divine judgments on people because of their sins. Deliverance came when people's repentance enabled God to turn from judgment to deliverance. Jeremiah knew that God could deliver Judah; but Jeremiah also believed that such deliverance depended on the people turning to God, and he saw no evidence of a genuine turning to God.

The history of prophecy shows that true prophets speak God's word even when the message is unpopular. False prophets are more likely to say what people want to hear. On other occasions, Jeremiah charged that false prophets cried, "Peace, peace; when there is no peace" (Jer. 6:14; 8:11). The people wanted to hear a message of deliverance and peace; prophets like Hananiah gave them what they wanted. Jeremiah persisted in declaring the word God had given him, no matter how unpopular the message (compare 1 Kings 22:14–17; Jer. 23:16–17; 2 Tim. 4:3).

In verse 9, Jeremiah proposed that the people apply to Hananiah's prophecy the classic Old Testament test for discerning true prophecy. Hananiah had predicted that deliverance would come in two years. Jeremiah proposed waiting and seeing if his prediction came true. If it didn't, Hananiah was a false prophet (see Deut. 18:21–22).

4. Hananiah's symbolic action (28:10–11)

10 Then Hananiah the prophet took the yoke from off the prophet Jeremiah's neck, and brake it.

11 And Hananiah spake in the presence of all the people, saying, Thus saith the LORD; Even so will I break the yoke of Nebuchadnezzar king of Babylon from the neck of all nations within the space of two full years. And the prophet Jeremiah went his way.

Earlier Jeremiah had put a yoke on his neck to show that the Judeans should submit to Nebuchadnezzar (Jer. 27:2–8). Jeremiah 28:11 shows that Jeremiah had continued to wear the yoke as a vivid reminder of his prophecy. Hananiah now seized the initiative by breaking the yoke on Jeremiah's neck. He announced that he did this as a striking way to reinforce his earlier prediction of deliverance from Babylon within two years.

For Bible students, the most puzzling part of verse 11 is the last line. Why did Jeremiah respond to Hananiah's bold act by silently leaving? Some have suggested that he left because he was afraid, but Jeremiah boldly faced greater threats than the one posed by Hananiah. Others have suggested that Jeremiah was confused by the boldness and seeming conviction of Hananiah's prediction and action in breaking the yoke. According to this view, Jeremiah was willing to concede for the time being that Hananiah might have a fresh word from the Lord.

The most likely explanation for Jeremiah's action was that he had not yet received a word from the Lord about how to respond. Earlier he had put on the yoke at the Lord's command (Jer. 27:2). True to his calling, Jeremiah waited for the Lord to speak.

5. The yoke of iron (28:12–14)

> 12 Then the word of the LORD came unto Jeremiah the prophet, after that Hananiah the prophet had broken the yoke from off the neck of the prophet Jeremiah, saying,
>
> 13 Go and tell Hananiah, saying, Thus saith the LORD; Thou hast broken the yokes of wood; but thou shalt make for them yokes of iron.
>
> 14 For thus saith the LORD of hosts, the God of Israel; I have put a yoke of iron upon the necks of all these nations, that they may serve Nebuchadnezzar king of Babylon; and they shall serve him; and I have given him the beasts of the field also.

Fresh instructions from the Lord came to Jeremiah. He was told to go and tell Hananiah what the Lord said. Hananiah had broken yokes of wood, but he only succeeded in making yokes of iron. The message of the iron yoke was to reinforce the Lord's earlier word to Jeremiah, which had been symbolized by the wooden yoke (Jer. 27:2–8). It not only repeated the gist of the earlier prophecy; it also strengthened it. If a wooden yoke symbolized subjection to Babylon by Judah and the other nations, an iron yoke only added to the strength of the symbol.

6. Judgment on Hananiah (28:15–17)

Armed with this fresh word from the Lord, Jeremiah confronted Hananiah. The Lord had not sent him as he had claimed. Jeremiah predicted Hananiah's death, which took place two months later.

II. Jeremiah's Letters to Exiles (Jer. 29:1–32)

1. The first letter (29:1–23)

Jeremiah wrote to those who had already been carried as captives into Babylon. False prophets were stirring up false hopes by promising that God would soon deliver them. Jeremiah advised them to settle down and make the best of their captivity. He assured them that God eventually would restore His people but that it would be seventy years.

2. Letter about Jeremiah (29:24–28)

Shemiah (shih MIGH uh), one of the exiles, resented Jeremiah's letter. He wrote to Zephaniah (zef uh NIGH uh), a priest in Jerusalem, advising that Jeremiah be treated as a crazy man.

3. Another letter from Jeremiah (29:29–32)

Instead of imprisoning Jeremiah, Zephaniah told the prophet about the letter from Shemiah. The Lord instructed Jeremiah to write to the exiles and tell them that God had condemned Shemiah for his lies to the exiles and his slander against Jeremiah.

APPLYING THE BIBLE

1. Giving the people what they want to hear. Israel, the northern kingdom, has fallen and been carried into captivity by Assyria. Judah stands alone, but Jeremiah continues to warn the leaders about the descending wrath of God upon the nation (29:1–14; 30:12–15).

Hananiah came on the scene prophesying what the nation's leaders wanted to hear (28:1–4). Jeremiah, God's prophet, said the Babylonian exile would last seventy years (29:10); but Hananiah, who told the leaders what they wanted to hear, declared it would last only two years (28:3). Yet Jeremiah was right for he told the people what God said, not what they wanted to hear. That's the mark of a true prophet.

Our people in our churches today need to hear the plain, undiluted, unvarnished Word of God from their preachers. "Thus saith the Lord" is what is needed, not "This is what I think!" Pious platitudes preached by pastors to people weighted down by their sins are not God's way of dealing with sin. It must be cut out by the divine scalpel if healing is to occur.

2. The Word of God desperately needed. For the first 150 years of American history, the Word of God was the basis for education, devotion and colonial government. Things have changed and not for the better.

The Bibles used in the colonies had been shipped in from England, but the American Revolution changed all that and the flow of Bibles to the people stopped. In 1777, Patrick Allison, chaplain of the Congress, placed before that body a petition for immediate relief. It was decided by a committee especially appointed that the matter was so critical that it should be brought before Congress, and 20,000 copies of the Bible were imported from Holland. The need arose once again in 1780 and Robert Aitken, publisher of *The Pennsylvania Magazine,* saw the need and quietly set out to do something about it. In 1781, Congress approved Aitken's request to print the Bibles needed, and the next year they came off the press.

The Word of God was the foundation upon which Judah's national life was founded. Heeding its instructions was the answer to Judah's problem. But, much like America today, they ignored it to their own hurt.

3. Faith in the midst of discouragement. Abraham Lincoln was once asked how he felt after an unsuccessful election. Lincoln replied that he felt like the little boy who had stubbed his toe in the dark; too old to cry, and it hurt too much to laugh.

A man once stopped to watch some boys in a sand-lot baseball game. When he inquired about the score, one of the boys said: "It's twenty-eight to nothing agin' us right now."

"My," the man asked, "Aren't you a bit discouraged?" "Oh, no," the boy replied. "We ain't been up to bat yet!"

No doubt Jeremiah was discouraged. He had faithfully proclaimed God's word to Judah, warning what was coming if they did not repent and turn to God. Even Hananiah publicly opposed Jeremiah in the house of the Lord, trying to discredit him before the priests and the people. Hananiah all but called God's prophet a liar; but in spite of all the discouragement he faced, Jeremiah remained faithful to God and His word and lived to see it fulfilled (28:12–17).

4. The key verses. The key verses for our lesson, and the key to a full, meaningful life, are Jeremiah 29:12–13: "Then shall ye call upon me, and ye shall go and pray unto me, and I will hearken unto you. And ye shall seek me, and find me, when ye shall search for me with all your heart."

But there was a thorn in God's promise that Judah could not accept: "When ye shall search for me with all your heart" (29:13). The holy city was full of idolatry. Wickedness of all kinds—adultery, lying, cheating, graft—abounded on all sides. In spite of God's promise to remove the curse from Judah if she repented, Judah refused to hear the word of the Lord (29:14) and plunged on toward national disaster.

Read Jeremiah's prophecy, then read your morning newspaper. What similarities do you see? Today's news seems as though it were taken from Jeremiah's prophecy. If God so dealt with Judah which was the very apple of His eye, how do you suppose He will deal with us? Repentance is our greatest need today!

TEACHING THE BIBLE

- *Main Idea:* Those who speak what we want to hear are not always speaking for God.
- *Suggested Teaching Aim:* To lead adults to describe true prophets.

A TEACHING OUTLINE

1. Use a Jeremiah monologue to introduce the Bible study.

2. Use a strip poster to guide the search for biblical truth.

3. Use brainstorming and case studies to help members give the truth a personal focus.

Introduce the Bible Study

IN ADVANCE, enlist a member to use the nine summary statements following the outline as the basis for a Jeremiah monologue. Call on the member to begin the study session.

Search for Biblical Truth

IN ADVANCE, prepare a strip poster containing the six points under "I. Clash Between Two Prophets (Jer. 28:1–17)." Place the first heading on the focal wall ("1. Hananiah's optimistic prophecy [28:1–4]") and use the material to provide the immediate background for the lesson.

Call for a volunteer to read 28:5–6. Place the second point on the focal wall ("Jeremiah's initial response [28:5–6]"). Ask: What was Hananiah's prophecy? What was Jeremiah's response? Why did Jeremiah respond in the way he did?

DISCUSS: What do you do when two equally sincere people differ about God's will?

Place the third point on the focal wall ("History of true prophecy [28:7–9]"). Call for a volunteer to read 28:7–9. Ask: What was the test of true prophecy? (If it came true.) Use the comments in "Studying the Bible" on these verses to show how Hananiah used Isaiah's prophecy of Jerusalem's deliverance from the Assyrians.

Place the fourth point on the focal wall ("4. Hananiah's symbolic action [28:10–11]"). Call on a volunteer to read 28:10–11. Ask: What did Hananiah do to show the force of his prophecy? (Broke yoke.) Why do you think Jeremiah responded as he did? (See "Studying the Bible.")

Place the fifth point on the focal wall ("5. The yoke of iron [28:12–14]"). Ask: What was the Lord's response to Hananiah's breaking the wooden yoke? What did this symbolic action mean?

Place the sixth point on the focal wall ("6. Judgment on Hananiah [28:15–17]"). Briefly point out that in this case God did not wait two years to show that Hananiah's prophecy was false. Hananiah died two months later as predicted by Jeremiah.

Give the Truth a Personal Focus

Give each member a piece of paper and a pencil. Ask them to write how believers today can distinguish between a true prophet and a false one. Ask members to share their ideas as you write them on a chalkboard or a large sheet of paper.

Organize the class in groups of two or three members. Ask them to write a brief case study about a modern false prophet. Ask them to read their case study to the class and let members tell why, based on the list, they would consider the person a false prophet.

Close in prayer, asking for courage to support those who do tell us the truth, even if it is not what we want to hear.

A Rebellious People

Basic Passage: Ezekiel 2:1–3:21

Focal Passages: Ezekiel 2:3–7; 3:4–11

Jeremiah and Ezekiel were contemporaries. Ezekiel began his ministry during the closing years of Jeremiah's long ministry. Jeremiah preached to the people in Judah. Ezekiel preached to the first group of exiles in Babylon (see 2 Kings 24:10–17). The call of Ezekiel to serve as a prophet is in Ezekiel 1–3. His call was similar in many ways to the call of Jeremiah in Jeremiah 1. Both were called to preach to rebellious people, and both were assured of divine strength for the difficult mission.

Study Aim: *To describe how God called and equipped Ezekiel to preach to a rebellious people*

STUDYING THE BIBLE

OUTLINE AND SUMMARY

I. Called to Preach to Rebellious People (Ezek. 2:1–3:3)

1. Hearing God's call (2:1–2)

2. Mission to rebellious people (2:3)

3. Called to be a prophet for God (2:4–5)

4. Fear not (2:6–7)

5. Eating the scroll (2:8–3:3)

II. Equipped for the Task (Ezek. 3:4–21)

1. Hardened hearers (3:4–7)

2. Strengthened messenger (3:8–9)

3. Spirit-led prophet to exiles (3:10–15)

4. A prophetic watchman (3:16–21)

As God's Spirit entered Ezekiel, God spoke to him (2:1–2). God sent Ezekiel to a people whose entire history was one of rebellion against God (2:3). Ezekiel was to speak God's word so that regardless of the people's response, they would realize that a prophet had been among them (2:4–5). Although Ezekiel would feel like someone in a brier patch filled with scorpions, he was not to fear the people, their words, or their looks (2:6–7). When Ezekiel obeyed God's command to eat a scroll filled with words of sadness and woe, the scroll tasted sweet (2:8–3:3). God told Ezekiel that foreigners who spoke another language would be more likely to obey God's word through Ezekiel than the people of Israel, who spoke the same language as the prophet (3:4–7). God promised to make the prophet's face and forehead hard enough to withstand the hard faces of the people (3:8–9). God sent Ezekiel as a Spirit-led spokesman to Jewish exiles (3:10–15). God told Ezekiel that he was a watchman who was called to warn the people of divine judgment for their sins (3:16–21).

I. Called to Preach to Rebellious People (Jer. 2:1—3:3)

1. Hearing God's call (2:1–2)

A central part of Ezekiel's call was the startling vision of God in Ezekiel 1:4–28. God's voice spoke to Ezekiel out of the vision. God's Spirit entered him as he heard God speak.

2. Mission to rebellious people (2:3)

> 3 And he said unto me, Son of man, I send thee to the children of Israel, to a rebellious nation that hath rebelled against me: they and their fathers have transgressed against me, even unto this very day.

The Lord addressed Ezekiel as "son of man" here and many times throughout the Book of Ezekiel. This title had a specialized meaning in Daniel 7:13–14 and in the New Testament references to this as a title for Jesus. The title as applied to Ezekiel does not have the meaning of the title in Daniel and in the New Testament. The words "son of man" as applied to Ezekiel stressed the humanity of the prophet. He repeatedly was confronted by visions and words of the exalted, eternal God; but the title reminded Ezekiel that he himself was a mere man who was privileged to be the spokesman for God Himself.

Verse 3 uses the words "rebel" and "rebellious" to describe the basic sin of the children of Israel. One or the other of these words occurs over and over in Ezekiel 2–3 to describe Israel's rebellion against God (2:3, 5, 6, 7, 8; 3:9, 26, 27). God had offered to Israel a unique relation with Him by offering them a covenant with Him. Their part of the covenant was to serve God only and to keep His commandments. They had rebelled against God by repeatedly breaking the covenant with God.

This was not something that had happened for the first time in Ezekiel's day. In God's call to Ezekiel, God accused Israel of having rebelled against Him throughout their history. The history of Israel from the golden calf until the exile had been a history of continual rebellion against God.

3. Called to be a prophet for God (2:4–5)

> 4 For they are impudent children and stiffhearted. I do send thee unto them; and thou shalt say unto them, Thus saith the Lord GOD.
>
> 5 And they, whether they will hear, or whether they will forbear, (for they are a rebellious house,) yet shall know that there hath been a prophet among them.

The word "impudent" literally means "hard of face." It describes a shameless person who brazenly refuses to lower his eyes before his accusers. "Stiffhearted" means a person of stubborn, unyielding will who refuses to give way even when found guilty. These were marks of the rebellious people to whom Ezekiel was sent.

God's commission was twofold: (1) Ezekiel was to speak in the name of the Lord God. (2) Regardless of the response of the people, they should know that a true prophet of God had been among them. The prophet's personal responsibility, in spite of the people's response, was emphasized also in 2:7 and 3:11.

(Passages like Ezek. 3:14–21; 18; and 33:1–20 stress the responsibility of the prophet to deliver God's warning and the responsibility of each person to respond.)

4. Fear not (2:6–7)

6 And thou, son of man, be not afraid of them, neither be afraid of their words, though briers and thorns be with thee, and thou dost dwell among scorpions: be not afraid of their words, nor be dismayed at their looks, though they be a rebellious house.

7 And thou shalt speak my words unto them, whether they will hear, or whether they will forbear: for they are most rebellious.

Compare these verses with Jeremiah 1:8, 17. Both Jeremiah and Ezekiel were called to preach to people who had rebelled against God. The same people rebelled at God's word and reacted against the prophets who spoke God's word. The prophets were tempted to cease their preaching in the face of angry looks and threatening words and actions. God warned Ezekiel that he would feel like someone thrown into a brier patch full of deadly scorpions.

God's command was twofold: (1) Don't be afraid of the rebellious people, their fierce looks, or threatening words. (2) Faithfully speak God's word—regardless of the response of the people to the message.

5. Eating the scroll (2:8–3:3)

God warned Ezekiel not to become rebellious like the people to whom God sent him. Instead he was to deliver God's message of judgment. This commission came in the form of a vision of a scroll filled with words of sadness and woe. God commanded Ezekiel to eat the scroll; and when he did, it tasted as sweet as honey.

II. Equipped for the Task (Ezek. 3:4–21)

1. Hardened hearers (3:4–7)

4 And he said unto me, Son of man, go, get thee unto the house of Israel, and speak with my words unto them.

5 For thou art not sent to a people of a strange speech and of an hard language, but to the house of Israel;

6 Not to many people of a strange speech and of an hard language, whose words thou canst not understand. Surely, had I sent thee to them, they would have hearkened unto thee.

7 But the house of Israel will not hearken unto thee; for they will not hearken unto me: for all the house of Israel are impudent and hardhearted.

Ezekiel was told to speak God's word to his own people who spoke the same language as he. On the surface, this would seem to be an easier task than if Ezekiel had to learn a foreign language and speak to foreigners. However, God told Ezekiel that a mission to foreigners would have been more successful than a mission to fellow Israelites. God said that foreigners who could not understand the language of the prophet would be more likely to hear and obey than would the Israelites, who fully understood the words of the prophet.

In verse 7, God clearly predicted that the Israelites would reject the message of Ezekiel. They had refused to listen to God; not surprisingly, they also would not listen to God's prophet. Such rejection of God's word by the guilty people would show them to be impudent and hard-hearted (see 2:4).

2. Strengthened messenger (3:8–9)

> 8 Behold, I have made thy face strong against their faces, and thy forehead strong against their foreheads.
>
> 9 As an adamant harder than flint have I made thy forehead: fear them not, neither be dismayed at their looks, though they be a rebellious house.

Chapter 3 is part of the same commission as chapter 2. The call itself is in chapter 2; chapter 3 includes the divine equipping of the prophet for his difficult mission. Compare Ezekiel 3:8–9 with Jeremiah 1:8, 17–19. When God called Jeremiah, He promised to make the prophet like a strong city, an iron pillar, and a brass wall. God used different figures to make the same promise to Ezekiel.

Ezekiel would be confronted with people of hard faces (the literal meaning of "impudent" in 2:4; 3:7). God promised to make Ezekiel's face even stronger and harder. God would make His prophet's forehead as hard as flint. This would enable him to confront the rebellious people and not flinch before their hardness.

The name "Ezekiel" means "God strengthens" or "God hardens." Some Bible scholars think that this passage may be the basis for the prophet's name. One of the marks of Ezekiel's ministry was his ability to outlast his opponents and not to be worn down by their attacks. The source of such strength and endurance was the Lord Himself. Ezekiel confronted the threats and attacks of opponents in the strength of the Lord.

3. Spirit-led prophet to exiles (3:10–15)

> 10 Moreover he said unto me, Son of man, all my words that I shall speak unto thee receive in thine heart, and hear with thine ears.
>
> 11 And go, get thee to them of the captivity, unto the children of thy people, and speak unto them, and tell them, Thus saith the Lord GOD; whether they will hear, or whether they will forbear.

Ezekiel was told to hear God's word and to receive it, first of all, into his own heart. Then he was to speak God's word to the exiles. This is one of many verses in Ezekiel that make clear that his message was for exiles. Ezekiel himself was among the exiles in Babylon (Ezek. 1:1). God used him to speak to his fellow exiles. Once again God stressed that Ezekiel was not responsible for how the people responded to the message. He was responsible for delivering the message.

Verses 12–15 show that Ezekiel 2:1–3:11 described God's call to Ezekiel from the vision of the wheels in Ezekiel 1:4–28. Ezekiel was inspired and led by God's Spirit during that exalted experience.

4. A prophetic watchman (3:16–21)

Seven days after the vision and call, God spoke again to Ezekiel. God told the prophet that he was like a watchman, whose task it was to warn Israel of coming judgment. God would not hold Ezekiel responsible for how people responded, but He would hold him accountable for warning them. (Ezekiel 18 stressed the responsibility of each hearer; see the lesson for Oct. 27.)

APPLYING THE BIBLE

1. Tongue-tied Christians. A fourth-grader by the name of Teddy England became literally tongue-tied. Curiosity got the better of the West Virginia lad when, one bitterly cold day, he put his tongue against an iron pole while waiting outside for the school bus. You guessed it! His tongue immediately froze to the pole and it was almost an hour before it occurred to someone to pour warm water on his tongue to loosen it. The tongue-tied Teddy learned a lesson he would never forget.

How many of us who claim the name of Christ are tongue-tied? Oh, not tongue-tied in the literal sense but hesitant and silent in sharing with others what God has done for us in Jesus Christ.

God called Ezekiel to share God's warning and plea for repentance with the exiles (1:1–3). (Francisco says Ezekiel's call came in 592 B.C. before the prophet was carried away into the Babylonian captivity in 597 B.C.). [1] Ezekiel was faithful to his call in the face of great opposition.

2. Let your light shine. Benjamin Franklin was an extraordinary visionary. He was trying to persuade his fellow Philadelphians to light the streets of their city, but with little success. Instead of arguing with them over the matter, he bought a beautiful, large lantern, polished the lens brightly and hung it in front of his house. He kept the wick well trimmed and the lantern brightly polished and it gave off a good light. By his own efforts, Franklin showed his townspeople what just one lantern would do; and soon they were following his example.

Jesus tells us to let our light of Christian witness shine when He says: "Let your light so shine among men, that they may see your good works, and glorify your Father which is in heaven" (Matt. 5:16). In both Jerusalem before the exile and in Babylon during the exile, Ezekiel was faithful to do this until his last prophecy in 570 B.C. (29:17).[2]

3. We have our great moments and some not so great. Some of the outstanding characters of the Bible served God faithfully at times, but were also disobedient at times. Is it not our autobiography too?

Adam and Eve were put in a garden of splendor, but their disobedience brought the sin-curse on the world. Noah was obedient in building the ark but guilty of drunkenness and incest with his daughter. Abraham was obedient when he left his home to follow God into the land of promise but disobedient when he took Hagar to his tent to "help" God fulfill His promise of a son.

Moses was finally obedient when he went back to Egypt at God's call to deliver His people from bondage but disobedient when he murdered the Egyptian. David was obedient in the manner in which he treated jealous King Saul, the Lord's anointed but disobedient when he committed adultery with Bathsheba and murdered her husband. Then there is Peter: obedient when he forsook his nets and followed Jesus but disobedient in denying his Savior.

Ezekiel's life, we can be sure, was not perfect; but he ranks among the faithful witnesses of the Bible who took a stand against the sins of his people and would not compromise (2:3–8). Obedience, faithfulness is the chief thing God requires of each of us.

4. Let the fire fall. Years ago in California's Yosemite Park, there was a thrilling ceremony that drew large crowds. High above the park on the mighty peak workmen would build a huge bonfire, adding wood all through the day. Just as full darkness fell, someone on the ground below would call up to the workmen, "Let the fire fall!" The huge cauldron of burning coals would then be pushed over the high cliff and fall like a molten river on the ground below as the people shouted and cheered.

Ezekiel calls day in and day out for the fires of repentance and spiritual awakening to fall upon the wicked people of God, but, alas, to no avail. They go on in their rebellion against God and pay a terrible price for it (3:4–11).

Our daily prayer for ourselves, our homes, our churches, and our nation ought to be, "Let the fire of God fall upon us and cleanse us as it cleansed Isaiah" (Isa. 6:5–7).

TEACHING THE BIBLE

- *Main Idea:* God calls us to be faithful, not successful.
- *Suggested Teaching Aim:* To lead adults to determine to be faithful in their witness for Christ.

A TEACHING OUTLINE

1. *Use an illustration to introduce the Bible study.*
2. *Use a matching exercise to begin the search for biblical truth.*
3. *Use Scripture search and brief lectures to examine the biblical passage.*
4. *Use a chart to compare Jeremiah and Ezekiel.*
5. *Use questions to make the study personal.*

Introduce the Bible Study

Use "Let your light shine" from "Applying the Bible" to introduce the Bible study.

Search for Biblical Truth

Copy the summary statements on one color of paper and the Scripture references on sheets of another color. Mix up both the statements and the references and place them at random on the wall around the room. Ask members to match the statement with the appropriate Scripture.

Point out that Ezekiel and Jeremiah were contemporaries but that Jeremiah prophesied in Judah and Ezekiel prophesied in Babylonia. Display a map and locate Jerusalem and Babylonia.

Ask members to look at Ezekiel 2:3. Ask what the title, "son of man" means when applied to Ezekiel. Ask members to check different translations to see how the phrase is translated. Use the comments on this verse in "Studying the Bible" to explain how it is used.

Ask members to find words that describe the children of Israel in this verse. (Rebellious, rebelled, transgressed.) Ask members to name some times in Israel's history when they rebelled.

Ask members to look at 2:4–5. Using the material in "Studying the Bible," explain "impudent" and "stiffhearted." Explain Ezekiel's call.

IN ADVANCE, prepare the following chart except the italicized phrases:

Two Prophets

	Jeremiah	Ezekiel
Sent to	*Judah*	*Babylonia*
People's Condition	*free*	*exiles*
People's Reaction	*rebellious*	*rebellious*
Prophet's Response	*faithful*	*faithful*
God's Command	*fear not; preach*	*fear not; preach*
God's Support	*strength*	*strength*

Ask members to look at Ezekiel 2:6–7 and Jeremiah 1:8, 17, and based on their study of Jeremiah last week, fill in the chart. (Their answers may differ somewhat and be correct.)

Ask members to look at Ezekiel 3:4–7. Ask: Why did God say it would be easier for Ezekiel to go to a people who spoke a foreign language? (They would respond; Jews would not.)

DISCUSS: Why did the Jews not listen? Why do we not listen?

Ask members to look at Ezekiel 3:6–9. Ask: How did God equip Ezekiel for his task?

DISCUSS: How does God equip His people today? What evidence do you see that He has equipped you for a special task?

Ask members to look at Ezekiel 3:10–11. Ask: What was Ezekiel's responsibility? (Proclaim all God told him.) What was Ezekiel to do if the people would not listen? (Deliver the message even if people did not respond.)

DISCUSS: What word would this passage speak to us about our responsibility to witness?

Give the Truth a Personal Focus

Ask: What enabled Ezekiel to be faithful in the face of great rejection and disappointment? (Let them respond. Consider this: Certainty of God's call to them, God's equipping him for the task.) Does God call us to a lesser degree of faithfulness than He called Ezekiel? (No.) What can we do to develop the same degree of commitment Ezekiel had?

Personal Responsibility

Basic Passage: Ezekiel 18

Focal Passages: Ezekiel 18:1–5, 7–13, 19–20

True repentance begins when we accept responsibility for our own sins. People often try to avoid accepting such responsibility. They try to shift the blame to someone other than themselves. The exiles to whom Ezekiel ministered were trying to blame earlier generations for their own moral and spiritual plight. God led Ezekiel to proclaim clearly the doctrine of personal responsibility.

Study Aim: *To explain what God revealed through Ezekiel about personal responsibility for sins*

STUDYING THE BIBLE

OUTLINE AND SUMMARY

I. Principle of Personal Responsibility (Ezek. 18:1–4)

II. The Principle Illustrated (Ezek. 18:5–19)

1. A righteous man (vv. 5–9)

2. The wicked son of a righteous man (vv. 10–13)

3. The righteous son of a wicked father (vv. 14–19)

III. Summary of the Principle (Ezek. 18:20)

IV. The Principle Applied to Changed Lives (Ezek. 18:21–32)

1. Two kinds of changes (vv. 21–24)

2. Charge that God is unjust (vv. 25–29)

3. Call to repentance (vv. 30–32)

God denied the claim of the people that they were suffering for the sins of their fathers (vv. 1–4). A righteous person fulfills God's commandments and lives (vv. 5–9). A wicked son of a righteous father suffers for his own sins (vv. 10–13). A righteous son of a wicked father is not punished for his father's sins (vv. 14–19). The principle holds: each person is responsible for his or her own actions (v. 20). A sinner can repent and live, and a righteous person can turn to sin and be punished (vv. 21–24). Although the people accused God of being unjust, they were the ones who were unjust (vv. 25–29). God calls sinners to repent, and they receive a new heart and spirit (vv. 30–32).

I. Principle of Personal Responsibility (Ezek. 18:1–4)

1 The word of the LORD came unto me again, saying,

2 What mean ye, that ye use this proverb concerning the land of Israel, saying, The fathers have eaten sour grapes, and the children's teeth are set on edge?

3 As I live, saith the Lord GOD, ye shall not have occasion any more to use this proverb in Israel.

4 Behold, all souls are mine; as the soul of the father, so also the soul of the son is mine: the soul that sinneth, it shall die.

Ezekiel 18 begins with God calling attention to a proverb or popular saying, "The fathers have eaten sour grapes, and the children's teeth are set on edge." The saying probably originated in Judah, where it was condemned by Jeremiah (Jer. 31:29). Ezekiel encountered the saying among the Jewish exiles in Babylon. God spoke through the prophet to demand that the people cease using this saying.

The people of Israel were using the saying to blame their forefathers for their own plight. The people implied that they were being made to suffer for sins of earlier generations, not for any sins of their own. They said that their fathers had eaten sour grapes (committed great sins against God); yet their children were left with the bitter aftertaste (the bitter harvest of their fathers' sins).

Verse 4 affirms two basic truths: (1) All people belong to God in the sense of being accountable to Him. (2) Each person is individually accountable to God for personal actions. Applied to the saying in verse 2, verse 4 means that each person must answer for personal sins, not for the sins of one's parents.

II. The Principle Illustrated (Ezek. 18:5–19)

Verses 5–19 provide three illustrations of the principle: (1) a righteous man (vv. 5–9), (2) the wicked son of the righteous man (vv. 10–13), and (3) the righteous son of the wicked man (vv. 14–19).

1. A righteous man (vv. 5–9)

> 5 But if a man be just, and do that which is lawful and right,
>
> 7 And hath not oppressed any, but hath restored to the debtor his pledge, hath spoiled none by violence, hath given his bread to the hungry, and hath covered the naked with a garment;
>
> 8 He that hath not given forth upon usury, neither hath taken any increase, that hath withdrawn his hand from iniquity, hath executed true judgment between man and man,
>
> 9 Hath walked in my statutes, and hath kept my judgments, to deal truly; he is just, he shall surely live, saith the Lord GOD.

Verses 5–9 describe a righteous person by the standards of the Old Testament Law. The description begins and ends with general statements (vv. 5,9a). In between is a list of thirteen specific examples of Old Testament righteousness.

The examples in verse 6 condemn idolatry and sexual immorality. The five examples in verse 7 deal with treatment of the poor. The righteous person avoids oppression and violence and provides food and clothing for the needy. Returning a debtor's pledge means giving back an item that the debtor had used as a pledge to repay a loan (Exod. 22:26–27).

The theme of merciful treatment of others continues in verse 8. An Israelite could charge interest on a loan to a foreigner but could not charge interest to a fellow Israelite (Deut. 23:19–20). A righteous person did not practice "usury" or in any way gain a personal "increase" from the misfortune of a fellow Israelite. A righteous person would not be involved in iniquity but would always deal fairly with others.

Such a person would be truly just or righteous by Old Testament standards. When God gave the Law through Moses, He promised life to those who kept the Law and death to those who persistently disobeyed. The description of life and death in passages like Deuteronomy 30 shows that "life" in passages like Ezekiel 18 referred to a long, happy life in fellowship with God. "Death" referred to calamity and destruction.

If we had only passages like verses 3–9, we might conclude that righteous people earn their salvation by their own goodness. We need to keep in mind that the full revelation of God in Christ clearly teaches that salvation from sin and spiritual death is by grace through faith in Christ. Also remember that Ezekiel ministered when Israel lived under the Law given at Mount Sinai.

2. The wicked son of a righteous father (vv. 10–13)

> 10 If he beget a son that is a robber, a shedder of blood, and that doeth the like to any one of these things,
>
> 11 And that doeth not any of those duties, but even hath eaten upon the mountains, and defiled his neighbour's wife,
>
> 12 Hath oppressed the poor and needy, hath spoiled by violence, hath not restored the pledge, and hath lifted up his eyes to the idols, hath committed abomination,
>
> 13 Hath given forth upon usury, and hath taken increase: shall he then live? he shall not live: he hath done all these abominations; he shall surely die; his blood shall be upon him.

Suppose that the righteous man of verses 5–9 had a wicked son who was the exact opposite of his father. Verses 10–13 describe such a sinful son. He is described as completely evil. He did not do the good that his father did; instead, he did all the sins from which his father refrained. He was not only a violent man and a robber, but he literally shed the blood of others.

What would be the fate of such a wicked person? Would the righteousness of his father avail to shield the sinful son from the responsibility for the son's sins? The answer is, "He shall surely die; his blood shall be upon him" (v. 13). The last part of that condemnation was used in the Old Testament as a way of saying that he was personally responsible for his own death.

3. The righteous son of a wicked father (vv. 14–19)

Then suppose that the wicked man of verses 10–13 had a son who saw his father's sins and decided to live a righteous life. Such a righteous son is described in verses 14–17. God stressed that such a righteous son would not be punished for his father's wickedness. Verses 17–18 declare that the wicked man would die for his own sins but that the righteous son would surely live.

> 19 Yet say ye, Why? doth not the son bear the iniquity of the father? When the son hath done that which is lawful and right, and hath kept all my statutes, and hath done them, he shall surely live.

The people of Ezekiel's day claimed to be children of wicked fathers. Thus they professed to be like the man in verses 14–18. Their fathers had been wicked, but they professed to be righteous. According to them, they were suffering for the sins of their fathers.

The fallacy in their analysis was that they were not righteous. Their fathers had been wicked. That much was true. What they failed to admit was that they too were sinners. Rather than being righteous descendants of evil forefathers, they were sinful descendants of sinful forefathers. Verse 19 insists that if they had been righteous, as they professed to be, they would not be punished unjustly for their fathers' sins.

III. Summary of the Principle (Ezek. 18:20)

> 20 The soul that sinneth, it shall die. The son shall not bear the iniquity of the father, neither shall the father bear the iniquity of the son: the righteousness of the righteous shall be upon him, and the wickedness of the wicked shall be upon him.

Verse 20 sums up the main theme of verses 1–19. The popular saying of verse 2 is wrong. Sons do not die for the sins of their fathers. Verse 20 adds a point not made earlier. What about righteous fathers who have sinful sons? Verse 20 says that the fathers are not punished for the sins of their children. God will hold each person responsible for his own sins.

The teaching of personal responsibility in Ezekiel 18 was the clearest statement of this divine truth that had been made up to that time. The New Testament makes it even stronger and clearer. God does not deal with people in a mass but as individuals.

This biblical truth should not be viewed in isolation from related truths. The truth of personal responsibility does not deny that individuals are influenced for good and for evil by those who went before them as well as by their contemporaries. The point of Ezekiel 18 is that such influences do not fix our fate. We are not submerged in some mass of humanity and held accountable for what others do or have done. We are not held in the grip of some fate determined by the sins of others.

IV.The Principle Applied to Changed Lives (Ezek. 18:21–32)

1. Two kinds of changes (vv. 21–24)

The principle that was illustrated by succeeding generations was applied to changes within one person's life. If a sinful man repented and changed his life, he would not die (vv. 21–23). By the same token, if a man of righteous actions became a reprobate, he would be punished for his sins (v. 24).

2. Charge that God is unjust (vv. 25–29)

The people accused God of being unjust. God replied that what had been said thus far showed how fair God was. He charged that they were the ones guilty of being unjust, not He.

3. Call to repentance (vv. 30–32)

God called Israel to repent and turn from their sins. They were admonished to receive from God a new heart and a new spirit. Because God takes no pleasure in seeing the wicked punished, He pleads with sinners to turn to Him and live.

1. Not guilty? Four elderly men were playing poker in the backroom of the general store when, suddenly, the sheriff broke through the door exclaiming, "Ah ha, finally I have caught you gambling!" The first man said he had just dropped in to talk. The second said he was "just visitin'." The third said he had just come in out of the cold to warm at the stove. But the fourth was caught red-handed with the cards in his hands.

With a satisfied smile of victory on his face the sheriff declared, "Well, you can't deny you were playing," to which the man replied, "Now, sheriff, who would I be playing with?"

Those to whom Ezekiel preached blamed everyone else for their sins. They were not responsible. They had neither sin nor guilt. Their tragedies had befallen them because of the sins of their fathers and forefathers (18:1–2). But Ezekiel told them clearly that their plight was due to their sins. They could not blame others. They were guilty before God.

How often we play the "blame game." We blame heredity, environment, lack of opportunity, the wrong associates for our wrongdoing. Indeed, these things may contribute to our sinful ways; but we, alone, are responsible before God. We always could have said no to temptation.

2. The curse of death. On Monument Avenue in historic Richmond, Virginia, the visitor will be impressed with the equestrian statues in the middle of the broad avenue. They tell a good deal about the Confederate leaders in the War between the States. If the rider died a natural death, such as General Robert E. Lee, the horse's four hooves are all on the ground. If two hooves are in the air, the rider died in battle. If just one hoof is raised, the rider died from wounds suffered in battle.

What is the cause of death in our world? What was the cause of death in Ezekiel's day? Verse 4 gives us the answer, and it is the same thing that caused the death of Adam and locked him out of the garden and away from the presence of God: S–I–N! But Jesus, through His resurrection, is the victorious answer to death. For the believer death is not final. It is only a passage to the Father's house.

3. Righteousness demonstrated. A young lawyer negotiated a contract of which he was rather proud. When he took the contract to an older, wiser lawyer, the friend said: "John, this is a well-drawn contract. You have insured your client's rights, but you have completely overlooked the other person's rights. No contract is worthy that overlooks the rights of the other person."

Our lesson today addresses the matter of righteousness—rightness—with God. Righteousness is faith in action that expresses itself both to God and man. The Jews thought of righteousness as a set of negatives—what they should not do (Exod. 20): "Thou shalt not kill"; "Thou shalt not commit adultery," and so forth. But Ezekiel defined righteousness as a positive response to God which expresses itself in purity of life and compassion toward others (18:5–13).

4. Sin finds us out. In San Antonio, Texas, some teenagers broke into a convenience store one night after the store had closed. They took what they wanted and then pulled out the video camera that had been taping their nefarious deed and took it with them. Returning to one of the boy's homes, they began to examine their loot. When the police knocked on the door, for they had a pretty good idea who had committed the crime, they recovered everything, including the camera with the faces of the boys plainly visible on the tape!

Sin always finds us out. We can run from God, but we can't hide from Him. This was Ezekiel's message to a rebellious people. They were guilty before God.

TEACHING THE BIBLE

- *Main Idea:* We are responsible for our sin.
- *Suggested Teaching Aim:* To lead adults to identify ways they will take responsibility for their sin.

A TEACHING OUTLINE

1. Use a graffiti wall to introduce the Bible study.

2. Use an illustrated lecture to guide the Bible study.

3. Use listing and group discussion to make the Bible study personal.

Introduce the Bible Study

Make a graffiti wall by placing a large sheet of paper on the wall. Provide colored markers. As members enter, ask them to go to the wall and write their favorite proverbs.

Read some or all of the proverbs and ask: How much truth is in these proverbs? Are they all true? mostly true? false? Point out that in general proverbs are true, but they express generalities and are not always true specifically.

Search for Biblical Truth

Read the proverb from Ezekiel 18:2. Point out that in a sense this is true, but that the people were using it to deny personal responsibility for their sins. Use the material in "Studying the Bible" for 18:1–4 to explain how the people were using the proverb and Ezekiel's response to this proverb. Point out the two basic truths affirmed in 18:4.

Using the graffiti wall, write *Three Illustrations.* Under it write *A righteous person (18:5–9).* Ask members to identify the nine specific examples of a righteous person found in 18:7–8. Suggest that members read these in modern translations. Point out that the examples in these verses deal with treatment of the poor. This was Ezekiel's way of describing a righteous person.

Point out clearly that the New Testament shows we are saved by our relationship to Jesus. While this does not excuse us from acts of mercy, it does make our salvation dependent on faith in Christ rather than good deeds. However, any person who has had a genuine relationship with Jesus will most certainly perform similar acts of mercy mentioned in these verses. Our relationship with Christ makes us more responsible for helping others, not less.

Write *The wicked child of a righteous person (18:10–13)* on the graffiti wall. Point out that this is a second example used by Ezekiel to explain the proverb. Ask a volunteer to read 18:10–13. Point out that the person's actions made the child responsible for the punishment received.

Write *The righteous child of a wicked person (18:14–19)* on the graffiti wall. Point out that this is a third example used by Ezekiel to explain the proverb. Ask a volunteer to read 18:19. Explain that the exiles claimed they were suffering for their parents' sins. Although their parents were evil, God was not punishing them for their parents' sins but for their sins. As Bob Dean says, "Rather than being righteous descendants of evil forefathers, they were sinful descendants of sinful forefathers."

Call on a volunteer to read 18:20 as a summary of the truth of individual responsibility in the Old Testament. Point out that we can break free of our past even if our parents and ancestors were great sinners and did horrible things. Point out, too, that even if our parents and ancestors were great spiritual leaders, we cannot count on their spirituality to give us a right standing with God.

Give the Truth a Personal Focus

Ask members to suggest some popular misconceptions they have heard from people about salvation. (For example, "My father was a preacher, so that makes me a Christian.") Write these on the graffiti wall. Point out that our relationship with Christ is determined by our response to Him.

Ask members to suggest steps they can take to assume responsibility for their sin. Encourage them to do this so they can confess it and receive forgiveness.

November

3

1996

A Portrayal of Doom

Basic Passage: Ezekiel 3:22–5:17

Focal Passage: Ezekiel 4:1–13

Ezekiel's prophecies fall into two main groups: (1) those before the fall of Jerusalem and (2) those after the fall of Jerusalem. Before Jerusalem fell, many exiles cherished false hopes of deliverance. During those years, God led Ezekiel to declare words of judgment. After Jerusalem fell, God gave the prophet many words of hope. Today's Bible passage describes events before Jerusalem fell. Thus it is a portrayal of doom that predicted coming judgment on Jerusalem.

Study Aim: *To tell how Ezekiel's actions and words were a portrayal of doom on Jerusalem*

STUDYING THE BIBLE

OUTLINE AND SUMMARY

I. A Silent Prophet (Ezek. 3:22–27)

II. Symbols and Words of Judgment (Ezek. 4:1–5:17)

1. The siege of Jerusalem (4:1–3)

2. The length of punishment (4:4–8)

3. Starvation and unclean conditions (4:9–17)

4. Jerusalem's terrible fate (5:1–17)

God told Ezekiel to remain silent except when God opened his mouth to speak (3:22–27). God led the prophet to depict the coming siege of Jerusalem using a brick and an iron pan (4:1–3). God told Ezekiel to signify the length of the punishment of Israel and Judah by lying on his side a certain number of days (4:4–8). God commanded Ezekiel to eat meager rations cooked in an unclean way to signify the coming siege and exile (4:9–17). God told Ezekiel to portray the fate of the people of Jerusalem by cutting his hair and disposing of it in certain ways (5:1–17).

I. A Silent Prophet (Ezek. 3:22–27)

The hand of the Lord led Ezekiel to see the same vision of God's glory that he had described in chapter 1. The Spirit entered him and spoke to him. God told the prophet to go inside his house, where he would be bound. God told him that he was to remain at home and be silent except when God opened his mouth to speak.

II. Symbols and Words of Judgment (Ezek. 4:1–5:17)

1. The siege of Jerusalem (4:1–3)

> 1 Thou also, son of man, take thee a tile, and lay it before thee, and portray upon it the city, even Jerusalem.
>
> 2 And lay siege against it, and build a fort against it; and cast a mound against it; set the camp also against it, and set battering rams against it round about.

God instructed Ezekiel, whom he called "son of man," to do something that would be a sign of the coming siege of Jerusalem. The prophets often spoke the words of God to the people, but many prophets also used object lessons to communicate the truth of God's message. Ezekiel 4:1–3 describes one of the many times when the Lord instructed Ezekiel to use some form of prophetic symbolism.

The word "tile" refers to one of the clay bricks that were a common building material in that day. This was not a kiln-baked brick, but a sun-dried brick. The Lord told Ezekiel to draw or portray on the brick the city of Jerusalem. Drawing or writing on clay bricks was a common practice. While the clay was still soft, a sharp instrument called a stylus could be used to make an impression on the clay.

The Babylonian brick was larger than most modern bricks. It was twelve inches long, twelve inches wide, and three inches thick. Thus Ezekiel could draw enough of the familiar Jerusalem skyline to enable the exiles to recognize it.

Ezekiel was not only to show the city; he was to show the features of a city under siege. Bible commentators discuss whether Ezekiel was to draw the siege on the brick, or whether he was to make models to place around the brick. In either case, the people would recognize that the sign meant that the city of Jerusalem was to come under siege.

Ancient cities used fortified walls as a defense against enemies. Therefore, an enemy army would lay siege to a city. They would cut off the city from outside sources of help, food, and water. They tried to break through the fortified walls with siege weapons.

Verse 2 lists various things used in a siege. The word "fort" was used in 2 Kings 25:1 to describe offensive towers that Nebuchadnezzar (neb yoo kad NEZZ ur) built around besieged Jerusalem. These were manned by archers and sometimes had a built-in battering ram. The word "mound" referred to the heaped-up earth that the invaders used to put them on the same level with the defenders of the wall. The "camp" referred to the camp of the besieging army. The "battering rams" were used to try to break down the gates of the city or some weak place in the wall.

> 3 Moreover take thou unto thee an iron pan, and set it for a wall of iron between thee and the city: and set thy face against it, and it shall be besieged, and thou shalt lay siege against it. This shall be a sign to the house of Israel.

Next the Lord told Ezekiel to get an "iron pan." This was probably a saucer-shaped piece of iron used for baking bread. Ezekiel was told to set the piece of iron between himself and the portrayal of the besieged city.

The meaning of this object lesson is not explained in the Bible. A number of possible interpretations have been given: One view is that the iron symbolized the severity of the siege and the impossibility of escape. Another view is that it symbolized the wall of sin erected between the people and God. Yet another view is that the iron was protection for Ezekiel while he declared judgment on the condemned city.

2. The length of punishment (4:4–8)

> 4 Lie thou also upon thy left side, and lay the iniquity of the house of Israel upon it: according to the number of the days that thou shalt lie upon it thou shalt bear their iniquity.

5 For I have laid upon thee the years of their iniquity, according to the number of the days, three hundred and ninety days: so shalt thou bear the iniquity of the house of Israel.

6 And when thou hast accomplished them, lie again on thy right side, and thou shalt bear the iniquity of the house of Judah forty days: I have appointed thee each day for a year.

7 Therefore thou shalt set thy face toward the siege of Jerusalem, and thine arm shall be uncovered, and thou shalt prophesy against it.

8 And, behold, I will lay bands upon thee, and thou shalt not turn thee from one side to another, till thou hast ended the days of thy siege.

The Lord laid on Ezekiel the iniquity of the people. The word "bear" used in verses 6–7 is the same word used in Isaiah 53:12 of the Suffering Servant who bore away sins through His own suffering and death. No such claim is made for Ezekiel. He bore their sins in the sense of representing their sins through what he said and did.

Bible students have had trouble agreeing on dates that literally match the 390 years for the iniquity of the Northern Kingdom and the 40 years for the iniquity of the Southern Kingdom. Although the days were clearly to represent years, some feel they were not intended to match specific dates. Instead, they were to stress a very long period of punishment for Israel and a shorter period for Judah. Among those views that take the years literally, one explanation adds the 390 to 40 to equal 430 years, which are measured from 597 B.C. (when Nebuchadnezzar carried King Jehoiachin [jih HOY uh kin] into captivity) to 167 B.C. (the Maccabean [mak uh BEE uhn] revolt).

Notice how God used objects and actions to portray the coming doom. According to verse 7, Ezekiel was to set his face toward the siege of Jerusalem. Apparently this meant that during the last forty days, he was to face the brick and iron pan that represented the siege of the city. With an unbared arm, the prophet was to speak against the city.

Verse 8 might mean that Ezekiel spent every hour of every day lying on his side for 430 days. If he had, he would have had difficulty in doing what is described in 4:9–5:4. Probably, Ezekiel spent some time every day lying on his side to fulfill the command of verses 4–8; however, he was up at least long enough to fulfill later commands.

3. Starvation and unclean conditions (4:9–17)

9 Take thou also unto thee wheat, and barley, and beans, and lentils, and millet, and fitches, and put them in one vessel, and make thee bread thereof, according to the number of the days that thou shalt lie upon thy side, three hundred and ninety days shalt thou eat thereof.

10 And thy meat which thou shalt eat shall be by weight, twenty shekels a day: from time to time shalt thou eat it.

11 Thou shalt drink also water by measure, the sixth part of an hin: from time to time shalt thou drink.

12 And thou shalt eat it as barley cakes, and thou shalt bake it with dung that cometh out of man, in their sight.

> 13 And the LORD said, Even thus shall the children of Israel eat their defiled bread among the Gentiles, whither I will drive them.

During the 390 days, Ezekiel was to cook and eat a meager diet. He was to do this in such a way that the people would see what he was doing. This was obviously intended as another object lesson. The lesson is spelled out in verse 13. Part of their punishment was to eat a limited diet in an unclean way.

The kind of food and the amounts of food and water illustrated starvation conditions. The only bread available was made from a mixture of cheap grains. The word translated "meat" in verse 10 did not mean "flesh," but "food." Verse 12 makes clear that the only food was made from the cheap grains into barley cakes. The twenty shekels weight of food per day amounted to about one-half pound and the sixth of a hin of water was less than a quart. Thus he was on a diet of limited bread and water.

The real problem for faithful Jews, however, was that the food was prepared in an unclean way according to the law. The Mosaic Law had strict rules about disposing of human excrement (Deut. 23:12–14), rules that people today follow for proper health and sanitation. The idea of cooking with human excrement, therefore, was revolting to Ezekiel. After Ezekiel objected, God allowed him to use cow manure instead (4:14–15). This was still considered unclean enough that the object lesson of verse 13 was preserved.

God also used the object lesson to describe the starvation conditions that would exist during the siege of Jerusalem (4:16–17).

4. Jerusalem's terrible fate (5:1–17)

God told Ezekiel to use a razor to cut his hair and beard. He was then to divide the hair into three parts: one part was burned; another was tossed into the air and cut with a knife; and a third part was tossed into the wind. A few hairs were to be put in Ezekiel's robe, but even some of these were thrown into the fire. God explained that these acts symbolized the terrible judgment God was sending against the people of Jerusalem for their sins. A third of the people would die of famine and pestilence. A third would be slain by the enemy. A third would be scattered, but many of these would fall by the sword. These punishments would be signs to the nations of the judgment of God on persistent sin.

APPLYING THE BIBLE

1. The silent prophet. I know a pastor who appeared in his pulpit one Sunday morning and asked the congregation to stand after the song service had ended. "God has not given me anything to say to you this morning, so we will be dismissed," he said to the startled audience!

At least he was honest! I cannot say why God had not given the pastor a word for the people. Perhaps the pastor had not carefully sought for it. Or could it be that silence itself was the message for people who have a habit of sitting down and tuning out the words being spoken?

But our lesson points out today (3:22–27) that God commanded Ezekiel to be silent and not speak to the people until He gave the prophet the message to declare. Any preacher who is "worth his salt" can come up with a pretty good sermon for Sunday morning without much effort. But here is the acid test of true preaching: Is it God's word for His people that day?

2. Preaching by symbolism. Ezekiel was given a vision of the destruction of Jerusalem, and he was to act out that vision (4:1–5:17). Jesus, of course, was the master when it came to using object lessons. His parables fall into a category similar to that used by Ezekiel, except our Lord spoke His parables—His comparisons. The Gospels say that "Jesus taught nothing except by parables." The wise preacher will use symbols, object lessons, and illustrations to get across eternal truths.

I knew a pastor of a large church who carried the object lessons method a bit too far, however. On Sunday he announced he would preach on Jonah. At the beginning of the sermon, he introduced Jonah being cast into the sea by jumping into the baptistry. The preacher remembered, however, when he was in mid–air, that the custodian had filled the baptistry for the evening baptismal service! You guess the rest of how the service proceeded!

3. The ministry of suffering. F. Townley Lord, a London pastor who once served as president of the Baptist World Alliance, told about what he called "the bravest Christian I ever knew." The man was a pastor in Wales. Two years after he married, his wife died in childbirth. He remarried sometime later and joy returned to the parsonage; but she died, too. The pastor later developed rheumatoid arthritis. Then on top of it all, he became blind.

When he was asked to preach on the radio, he chose to preach on the ministry of suffering.

Ezekiel suffered greatly, but not for his wrongdoings. He suffered in obedience to God to reveal to the disobedient Jews what would befall their beloved but rebellious holy city. Ezekiel's suffering was for the glory of God and the warning of the people. Should we not use our afflictions which are but for a moment in the same manner?

4. God sick of sin. In his life of Henry Drummond (1851–1897), author of *The Greatest Thing in the World* (a study of 1 Corinthians 13), Old Testament scholar George Adam Smith (1856–1942) tells of coming unannounced upon the professor one day. Drummond, who had just spoken at one of his university meetings, was leaning with his head bowed against the mantelpiece. He was looking into the fire with a worn and haggard face. When Smith asked Drummond if he was tired, he replied, "No, not very, but oh, I am sick of the sin of these men. How can God bear it?"

God was sick of the sins of His rebellious people. He hated their sins, but He loved them. He chastised them not because he hated them, but because He loved them and wanted to redeem them. This was Ezekiel's message, and it is the message our world needs to hear from God's prophets today. He is sick of our sins; but in Christ, He loves us with an eternal love.

5. Pierced by arrows of our own making. There is a telling legend about a once-mighty eagle which had flown in the high places. Wounded by an arrow, the eagle lay dying on a rock. As its life blood trickled away, the eagle was saddened even more when it noticed that the feather that had guided the arrow with deadly accuracy was from its own wing.

There is no getting away from it: We reap what we sow. It is both a natural law and a spiritual law. God's people had rebelled against Him. The Northern Kingdom had been destroyed and exiled. In his vision, Ezekiel saw Jerusalem destroyed to rubble. But the people had been warned repeatedly across the years to repent and return to God, all to no avail.

Sin—theirs, yours, mine—is the costliest thing imaginable. It has not changed: we reap what we sow!

TEACHING THE BIBLE

Main Idea: God brings devastation on people who ignore His warnings.

Suggested Teaching Aim: To lead adults to examine their lives to see if they are rejecting God's warnings.

A TEACHING OUTLINE

1. *Use an illustration to introduce the Bible study.*
2. *Use a "tile" to visualize the lesson.*
3. *Use a chart explaining Ezekiel's symbols to guide the search for biblical truth.*
4. *Use a "tile" to appeal to members to examine their lives to see if they are rejecting God's warnings.*

Introduce the Bible Study

Use "Pierced by arrows of our own making" to introduce the Bible study.

Search for Biblical Truth

Enlist two readers to read the summary statements alternately to set the context for the lesson. Briefly summarize Ezekiel 3:22–27.

IN ADVANCE, make a 12-by-12-by-3-inch "tile" from cardboard or heavy paper. Draw on it the outline of an ancient city to represent Jerusalem. On a chalkboard or a large sheet of paper write the following (do not write italicized words):

Ezekiel's Symbols	
Tile	*12x12x3-inch sun dried brick*
Lay siege	*cut off city from outside help*
Mound	*heaped up earth built by invaders*
Camp	*camp of the besieging army*
Battering ram	*used to break down city gates*
Iron pan	*symbolized severity of siege or wall of sin erected by people*
Lying on his side	*symbolized the years the nation would be in exile*
Preparing unclean food	*symbolized the food to be eaten during siege*

Call for a volunteer to read 4:1–3. Ask members to list the symbols Ezekiel used in these verses and write them on the chart. Use the material in Studying the Bible to explain each of these. (Members' responses may differ some from above and still be correct.) Ask: What was the advantage of using symbols instead of just telling the people outright what was going to happen? What Teacher in the New Testament also used symbols to get His message across to the common people?

Call for a volunteer to read 4:4–8. Ask: What is the symbol in these verses? (Lying on his side.) How many days was Ezekiel to do this? (390 plus 40.) Explain the two possibilities that (1) the days were not intended to match specific dates but stressed a very long period of punishment, or (2) that some suggest the two numbers could be added together (430 years) and indicate the freedom in the Maccabean revolt (167 B.C.).

Explore whether Ezekiel spent every hour of every day in this position or whether he spent part of the day doing this and part doing other activities (see 4:9–5:4).

Call for a volunteer to read 4:9–13. Ask for the symbol. (Preparing and eating unclean food.) Use the material on these verses in "Studying the Bible" to prepare a brief lecture to explain the following: (1) Ezekiel was to prepare this food for 390 days; (2) he was to eat a half-pound of cheap grain and drink less than a quart of water a day for over a year; (3) he was to prepare the food by using animal manure as fuel which was considered unclean. Point out that in spite of all Ezekiel did, the people ignored God's warnings and the city of Jerusalem was destroyed in 587 B.C.

DISCUSS: Why do you think the Jews ignored God's warnings?

Give the Truth a Personal Focus

Ask: What warnings has God given us? How has He communicated His warnings to us individually and as a nation? Why do we ignore God's warnings?

Ask members to examine their lives to see if they are ignoring God in any area of their lives. Remind them that God does give many appeals to us. On the brick you displayed earlier, use a marking pen to write: *Repent!* Remind members that God still calls for us to repent.

Jerusalem Falls

Basic Passage: 2 Kings 24–25

Focal Passage: 2 Kings 24:20–25:12

The unbelievable happened. Jerusalem fell to an enemy. For years, the prophets Jeremiah and Ezekiel had predicted that this would happen as punishment for the people's sins. Other prophets had predicted that God would never allow an enemy to capture the holy city. However, the unpopular prophesy of Jeremiah and Ezekiel was fulfilled. The biblical account of the fall is recorded in 2 Kings 24–25.

Study Aim: *To describe events related to the fall of Jerusalem*

STUDYING THE BIBLE

OUTLINE AND SUMMARY

I. The Final Years of Judah (2 Kings 24:1–20)
- **1. Jehoiakim (24:1–7)**
- **2. Jehoiachin (24:8–17)**
- **3. Zedekiah (24:18–20)**

II. The Fall of Jerusalem (2 Kings 25:1–21)
- **1. The siege of Jerusalem (25:1–3)**
- **2. Capture of Zedekiah (25:4–7)**
- **3. Destruction of Jerusalem (25:8–10)**
- **4. The fate of the survivors (25:11–12)**
- **5. The temple treasures (25:13–17)**
- **6. Execution of leaders (25:18–21)**

III. Later Events (25:22–30)
- **1. Gedaliah as governor (25:22–26)**
- **2. Jehoiachin in Babylon (25:27–30)**

When Jehoiakim (jih HOY uh kim) rebelled against Nebuchadnezzar (neb yoo kad NEZZ ur), God sent raiders into Judah as punishment (24:1–7). After Nebuchadnezzar besieged Jerusalem, King Jehoiachin (jih HOY uh kin) surrendered and he and others were carried into exile (24:8–17). King Zedekiah's (zed uh KIGH uh) rebellion against the Babylonians ushered in God's judgment on Jerusalem (24:18–20). During the siege of Jerusalem the people ran out of bread (25:1–3). Zedekiah tried to flee, but he was captured and blinded after he watched his sons being executed (25:4–7). The Babylonians then burned the temple and houses of Jerusalem, and tore down the wall (25:8–10). Most of the survivors were taken into exile (25:11–12). The temple treasures were plundered (25:13–17). The remaining leaders were executed (25:18–21). Nebuchadnezzar's governor Gedaliah (ged uh LIGH uh) was assassinated (25:22–26). Years later, Jehoiachin was treated more kindly by the new Babylonian king (25:27–30).

I. The Final Years of Judah (2 Kings 24:1–20)

1. Jehoiakim (24:1–7)

The evil reign of Jehoiakim is attested to not only by 2 Kings 23:35–37 but also by many passages in Jeremiah (for example, see Jer. 36). During Jehoiakim's reign, a power struggle took place between Egypt and Babylonia. After a great Babylonian victory, Jehoiakim shifted his allegiance to Nebuchadnezzar, king of Babylon. Then after another battle, which caused Nebuchadnezzar to retreat temporarily, Jehoiakim rebelled against the Babylonians. As punishment for the sins of Judah, God sent raiders into Judah. Among these were the Chaldeans (kal DEE uhnz), another name for the Babylonians. By the end of Jehoiakim's evil reign of twenty-five years, Babylonia had defeated the Egyptians. All the Middle East, including Judah, lay open to the might of Nebuchadnezzar. After Jehoiakim's death, he was succeeded by his son Jehoiachin.

2. Jehoiachin (24:8–17)

Shortly after the eighteen-year-old Jehoiachin became king, Nebuchadnezzar's army besieged Jerusalem. After a reign of only three months, Jehoiachin surrendered to Nebuchadnezzar. He, his family, and many of the leading people were carried into exile in Babylonia. Nebuchadnezzar placed Zedekiah on the throne. Treasures from the temple were also taken; however, at this time in 597 B.C., the city and the temple were not destroyed.

3. Zedekiah (24:18–20)

Zedekiah's eleven-year reign spanned the time between the surrender of the city by Jehoiachin and the fall and destruction of the city. He continued Jehoiakim's evil practices.

> 20 Zedekiah rebelled against the king of Babylon.

Zedekiah reigned during a power struggle between Babylonia and Egypt outside Judah, and between pro-Babylonian and pro-Egyptian voices within Judah (see Jer. 37:5). Jeremiah was seen as pro-Babylonian because he advised Zedekiah not to rebel against Nebuchadnezzar (see Jer. 27:1–15). Jeremiah spoke about politics, but he was not speaking as a political adviser. He was speaking as a prophet who said that Babylon would be the instrument of divine wrath against the sins of Judah.

The Book of 2 Kings was placed by the Hebrews among the Prophets. They did this because although it is a book of history, it is a book of prophetic history. That is, the writers wrote from a perspective of faith in God. Here is the explanation given in 2 Kings 24:30 for the ruin that came to Jerusalem after Zedekiah rebelled: "For through the anger of the LORD it came to pass in Jerusalem and Judah, until he had cast them out from his presence, that Zedekiah rebelled against the king of Babylon."

II. The Fall of Jerusalem (2 Kings 25:1–21)

1. The siege of Jerusalem (25:1–3)

> 1 And it came to pass in the ninth year of his reign, in the tenth month, in the tenth day of the month, that Nebuchadnezzar king

of Babylon came, he, and all his host, against Jerusalem, and pitched against it; and they built forts against it round about.

2 And the city was besieged unto the eleventh year of king Zedekiah.

3 And on the ninth day of the fourth month the famine prevailed in the city, and there was no bread for the people of the land.

Ezekiel 4:1–3 was fulfilled in the siege of Jerusalem, which began in the ninth year of Zedekiah or 588 B.C. Some of the same words from Ezekiel appear in the description of 2 Kings. As we noted in the lesson for November 3, the "forts" were offensive towers. The towers put the Babylonian archers level with the Jewish defenders on the wall.

Verse 3 mentions one outcome of the siege as starvation. Passages like Ezekiel 4:9–17 had predicted this. Ezekiel predicted that the starvation would become so terrible that some people would resort to cannibalism, even eating dead members of their own family (Ezek. 5:10; compare 2 Kings 6:25–29).

The siege lasted for nineteen months. The fact that it lasted so long was due to a diversionary raid by the Egyptians that caused Nebuchadnezzar to lift the siege temporarily (Jer. 37:5). This intervention by Egypt raised false hopes. The enemies of Jeremiah used it to try to bolster Zedekiah's will to resist Nebuchadnezzar. Jeremiah warned that the respite was only temporary, as indeed it proved to be (see Jer. 37–39 for the prophet's account of these terrible times).

2. Capture of Zedekiah (25:4–7)

4 And the city was broken up, and all the men of war fled by night by way of the gate between two walls, which is by the king's garden: (now the Chaldees were against the city round about:) and the king went his way toward the plain.

5 And the army of the Chaldees pursued after the king, and overtook him in the plains of Jericho: and all his army was scattered from him.

6 So they took the king, and brought him up to the king of Babylon to Riblah; and they gave judgment upon him.

7 And they slew the sons of Zedekiah before his eyes, and put out the eyes of Zedekiah, and bound him with fetters of brass, and carried him to Babylon.

When the city wall had been breached, King Zedekiah and his army escaped the tight siege by stealing out of the city at night through one of the gates. They fled toward the plain of the Jordan. Nebuchadnezzar's army pursued the Judeans. When the Chaldeans overtook Zedekiah on the plains of Jericho, the Judean soldiers fled for their lives.

The hapless king was taken to the headquarters of Nebuchadnezzar. A terrible judgment was meted out to Zedekiah. While he watched helplessly, his sons were executed. This terrible sight was the last thing he ever saw, because his captors immediately put out his eyes. Then they bound him and carried him to Babylon.

3. Destruction of Jerusalem (25:8–10)

8 And in the fifth month, on the seventh day of the month, which is the nineteenth year of Nebuchadnezzar king of Babylon, came Nebuzaradan, captain of the guard, a servant of the king of Babylon, unto Jerusalem:

9 And he burnt the house of the LORD, and the king's house, and all the houses of Jerusalem, and every great man's house burnt he with fire.

10 And all the army of the Chaldees, that were with the captain of the guard, brake down the walls of Jerusalem round about.

Nebuchadnezzar then sent Nebuzaradan (NEB yoo zahr AY dan), the captain of the guard and his army, back to Jerusalem. Because the army of Judah had fled with the king, the city was undefended. The Chaldeans entered the city easily and proceeded to destroy it. The captain of the guard began by burning the temple. Then he burned the king's palace, and finally burned all the houses of the city. The time was 586 B.C.

Then the army destroyed the wall around Jerusalem. In those days, a city without a wall could not be defended against attack. This explains the concern of Nehemiah for rebuilding the wall after the Jews returned to Jerusalem years later.

The Babylonians had lost patience with Jerusalem. They had besieged and captured it eleven years earlier but had not destroyed the city and its walls. Now they ensured that Jerusalem would no longer be capable of mounting any opposition to Babylonian rule.

4. The fate of the survivors (25:11–12)

11 Now the rest of the people that were left in the city, and the fugitives that fell away to the king of Babylon, with the remnant of the multitude, did Nebuzaradan the captain of the guard carry away.

12 But the captain of the guard left of the poor of the land to be vinedressers and husbandmen.

In order further to ensure no further Jewish revolts, the Babylonians carried most of the survivors into exile in Babylon. This included some who had earlier surrendered to the Babylonians as well as most of the rest of the population. Only the poorest of the land were allowed to stay in order to tend the vineyards.

5. The temple treasures (25:13–17)

The Babylonians plundered the temple of its treasures. The wealth that had been accumulated during the time of Solomon was carried to Babylon.

6. Execution of leaders (25:18–21)

Not all the survivors were carried into exile. Some of the leading captives were taken to Nebuchadnezzar's headquarters and executed. This included the chief priest and temple leaders, military leaders, and government advisers.

III. Later Events (2 Kings 25:22–30)

1. Gedaliah as governor (25:22–26)

Judah no longer had a ruling king, so Nebuchadnezzar appointed Gedaliah as governor of Judah. Some of the soldiers who had fled came to Gedaliah. He tried to persuade them to remain obedient to the Babylonians, but they killed him and fled to Egypt.

2. Jehoiachin in Babylon (25:27–30)

Jehoiachin had been a captive in Babylon for thirty-seven years when Evil-merodach (EE vil-mih ROH dak) became king of Babylon. As a goodwill gesture, he changed Jehoiachin from a prisoner to a guest in the king's house. Jehoiachin, of course, was still not reigning in Judah; and he was still under close Babylonian control, but he was at least treated more kindly.

APPLYING THE BIBLE

1. While the king slept. On the eve of the French Revolution (1789–1799), King Louis XVI presided over the opening of the States General. His intention in calling the meeting was to provide money for his bankrupt government. The Bishop of Nancy delivered a rousing sermon on the appalling condition of the people whose lifeblood had been drained away by a selfish monarchy. But as the Bishop preached, the king slept; and, as one writer put it, the sermon was "punctuated by the royal snores!" Later, both King Louis and his queen, Marie Antoinette, were sent to the guillotine.

Jeremiah and Ezekiel have been warning the kings of Judah for years to call their people to repentance and a return to God. But they have slept through those warnings and now Jerusalem's doom is sealed (2 Kings 25:1–21).

2. Judah's dash to destruction. There is a moving painting by French artist/sculptor Francois Rude (1784–1855) which shows the gray dawn with opposing armies near. A watchman has been placed on the outskirts of the city and on him depends the safety of the city. But, alas, the watchman is asleep! Napoleon, passing by, removes the careless soldier's weapon and stands guard himself.

Where are Judah's watchmen? With the Babylonians battering Jerusalem's walls, where are the watchmen to call upon Judah to repent? The voice of the prophets is now silenced. Judah is on a mad dash toward destruction. The days of warning are passed.

Is our world on that same course today? Many think so. Our sins are coming home to roost. We are destroying ourselves. How much longer can America and our world continue when God has been shut out? The picture of Judah in today's lesson closely parallels the condition of our world today. But, thank God, there is hope and that hope rests in Jesus Christ.

3. Key verse. The key verse for our lesson is Jeremiah 13:17. Read it and note the grief of God; darkness on the nation descends (v. 16); the nation is stumbling toward destruction (v. 16); hope is overwhelmed by the clouds of despair (v. 16); God weeps over their rebellious spirit (v.

17); His eyes weep bitterly (v. 17); the Lord's flock will be taken captive (v. 17).

What a tragic thing it is to grieve God! To think that He who is the very essence of joy and peace can and does weep over the sins of His people is almost too much for us to comprehend. But it is another evidence of His eternal love that will not forsake us.

Do our actions and attitudes grieve God? Does He weep over what He witnesses in our churches, our nation? He does, and Paul confirms this when he writes in Ephesians 4:30: "And grieve not the holy Spirit."

4. Two great prophets. Jeremiah and Ezekiel were God's spokesmen during the fall of Jerusalem, the darkest days of Judah's history.

In 1809 when Napoleon was ravaging Europe and the clouds of despair hung over the entire continent, God was still at work. In that year some of history's most notable men were born: scientist Charles Darwin; Abraham Lincoln, who would lead America through its darkest days; England's great Christian prime minister William Gladstone; Alfred Lord Tennyson, perhaps England's greatest poet; American poets Edgar Allen Poe and Oliver Wendell Holmes; composer Felix Mendelssohn; and Cyrus McCormick, the inventor of the grain reaper.

In our darkest days God is with us to give us courage and hope. That hope often comes through some friend God sends to us to put his or her hand on our shoulder and say to us: "Commit thy way unto the LORD; trust also in him; and he shall bring it to pass" (Ps. 37:5). (The 37th Psalm was said to be Lincoln's favorite Scripture passage.)

5. "Crazy Bell." How many telephones do you have in your home or office? Alexander Graham Bell, the inventor of the telephone, was called "Crazy Bell" by his contemporaries because he believed people could communicate over a wire through a thing he called a telephone. The parents of the girl Bell hoped to marry said he could never marry their daughter until he quit wasting his time working on the "crazy" invention. But Bell persisted, even when Western Union rejected his telephone because it was only an "electrical toy." On May 7, 1876, Bell was granted a patent for his telephone, and on May 10 it carried its first intelligible sentence from the top floor of a Boston boarding house.

All prophets/preachers who declare the Word of God in power and truth are called senseless and foolish by an unbelieving world. Jeremiah and Ezekiel were spurned, criticized, and mocked when they prophesied the impossible: the destruction of Jerusalem.

TEACHING THE BIBLE

- *Main Idea:* God's promised judgment will come at last.
- *Suggested Teaching Aim:* To lead adults to determine why God destroyed Jerusalem

A TEACHING OUTLINE

1. Use an illustration to introduce the Bible study.
2. Use a study guide to guide the search for biblical truth.
3. Use listing to help members give the truth a personal focus.

Introduce the Bible Study

Use "While the king slept" from "Applying the Bible" to introduce the Bible study.

Search for Biblical Truth

IN ADVANCE, prepare the following:

Study Guide—2 Kings 24–25		
1.	Who was the first evil Judean king subdued by Nebuchadnezzar?	(24:1–7)
2.	Who was king of Judah when Nebuchadnezzar first removed vessels from the temple?	(24:8–17)
3.	Who was king of Jerusalem when Jerusalem finally fell to the Babylonians?	(24:18–20)
4.	How long did the Babylonians besiege the city?	(25:1–3)
5.	How did the siege affect the people of Jerusalem?	(25:3)
6.	What was Zedekiah's reaction to the fall of the city?	(25:4)
7.	What did Nebuchadnezzar do to punish Zedekiah?	(25:5–7)
8.	What did the Babylonian army do to Jerusalem?	(25:8–10)
9.	Whom did the Babylonians carry to Babylonia?	(25:11)
10.	Who was left in Judah to take care of the vineyards?	(25:12)
11.	What happened to Gedaliah, the man appointed as governor of Judah?	(25:22–26)
12.	How did Evil-merodach treat Jehoiachin?	(25:27–30)

The following are correct answers: **1.** Jehoiakim. **2.** Jehoiachin. **3.** Zedekiah. **4.** Approximately a year and a half. **5.** Famine. **6.** Fled. **7.** Killed his sons as he watched and then put out his eyes. **8.** Burned temple and all great houses and broke down the city wall. **9.** The people left in the city and those who had deserted to the Babylonians. **10.** The poor. **11.** Judean solders. **12.** Treated him kindly.

You can use this study guide in several ways. (1) Make copies for each person present and let them find the answers individually. Then let them suggest the answers and go over the questions as a group. (2) Organize members in groups of two to three people and proceed as mentioned in (1) above. (3) Ask the questions aloud instead of distributing the study guide to each person. (4) Prepare copies for each person present and then present a lecture in which you answer these questions. Ask members to write down their answers and check them after your lecture and group discussion.

Conclude by using these discussion questions:

DISCUSS: Is God being fair when he allows innocent people to suffer because the majority are evil and disobey Him? Why do we want to listen to the prophets who promise us good and refuse to listen to those who warn us of God's judgment? What do you do when God allows your enemies to defeat you?

Give the Truth a Personal Focus

Ask members to list reasons why God destroyed Jerusalem. Write these on a chalkboard or a large sheet of paper. Then ask them how many of the reasons they see present in our nation. Lead in a prayer of confession that they will be the kind of people God wants in His kingdom to preserve and save society.

A Cry of Anguish

Basic Passage: Lamentations

Focal Passages: Lamentations 5:1–10, 19–22

The Bible deals with the fall of Jerusalem in different ways. The prophet Ezekiel used object lessons to point to the siege and fall. The Book of 2 Kings describes what happened before, during, and after the fall of the city. The Book of Lamentations records the anguished cry of one who experienced the fall.

Study Aim: *To empathize with the prayer of Lamentations 5*

STUDYING THE BIBLE

OUTLINE AND SUMMARY

I. Misery of the Ruined City (Lam. 1:1–22)

II. God's Anger and One Sufferer's Grief (Lam. 2:1–22)

III. Faithless People and Faithful God (Lam. 3:1–66)

IV. From a Golden City to a Ruined City (Lam. 4:1–22)

V. Prayer for God to Remember and Renew (Lam. 5:1–22)

1. Remember, O Lord (5:1)

2. Strangers in their own land (5:2–5)

3. Punished for sin (5:6–7)

4. Slaves of slaves (5:8–13)

5. Grief and disgrace (5:14–18)

6. O Lord, why? (5:19–20)

7. Restore and renew us (5:21–22)

Jerusalem after the fall was like a grieving widow (chap. 1). The intense sufferings of Jerusalem were the results of divine wrath (chap. 2). Although the people had been unfaithful to God, His faithfulness was great (chap. 3). Jerusalem had gone from golden days to total ruin (chap. 4). The writer prayed for God to remember His people (5:1). They were strangers in the land God had given them (5:2–5). Their forefathers had sinned, but so had they by trusting in foreign alliances (5:6–7). The people had become slaves of people who were slaves themselves (5:8–13). Their disgrace was epitomized in the ruin of the temple (5:14–18). The writer asked the sovereign Lord why He had forsaken His people (5:19–20). He prayed that God would restore and renew His people (5:21–22).

I. Misery of the Ruined City (Lam. 1:1–22)

The setting was after the destruction of Jerusalem. The city was like a grief-stricken widow (vv. 1–11). Then the widow cried out to passersby for sympathy (vv. 12–19) and to God for deliverance (vv. 20–22).

II. God's Anger and One Sufferer's Grief (Lam. 2:1–22)

The terrible destruction that came to Jerusalem was the result of God's anger (vv. 1–10). One sufferer expressed his grief and shame over the sufferings of Jerusalem (vv. 11–17). He called on Jerusalem to cry out to God (vv. 18–22).

III. Faithless People and Faithful God (Lam. 3:1–66)

The author expressed the personal affliction he had suffered as a result of God's wrath (vv. 1–18), but he expressed his hope in the goodness and faithfulness of God (vv. 19–39). He called the people to pray, repent, and place their hope in God (vv. 40–66).

IV. From a Golden City to a Ruined City (Lam. 4:1–22)

The golden city went through the horrors of the siege and fall (vv. 1–10). The sins of the prophets and priests brought on them the wrath of God (vv. 11–16). The hope of help from other nations proved vain, and efforts to escape failed (vv. 18–20). Eventually Zion's exile would end, but God would judge Edom (vv. 21–22).

V. A Prayer for God to Remember and Renew (Lam. 5:1–22)

1. Remember, O Lord (5:1)

1 Remember, O LORD, what is come upon us: consider and behold our reproach.

"Remember" was a key word in the prayer of Moses after the children of Israel had worshiped the golden calf. Moses asked God to remember His promises to Abraham, Isaac, and Jacob (Exod. 32:13). The people had forgotten God and broken the covenant. They did not deserve God's mercy and continued care, but Moses dared to pray that God would forgive their sins and renew His covenant with them. The history of Israel had been a long history of forgetting God. Eventually, judgment came just as the prophets had foretold. Now a man of faith asked God to remember and to take notice of His people and their plight.

Tradition says that Jeremiah was the one who wrote Lamentations. His name is on the superscription in many editions of the Bible. Although the writer did not mention his name in the text of the book itself, we know that Jeremiah delivered a lament on an earlier occasion of national grief (2 Chron. 35:24–25). We also know that the Book of Jeremiah contains passages that sound like the Book of Lamentations (see Jer. 9:10–22; 15:5–14).

2. Strangers in their own land (5:2–5)

2 Our inheritance is turned to strangers, our houses to aliens.

3 We are orphans and fatherless, our mothers are as widows.

4 We have drunken our water for money; our wood is sold unto us.

5 Our necks are under persecution: we labour, and have no rest.

Verse 1 called on God to consider their shame and reproach. Verses 2–5 focus on the shame of seeing their enemies in the land that God had given them. The promised land was their inheritance (Deut. 4:21). Now their land and their houses had been turned over to foreigners.

Orphans and widows were recognized as the most defenseless members of ancient society. After the fall of Jerusalem, no doubt many of the survivors were literally orphans and widows; but all of them were as helpless as orphans and widows.

The invaders forced them to pay for water from their own wells and for wood from their own trees. The ruthless tyrants treated the Jews like slave laborers. The words "no rest" mean more than that they were allowed little time to rest from toil. When Israel had entered Canaan, God promised that He would give them "rest" from all their enemies. "Rest" was defined as the ability to dwell in the land in safety (Deut. 12:10; see also Deut. 25:19).

3. Punished for sin (5:6–7)

> 6 We have given the hand to the Egyptians, and to the Assyrians, to be satisfied with bread.
>
> 7 Our fathers have sinned, and are not; and we have borne their iniquities.

On the surface, verse 7 seems to be an attempt to blame earlier generations for the plight of the generation alive when Jerusalem fell. God had spoken through Ezekiel to condemn such an attempt to deny personal responsibility (Ezek. 18; see the lesson for Oct. 27). Jeremiah 31:29 issued a similar warning.

When verse 7 is read with the whole passage, we see that the writer was not trying to blame everything on earlier generations. For one thing, verse 16 says, "Woe unto us, that we have sinned!" Likewise, verse 6 uses "we," not "they" to describe the futile attempts to survive by making alliances with Egypt and Assyria (uh SIRH ih uh). Taken together, verses 6–7, 16 teach that all of us are subject to bad influences, but each person is responsible for individual sins.

4. Slaves of slaves (5:8–13)

> 8 Servants have ruled over us: there is none that doth deliver us out of their hand.
>
> 9 We gat our bread with the peril of our lives because of the sword of the wilderness.
>
> 10 Our skin was black like an oven because of the terrible famine.

The word "servants" is literally "slaves." These "slaves" were the Babylonian (bab uh LOH nih uhn) officials who controlled the lives of the survivors in Judah. The common people were subject especially to the lower officials, who were cruel and crude. The sorry plight of the Jews was that they were treated like slaves, totally under the control of people who were themselves slaves. They had no one to whom to address their grievances or to turn to for help.

Verses 9–10 describe the terrible famine after the invaders' victory. Little food was left for the survivors. They risked their lives when they went into the fields to gather food. Bands of robbers preyed on the people. Their bodies shriveled and dried with starvation. Women were raped

(v. 11). Rulers were hanged. Elders were dishonored (v. 12). Young men and even children were assigned to work details (v. 13).

5. Grief and disgrace (5:14–18)

Normal life had ceased. The elders no longer met to administer justice and to enjoy life. The music of the young was no more (v. 14). Joy had ceased, and dancing had been replaced with mourning (v. 15). They no longer had a king. Their woes were the result of their sins (v. 16). They had lost heart and vision (v. 17). Worst of all, wild animals roamed the ruins of the former site of the holy temple, Mount Zion (v. 18).

6. O Lord, why? (5:19–20)

> 19 Thou, O LORD, remainest for ever; thy throne from generation to generation.
>
> 20 Wherefore dost thou forget us for ever, and forsake us so long time?

The writers of the Bible often asked God "Why?" They were people of faith, because people of faith take everything to God in prayer. Thus the question of verse 20 expresses the honest perplexity of people of faith when they confront situations that do not seem to fit their understanding of God.

The writer praised God as the eternal King and Sovereign forever over all things. However, this confession of faith did not seem to match what God's people were going through. Why was the sovereign, eternal King of the universe allowing His people to suffer so? Had He forgotten them? Had He forsaken them?

7. Restore and renew us (5:21–22)

> 21 Turn thou us unto thee, O LORD, and we shall be turned; renew our days as of old.
>
> 22 But thou hast utterly rejected us; thou art very wroth against us.

The writer had begun the prayer by asking God to remember and take notice of His people's plight. He had confessed that they had sinned and that their troubles were expressions of God's wrath. Thus in a sense he had answered part of his own question of verse 20. God had turned from them only after they repeatedly had turned from Him. Thus, the writer prayed that God would turn them back toward Him.

Verse 21 is like a prayer for a new heart and a new spirit. Sin had so twisted and perverted the people that they were incapable of reforming their lives. They needed to turn to God, but they could do this only as His Spirit helped them to be changed. Verse 21 is also a prayer for renewal. The writer longed for the life and joys of former days when the people walked with God.

Verse 22 has puzzled Bible students. When this passage is used in Jewish worship, it has become traditional to reverse the order of verses 21 and 22 so that the reading ends with verse 21. But the Bible text ends with verse 22. At the time the writer's prayers seemed not to have been answered. The people were still suffering at the hands of their oppressors. A time of deliverance remained only a distant hope.

People of faith in every generation must live in hope of promises that have not yet been fulfilled. We struggle with the evils and sorrows of our times in light of our faith in a God of power and goodness. We often ask God why certain things happen or don't happen. God seldom explains His ways to us. Thus we join the writer of Lamentations 5 in expressing our trust and hope in God—even in hard times. We continue to trust, pray, and praise even while we have questions that we cannot answer.

APPLYING THE BIBLE

1. The grieving widow. I know a fine Christian woman whose husband of forty years died one year ago. Obviously, it has been a very hard year for her. Although her children live nearby, she finds little comfort. She is active in her church, but church friends have not been able to give much solace. Her weight has dropped. Her shoulders are drooped. Her face is strained and tired-looking. Her sorrow is devastating her. We understand this, for we know that only time and the grace of God will bring comfort to her.

This is the picture of Jerusalem. She is a grieving widow (chap. 1). Her destruction had been catastrophic under the cruel hand of the Babylonians. As our writer comments Jerusalem had gone from her golden days to total ruin (chap. 4). In 1:2 the grief of Jerusalem, the grieving widow, is tragically described: "She weepeth sore in the night, and her tears are on her cheeks: among all her lovers she hath found none to comfort her." It is, indeed, a sad picture of a broken but once-beautiful and splendid city.

2. To sing again. The people of the Harz Mountains of Germany are well-known for raising beautiful singing canaries. When World War I broke out, the canaries could no longer be shipped to the United States although there was a demand for them. But a Harlem, New York, dealer had an answer. He bred domestic canaries, put them in a dark room where there would be no distractions, and played the songs sung by the Harz Mountain canaries. This was done daily over a period of time until the domestic birds learned to sing with matchless beauty.

The song has gone from Jerusalem. Darkness, desolation are all around. There is loud weeping where once there was robust joy. God let the city be destroyed and the people carried into captivity that they might learn a new song—one to the glory of God alone!

3. Is God still alive? Frederick Douglas and Sojourner Truth are well-known for their stand against slavery. Once, in 1847, when Douglas was addressing an antislavery convention at Salem, Illinois, he described how long freedom was in coming to the slaves and how much his people had suffered. Sojourner Truth, the powerful and aged African-American leader who was well-known among the black people, cried out: "Frederick! Frederick! Is God dead?"

We see the desolation of the city, but we know that God is still alive and will not forever turn His back on His people. The opening words of chapter 5 powerfully express this faith in the faithfulness of God: "Remember, O Lord, what is come upon us: consider, and behold our reproach."

Our lesson writer says: "Eventually, judgment came just as the prophets had foretold. Now a man of faith asked God to remember and to take notice of His people and their plight."

4. Sin will not stay hidden. A minister tells of a story that came out of his boyhood. He was given a basket of popcorn by his mother and told to go to the field and plant it. After a couple of hours under the broiling sun, the basket seemed to contain as many seeds as it did when he began. So, to end the seemingly eternal task: he dug a hole at the end of one row and dumped the remaining seeds in it. But his mother knew when he returned to the house that he had not been gone long enough to do the job.

"Jake," she said, "if you have told me a lie about planting the corn, it will tell on you." And it did! The weather soon turned warm and the gentle rain fell and the mother discovered the truth. Marching Jake to the field, she showed him the thick shoots of popcorn coming up at the end of the row. "The corn will always tell on you," she sternly told him.

Sin always tells. It cries out to condemn us. It cannot forever be forgotten or hidden. For decades Jerusalem and Judah's people had been warned, but they had refused to heed the warnings to repent and turn to God. Now, their sins have found them out and destruction and misery lie all about them (5:6–18).

5. No help yet. A United States military airplane crashed in the desert of Africa in 1943, during World War II. When it was found seventeen years later, the pilot had written in his logbook on the first day after the crash, "Yesterday we went through hell!" Seven days later, the last entry read, "No help yet!"

The writer of Lamentations prays for better days for Jerusalem, and he still has hope; but it does shine very brightly amidst the desolation (5:21–22). Help will come and hope will return but only after years of captivity and sorrow.

Our prayer for ourselves and our world must be for spiritual revival. We must hold on to our hope until that day comes.

TEACHING THE BIBLE

- *Main Idea:* God punishes His people for their sins.
- *Suggested Teaching Aim:* To lead adults to identify how not to become discouraged when they feel God has forsaken them.

A TEACHING OUTLINE

1. Use an illustration to introduce the Bible study.

2. Use three readers to summarize the background material.

3. Use brief lectures and group discussion to search for biblical truth.

4. Use a writing project to help members give the truth a personal focus.

Introduce the Bible Study

Use "Is God still alive?" from "Applying the Bible" to introduce the Bible study.

Search for Biblical Truth

Read the eleven summary statements to set the context for the study. **IN ADVANCE,** copy the material contained in the paragraph in outline points I–IV. Distribute one of the paragraphs to four members and ask them to read it aloud to the class.

Ask a volunteer to read Lamentations 5:1. Explain the importance of "remember" in Israel's history.

Use the material in "Studying the Bible" to explain the traditional connection of Jeremiah with this Book.

Ask members to open their Bibles to 5:2–5. Explain that these four verses describe their loss. Write ***Lost . . .*** on a chalkboard or a large sheet of paper. Ask members to describe what the people lost in each of the verses. As they do, write a one-word summary beneath the word ***Lost . . .*** (5:2—property; 5:3—fathers; 5:4—money; 5:5—freedom). As you discuss 5:5, explain the use of the word "rest."

Call for a volunteer to read 5:6–7. Use the material in "Studying the Bible" to explain how each person is responsible for individual sins.

Call for a volunteer to read 5:8–10. Use "Studying the Bible" to identify "slaves." Point out that these Babylonian officials who ruled them were no better than slaves. What made the situation so bad was that they had no one to whom they could address their grievances or turn to for help.

Call for a volunteer to read 5:19–20. Ask: What do these verses affirm about God? (He will reign forever.) What one word can summarize 5:20? ("Why?") Use the material in "Studying the Bible" to explain how people of faith take everything to God in prayer.

DISCUSS: If God is our eternal, sovereign King, why does He allow His people to suffer so horribly? Why do some people experience grave punishment for their sins while others who are seemingly worse sinners get by relatively easily?

Ask a volunteer to read 5:21–22. Ask members to read 5:21 in different translations and then paraphrase it. Write the paraphrase on a chalkboard or a large sheet of paper.

Point out the difficulty of 5:22 and the way the verse is handled in Jewish worship services. However, use the explanation in "Studying the Bible" to explain why the book ends as it does.

DISCUSS: What do we do when it seems that God has rejected us forever? What can we do to develop faith to keep us through those times when we cannot see?

Give the Truth a Personal Focus

Distribute paper and pencils to all members. Ask them to compose a lament which expresses their feelings about their personal situation or the state of our nation. They may work in groups or individually.

Call on volunteers to read their laments. Ask members to list steps they can take when they face difficult days and feel God has forsaken them. Write these on a chalkboard or a large sheet of paper. Ask them to choose one or more of these and to discuss ways they can put these steps into practice. Close in prayer that they will not give up when they feel discouraged.

God's Power to Restore

Basic Passage: Ezekiel 37

Focal Passages: Ezekiel 37:1–12, 14

Two themes dominate the Book of Ezekiel: judgment and hope. Before Jerusalem fell, Ezekiel preached sure judgment on the wicked people. This message countered the false assurances of prophets who kept saying that God would never allow Jerusalem to fall. After the city fell, many despaired. During those dark days, Ezekiel preached a message of restoration and hope. Ezekiel 37 records his most familiar message in the latter category.

Study Aim: *To explain how the vision of the dry bones teaches God's power to restore*

STUDYING THE BIBLE

OUTLINE AND SUMMARY

I. Life for Dry Bones (Ezek. 37:1–14)
- **1. A vision and a question (vv. 1–3)**
- **2. God's command and promise (vv. 4–6)**
- **3. Preaching to the bones and to the wind (vv. 7–10)**
- **4. Israel's hopeless plight (v. 11)**
- **5. God's wonderful promises (vv. 12–14)**

II. Two Sticks Joined as One (Ezek. 37:15–28)
- **1. Prophecy of a reunited people (vv. 15–22)**
- **2. A covenant of peace (vv. 23–28)**

After God showed Ezekiel a vision of dry bones, God asked him if the bones could live (vv. 1–3). God commanded the prophet to preach to the bones, and He promised that the bones would become living human beings (vv. 4–6). Ezekiel preached to the bones, and they joined together as skeletons; then he preached to the wind, and the skeletons became living human beings (vv. 7–10). The bones represented the exiled Jews, who felt hopeless and dead (v. 11). God promised to raise them from the death of the exile (vv. 12–14). God used an object lesson of two sticks to predict the reunion of Judah and Israel (vv. 15–22). God promised to abide with His changed people in a covenant of peace (vv. 23–28).

I. Life for Dry Bones (Ezek. 37:1–14)

1. A vision and a question (vv. 1–3)

1 The hand of the LORD was upon me, and carried me out in the spirit of the LORD, and set me down in the midst of the valley which was full of bones,

2 And caused me to pass by them round about: and, behold; there were very many in the open valley; and, lo, they were very dry.

Ezekiel's vision of the valley of dry bones is the most familiar passage in the book. As in earlier visions, the hand of the Lord was laid on

Ezekiel in a special way (1:3; 3:14; 8:1). The Spirit of the Lord was instrumental in this and earlier visions of the prophet (2:2; 3:12, 14, 24; 8:3; 11:1, 5).

The vision of chapter 37 was of a place littered with human bones. The place resembled the site of a battle in which many had been killed and their bodies left unburied. These bodies had lain in the open for a long time. Not only was no flesh left on the bones but also the bones had been dried by the sun and scattered by birds and animals.

> 3 And he said unto me, Son of man, can these bones live? And I answered, O Lord GOD, thou knowest.

As Ezekiel pondered this vision, God asked, "Can these bones live?" From a human point of view the obvious answer was no. Ezekiel, however, had seen what God could do. He, therefore, answered, "O Lord GOD, thou knowest." This was a wise answer. Ezekiel did not answer either yes or no. To have said no would have been to deny the power of God. To have answered yes would have been to presume that God would choose to act. So Ezekiel said in effect, "You know whether You will choose to exercise Your power to make them live."

2. God's command and promise (vv. 4–6)

> 4 Again he said unto me, Prophesy upon these bones, and say unto them, O ye dry bones, hear the word of the LORD.

Imagine the scene. Ezekiel saw himself standing in a place littered with bones, and God told him to preach to the bones. Ezekiel knew the feeling of preaching to people who were as unresponsive as if they were dead. Now the Lord was calling him to preach to dry bones.

For Ezekiel to respond to this command, he needed to believe that God could do great things through His word. The Hebrews viewed a person's words as an extension of the person. Thus God's words were God Himself at work through His words.

> 5 Thus saith the Lord GOD unto these bones; Behold, I will cause breath to enter into you, and ye shall live:
>
> 6 And I will lay sinews upon you, and will bring up flesh upon you, and cover you with skin, and put breath in you, and ye shall live; and ye shall know that I am the LORD.

Part of the power of this chapter is the repeated use of a Hebrew word that can be translated "breath," "wind," or "spirit." The word is translated "breath" in verses 5, 6, 9, 10. It is translated "wind" three times in verse 9. The same word is translated "spirit" in verses 1 and 14.

The miracle of giving breath or life to these dead bones was possible only by God breathing into them His life-giving Spirit. This is made explicit in the interpretation of the vision in verse 14. Only God could make dead bones live. He would accomplish this by the power of His word and His Spirit. When this miracle would take place, God said, "Ye shall know that I am the LORD." The "ye" refers to Ezekiel and to the dead who were made alive.

3. Preaching to the bones and to the wind (vv. 7–10)

> 7 So I prophesied as I was commanded: and as I prophesied, there was a noise, and behold a shaking, and the bones came together, bone to his bone.

The words "noise" and "shaking" may refer to an earthquake, or the words may refer to the rattling sound of many bones being joined together. At this point, the bones became skeletons still lying on the ground. No sinews or flesh had yet appeared, nor had the bodies stood up. The bones were still dry and dead, but they were joined together.

> 8 And when I beheld, lo, the sinews and the flesh came up upon them, and the skin covered them above: but there was no breath in them.

Verse 8 describes how the skeletons became bodies as sinews, flesh, and skin covered the bones. Verse 8 also says that the bodies were dead because no breath was in them.

> 9 Then said he unto me, Prophesy unto the wind, prophesy, son of man, and say to the wind, Thus saith the Lord GOD; Come from the four winds, O breath, and breathe upon these slain, that they may live.
>
> 10 So I prophesied as he commanded me, and the breath came into them, and they lived, and stood up upon their feet, an exceeding great army.

The miracle had two phases. In phase one, the prophet preached to the bones and they became bodies. The bones were joined to become skeletons, which were then given sinews, flesh, and skin. However, they still were only dead bodies. Phase two is described in verses 9–10.

In verses 7–8, Ezekiel had preached the word of God to the bones. Now he was told to preach to the wind. As already noted, "wind" and "breath" are the same word translated "spirit." Preaching to the wind was like summoning the Spirit of God to blow or breathe life into the dead bodies. When Ezekiel obeyed the command of God, breath came into the dead bodies. They came to life and stood up like a great army.

Ezekiel 37 uses symbols from the biblical account of creation. In the beginning, God created all things by speaking the word that called all things into being (Gen. 1). His creation of life is described as God breathing into man the breath of life (Gen. 2:7). As in creation, the emphasis is on the fact that only God could create life.

4. Israel's hopeless plight (v. 11)

> 11 Then said he unto me, Son of man, these bones are the whole house of Israel: behold, they say, Our bones are dried, and our hope is lost: we are cut off for our parts.

The dry bones were identified as not only the exiles from Judah, who had been carried into captivity by the Babylonians (bab un LOH nih uhns), but also the survivors of the fall of the Northern Kingdom to the Assyrians (uh SIHR ih uhns). The rest of chapter 37 (vv. 15–28) makes this clear. The defeat of Israel and Judah, especially the fall of Jerusalem, had dealt a terrible blow to the survivors. Powerful enemies had overwhelmed the people of God and taken them as helpless captives into heathen lands. By the standards of the day, this meant that their God was powerless and their plight was hopeless.

When Ezekiel shared this vision with them, the exiles could identify with the dry bones. They felt that their plight was hopeless. They had no more prospects of a meaningful future than the bleached bones had of coming to life again. (See Ps. 137 for another example of how the exiles felt.)

5. God's wonderful promises (vv. 12–14)

> 12 Therefore prophesy and say unto them, Thus saith the Lord GOD; Behold, O my people, I will open your graves, and cause you to come up out of your graves, and bring you into the land of Israel.
>
> 13 And ye shall know that I am the LORD, when I have opened your graves, O my people, and brought you out of your graves,
>
> 14 And shall put my spirit in you, and ye shall live, and I shall place you in your own land: then shall ye know that I the LORD have spoken it, and performed it, saith the Lord.

The vision was not given as a secret message for Ezekiel to keep to himself. The purpose of the vision was to reinforce the message that runs through the closing chapters of Ezekiel. God promised to bring the helpless, hopeless people out of the graves of the exile and restore them to their land.

In Ezekiel's vision, he was told to preach to dry bones lying in the open. In verses 12–14, he was to preach to people who saw themselves as though they were dead and buried. Whether unburied or buried, the dead are hopelessly dead. Ezekiel was told to preach a message of life and hope to people who saw themselves as cut off from life as if they were dead.

From a human point of view, their plight was as hopeless as the plight of the dead. But the God of the living and the dead can bring the dead back to life—whether as lifeless unburied bones or buried bodies. God promised to put His life-giving Spirit in them and they would live. When they lived, they would know that this was the work of the Lord.

Ezekiel 37 uses not only the language of creation but also the language of resurrection. When I study this passage, I think of John 11. From a human point of view, Lazarus (LAZ uh ruhs) could not be brought back to life. After all, he had been dead four days when Jesus arrived at Bethany. The stench of death surrounded the place of burial, yet Jesus called Lazarus back to life (John 11:38–44). The common teaching is that God has power to restore us from death unto life, from despair to hope.

II. Two Sticks Joined as One (Ezek. 37:15–28)

1. Prophecy of a reunited people (vv. 15–22)

God told Ezekiel to write on one stick a name representing Judah and on another stick a name representing Israel. Then he was to join the two by holding them in one hand. When the people asked what this meant, Ezekiel was to tell them that God was going to make Judah and Israel one by holding them in His hand. God promised to restore some survivors of both Israel and Judah and to reunite them in one nation with one king.

2. A covenant of peace (vv. 23–28)

The reunited people would no longer worship idols but would walk in God's ways under the reign of a descendant of David. God promised to abide with His people in a covenant of peace.

APPLYING THE BIBLE

1. Even in tragedy, God is near. An old mariner's chart drawn in 1525 is on display in London's British Museum. It is not known who drew it, but it shows both the hopes and fear of ancient sailors. Over a vast unexplored area, the original mapmaker wrote: "Here be giants"; "Here be dragons." Sometime later the chart fell into the hands of scientist Sir John Franklin who marked through the foreboding warning and wrote across the map, "Here be God!"

In Ezekiel's vision there was nothing to be seen but death: dry, bleached bones. But in that place of utter desolation and death, God met Ezekiel (vv. 1–3). God was there even in the most unlikely place. Whatever our sorrow or need, or however impossible our situation appears to be, remember: "God is here, too."

2. Nothing impossible for God. Years ago, when construction workers were building a bridge across a portion of New York's harbor, they were seeking a base for one of the buttresses to hold up the bridge. In the process, they struck an old ship that had sunk loaded with bricks and stones, but every effort to lift it out of the way failed. Then a young engineer had a brilliant idea. Divers were sent down to hook large chains to the sunken ship, and those chains were tied to large barges on the surface. Then they waited for the tide to rise. As the mighty tide from the Atlantic rose, the old ship shivered and shook and finally was brought up.

In the valley of dry bones, Ezekiel looked on what he must have believed to be an impossible situation. "Can these bones live?" God asked (v. 3). Ezekiel could not answer yes or no: "O, Lord GOD, Thou knowest," was the only answer he could give to what appeared to be an impossible situation (v. 3).

There is a lesson here for us: However great our problems may be, they are not too great for God to handle. In answer to our fervent prayers He will either remove the obstacle or give us the grace to handle it. Either way it will be all right.

3. Preaching to dry bones. Ezekiel was commanded to preach to the dry bones. Don't you suppose he thought, "How foolish"? But his faith expressed itself; he did as he was commanded, and God did the rest. But what if Ezekiel had not exerted his faith and believed God? Sometimes God works sovereignly without help from anyone, but at other times he works through His people to accomplish His purposes. Remember how He used the virgin Mary.

For many years Dr. J. B. Tidwell taught Bible at Baylor University in Waco, Texas. As a young student, called by God to preach, poor and struggling with a young family, Tidwell faced great difficulties. One night as he was trying to prepare for Greek class the following day, he walked the floor with his Greek book in one hand and his crying baby in the other arm. Finally, he put the baby down and wrote across the first page of the Greek book: "J. B. Tidwell plus God Equals Enough!"

What a testimony! And what an example for us to follow in hard times!

4. New life. Jonathan Edwards (1703–1758) was a colonial Congregational minister used mightily by God to ignite a revival known as the Great Awakening. His sermon, "Sinners in the Hands of an Angry God," was particularly influential. Thousands were saved and many colonial churches that were steeped in dead liturgy and formality were revived.

Before Edwards preached his sermon that had such a powerful impact, he had not eaten for three days or slept for three nights. Over and over again he prayed, "God, give me New England! Give me New England!" It is said that when he walked into his pulpit to preach, the people felt they were looking into the face of God and conviction for sins fell mightily upon them even before he opened his mouth! Spiritually dead people in that church were born again, and revival fire swept the colonies and even spread into Europe. It was all done by the power of God. In his vision, Ezekiel was told by God that the dead bones would live and that He would give new life to both Judah and Israel (vv. 5–6). As Ezekiel preached he saw, in his vision, the bones coming together and God's fresh breath of life being breathed into them (vv. 7–10).

Spiritual deadness fills our lives and churches, but God can give us and them this new spiritual life if we seek Him with all our hearts. Ezekiel's vision also reminds us that through Jesus Christ there is abundant hope for the hopeless (vv. 11–22).

TEACHING THE BIBLE

- *Main Idea:* The vision of the dry bones teaches that God has the power to restore His people.
- *Suggested Teaching Aim:* To lead adults to identify ways God is working in their lives to restore them to a closer relationship with Him.

A TEACHING OUTLINE

1. Use an illustration to introduce the study.

2. Use a matching test to set the context.

3. Use brief lectures, questions, and group discussion to search for biblical truth.

4. Use a drawing exercise to help members describe how God is working in their lives.

Introduce the Bible Study

Use the illustration, "Even in tragedy, God is near" from "Applying the Bible." Lead in a prayer that the lesson will help them see how God is at work in their lives to restore them to a closer relationship with Himself.

Search for Biblical Truth

IN ADVANCE, make a matching test by copying the seven summary statements in one column and the seven references in a second column. Place this on members' chairs and ask them to complete it as they arrive. Read the correct answers at this point to describe the context from which the focal passage comes.

Call for a volunteer to read Ezekiel 37:3. Ask: What options were open to Ezekiel to respond to God's question? (See "Studying the Bible.")

DISCUSS: What lessons can we learn about responding to God from Ezekiel's response?

Call for a volunteer to read 37:4–6. Explain that the same Hebrew word is translated "breath," "wind," or "spirit." Ask members to scan 37:1–14 to find references to these three words. ("Breath"—37:5, 6, 9, 10; "Wind"—37:9 [3 times]; "Spirit"—37:1, 14.) Point out that the miracle of giving breath or life to these dead bones was possible only because God breathed His breath, or Spirit, into them.

Call for a volunteer to read 37:7–10. Explain that "shaking" can refer to an earthquake or to the rattling sound of many bones being joined together.

Ask members to look at 37:9–10 and answer the following: (1) What did God tell Ezekiel to do? (Prophesy.) (2) To whom was he to prophesy? (Wind = Spirit.) (3) What was the wind to do? (Breathe on the dead bodies.) (4) What did the bodies do to prove they were alive? (Stood up.)

DISCUSS: What similarities do you see between this experience and the experience of creation?

Call for a volunteer to read 37:11–12, 14. Point out that it was not until after the bodies came alive that God explained His miracle. Ask members to examine 37:12, 14 and explain what the purpose of the miracle was. (God will bring hopeless exiles from their "grave" and restore them to their land.)

Give the Truth a Personal Focus

Distribute to members a sheet of paper and pencil. Ask them each to draw a stick figure to portray where they feel like they are in their spiritual lives—dry, bleached, disjointed bones; bones together but without flesh, and so forth.

Allow volunteers to explain their drawings. Ask: What do we need to do to have the experience of wholeness in our spiritual lives? List suggestions on a chalkboard or a large sheet of paper.

Ask: What evidence do you see in your life that God has already begun the process of making you whole? What can you do to experience even more of the breath of God's Spirit?

Close in prayer that members will recognize God's working in their lives and claim even more of His Spirit.

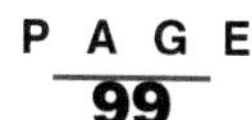

New Testament Personalities

DECEMBER
JANUARY
FEBRUARY

1996—1997

INTRODUCTION

The studies this quarter are about key personalities in the New Testament. The first five lessons are "Personalities of Jesus' Nativity and Early Life." The first lesson is about Zechariah and Elizabeth, the parents of John the Baptist. The second lesson is about Mary, the mother of Jesus. Lesson three focuses on the angels, the first group to hear the good news of Jesus' birth. Lesson four tells of the contrasting responses of the wise men and Herod. Lesson five shows how Simeon and Anna declared the infant Jesus to be the Messiah.

The second unit of four lessons portrays "Persons in Jesus' Ministry." These lessons focus on John the Baptist as the forerunner of Jesus; Mary and Martha as loyal friends of Jesus; Peter; who confessed Jesus as the Messiah and then rebuked Jesus for talking about His death; and Judas, who betrayed Jesus.

The third unit of four lessons describes some "Persons of the New Testament Church." The first lesson cites several examples of Barnabas as an encourager. The second lesson presents Stephen, the first Christian martyr. Lesson three is about Paul's loyal friends Priscilla and Aquila. Lesson four is about Timothy, whom Paul considered his son in the faith.

December

1

1996

Elizabeth and Zechariah

Basic Passages: Luke 1:5–25, 57–80

Focal Passages: Luke 1:5–13, 24–25, 59–64

We begin our studies of "New Testament Personalities" by looking at "Persons of Jesus' Nativity and Early Life." Luke begins the story with the announcement to Zechariah (zek uh RIGH uh) of the birth of John the Baptist. Although he and his wife were past the normal age for bearing children, they were to become the parents of the forerunner of the Messiah. When God chose to send His Son into the world, He chose people of true godliness to prepare the way.

Study Aim: *To tell the story of the announcement about and the birth of John the Baptist*

STUDYING THE BIBLE

OUTLINE AND SUMMARY

I. Announcement of the Birth of John the Baptist (Luke 1:5–25)

1. True righteousness (vv. 5–6)

2. Old and childless (v. 7)

3. Appearance of Gabriel (vv. 8–12)

4. Joyful news (vv. 13–17)

5. Too good to be true (vv. 18–23)

6. Elizabeth's joy (vv. 24–25)

II. Birth of John the Baptist (Luke 1:57–80)

1. His name is John (vv. 57–66)

2. Light in the darkness (vv. 67–79)

3. In the wilderness (v. 80)

Elizabeth and Zechariah were people of true righteousness (vv. 5–6). They were old and childless (v. 7). The angel Gabriel (GAY brih uhl) appeared to Zechariah as he offered incense in the temple (vv. 8–12). Gabriel told the old priest that their prayers had been answered (vv. 13–17). When Zechariah doubted the angel's words, he was struck speechless until the promise was fulfilled (vv. 18–23). Elizabeth hid herself until all would know that her days of barren reproach were over (vv. 24–25). When the child was born, the parents insisted that he be named John (vv. 57–66). Zechariah prophesied of the coming Messiah and of his son's role as forerunner (vv. 67–79). The child grew and went into the wilderness until his public work began (v. 80).

I. Announcement of the Birth of John the Baptist (Luke 1:5–25)

1. True righteousness (vv. 5–6)

5 There was in the days of Herod [HAIR uhd], the king of Judaea [joo DEE uh], a certain priest named Zacharias [zak uh RIGH uhs], of the course of Abia [uh BIGH uh]: and his wife was

of the daughters of Aaron [AIR'n], and her name was Elisabeth [ih LIZ uh beth].

6 And they were both righteous before God, walking in all the commandments and ordinances of the Lord blameless.

One of the characteristics of Luke's Gospel is the way Luke establishes the truth of the events of Jesus' coming, life, death, and resurrection (see Luke 1:1–4). For example, Luke described the historical setting of key events. Thus he set the events of Luke 1 within the years of the reign of Herod. In a similar way, the birth of Jesus took place when Caesar (see zur) Augustus (aw GUHS tuhs) issued a decree about taxation (Luke 2:1); and the ministry of John began in the days of Tiberias (tigh BIR ih uhs) Caesar (Luke 3:1).

Augustus, Tiberias, and Herod were the names of people of power and prestige in those days. But when God sent His Son into the world, He did not send Him into the mansions and palaces of the day. Luke 1–2 shows that God used people of true godliness through whom to bring the good news to the world.

God used people like Zechariah and Elizabeth to bring John into the world. He chose a humble and godly young woman like Mary to be the mother of Jesus (Luke 1:26–42) and a godly man like Joseph to act as His earthly father (Luke 2:1–7; see also Matt. 1–2). He chose to make the first announcement of the birth to humble shepherds (Luke 2:8–20). He chose people like Simeon (SIM ih uhn) and Anna to recognize the infant as the Messiah (Luke 2:21–40).

Elizabeth and Zechariah represent the true piety that existed in Israel. They were righteous in the best sense of the word, not in the sense of meticulous legalism. They were of priestly families, but they were different from the priestly families that controlled the temple for their own advantage.

2. Old and childless (v. 7)

7 And they had no child, because that Elisabeth was barren, and they both were now well stricken in years.

We know from Old Testament studies how a Hebrew couple viewed childlessness. Children were blessings of God who fulfilled their parents' hopes. A wife who could not bear children considered herself deprived of life's highest fulfillment. We remember the anguish of Hannah (HAN uh), her fervent prayers for a son, and her joy when Samuel was born (1 Sam. 1).

The plight of an elderly, childless couple was especially sad. Elizabeth and Zechariah were like Sarah and Abraham before the birth of Isaac. They had hoped and prayed for a child for many years. The older they grew, the less likely it became that they could ever have a child. In both cases, God showed His mercy by sending a son; and in both cases, the sons played key roles in the redemptive purpose of God.

3. Appearance of Gabriel (vv. 8–12)

8 And it came to pass, that while he executed the priest's office before God in the order of his course,

9 According to the custom of the priest's office, his lot was to burn incense when he went into the temple of the Lord.

10 And the whole multitude of the people were praying without at the time of incense.

11 And there appeared unto him an angel of the Lord standing on the right side of the altar of incense.

12 And when Zacharias saw him, he was troubled, and fear fell upon him.

Verses 8–9 describe a high moment in the life of Zechariah as a priest. Priests were chosen by lot to officiate at certain rituals; and because there were so many priests, no one offered incense more than once. So this was Zechariah's big day—when he served at the altar of incense. The incense symbolized the prayers of the priest and people going up to God. Therefore, while Zechariah was inside offering the incense, the people were praying outside the area in which the priests served.

This would have been a high point in the life of Zechariah under normal circumstances; but, as he officiated, suddenly Zechariah saw an angel of the Lord standing beside the altar. The old priest was troubled and terrified by this heavenly messenger.

4. Joyful news (vv. 13–17)

13 But the angel said unto him, Fear not, Zacharias: for thy prayer is heard; and thy wife Elisabeth shall bear thee a son, and thou shalt call his name John.

The angel quickly reassured the old priest by quieting his fears. The angel told him that his prayers had been heard and that Elizabeth would bear a son, whose name would be John.

Just as verse 6 tells us that Elizabeth and Zechariah were righteous people, verse 13 presents them as people of prayer. This is not surprising, because true righteousness grows out of a personal relation with God. We might assume from verse 13 that Elizabeth and Zechariah had prayed only for a child of their own. They had surely prayed for a child of their own; but as good Israelites, they also prayed for the Messiah's coming.

The angel's words show that God answered both prayers. The old couple would find new joy in the birth of a son (v. 14). His mission involved a special commitment and the filling of God's Spirit (v. 15). He would turn many to the Lord (v. 16). His mission was to go before the Messiah and "to make ready a people prepared for the Lord" (v. 17).

5. Too good to be true (vv. 18–23)

Zechariah questioned how such a thing could take place (v. 18). The angel, who revealed his name to be Gabriel, said that he had been sent with this good news (v. 19). However, because Zechariah had doubted the good news, he was to be unable to talk until the promise was fulfilled (v. 20). Because Zechariah was taking so long in the court of the priests, the people outside were wondering what had happened to him (v. 21). When the priest finally came outside, he was unable to talk; and the people concluded that he had seen a vision (v. 22). Zechariah filled out his term of service at the temple and returned home (v. 23).

6. Elizabeth's joy (vv. 24–25)

> 24 And after those days his wife Elisabeth conceived, and hid herself five months, saying,
>
> 25 Thus hath the Lord dealt with me in the days wherein he looked on me, to take away my reproach among men.

Elizabeth withdrew from crowds during the first five months of her pregnancy. During her barren years as a wife, she had seen many looks and perhaps heard words of reproach about her childlessness. She did not want to endure any more of these when she was actually pregnant. Thus she avoided people until she was a mother or at least until her pregnancy was apparent to all who saw her.

II. Birth of John the Baptist (Luke 1:57–80)

1. His name is John (vv. 57–66)

Elizabeth's day of joy was fulfilled when she gave birth to a son, and her neighbors and relatives came to rejoice with her because of God's mercy toward her (vv. 57–58).

> 59 And it came to pass, that on the eighth day they came to circumcise the child; and they called him Zacharias, after the name of his father.
>
> 60 And his mother answered, Not so; but he shall be called John.
>
> 61 And they said unto her, There is none of thy kindred that is called by this name.
>
> 62 And they made signs to his father, how he would have him called.
>
> 63 And he asked for a writing table, and wrote, saying, His name is John. And they marvelled all.
>
> 64 And his mouth was opened immediately, and his tongue loosed, and he spake, and praised God.

Consider how often God began some new phase of His work with the birth of a child. We think, for example, of Isaac, Moses, and Samuel. The same kind of newness came with the birth of John the Baptist and even more so with the birth of Jesus.

The naming of a child had special meaning in Bible times. Picture the scene. The child was circumcised as a descendant of Abraham on the eighth day (Gen. 17:9–14). Relatives and friends assumed that the child would be named for his father. Elizabeth objected. She emphatically declared that the child would be called John. Relatives reminded her that no one else in the family was named John.

Zechariah, who had been unable to talk since the day he saw Gabriel in the temple, was asked about the child's name. When he was given something to write on, Zechariah wrote, "His name is John." When he wrote those words according to the commandment of God from Gabriel, Zechariah's speech returned; and he proceeded to praise the Lord. When word of these amazing events spread throughout the hill country of Judea, people were amazed (v. 65).

They wondered what sort of special child would be born under such miraculous circumstances (v. 66).

2. Light in the darkness (vv. 67–79)

Zechariah, filled with the Holy Spirit, praised and blessed God for visiting and redeeming His people (vv. 67–68). His inspired words focused on the coming of the Messiah as foretold by the prophets (vv. 69–75). Zechariah also predicted that his son would play a key role in preparing the way for the Lord (vv. 76–79).

3. In the wilderness (v. 80)

John grew as a child and went into the wilderness to prepare for his own crucial mission.

APPLYING THE BIBLE

1. Humble and righteous people. God has always used humble and righteous people to accomplish His purpose and get His work done. He often bypasses the rich and powerful and lays His hands on the poor and humble. Zechariah and Elizabeth were two such people. Humble, poor, righteous—they were just the kind of people God needed to do His work (vv. 5–6).

Think of the people who have touched your life the most for God. Have they not been people like this? A Sunday School teacher who was not the best educated, a humble pastor who was faithful in declaring the Word of God but who was lacking in some skills, godly parents who had not been college educated but who loved Jesus with all their hearts and pointed you in the right direction—on these people God builds His kingdom.

2. Faithful to God's call. William Booth founded the Salvation Army. When Booth asked his Methodist Conference to appoint him and his wife to minister to London's derelicts and outcasts, his request was denied. Walking out of the conference, he and his wife went to London's outcasts, preached the gospel to them, and fed and clothed the hungry and needy. God used them mightily.

God came to Zechariah while he was faithfully performing the ministry to which God had called him. God came to Zechariah, through the angel, and appointed Zechariah to a high and nobler calling: He would father John, who would prepare the way for the Messiah (vv. 8–13). God uses those who are faithful and busy at work for Him, bypassing the idle and unfaithful.

3. The ministry of angels. Billy Graham says there is more said in the Bible about angels than about the devil or demons. Thank God for the daily ministry of the angels on behalf of God's people (Heb. 1:13–14). It was an angel named Gabriel (vv. 13, 19) who appeared to Zechariah to announce the good news that Zechariah would father John.

There is more being written today about angels than ever before. It seems that Christians are becoming more keenly aware of the ministry of angels on their behalf.

In his book *Angels, Angels, Angels: God's Secret Agents,* Billy Graham tells a story that once appeared in *Reader's Digest.* One cold, snowy night, a noted Philadelphia neurologist heard a knock at his door. Opening the door, he found a little girl poorly dressed and deeply distressed. She asked the doctor to come to her home and help her sick mother. Although the doctor protested because it was so cold, he reluctantly went to a poor tenement house with the little girl. He found her mother desperately ill. The doctor ministered to the mother and then complimented her on the insight and persistence of her daughter. Shocked, the mother told the doctor her daughter had died a month ago and that her clothes were still hanging in the closet! When the doctor opened the closet, he found the very clothes and shoes the girl had worn, perfectly dry and unexposed to the elements! Graham asks, "Was this the work of God's angels on behalf of the sick."[1]

What we attribute to luck or good fortune or coincidence is, in my judgment, the ministry of God's angels among us.

Graham also tells about a Persian Christian who was selling Bibles. When asked if he had a right to sell Bibles, he replied: "Why, yes, we are allowed to sell Bibles anywhere in this country." The man looked puzzled and asked, "How is it, then, that you are always surrounded by soldiers? I planned three times to attack you, and each time, seeing the soldiers, I left you alone. Now I no longer want to harm you." Graham asks, "Were those soldiers heavenly beings?"[2]

What, too often, we believers mark up to circumstances or "good luck" is more than that. How often must the angels of God, unseen by us, surround and protect us?

4. News too good to be true. When the angel broke the news to Zechariah (v. 13) and Elizabeth (vv. 24–25) that they were to have a son, it was news too good to be true and certainly too good to keep to themselves (vv. 57–80).

Have you ever prayed for a thing that burdened you and, although you doubted at times that your prayers would be answered, God mercifully gave you the thing for which you asked? What was your response? As did Zechariah and Elizabeth, did you thank God and rejoice with a heart full of praise? Did you share the news that was too good to keep with some struggling friend to strengthen his or her faith? Or did you lock it up in your heart, afraid that someone would call you foolish? Our response ought to be obvious. God's news is too good to keep quiet about.

TEACHING THE BIBLE

- *Main Idea:* God chooses righteous people to do His work.
- *Suggested Teaching Aim:* To lead adults to identify what they need to do to prepare their lives so God can use them.

A TEACHING OUTLINE

1. Use an illustration to introduce the lesson.
2. Use a chalkboard or a large sheet of paper to guide members' search of the Scripture.
3. Use Scripture search.
4. Use questions to help members give the truth a personal focus.

Introduce the Bible Study

Use "Faithful to God's call" in "Applying the Bible" to introduce the Bible study.

Search for Biblical Truth

Write the nine Scripture references of the background Scripture on a chalkboard or a large sheet of paper and ask members to write a one-sentence summary for each reference. (This could be an activity for early arrivals.)

Ask members to think through biblical history and identify some times that God began a new phase of his work with the birth of a child. (Examples: Isaac, Moses, Samuel, John, Jesus.)

Write *Zechariah* and *Elizabeth* on a chalkboard or large sheet of paper. Ask members to list what they know about these two people and list this information under each name.

Ask a volunteer to read Luke 1:5–7. Ask members to identify the two words in these verses that describe Zechariah and Elizabeth. ("Righteous" and "childless.")

Ask: What evidence can you find that they were righteous? How did childlessness affect their lives?

On a chalkboard or a large sheet of paper write the following words in bold. (You will add italicized information later.)

Priests	*Chosen by lot to officiate at certain rituals; this was Zechariah's chance of a lifetime.*
Incense	*Symbolized prayers of the priest and people ascending to God.*
Angel	*Angel Gabriel told him they would have a son.*
Prayers	*Both the prayers of Zechariah in the temple and their prayers earlier for a son.*
Good News	*Angel announced they would have a son and name him John.*

Ask members to examine 1:8–13 and suggest information about each of these words based on the text. The italicized statements above are possible responses; your members' responses may vary and still be correct.

Ask the class to read 1:24–25. Write on a chalkboard or a large sheet of paper: "Why did Elizabeth hide herself for the first five months?" (See "Studying the Bible.") Ask members to list words that they think would describe Elizabeth's feelings during this time.

Ask members to look at 1:59–64. Ask: What did the people want to name the baby? (Zechariah, after his father.) Who objected? (Elizabeth.) Why did Zechariah not object? (Apparently he could neither hear nor speak—the people had to make signs to him [1:62].) What was his first reaction after he was able to speak? (Praised God.)

Give the Truth a Personal Focus

Ask: Why do you think God chose Zechariah and Elizabeth? What part did the way they lived contribute to God's choosing them? How does the way we live affect God's choosing us for tasks today?

Ask members to list qualities of a righteous person. (To encourage more answers, let members work in groups of two or three.) Write these on a chalkboard or a large sheet of paper.

Give members paper and a pencil and ask them to list elements in their lives that keep them from being referred to as "righteous." Assure them that they alone will see the paper. Challenge them to eliminate these obstructions so God can use them to accomplish His purpose. Close in prayer.

---

1. Billy Graham, *Angels, Angels, Angels,: God's Secret Agents* (Waco, Tex.: Word Books, 1975), 17.

2. Ibid.

Mary, Mother of Jesus

Basic Passage: Luke 1:26–56
Focal Passage: Luke 1:26–42

Luke 1 records two special birth announcements by the angel Gabriel (GAY brih uhl). He told Zechariah (zek uh RIGH uh) about the birth of John, and he told Mary about the birth of Jesus. Mary was a young woman of true piety. She responded to Gabriel with candor and with humble trust in God. As a result, she became a channel of blessing by giving birth to Jesus, the Son of God.

Study Aim: *To show how Mary's response to the angel's announcement revealed the kind of person she was*

STUDYING THE BIBLE

OUTLINE AND SUMMARY

I. Announcement of the Birth of Jesus to Mary (Luke 1:26–38)
1. **The angel Gabriel sent to the virgin Mary (vv. 26–30)**
2. **Gabriel's announcement (vv. 31–33)**
3. **Mary's question and Gabriel's answer (vv. 34–35)**
4. **Mary's response to a call to trust (vv. 36–38)**

II. Mary's Visit to Elizabeth (Luke 1:39–56)
1. **Elizabeth's prophecy (vv. 39–45)**
2. **Mary's words of praise (vv. 46–56)**

The angel Gabriel appeared to Mary and told her that she was specially favored among women (vv. 26–30). Gabriel explained that Mary would conceive and bear a son who would be the Messiah (vv. 31–33). When Mary—who was a virgin—asked how this could be, Gabriel said that the Holy Spirit would overshadow her in such a way that the child would be the Son of God (vv. 34–35). After Gabriel reminded Mary that nothing is impossible for God, Mary expressed submissive trust in God (vv. 36–38). When Mary visited Elizabeth, the older woman declared Mary blessed for what God would do through her (vv. 39–45). Then Mary herself praised God for using a lowly person for such an exalted purpose (vv. 46–56).

I. Announcement of the Birth of Jesus to Mary (Luke 1:26–38)

1. The angel Gabriel sent to the virgin Mary (vv. 26–30)

26 And in the sixth month the angel Gabriel was sent from God unto a city of Galilee [GAL ih lee], named Nazareth [NAZ uh reth],

27 To a virgin espoused to a man whose name was Joseph, of the house of David; and the virgin's name was Mary.

In the sixth month of Elizabeth's pregnancy, God sent Gabriel to Nazareth, where Mary and Joseph lived. This couple was betrothed to each other. A betrothal was something like a modern engagement, except that it was more binding. The couple were not yet married and did not live together, but they had committed themselves to become husband and wife. Thus Mary was a virgin at the time of Gabriel's visit.

> 28 And the angel came in unto her, and said, Hail, thou that art highly favoured, the Lord is with thee: blessed art thou among women.
>
> 29 And when she saw him, she was troubled at his saying, and cast in her mind what manner of salutation this should be.
>
> 30 And the angel said unto her, Fear not, Mary: for thou hast found favour with God.

Mary was troubled by the angel's greeting. She wondered what the greeting meant. Over the centuries, people have pondered the meaning of verses like verse 28. One thing to notice is that the word "favour" in verse 30 is the word usually translated "grace." The verb form of the same word appears in verse 28. Mary was one upon whom the Lord shed His grace by choosing her for a special mission. God blessed her by making her a channel of blessings to others.

2. Gabriel's announcement (vv. 31–33)

> 31 And, behold, thou shalt conceive in thy womb, and bring forth a son, and shalt call his name JESUS.
>
> 32 He shall be great, and shall be called the Son of the Highest: and the Lord God shall give unto him the throne of his father David:
>
> 33 And he shall reign over the house of Jacob for ever; and of his kingdom there shall be no end.

The angel explained to Mary the meaning of his puzzling greeting. She was to bear a son whose name would be Jesus, which means "the Lord saves." When an angel later spoke to Joseph, he told Joseph to "call his name JESUS: for he shall save his people from their sins" (Matt. 1:21).

Gabriel used the word "great" to describe both John and Jesus (vv. 15, 32). However, the further descriptions of John and Jesus show that Jesus was by far the greater. He would be "the Son of the Highest." Verse 35 uses the title "Son of God." Luke 1:32–33 shows that Jesus would be the Messiah, the Anointed One who came as a descendant of David to establish an eternal kingdom. In the background is the basic promise to David in 2 Samuel 7:13–16 and other passages like Psalm 2:7 and Isaiah 9:6–7.

3. Mary's question and Gabriel's answer (vv. 34–35)

> 34 Then said Mary unto the angel, How shall this be, seeing I know not a man?
>
> 35 And the angel answered and said unto her, The Holy Ghost shall come upon thee, and the power of the Highest shall overshadow thee: therefore also that holy thing which shall be born of thee shall be called the Son of God.

People of faith in the Bible were open and honest in their conversations with God and with messengers from God. Such candor was an expression of faith, not doubt. Mary was awed by the angel's presence and puzzled by his words; however, she still asked the obvious question: How could she bear a child when she was a virgin?

Verse 35 is the Bible's answer to her question and to the questions that others have asked about this miracle. Even with the angel's answer, the virgin birth remains a supernatural miracle that defies human explanations. However, verse 35 tells us some crucial facts about this miracle.

For one thing, the language of the Bible does not describe God as a male partner in a sexual union; rather, the language is that of Genesis 1, where the Spirit of God was active in creation. John's conception had its Old Testament parallel in Isaac, the child of promise born to Abraham and Sarah in their old age; but the conception of Jesus had its parallel in the miracle of divine creation.

Another thing to keep in mind is that Jesus was born to a virgin, but He *was born*. Some ancient stories told of divine beings that sprang full-grown into life. This was not the way God chose to send His Son into the world. Jesus was divinely conceived; but once conceived, He was formed within Mary's womb and was born through the normal processes of birth. Thus there was a blending of the divine and the human in Jesus' conception and birth, just as there was throughout His life and ministry.

Most important, verse 35 declares that Jesus was uniquely the Son of God. "My beloved Son" is the title God used in describing Jesus at His baptism and at the transfiguration (Matt. 3:17; 17:5). Paul wrote that Jesus was "declared to be the Son of God with power, according to the spirit of holiness, by the resurrection from the dead" (Rom. 1:4). The virgin birth also testifies to the unique sonship of the One conceived in and born to the virgin Mary.

4. Mary's response to a call to trust (vv. 36–38)

> 36 And, behold, thy cousin Elisabeth, she hath also conceived a son in her old age: and this is the sixth month with her, who was called barren.
>
> 37 For with God nothing shall be impossible.

Gabriel's words in verses 36–37 were a call for Mary to believe the miracle he had described in verse 35. Gabriel told Mary about the pregnancy of her relative Elizabeth. Mary knew that Elizabeth was old and had been barren. If she was to have a child, it must be because God was giving her a child. Mary knew how God had given Isaac to Abraham and Sarah when they were old. The angel's words in verse 37 reflect the rhetorical question that God asked Abraham before that miracle took place: "Is any thing too hard for God?" (Gen. 18:14).

As we have already noted, the births of Isaac and John the Baptist involved a miracle; but the miracle was less spectacular than the birth of Jesus. Isaac and John were born to women who were old and barren, but each had a human father. Gabriel mentioned these miracles to challenge Mary to believe that God would do an even greater miracle by causing her to have a son without a human father.

38 And Mary said, Behold the handmaid of the Lord; be it unto me according to thy word. And the angel departed from her.

The word "handmaid" is literally "slave." In that day of slavery, a slave was totally submissive and obedient to his or her master. Mary used this word to express her obedient submission to the will of the Lord. She probably had many questions about how the miracle would happen, how Joseph would respond, and how she could raise Jesus, the Son of God. However, she trusted God to accomplish His word; thus, she placed herself in His hands to work out His will.

II. Mary's Visit to Elizabeth (Luke 1:39–56)

1. Elizabeth's prophecy (vv. 39–45)

39 And Mary arose in those days, and went into the hill country with haste, into a city of Juda;

40 And entered the house of Zacharias, and saluted Elisabeth.

Soon after Gabriel's announcement to Mary, she made a trip to the home of Zechariah and Elizabeth. Since Mary lived in Nazareth in Galilee, this trip involved a journey of many miles to the south to the hill country of Judea (joo DEE uh). The angel's words in verse 36 probably were what encouraged Mary to make this long journey. Mary was further encouraged by what happened during her visit with Elizabeth.

41 And it came to pass, that, when Elisabeth heard the salutation of Mary, the babe leaped in her womb; and Elisabeth was filled with the Holy Ghost:

42 And she spake out with a loud voice, and said, Blessed art thou among women, and blessed is the fruit of thy womb.

As soon as Mary greeted her, Elizabeth felt the child leap in her womb; and she was filled with the Holy Spirit. Zechariah had no doubt told Elizabeth what Gabriel had said about John and also about Jesus (Luke 1:13–17). She had heard the prophecy of her husband after the birth of John (Luke 1:68–70). Thus Elizabeth's words to Mary reflected the theme of the superiority of Mary's son to her own.

Elizabeth called Mary "the mother of my Lord" (v. 43) and blessed Mary for believing what God had said to her (v. 45). She interpreted her own child's leaping in the womb as a sign of joy over these events (v. 44). Elizabeth's words in verse 42, like Gabriel's in verse 28, were used in later centuries to exalt Mary to a divine-like role of her own. This misses the point not only of these passages but also of the whole New Testament. Mary was a recipient of grace, not a source of grace. Her blessedness was the blessedness of one who became a willing channel of divine blessings to others by becoming the mother of Jesus.

2. Mary's words of praise (vv. 46–56)

Mary's response in verses 46–55 reflects the same kind of humble trust seen in verse 38. The passage is a hymnlike poem of praise (vv. 46–47). Mary rejoiced that God had regarded her low estate. This was the basis on which she would be called blessed by future generations (vv. 48–49). What had happened to Mary was a sign of what God was doing among His people (vv. 50–53) and on behalf of His servant Israel (vv. 54–55).

Mary stayed with Elizabeth for three months before returning home (v. 56).

APPLYING THE BIBLE

1. Who is Gabriel? The name means "strong man of God." He appears four times in the Bible, each time bringing a message from the Lord: twice in the Old Testament to Daniel (8:15–27; 9:20–27); twice in the New Testament to announce the births of John the Baptist (Luke 1:8–20) and Jesus (Luke 1:26–38).

2. The joy of the virgin. What joy an approaching wedding brings to the prospective bride and groom if they are followers of Jesus. Many marriages today do not last because they have no spiritual foundation. The joy of the wedding is too frequently followed by the sorrow of divorce. Many young couples today are living together outside of marriage, giving their virtue and youth to a relationship that has little if any chance of truly being a joyous one.

The joy of Mary abounded as she looked forward to becoming a bride. She was a virgin engaged, or espoused, to Joseph. On top of the joy of her forthcoming wedding came the unexpected joy announced to her by Gabriel (vv. 28–33).

Mary's virtue and purity are worthy examples for every young woman today to emulate.

3. Troubling news. At times, through His word and through circumstances that befall us, God breaks in upon us to bring great joy. But at other times He troubles us with His revelations. Mary was full of joy at the angel's announcement, but she was also troubled: "She was troubled at his saying . . . How shall this be, seeing I know not a man?" (vv. 29, 34). But God never leaves us without comfort when we are deeply troubled, and Gabriel had the comfort Mary needed (v. 35).

Are you troubled at what is happening to you today? Take it to Jesus. He will give you grace to bear up under it and turn your heartache into happiness.

4. Nothing impossible to God. God is not limited in His power to act. Mary wondered how these things could possibly come to pass, but Gabriel reminded her of what this Jewish maiden already knew: "For with God nothing shall be impossible" (v. 37).

Niccolo Paganini (Pag uh NEE nee; 1782–1840), one of the greatest violinists of all time, stepped before an audience one day to play. Much to his horror it was only then he realized the violin he held in his hand was not the fine and valuable one he always used. Excusing himself for a minute, he went behind the curtains to get his valuable violin, only to discover it had been stolen and replaced with the cheap imitation. Going back on stage, he explained to the large audience what had happened and then told them they would hear what Paganini could do with the cheap violin. "Music is not in the instrument but in the soul," he explained, and then proceeded to thrill his audience with one of his best performances ever. Nothing was too much for the master violinist.

Mary discovered, and we need to rediscover, that nothing is impossible with God. Our Lord and Savior Jesus Christ is our Alpha and Omega and everything in between!

5. Doing the will of God. Jesus taught us to pray, "Thy kingdom come, Thy will be done on earth as it is in heaven."

Tennyson wrote: "Our wills are ours, we know not how; our wills are ours, to make them thine." Dante, the greatest poet of the Middle Ages, wrote: "His will is our peace."

Mary was troubled by the angel's announcement. She did not know all that was involved in the miracle God would perform and how He would use her to accomplish His will. She quietly submitted to God's will for her life (v. 38).

Knowing the will of God is not always easy, even for those who are eager to do it. But in faith we place our hands in the hand of God and move on, only to discover, as Martin Luther put it, that God has led us "like a poor blind mule."

Scottish evangelist Henry Drummond (1851–1897) shares some insights on discovering the will of God in matters that concern us: Pray; think; talk to wise Christians; do your duty faithfully in the things you know to do; when decisions must be made, make them and move on; never reconsider the decision when it is made—have no fellowship with doubt; and, finally, you will probably not discover until later—perhaps long afterward—that God has led you all the way.

As Mary prayed, so let us pray, "Be it unto me according to Thy word."

TEACHING THE BIBLE

- *Main Idea:* Mary's willingness to be used by God enabled her to be a part of God's plan of the ages.
- *Suggested Teaching Aim:* To challenge adults to be willing to let God use them in His great plan.

A TEACHING OUTLINE

1. Use an illustration to introduce the lesson.
2. Use a chart to see just how special Jesus' birth was and how it differed from other miraculous human births.
3. Use a poster to highlight the suggested teaching aim.
4. Use group discussion to guide the Bible study.
5. Use group discussion to challenge members to be willing to let God use them in His great plan.

Introduce the Bible Study

Use "Nothing impossible to God" from "Applying the Bible" to introduce the lesson. Point out that Mary, the mother of Jesus, is a beautiful demonstration of what God can do with people who are willing to let God use them.

Search for Biblical Truth

Write on a chalkboard or a large sheet of paper: *Isaac, John the Baptist,* and *Jesus.* Ask members to suggest how the births of these three were similar and different. Write members' comments opposite each name.

Suggest that all three births were miraculous but that Jesus' birth differed from Isaac's and John's because they had a human father; Jesus did not.

DISCUSS: Why do you think God chose to have His Son born to a virgin?

On a large sheet of paper, write the Suggested Teaching Aim. Mount this on the focal wall.

Ask a volunteer to read Luke 1:26–30. Ask members what this passage reveals about the kind of person Mary was. Ask: What does Gabriel's appearing to Mary indicate about Mary? (She was the best choice God could find; she was favored by God.)

Ask a volunteer to read 1:31–33. Ask: What do we learn about Mary from these verses? (She was not pregnant at the time Gabriel appeared. She would give birth to a Son whose name was going to be Jesus.)

DISCUSS: How does the name God chose for His Son indicate His task?

Ask a volunteer to read 1:34–35. Ask: What do we learn about Mary from these verses? (She felt free to question the angel. She was awed by the angel's presence and words. She affirmed that she had not had sexual relations prior to this event. She would become pregnant through the creative action of the Holy Spirit.)

DISCUSS: Why do you think God chose Mary to be the mother of His Son? What qualities do you think set her apart from other women? Was she more "holy" than others? How do you think God created the Child in Mary?

Ask a volunteer to read 1:36–38. Ask: What do we learn about Mary from these verses? (She was related to Elizabeth in whom God was also working. Mary willingly agreed to be used by God in this special manner.)

DISCUSS: Could Mary have refused to become the mother of Jesus? Did she have a choice in the matter?

Call for a volunteer to read 1:39–42. Ask: What do we learn about Mary from these verses? (She felt the need to see Elizabeth and stay with her for a while. She received Elizabeth's blessing.)

Give the Truth a Personal Focus

Ask members to list characteristics Mary had that equipped her to be used by God in this special way. Ask: Which of these characteristics do you have? Which would you like to have? What steps do you need to take before God can use you to accomplish His purpose?

Read the "Suggested Teaching Aim" from the poster. Challenge members to be willing to let God use them in His great plan. Close in a time of prayerful commitment.

The Shepherds

Basic Passage: Luke 2:1–20

Focal Passage: Luke 2:8–20

Luke 2:1–20, the most familiar of the Christmas passages, records the birth of Jesus and the announcement of the good news to the shepherds. We don't know the names of these shepherds, but we do learn a number of great lessons from the biblical account about them.

Study Aim: *To name lessons we can learn from the biblical account of the shepherds*

STUDYING THE BIBLE

OUTLINE AND SUMMARY

I. The Birth of Jesus (Luke 2:1–7)
- **1. The taxation decree (vv. 1–3)**
- **2. The trip to Bethlehem (vv. 4–5)**
- **3. Born and laid in a manger (vv. 6–7)**

II. Announcement to the Shepherds (Luke 2:8–14)
- **1. Good news for all people (vv. 8–10)**
- **2. Savior, Christ the Lord (vv. 11–12)**
- **3. Glory to God and peace to people (vv. 13–14)**

III. Witnesses of the Good News (Luke 2:15–20)
- **1. The shepherds' response (vv. 15–16)**
- **2. Spreading the news (vv. 17–18)**
- **3. Aftermath (vv. 19–20)**

Caesar (SEE zur) Augustus (aw GUHS tuhs) decreed that all people in the Roman Empire should be taxed (vv. 1–3). Joseph traveled to his ancestral home in Bethlehem (BETH lih hem) with Mary, who was soon to give birth (vv. 4–5). Jesus was born in Bethlehem and laid in a manger (vv. 6–7). An angel announced to shepherds good news of great joy for all people (vv. 8–10). The angel announced the birth of the Savior, Christ the Lord (vv. 11–12). A heavenly host spoke of glory to God and peace to people, upon whom God bestowed His good will (vv. 13–14). The shepherds quickly obeyed by going and finding Jesus (vv. 15–16). Then they told others what the angels had told them (vv. 17–18). Mary treasured all these things in her heart, and the shepherds returned praising God for all they had seen and heard (vv. 19–20).

I. The Birth of Jesus (Luke 2:1–7)

1. The taxation decree (vv. 1–3)

The head of the Roman Empire, Caesar Augustus, issued a taxation decree for all his domains, which included the civilized world of the day (v. 1). Cyrenius (sigh REE nih uhs) was governor of Syria (SIHR ih uh) at the time (v. 2). The decree called for each person to be enrolled in the city of his ancestors (v. 3).

2. The trip to Bethlehem (vv. 4–5)

Since Joseph's ancestral roots were in Bethlehem, the city of David, Joseph traveled to Bethlehem from Nazareth (NAZ uh reth) in Galilee (GAL ih lee), where he was living at the time (v. 4). Joseph took with him Mary, who was due to deliver her child (v. 5).

3. Born and laid in a manger (vv. 6–7)

When the time came for Jesus to be born, Mary gave birth. She wrapped the infant in swaddling clothes and laid him in an animal's feeding trough, because they had found no room in an inn.

Cameo of Augustus Caesar. Credit: Bill Stephens.

II. Announcement to the Shepherds (Luke 2:8–14)

1. Good news for all people (vv. 8–10)

8 And there were in the same country shepherds abiding in the field, keeping watch over their flock by night.

9 And, lo, the angel of the Lord came upon them, and the glory of the Lord shone round about them: and they were sore afraid.

10 And the angel said unto them, Fear not: for, behold, I bring you good tidings of great joy, which shall be to all people.

After Jesus was born, an angel announced the good news of Jesus' coming to a group of shepherds tending their flocks at night near Bethlehem. The earlier announcements of Gabriel had been to individuals who were personally involved in the dawning of God's new day—Zechariah (zek uh RIGH uh) and Mary. The announcement to the shepherds was the first public proclamation of the good news of the Savior's coming.

The angel told the shepherds "good tidings of great joy, which shall be to all people." This universal gospel is one of the strongest themes in the two books of the New Testament written by Luke. Some religious people tried to exclude certain individuals and groups from the circle of God's love. The good news of God in Christ is that no person or group is excluded.

This message was acted out when God chose to proclaim the good news first to shepherds. Shepherds were among the lowest groups on the social scale. Thus the first public proclamation of the gospel was to people of no social standing. By sending the message first to shepherds, God signified the truth that the good news is for everyone.

2. Savior, Christ the Lord (vv. 11–12)

11 For unto you is born this day in the city of David a Saviour, which is Christ the Lord.

The good news of the angel focused on the One whose coming was heralded. The angel used three titles that describe Him: Savior, Christ, Lord.

The word "Savior" was familiar to Jews and Gentiles. It meant "healer, deliverer, benefactor." It was a title often claimed for great men of the day. For example, Caesar Augustus was called a "savior." As used of Jesus, it refers to the divine Savior who came to save sinners from sin and death (Matt. 1:21).

The title "Christ" is the Greek equivalent of the Hebrew "Messiah." These words mean "Anointed One." Because the selection of kings often involved being anointed with oil, the term was a way of referring to a king. Because of God's promise to David that one of his descendants would reign over an everlasting kingdom, the Israelites hoped for the coming of the Messiah (2 Sam. 7:13–16; Luke 1:32–33).

The word "Lord" means "master." The word was used in the Greek translation of the Old Testament to represent the personal name of God. Thus it speaks of the divine nature of the One who was born. "Jesus Christ is Lord" became a basic expression of faith in Jesus as Lord (Rom. 10:9; 1 Cor. 12:3).

> 12 And this shall be a sign unto you; Ye shall find the babe wrapped in swaddling clothes, lying in a manger.

These words of the angel were not just about how to locate the infant. They were about a sign that the angel's message was true. Jesus was not born in a king's palace, but in a place where an animal's feeding trough became His first bed. This shows that this King is a humble, loving Savior. The shepherds could perhaps begin to see why the first public announcement of His birth was to lowly people such as they.

3. Glory to God and peace to people (vv. 13–14)

> 13 And suddenly there was with the angel a multitude of the heavenly host praising God, and saying,
>
> 14 Glory to God in the highest, and on earth peace, good will toward men.

The angel was joined by other angels to praise God for what was happening. Their words of praise focus on two things. The coming of Christ meant that all glory was due to God, who had sent His Son as Savior. It also meant peace for benighted humanity. Centuries before, Isaiah had prophesied the coming of a Child who would be called "the Prince of Peace" (Isa. 9:6). He provides peace with God and with fellow believers, and His coming ensures a time when peace shall prevail among all God's creatures.

The word translated "good will" is always used in the Bible of God's good will. Thus the point in verse 14 seems to be that God gives the gift of peace because of His good will or grace toward sinful humanity.

II. Witnesses of the Good News (Luke 2:15–20)

1. The shepherds' response (vv. 15–16)

> 15 And it came to pass, as the angels were gone away from them into heaven, the shepherds said one to another, Let us now go

even unto Bethlehem, and see this thing which is come to pass, which the Lord hath made known unto us.

16 And they came with haste, and found Mary, and Joseph, and the babe lying in a manger.

After the angels disappeared from sight, the shepherds talked together about what to do. No one argued that they had seen only an hallucination. Instead they agreed that the message of the angels was God's revelation to them. They also agreed that they should go into Bethlehem and see the new King of whom the angel had spoken. They quickly followed up on their decision. As a result, they found Mary, Joseph, and Jesus. Just as the angel had said, the baby was lying in a manger.

The shepherds are good examples of how people should respond to God's word: (1) They accepted the message as being from God. (2) They obeyed God's word. (3) They did so quickly. As a result, they found what God had for them.

2. Spreading the news (vv. 17–18)

17 And when they had seen it, they made known abroad the saying which was told them concerning this child.

18 And all they that heard it wondered at those things which were told them by the shepherds.

After they had seen Jesus, the shepherds began to tell others what they had seen and heard. Specifically, they bore witness to what the angel had told them about the One who was Savior, Christ the Lord. The people of Bethlehem wondered at the things that the shepherds told them.

God gave the shepherds three special privileges: (1) They heard the first public announcement of the Savior's birth. (2) They were the first—other than Mary and Joseph—to see Jesus. (The wise men came later. See the lesson for Dec. 22.) (3) They were the first human witnesses of the good news of Jesus' birth.

God could have chosen any person or group to receive such special privileges. The fact that He chose shepherds underscores the purpose of Christ's coming. He came for all people; but only those who realize their humble status are open to hear, receive, and tell the good news of the Savior.

3. Aftermath (vv. 19–20)

19 But Mary kept all these things, and pondered them in her heart.

20 And the shepherds returned, glorifying and praising God for all the things that they had heard and seen, as it was told unto them.

Verse 19 gives a rare insight into Mary's inner thoughts. She locked all these things away in her memory, and she gave considerable thought to all that she had experienced. A similar insight is mentioned after Jesus' trip to the temple at the age of twelve (Luke 2:51). At the time these things happened, Mary believed that God wanted her to keep them to herself. However, many Bible students think Mary was one of the eyewitnesses whom Luke consulted when he wrote the Gospel (Luke 1:1–4).

She was the only human witness of some of the wondrous things recorded in Luke 1–2.

Verse 20 provides a final glimpse of the shepherds. What a night they had had. They had been quietly tending their flocks when God drew them into the center of His redemptive purpose. They appear only here in the Bible, but they stand as models of how to hear and respond to God's word. Their final response to all they had seen and heard was to go on their way glorifying and praising God.

APPLYING THE BIBLE

1. Who was Caesar Augustus? "Caesar" was the family name of Julius Caesar, who ruled Rome from 49 to 44 B.C. Eventually, his name came to be used as a title. Octavian, Caesar's nephew and adopted son, took his uncle's name and also the title of Augustus, meaning "exalted" or "sacred." In Russian, "Caesar" is "Czar" and in German it is "Kaisar." Caesar Augustus was the founder of the Roman Empire. He was ruler of the empire, including Palestine, when Jesus was born. He issued the tax decree that brought Mary and Joseph to Bethlehem (vv. 1–3).

2. Did Luke make a mistake? Luke said Cyrenius was governor of Syria (v. 2) and that Herod was king of Galilee (Matt. 2:1) when Jesus was born. Historians know from other sources that Herod died in 4 B.C. Some historians once rejected Luke's statement, for Cyrenius ruled Syria from A.D. 6–9. But Luke was right. An inscription unearthed by archeologists revealed that Cyrenius (Quirinius in Latin) ruled Syria twice—the first time during the reign of Herod (Luke 2:1; Matt. 2:1). The unearthed inscription also showed Cyrenius ruled Syria between 10 and 7 B.C. Even the archaeologist's spade proves the trustworthiness of the Scriptures!

3. On to Bethlehem. A census was taken every fourteenth year by Roman authorities. It fulfilled two purposes: information for calling men for military service, and for taxation purposes. The second of these was the chief reason it was taken in captive nations such as Israel. Only by doing this were they able to guarantee the people in Rome "bread and circuses" at no cost to themselves. Being a descendant of David, Joseph (v. 2) took his "betrothed" wife (Mary), to Bethlehem, the home of David, to enroll.

One can only imagine the discomfort of Mary during the hard journey. Her time for delivery was at hand. Mary's suffering through the ordeal would only be the beginning of a life of heartbreak and suffering. Although we do not worship Mary, she certainly deserves our deepest love and respect.

4. The humble birth. P. O. Bershell has written: "Other babes were born and cried that very night to live and died unheralded. The world did not know that the cry of this babe in Bethlehem was God's answer to the piteous cry of humanity."

The birth of princesses or princes has often been marked in unique ways: the roar of guns, strains of music, the waving of flags, or by blazing bonfires. But for the King of kings and the Lord of lords who would redeem those trusting in Him, there was no earthly honor. God quietly stepped down from heaven, was cradled in a virgin's tender arms, and placed in a manger—all witnessed only by Joseph, Mary, and the dumb animals of the stall (vv. 6–7). But heaven sang at the holy birth!

5. The shepherds. Observe that the first to hear the good news announced by the angels were poor, humble shepherds. Often God works in and through His humble followers to reveal His eternal truth while He passes by an educated, sophisticated world that won't believe. What value there is in a humble heart, and how greatly we ought to pursue it! When they heard the announcement from the angels, the shepherds immediately did as they were told: they went to Bethlehem to "see this thing which is come to pass, which the Lord hath made known unto us" (vv. 15–16). No doubting; no hesitation; no reluctance, they obeyed immediately. Their faith ought to characterize us, for we know much more about the Savior than they did.

6. The songs of Christmas. Christmas is a season for singing and rejoicing. In our churches all across the land, church congregations will join in singing "O Little Town of Bethlehem," "Silent Night, Holy Night," "O Come All Ye Faithful," and others. Against this backdrop, "Jingle Bells" and "Rudolph, the Red-Nosed Reindeer" are shallow. But no Christmas cantata can match the one sung by the angelic choir on the plains of Judea to a simple group of shepherds: "Glory to God in the highest, and on earth peace, good will toward men" (vv. 13–14).

7. Back to work. After the great and heavenly encounter with the angels and the Christ-child, Luke says: "And the shepherds returned, glorifying and praising God" (v. 20). Touched by Christ and lifted by a heavenly blessing they returned to their lowly tasks, but the shepherds were never again the same.

So it must be with us. When we worship and are blessed, we are not to enter some monastery to ponder what we have experienced. No, we are to return to our daily work sharing the good news with others (vv. 17, 19).

TEACHING THE BIBLE

- *Main Idea:* We can learn many lessons from the biblical account of the angels appearing to the shepherds.
- *Suggested Teaching Aim:* To lead adults to name lessons they can learn from the biblical account of the shepherds.

A TEACHING OUTLINE

1. Introduce the Bible study by sharing an illustration.

2. Use a Pretest-Posttest to help members learn.

3. Use brief lectures, group discussion, and listing to examine the focal passage.

4. Use an illustration to "Give the Truth a Personal Focus."

Introduce the Bible Study

Use "The Shepherds" from "Applying the Bible" to introduce the lesson. Point out that in New Testament times shepherds were on the lowest level of society. God's choice of them as the first persons to hear the good news of Jesus' birth carries a message as to the people Jesus came to save.

Search for Biblical Truth

Prepare the following Pretest-Posttest and give to members. Tell them that no one else will see their paper.

Pretest-Posttest

Pretest		Posttest
	1. To whom was the first public announcement made of Jesus' birth?	
	2. Where did these people rank on the social ladder?	
	3. Why did the angel tell them not to fear?	
	4. What was the good news promised by the angel?	
	5. What was their response to the angel's message?	
	6. What did they do after they saw the Baby?	
	7. What was their final response to all they saw?	

Answers: **1.** Shepherds (2:8). **2.** Low. **3.** Angels brought good tidings (2:10). **4.** Jesus was born (2:11). **5.** Went to Bethlehem (2:15). **6.** Spread good news (2:17–18). **7.** Praised God (2:20).

Call for a volunteer to read Luke 2:8–10. Summarize the material in "Studying the Bible" on Luke 2:1–7 to give the background. Ask test questions 1–3. Ask: What lessons can we learn from these verses? (Among others: No person is excluded from hearing the good news of God.) Write members' response on a chalkboard or a large sheet of paper.

Call for a volunteer to read 2:11–14. Ask: What three titles did the angel use to describe Jesus? (Savior, Christ, Lord.) Use the material in "Studying the Bible" to explain the significance of these three titles. Ask: What did the angel say belonged to God? (Glory.) To people? (Peace, good will.) Answer test question 4. Ask: What lessons can we learn from these verses? Add these to your list.

Call for a volunteer to read 2:15–16. Point out that the shepherds are good examples of how people should respond to God's Word. (See "Studying the Bible".) Answer question 5. Ask members to share their response to question 6. Ask: What lessons can we learn from these verses? Add these to your list.

Call for a volunteer to read 2:17–20. Ask: What was the shepherds' reaction to what they had seen? (Told everyone.) Using "Studying the Bible," point out the three special privileges God gave the shepherds. Ask: What was Mary's reaction to all of this? Answer test questions 6 and 7. Ask: What lessons can we learn from these verses? Add these to your list.

Ask members to cover their pretest answers and take the posttest.

Give the Truth a Personal Focus

Ask members to review the list of lessons. Ask them to identify those that would apply to them today. Ask them to select as many as they would be willing to try to apply to their lives this coming week.

Share "Back to Work" from "Applying the Bible." Close with a time of commitment that members will be able to take what they have learned today back to their world of work.

The Wise Men and Herod

December

22

1996

Basic Passage: Matthew 2

Focal Passages: Matthew 2:1–12, 16

Matthew 2 tells of two different responses to the coming of the Son of God. The positive response was the worship of the wise men. They represent all who come to the Lord Jesus with reverent faith. The negative response was Herod's (HAIR uhd) attempt to have Jesus killed. His rejection represents all who refuse to come to the Lord Jesus with reverent faith.

Study Aim: *To contrast the responses of the wise men and Herod to the coming of Christ*

STUDYING THE BIBLE

OUTLINE AND SUMMARY

I. The Coming of the Wise Men to Worship Jesus (Matt. 2:1–11)

1. Searching for the King of the Jews (vv. 1–2)

2. Herod the tyrant (v. 3)

3. Fulfilled prophecy (vv. 4–6)

4. Following the star (vv. 7–10)

5. Worshiping the King (v. 11)

II. Deliverance of Jesus from Herod (Matt. 2:12–23)

1. A warning to the wise men about Herod (v. 12)

2. Flight to Egypt (vv. 13–15)

3. Massacre in Bethlehem (vv. 16–18)

4. From Egypt to Nazareth (vv. 19–23)

Wise men came from the east to Jerusalem to worship the King of the Jews because they had seen a star heralding His birth (vv. 1–2). Herod and the people of Jerusalem were troubled when they heard this (v. 3). When Herod asked where the King was born, religious advisors quoted Micah 5:2, which predicted the Messiah's birth in Bethlehem (vv. 4–6). After being asked by Herod to report where they found the new King, the wise men followed the star with joy (vv. 7–10). They found the young child, gave Him expensive gifts, and worshiped Him (v. 11). When God warned the wise men about Herod, they left the country without Herod's knowledge (v. 12). When God warned Joseph about Herod, Joseph obeyed God and took Mary and Jesus to Egypt (vv. 13–15). Herod discovered that the wise men were gone, and he ordered the murder of all the boys in Bethlehem two years of age and under (vv. 16–18). After Herod died, God told Joseph to return to Israel, and Joseph settled in Nazareth (NAZ uh reth) because Herod's ruthless son ruled in Judea (joo DEE uh, vv. 19–23).

I. The Coming of the Wise Men to Worship Jesus (Matt. 2:1–11)

1. Searching for the King of the Jews (vv. 1–2)

1 Now when Jesus was born in Bethlehem of Judaea in the days of Herod the king, behold, there came wise men from the east to Jerusalem,

2 Saying, Where is he that is born King of the Jews? for we have seen his star in the east, and are come to worship him.

The ones who came seeking Jesus were a combination of wise men and priests from some country to the east of Judea, probably Persia. These particular wise men had some knowledge of Jewish traditions. From their homes in the East, they had seen a heavenly sign that they believed heralded the birth of the King whom the Jews were expecting. Thus they made the long trip to Judea.

They went to Jerusalem, the capital of Judea, and announced that they had come to worship the One who was born as King of the Jews. Just as the shepherds signified that the good news was for all people, so did the wise men. Although the shepherds were of lowly social status, they were at least Jews. The wise men were Gentiles. Their coming to worship Jesus at the beginning of His life foreshadowed the later coming of many Gentiles to join with believing Jews in worshiping Jesus as Lord.

2. Herod the tyrant (v. 3)

3 When Herod the king had heard these things, he was troubled, and all Jerusalem with him.

The reigning king in Judea was Herod the Great. He was a half-Jew who had connived his way into being granted the title "king" by the Roman overlords of the Jews. Herod was absolutely ruthless in how he got his title and how he kept it. He lived with the suspicion that others were conspiring to steal his throne. This paranoia focused on his own family. Over the years, he had executed his wife, his brother-in-law, and several of his sons because he suspected them of plotting to replace him.

These backgound facts about Herod shed light on verse 3. No wonder Herod was troubled to hear that someone had been born to be King of the Jews. The people of Jerusalem were troubled because they knew that such news might unleash from Herod another bloody purge.

3. Fulfilled prophecy (vv. 4–6)

4 And when he had gathered all the chief priests and scribes of the people together, he demanded of them where Christ should be born.

5 And they said unto him, In Bethlehem of Judaea: for thus it is written by the prophet,

6 And thou Bethlehem, in the land of Juda, art not the least among the princes of Juda: for out of thee shall come a Governor, that shall rule my people Israel.

Herod asked religious authorities and scholars where the Christ was to be born. They referred Herod to Micah 5:2, which predicted that the Messiah would be born in Bethlehem. Although Bethlehem was only a small village, it would receive lasting importance as not only the home of David but also the birthplace of the Messiah.

Verse 6 also contains a reference to 2 Samuel 5:2. The Old Testament verse was a commission to David to rule as a shepherd over Israel. The word "rule" in Matthew 2:6 means "to be a shepherd to." Thus verse 6 not only foretold where the Messiah was to be born but also the kind of King He was to be. He was to be a Shepherd-King.

4. Following the star (vv. 7–10)

> 7 Then Herod, when he had privily called the wise men, inquired of them diligently what time the star appeared.
>
> 8 And he sent them to Bethlehem, and said, Go and search diligently for the young child; and when ye have found him, bring me word again, that I may come and worship him also.

Herod summoned the wise men to a secret conference. Herod's later actions show that he was trying to use the wise men in a plan to kill the new King (v. 16). Thus his words in verse 8 express blatant hypocrisy.

> 9 When they had heard the king, they departed; and, lo, the star which they saw in the east, went before them, till it came and stood over where the young child was.
>
> 10 When they saw the star, they rejoiced with exceeding great joy.

Some facts about the star are clear, but much remains a mystery. The wise men saw the star from their homes in the East and believed it heralded the birth of the King of the Jews (v. 2). Verse 9 tells us that the star led the wise men as they left Jerusalem. Verse 10 describes their great joy at seeing the star. This may mean either that the star had not been visible since they first saw it over Judea; or it may mean that the star, which had been stationary, now began to move. In any case, God used this star to guide the wise men first to Judea and eventually to Bethlehem.

5. Worshiping the King (v. 11)

> 11 And when they were come into the house, they saw the young child with Mary his mother, and fell down, and worshipped him: and when they had opened their treasures, they presented unto him gifts; gold, and frankincense, and myrrh.

A number of ancient traditions about the wise men have found their way into modern Christmas practices. These traditions picture three kings bringing gifts to Jesus on the night of His birth.

The Bible does not have the wise men arriving on the night of His birth. The shepherds did, but not the wise men. Verse 11 refers to the wise men coming into "the house." Verses 8, 9, and 11 refer to Jesus as "the young child." This is a different word from the "babe" that the shepherds found in the manger (Luke 2:16).

Nowhere in the Bible are we told that there were three wise men. The assumption of three wise men comes from the fact that there were three gifts.

The Bible does not picture the wise men as kings. It definitely does not tell us their names, as some traditions do. Only two people in Matthew 2 were called "king"—Jesus and Herod. Wise men were sometimes advisors to kings, but not kings themselves. Greco-Roman literature contains accounts of wise men paying special visits to kings. Matthew 2 tells of some wise men who paid a special visit to the King of kings. They came bearing gifts and to worship Him. Gold was a gift worthy of a king. Frankincense and myrrh were expensive spices that were greatly prized.

The long-range significance of their coming was the picture of Gentiles coming to accept and worship the Jewish Messiah as the Savior of the world. The fact that they were wise men says that anyone who is truly wise will follow these wise men's example and worship Christ as Lord.

II. Deliverance of Jesus from Herod (Matt. 2:12–23)

1. A warning to the wise men about Herod (v. 12)

> 12 And being warned of God in a dream that they should not return to Herod, they departed into their own country another way.

Earlier the wise men had apparently taken Herod at face value when he asked them to report to him so he could also worship the new King (v. 8). Before they could report back to Herod, God warned them in a dream not to return to Herod. These men showed their wisdom by obeying God. Thus they departed Judea by another route.

2. Flight to Egypt (vv. 13–15)

God also warned Joseph in a dream that Herod was determined to destroy Jesus. Joseph immediately obeyed God's command to take Mary and Jesus to Egypt, where they would be safe until Herod was dead.

3. Massacre in Bethlehem (vv. 16–18)

> 16 Then Herod, when he saw that he was mocked of the wise men was exceedingly wroth, and sent forth, and slew all the children that were in Bethlehem, and in all the coasts thereof, from two years old and under, according to the time which he had diligently enquired of the wise men.

Herod was outraged when the wise men failed to return with the exact location of the child in Bethlehem. In a terrible rage, the ruthless king ordered the murder of all small boys in Bethlehem. (The form of "the children" shows that male children were meant.) Herod hoped in this way to include the young King. As we have already noted, Herod had slaughtered many people to preserve his throne. If a king would execute his own family members, he would have no qualms about ordering the deaths of strangers.

Matthew explains that Herod chose two years based on what the wise men had told him about when they first saw the star (v. 8). We don't know what they told him, but it must have been no more than two years earlier. Herod probably added some time to ensure killing Jesus.

Verses 17–18 show that this massacre fulfilled the spirit of Jeremiah 31:5.

4. From Egypt to Nazareth (vv. 19–23)

After Herod died, God appeared to Joseph in a dream and told him to return to Israel (vv. 19–20). When Joseph heard that Archelaus (ahr kih LAY uhs), one of Herod's ruthless sons, ruled in Judea, Joseph took Mary and Jesus to Nazareth in Galilee (GAL ih lee, vv. 20–23).

APPLYING THE BIBLE

1. The star. A bright star guided the wise men from Persia. Perhaps it was a conjunction of Jupiter and Saturn. Tacitus, a Roman historian, relates an old Jewish tradition that Saturn was said to protect the Jews. Babylonian astrologers reckoned Saturn to be the special star of both Syria and Palestine. P. Schnabel, a German astronomer, deciphered from ancient Babylonian writings that in 7 B.C. the conjunction of the planets was observed for a period of five months. Who has the answer? Only God does. But it was a miracle nonetheless and led the Gentile wise men to the Savior. That, it seems, is the greatest miracle of all! [1]

2. For all people. Angels led the Jewish shepherds to Jesus, and the miraculous star led the Gentile wise men to Jesus. Although it was a foreshadowing of a Savior for all the world, it took the Jewish believers years to accept this.

At this season of the year when we take special offerings for missionary work around the world, let us give generously, realizing that our Lord is not only for the Americans but for everyone who will believe. The world is drowning in its sin and dying lost without a Savior. But Christians know the secret that makes a difference.

3. Herod the tyrant. History reveals many tyrants, from Nero, Genghis Khan, and Napoleon on down to Hitler, Stalin, and Mussolini—only to mention a few. Stalin and Hitler alone had multiplied millions of innocents killed.

Herod was a blood-thirsty tyrant, as history records. When he learned that the Messiah was born in Bethlehem, Herod, fearing for his authority, told the wise men to find this new King of the Jews that he (Herod) might go and worship Him (vv. 2–8). Rather, Herod intended to kill the newborn King (vv. 13, 16) and sent his cohorts to kill all the boy babies two years old and under (v. 16). Then there appears the sad refrain of Rachel, the mother of Israel, weeping for her children (v. 18). Despots like Herod will someday answer to Almighty God. But will we? for we are all sinners. Jesus was spared from being slain, for an angel had warned Joseph in a dream to flee to Egypt for safety (vv. 13–15). It was another miracle that marked the birth of the Savior.

4. Going home another way. The wise men were led by God. Although they were pagan Gentiles, God used them in His plan. God is sovereign, and He uses whom He chooses. We ought to be cautious in judging whom God can use and whom He cannot use. He neither needs our advice nor criticism about the vessels He chooses for His service. In a dream, the wise men were warned not to return to Herod. Perhaps his duplicity had revealed itself to them, for they were "wise men." Anyway, verse 12 says: "They departed into their own country another way."

5. Return to Nazareth. We cannot tell for sure how long Mary and Joseph had been gone from their home in Nazareth. Luke writes that Jesus was circumcised on the eighth day (Luke 2:28); presented to the Lord in the temple at Jerusalem (v. 22–24); and then was taken to Egypt to escape Herod. Jesus next appears in the temple as a twelve-year-old. (2:41–50).What a glorious homecoming it must have been as friends and relatives gathered about them in their humble home. Luke is silent about the years in Egypt (2:39).

A few years ago, I was in the small town of Nazareth. As our group of tourists walked down the street, I looked back and saw a boy about twelve years of age, carrying a board across the street just as Jesus did two thousand years ago as he worked alongside Joseph in the carpenter's shop (Matt. 13:55). It was a moving experience to think of the boy Jesus, with callouses on His hands from honest work, whose precious hands would all-too-soon be nailed to a cross.

TEACHING THE BIBLE

- *Main Idea:* Those who are truly wise will come to Christ.
- *Suggested Teaching Aim:* To lead adults to follow the wise men's example and worship Christ.

A TEACHING OUTLINE

1. *Use an illustration to introduce the Bible study.*
2. *Use a poster to identify characters in the birth story.*
3. *Use an advance assignment to examine Herod.*
4. *Use a reading to describe the feelings of God toward the death of the children.*

Introduce the Bible Study

Use "The star" from "Applying the Bible" to introduce the Bible study. Point out that the star and the wise men point to God's personal involvement in the birth of Jesus.

Search for Biblical Truth

On a chalkboard or a large sheet of paper make a poster entitled: *Characters in the Birth of Jesus.* Ask: How many wise men does Matthew say came to see Jesus? Point out that Matthew does not say how many came; we normally assume there were three because they brought three gifts.

Ask a volunteer to read Matthew 2:1–2. Point out the following about the wise men: they were priests/astrologers; they possibly were from Persia, or what had been Babylon when the Jews had been in captivity; they were Gentiles, and their coming foreshadowed the later coming of many Gentiles to worship Jesus. Write *wise men* on the poster.

Call for a volunteer to read 2:3. **IN ADVANCE,** enlist a member to read about "Herod," in the *Holman Bible Dictionary,* pages 639–40 (or another Bible dictionary) and give a two- to three-minute report on Herod. Or use "Herod the tyrant" in "Applying the Bible." Emphasize how suspicious and mean Herod was. Write *Herod* on the poster.

Call for a volunteer to read 2:4–6. Ask: To whom did Herod turn to find the answer to the wise men's question? (Chief priests and scribes.) Where did they say the Messiah would be born? (Bethlehem.) What Scripture did they quote? (Mic. 5:2.) Use "Studying the Bible" to explain how 2:6 tells where the Messiah would be born and what kind of King He would be. Write *chief priests* and *scribes* on the poster.

Call for a volunteer to read 2:7–12. Explain that the wise men probably arrived as much as eighteen months to two years after Jesus was born because Jesus now lived in a house (2:11) with Mary. Point out how God warned them in a dream not to return to Herod. Write *Mary* on the poster.

Call for a volunteer to read 2:16. **IN ADVANCE,** make copies and enlist three readers to read the copy on the following page.

Give the Truth a Personal Focus

Challenge members to respond as the wise men to Jesus' birth, not as Herod.

---

1. Werner Keller, *The Bible History: A Confirmation of the Book of Books* (New York: Morrow and Co., 1956), 345–54.

All the Babies Are Dead!

1: All the babies are dead!
2: Pain.
3: Dread.
2: Terror.
3: Fear.
1: All the babies are dead!
3: All the male babies under two years of age.
2: So innocent.
3: So blameless.
2: So much joy—torn from us.
3: So much happiness—ripped from our hearts.
2: Why?
3: Why?
1: All the babies are dead!
2: Why this lifeless body in my arms?
3: Why this awful ache in my heart?
2: Is there no balm in Bethlehem?
3: Is there no cure for a broken heart?
1: All the babies are dead!
2: Who made Herod god that he could determine who lives and who dies?
3: Who gave him power to snuff out my joy, my hope for the future?
2: Who creates madmen like this to curse us with pain . . .
3: . . . dread . . .
2: . . . terror . . .
3: . . . fear?
1: All the babies are dead!
2: Where was God when this was going on?
3: Does He not care what happens to us?
2: Where was God when our sons were being slaughtered?
3: Was He powerless to do anything about it?
1: All the babies are dead!
2: But God's Son is still living.
3: His Son is safe.
2: Why?
3: Why?
1: All the babies are dead!
2: Whose Son is that who is dying there?
3: Whose Son is that with the blood running down His face?
2: Whose Son is that with the spear thrust through His side?
3: Whose Son is that with the nail prints in His hands and feet?
All: (Slight pause) *All* the babies are dead!

Simeon and Anna

Basic Passage: Luke 2:21–40

Focal Passages: Luke 2:22, 25–38

Of all the people connected with the birth and early life of Jesus, Simeon (SIM ih uhn) and Anna are probably the least known. Because they are not included in our traditional tellings of the Christmas story, many people have never heard of them. Students of the Bible, however, know that they played a key role in the early days of Jesus. Simeon and Anna represented Jews of true faith who had been looking for the Messiah's coming. They both testified that Jesus was the Messiah.

Study Aim: *To explain the significance of the testimonies of Simeon and Anna about Jesus*

STUDYING THE BIBLE

OUTLINE AND SUMMARY

I. Jesus Presented in the Temple (Luke 2:21–24)
- **1. Naming of Jesus (v. 21)**
- **2. Presented in the temple (vv. 22–24)**

II. The Witness of Simeon (Luke 2:25–35)
- **1. God's promise to Simeon (vv. 25–26)**
- **2. Simeon's blessing and testimony (vv. 27–32)**
- **3. Simeon's prophecy (vv. 33–35)**

III. The Witness of Anna (Luke 2:36–38)
- **1. Anna's devotion to God (vv. 36–37)**
- **2. Anna's testimony about Jesus (v. 38)**

IV. Jesus Growing Up in Nazareth (Luke 2:39–40)

Jesus was circumcised and named when he was eight days old (v. 21). Mary and Joseph presented him in the temple when Mary was purified and Jesus was dedicated (vv. 22–24). Simeon was a righteous man of faith, whom the Lord had promised that he would see the Messiah before he died (vv. 25–26). He took Jesus in his arms and testified that He was the fulfillment of that promise, a light to Israel and to the Gentiles (vv. 27–32). Simeon prophesied to Mary about the coming rejection of Jesus and of her own inner pain (vv. 33–35). Anna was an elderly woman who lived in the temple and spent her time fasting and praying (vv. 36–37). She gave thanks for Jesus and testified that He was Israel's Redeemer (v. 38). After the family returned to Nazareth (NAZ uh reth), Jesus grew in strength, wisdom, and the grace of God (vv. 39–40).

I. Jesus Presented in the Temple (Luke 2:21–24)

1. Naming of Jesus (v. 21)

When Jesus was eight days old, Joseph and Mary had Him circumcised according to the Scriptures (Gen. 17:9–14) and named Him Jesus as the angel had told them (Luke 1:31).

2. Presented in the temple (vv. 22–24)

22 And when the days of her purification according to the law of Moses were accomplished, they brought him to Jerusalem, to present him to the Lord.

Leviticus 12 describes how a woman was to be ritually purified after childbirth. The purification was to take place thirty-three days after the child's circumcision on the eighth day. A lamb was to be offered as a cleansing sacrifice. If a woman could not afford a lamb, the offering was to be two doves or young pigeons. Verse 24 implies that Mary offered two birds rather than a lamb.

When the Lord delivered the firstborn of the Hebrews from the final plague on Egypt, He prescribed that His people consider the life of any firstborn son as a special trust from God. As a sign of this, they were to consecrate each firstborn male animal or son to the Lord (v. 23; Exod. 13:2,14–16). According to Numbers 18:15–16, the redemption price for a son was five shekels.

These verses show two things about Mary and Joseph. First of all, they were people of faith and obedience. The passage stresses that they acted according to the law (vv. 22–24; see also vv. 27, 39). Second, verse 24 shows that they could not afford a lamb to offer as a sacrifice.

II. The Witness of Simeon (Luke 2:25–35)

1. God's promise to Simeon (vv. 25–26)

25 And, behold, there was a man in Jerusalem, whose name was Simeon; and the same man was just and devout, waiting for the consolation of Israel: and the Holy Ghost was upon him.

26 And it was revealed unto him by the Holy Ghost, that he should not see death, before he had seen the Lord's Christ.

Simeon was a righteous man with a deep devotion to God. His consuming goal in life was to see the Messiah. The words "the consolation of Israel" were used by the rabbis to describe the fulfillment of the messianic hope. Simeon looked forward to seeing the Anointed One of the Lord. Simeon was also a man who lived under the direction of the Spirit of God. The Spirit had revealed to Simeon that he would see the Messiah before he died.

2. Simeon's blessing and testimony (vv. 27–32)

27 And he came by the Spirit into the temple: and when the parents brought in the child Jesus, to do for him after the custom of the law,

28 Then he took him up in his arms, and blessed God, and said,

29 Lord, now lettest thou thy servant depart in peace, according to thy word:

30 For mine eyes have seen thy salvation,

31 Which thou hast prepared before the face of all people;

32 A light to lighten the Gentiles, and the glory of thy people Israel.

The Holy Spirit led Simeon to the temple at the same time that Mary and Joseph were presenting Jesus there. The word "parents" is used here and later in verse 41, when Mary and Joseph took Jesus to the temple at age twelve. Luke has already clearly shown that Jesus was miraculously conceived and born to the virgin Mary (Luke 1:26–38). Thus Luke was not claiming that Joseph was the biological father of Jesus. However, his words do show that God had entrusted to Joseph the role of earthly father of Jesus.

When Simeon saw the infant Jesus, the old man took Jesus in his arms and blessed God for fulfilling His promise to Simeon. He said that he could now die in peace because God's word had come true. Simeon declared that he had seen God's salvation. He obviously meant that he had seen the Messiah, who would be the instrument of God's deliverance.

Simeon's words of praise reflect the language of Isaiah about the promised Servant of God. Simeon echoed the promises of God through Isaiah that the Servant-Messiah would be a light to all people. He would fulfill the covenant with Israel and would also provide salvation for the Gentiles (see Isa. 42:6; 49:6; 52:10). The difference between Isaiah and Simeon was that Isaiah looked into the future and predicted the coming of such a One, and Simeon testified that the child Jesus *was* the promised One.

One of the characteristics of Luke 1–2 is that those connected with the coming of Christ uttered poetic words of praise and testimony about Jesus. Each spoke under the impulse of God's Spirit using words that have traditionally been called songs. We have the song of Elizabeth in Luke 1:42–45; the song of Mary in Luke 1:46–55; the song of Zechariah in Luke 1:67–79; the song of the heavenly host in Luke 2:14; and the song of Simeon in Luke 2:29–32. The common theme in all these songs is the exaltation of Jesus as the Messiah.

Another theme which is sounded in Simeon's song is that Jesus came not just as the Messiah of the Jews but also as the Savior of all people (see also Luke 2:10). The Gospel of Luke shows how Jesus laid the foundation for the Great Commission, and the Book of Acts shows how the Spirit of the Lord led the early believers to undertake a worldwide mission. We live in a dark world. Jesus came to be the Light of the world. None of us needs to continue to walk in darkness. None of us can remain silent when those all about us still walk in darkness.

3. Simeon's prophecy (vv. 33–35)

> 33 And Joseph and his mother marvelled at those things which were spoken of him.
>
> 34 And Simeon blessed them, and said unto Mary his mother, Behold, this child is set for the fall and rising again of many in Israel; and for a sign which shall be spoken against;
>
> 35 (Yea, a sword shall pierce through thy own soul also,) that the thoughts of many hearts may be revealed.

Although Joseph and especially Mary knew things about Jesus that others did not know, they were still amazed at what Simeon said. Perhaps it was the universal scope of the mission of Jesus that surprised them. Perhaps it was that this old man so quickly recognized who Jesus was.

Simeon then told Mary something else that she probably had not realized. Simeon predicted that Jesus' mission would create division and would lead to rejection by many. Then speaking directly to Mary, Simeon told her that all of this would be like the pain of a sword in her own soul.

Perhaps Simeon was still thinking of the Servant foretold by Isaiah and remembering that Isaiah predicted that He would be a Suffering Servant. Isaiah 53 says that the Servant would be despised and rejected among men, and would bear our sins through His own suffering and death. Few of Jesus' closest followers saw the meaning of the cross until after the Crucifixion and Resurrection, but Simeon predicted this universal Savior would fulfill His mission through suffering.

III. The Witness of Anna (Luke 2:36–38)

1. Anna's devotion to God (vv. 36–37)

> 36 And there was one Anna, a prophetess, the daughter of Phanuel [fuh NYOO uhl], of the tribe of Aser [AY sur]: she was of a great age, and had lived with an husband seven years from her virginity;
>
> 37 And she was a widow of about fourscore and four years, which departed not from the temple, but served God with fastings and prayers night and day.

Anna was known for two things: her great age and her great devotion to God. The "four score and four years may mean that she was a widow eighty-four years of age, or it may mean that she had been a widow for eighty-four years since her husband's death after seven years of marriage. In either case, she was well along in years. At this stage in her life, she never left the temple. Since the temple covered a large area with many rooms, she apparently found a place to sleep. However, she spent most of her time day and night fasting and praying. One cannot imagine any more intense personal devotion to God.

2. Anna's testimony about Jesus (v. 38)

> 38 And she coming in that instant gave thanks likewise unto the Lord, and spake of him to all them that looked for the redemption of Israel.

Anna came in while Simeon was holding Jesus in his arms and declaring Him to be the Messiah of Israel and the Savior of all people, who would fulfill His mission through suffering. Simeon was giving thanks to God for sending the Messiah. When Anna came in, she also gave thanks to God.

The tense of the verb "spake" shows that she continued to speak of Jesus as the Messiah. She did this not only while Jesus, Mary, Joseph, and Simeon were together, but also she continued to speak of Him to all who were looking for the One who would redeem Israel. Her words were similar to those used years later by the two men on the Emmaus Road, who said that they had trusted Jesus to be the One who would redeem Israel (Luke 24:21).

We have been studying "Persons of Jesus' Nativity and Early Life." With the exception of Herod, all of the others played positive roles in this divine drama. Simeon and Anna were no exceptions. They represented the highest and best of Old Testament religion. They were fervently looking for the Messiah. They both testified that Jesus was that Messiah, and Simeon also stressed that Israel's Messiah was the Savior of the world.

IV. Jesus Growing Up in Nazareth (Luke 2:39–40)

After doing all that the law required in Jerusalem, Joseph, Mary, and Jesus went to Nazareth in Galilee (GAL ih lee) (v. 39). Jesus grew up there: growing in strength and wisdom and having God's grace on Him (v. 40).

APPLYING THE BIBLE

1. The naming of Jesus. Jesus is given many titles in the New Testament; but His name is "Jesus," so named by the angel before He was born (Luke 1:31). There is much in a name. We carefully pick the name of our children, but Mary and Joseph had no part in naming Jesus. God named Him; and His name means, "Jehovah is salvation." It is the Greek form of "Joshua." He is the Christ—"the Anointed One," or "Messiah."

2. From poor people. Some of history's greatest luminaries came from poor homes. Martin Luther, the great reformer, was born among the mines of Germany. Shakespeare, the magnificent writer, was born in a humble home at Stratford-on-Avon, England. Columbus was born in poverty at Genoa. Lincoln was born in a log cabin. Some of our greatest preachers and teachers were from humble origins.

So it was with Jesus. Our lesson writer points out that, according to the Levitical law (Lev. 12), a woman was to give an offering of purification after childbirth—a lamb or young pigeons or two doves. Mary, it is implied, could not offer a lamb so she offered two birds. This says so much about the needy home into which He who owned the cattle of a thousand hills was born. As the late R. G. Lee pointed out: He was born in a borrowed barn; cradled in a borrowed crib; preached from a borrowed boat; fed a multitude with a borrowed lunch; was nailed to a borrowed cross; and laid in a borrowed tomb. He who had always from eternity laid His head on the bosom of His Father, had no place to lay His head.

Mary could not give a lamb, but all-too-soon she would yield up to the Father "the Lamb of God who takes away the sin of the world" (John 1:29, NRSV).

Oh! What a glorious Savior and what a blessed, selfless mother!

3. Blessed by the saints. Simeon was an old man, just and devout. God promised Simeon that he would not die before he had seen the Lord's Christ (vv. 25–26). Anna was an eighty-four-year-old widow who stayed at the temple fasting day and night. Both of them blessed the child Jesus.

Think back at the saints of God who have blessed you: a mother and father who loved Jesus; a pastor who faithfully preached God's Word to you; faithful Sunday School teachers who dealt with you lovingly and tenderly; college teachers who shared their wisdom with you; and friends in whom you confided your deepest secrets. As God used Simeon and Anna to bless the child Jesus, as well as His parents, so God continues to bless us and draw us nearer to Himself by the people He puts in our pathway. Like them, we are the hands God uses to bless and encourage others. Let us never, never forget it!

4. Dismissed! Simeon has seen the Savior as God had promised him. Now, in verse 29, he prays: "Lord, now lettest thou thy servant depart in peace, according to thy word." A marginal reading in the New International Version translates "now lettest . . . depart" as "now dismiss"! Simeon has had his prayer answered, and he is ready to go home. It is an interesting translation.

Some of our loved ones, critically ill and at death's door, hold on by pure determination, for they don't want to bring grief to their family. However, there is an appropriate time, on occasion, when, led by the Holy Spirit, it is appropriate to say to them, "Whenever you feel like going home to Jesus, it's all right."

On one occasion I was ministering to a woman critically ill in the hospital. Neither she nor her husband nor her daughter was a Christian. After I led them all to Jesus, I looked at her, heaving for breath, called her name, and said, "It's all right for you to go home." I asked her husband and daughter if it was all right with them, and through tears they embraced her and told her it was all right. A few weeks later she met her dear Savior face to face.

Simeon dismissed his spirit, as did his Savior years later, because all was finished and fulfilled. It was time to go home!

5. The dedication of children. In many of our churches, a red rose is placed on the altar table after a baby is born to church members. This calls attention to a happy event and focuses the church on its responsibility to the child. Also, many of our churches have "Baby Dedication Day" when all those children born in the previous year are brought forward, in the arms of their parents, for a prayer of blessing for the little ones and their parents as well. All of this is good and wholesome, for we must dedicate our little ones to Jesus until they are old enough to receive Him as their Savior on their own. Perhaps the chief value of this tender ceremony is that it reminds the parents of the children to do all they can do to rear the child in the nurture and admonition of the Lord.

Mary and Joseph were keenly aware of their responsibility to do this (see v. 22). Oh, that parents today would follow their example! How much heartache it would spare them and their children in later years.

TEACHING THE BIBLE

➧ *Main Idea:* Simeon and Anna's recognition of Jesus can encourage us to respond to Jesus.

➧ *Suggested Teaching Aim:* To lead adults to praise Jesus as did Simeon and Anna.

A TEACHING OUTLINE

1. Use a chart portraying the songs of Christmas to introduce the bible Study.
2. Use titles to help members summarize the Scriptures.
3. Use posters to guide members' search of the Scripture.
4. Use a poster to give the truth a personal focus.

Introduce the Bible Study

Write the Scripture references below on a chalkboard or a large sheet of paper. Ask members to suggest their favorite Christmas song. Then remind members that Luke's account of the birth of Jesus is also full of songs. Ask members to suggest the songs from Luke that they remember and write them opposite the Scripture reference. If members cannot identify the songs from memory, ask them to turn to the Scriptures and identify the singer. Ask: What is the one common theme that runs through all these songs? (Exaltation of Jesus as Messiah.) Write this on the poster. Your finished poster should resemble the following:

Songs of Christmas
Luke 1:42–45: *Song of Elizabeth*
Luke 1:46–55: *Song of Mary*
Luke 1:67–79: *Song of Zechariah*
Luke 2:29–32: *Song of Simeon*
Theme: *Exaltation of Jesus as the Messiah.*

Search for Biblical Truth

Ask members to look at 2:22 and suggest a title that would describe this verse. (Their response should be something like *Presented in the Temple.*) Use "Studying the Bible" to explain the purification/presentation process.

Ask members to look at 2:25–26 and suggest a title that would describe these verses. (*God's Promise to Simeon.*) Ask members to do the same for 2:27–32 (*Simeon's Blessing and Testimony*) and 2:33–35 (*Simeon's Prophecy.*) **IN ADVANCE,** make the following posters, leaving space to write in members' responses.

Simeon
Who was he?
When did he meet Jesus?
What did he do for and say to Jesus?
Where did he meet Jesus?
Why did he prophesy as he did?

Ask members to suggest answers to these questions; write their answers on the poster.

Ask members to look at 2:36–37 and 2:38 and suggest titles. (*Anna's Devotion to God* and *Anna's Testimony about Jesus.)* Ask members to suggest answers to the questions below:

Anna
Who was she?
When did she meet Jesus?
What two things was she noted for?
Where did she meet Jesus?
Why did she testify as she did?

Give the Truth a Personal Focus

Ask members to suggest why Simeon and Anna are important in the birth story. (Members' response should be similar to the "Main Idea" of the lesson: Simeon and Anna's recognition of Jesus can encourage us to respond to Jesus.) Ask: What kind of response do you need to make to Jesus? Use the following poster and ask members privately to respond to each question:

You
Where did you meet Jesus?
What have you done for Jesus?
How can you praise Jesus by the way you live?

John the Baptizer

Basic Passages: Mark 1:1–15; Luke 7:18–30
Focal Passages: Mark 1:4–11, 14–15; Luke

This lesson begins a four-lesson study on "Persc try." John the Baptist (literally "Baptizer") was born of Jesus (see the lesson for Dec. 1). John's bold pre and his baptism drew crowds, which he pointed to One After John was arrested, Jesus began His own ministry—a ministry at times puzzled John.

Study Aim: *To describe how John the Baptist set the stage for the ministry of Jesus*

January 5 1997

STUDYING THE BIBLE

OUTLINE AND SUMMARY

- **I. The Beginning of the Gospel (Mark 1:1–15)**
  - **1. The gospel and John's ministry (1:1–6)**
  - **2. John and the One mightier than he (1:7–8)**
  - **3. Baptism of Jesus (1:9–11)**
  - **4. Temptations of Jesus (1:12–13)**
  - **5. Jesus preaching the gospel (1:14–15)**
- **II. When John Was in Prison (Luke 7:18–30)**
  - **1. John's question (7:18–20)**
  - **2. Jesus' answer (7:21–23)**
  - **3. Jesus' commendation of John (7:24–30)**

John the Baptist prepared for the Messiah by preaching repentance and baptizing those who repented (Mark 1:1–6). John pointed to One mightier than he, who would baptize with the Holy Spirit (Mark 1:7–8). When Jesus was baptized, the Spirit descended on Him and a voice from heaven declared Him to be God's Son and Servant (Mark 1:9–11). Jesus was driven into the wilderness by the Spirit, where he was tempted by Satan, after which angels ministered to Him (Mark 1:12–13). After John's arrest, Jesus preached that people should repent and believe because the kingdom was at hand (Mark 1:14–15). From prison John sent his disciples to ask Jesus if He was the coming One, or should they look for another (Luke 7:18–20). Jesus told John's disciples to describe Jesus' ministry of healing, helping, and preaching to John (Luke 7:21–23). Jesus commended John as more than a prophet, but noted that he did not see the fulfillment of the kingdom to which he had pointed (Luke 7:24–30).

I. Beginning of the Gospel (Mark 1:1–15)

1. The gospel and John's ministry (1:1–6)

The Gospel of Mark is introduced with the words, "The beginning of the gospel of Jesus Christ, the Son of God" (v. 1). Mark's account of the

pel begins with the work of John the Baptist, who fulfilled Malachi
:1 and Isaiah 40:3 (vv. 2–3).

4 John did baptize in the wilderness, and preach the baptism of repentance for the remission of sins.

5 And there went out unto him all the land of Judaea [joo DEE uh], and they of Jerusalem, and were all baptized of him in the river of Jordan, confessing their sins.

John's ministry focused on preaching repentance and baptizing those who repented. Luke 3:7–14 gives an example of his preaching. He called on people to turn from their sins, and he expected them to begin to do what was right. John's mission was to prepare the way for the Messiah. He called on people to prepare themselves by repenting of their sins and receiving God's forgiveness. As a sign of their repentance and forgiveness, John baptized them in the Jordan River.

Judaism had a number of washings, but the closest thing to John's baptism was proselyte baptism. When Gentiles were converted to Judaism, they were required to be baptized. This baptism was only for Gentile converts, and John insisted that Jews also needed to repent and be baptized. Gentile converts immersed themselves, whereas John immersed those who came to him in repentance. This seems to be where he got his name "the baptizer."

6 And John was clothed with camel's hair, and with a girdle of a skin about his loins; and he did eat locusts and wild honey;

Luke 1:80 tells us that John lived in the wilderness from an early age. His food was what he could forage in that bleak region. His clothing and appearance reminded people of Elijah the prophet (2 Kings 1:8). Malachi 4:5–6 had predicted that God would send Elijah the prophet before the day of the Lord. John was the fulfillment of that promise.

2. John and the One mightier than he (1:7–8)

7 And preached, saying, there cometh one mightier than I after me, the latchet of whose shoes I am not worthy to stoop down and unloose.

8 I indeed have baptized you with water: but he shall baptize you with the Holy Ghost.

When John preached, he pointed beyond himself to One mightier than he. A slave or servant would unloose the latchet of a guest's sandals, but John said that he was unworthy to serve the coming One even in such a lowly way. John said that his baptism in water foreshadowed a baptism of the Spirit. The One to whom he pointed would perform this Spirit baptism. When God sent His Spirit at Pentecost, He inaugurated an age when the risen Lord continued His work in His people through His Spirit.

3. Baptism of Jesus (1:9–11)

9 And it came to pass in those days, that Jesus came from Nazareth [NAZ uhr reth] of Galilee [GAL ih lee], and was baptized of John in Jordan.

10 And straightway coming up out of the water, he saw the heavens opened, and the Spirit like a dove descending upon him:

11 And there came a voice from heaven, saying, Thou art my beloved Son, in whom I am well pleased.

Jesus prepared to launch His own ministry by coming to John for baptism. He obviously had no sins to confess, so why did He come? He came to identify with the sinners He had come to save and to picture His coming death and resurrection. The words from heaven echo Psalm 2:7 and Isaiah 42:1. One of these declares the Messiah to be the Son of God; the other shows that the Son of God would fulfill His mission as the Servant who suffers.

This is one of the Bible passages that depicts God the Father, God the Son, and God the Holy Spirit. One God has revealed Himself as Father, Son, and Spirit. The doctrine of the Trinity remains a mystery, but it matches the revelation of the Scriptures and our own experiences. We know God as Creator and Father to whom we pray; as Son who lived, died, and was raised for our salvation; and as Spirit who is with us and among us.

4. Temptations of Jesus (1:12–13)

Mark does not describe the temptations as Matthew (4:1–11) and Luke (4:1–13) do. He tells us that the Spirit drove Jesus into the wilderness, where He was tempted by Satan, after which the angels ministered to Him.

5. Jesus preaching the gospel (1:14–15)

14 Now after that John was put in prison, Jesus came into Galilee, preaching the gospel of the kingdom of God,

15 And saying, The time is fulfilled, and the kingdom of God is at hand: repent ye, and believe the gospel.

Mark 6:14–29 tells about John's arrest, imprisonment, and execution. Herod Antipas arrested John because the bold preacher had denounced Herod and Herodias for their immoral marriage. Mark 1:14 says that Jesus launched His ministry after John was arrested. John was the forerunner of Jesus by his preaching and also by his suffering and death. Jesus too would be arrested and killed, but His death would atone for the sins of the world.

Mark 1:15 gives us the gist of what Jesus preached. He preached that the decisive time in God's redemptive plan had arrived. God's time was fulfilled. His reign was to be declared and offered to all people. Jesus' life, death, and resurrection were the heart of God's saving work. The future for which we hope is rooted in what God has already done in history through His Son, our Savior.

As John had called people to repent in preparation for the Coming One, Jesus called people to repent and believe because He was that One. Repentance and faith describe the human response to God's grace in Christ. These represent two sides of the same thing. *Repent* means to turn from sin, and *believe* means to turn to the Lord (see Acts 20:21).

II. When John Was in Prison (Luke 7:18–30)

1. John's question (7:18–20)

18 And the disciples of John shewed him of all these things.

Luke 7:18–30 took place some time after John was imprisoned. While he was there, Jesus was engaged in His ministry of preaching, healing, and helping. John had loyal followers who served as his disciples. They reported to John what Jesus was doing. "These things" refers to things like those recorded in Luke 7:1–17: healing the centurion's servant and restoring to life the son of the widow of Nain.

> 19 And John calling unto him two of his disciples sent them to Jesus, saying, Art thou he that should come? or look we for another?
>
> 20 When the men were come unto him, they said, John the Baptist hath sent us unto thee, saying, Art thou he that should come? or look we for another?

Why would John, who had so boldly preached Jesus as the Messiah, ask such a question? John seems to have been puzzled by the kind of ministry Jesus was performing. John had pictured the Messiah vindicating the righteous and punishing the wicked (Luke 3:17). Instead a righteous man like John languished in prison while the evil Herod and Herodias lived in luxury and security. Meanwhile Jesus was quietly going about helping needy people. John was puzzled because Jesus' actions did not match John's expectations.

2. Jesus' answer (7:21–23)

> 21 And in that same hour he cured many of their infirmities and plagues, and of evil spirits; and unto many that were blind he gave sight.
>
> 22 Then Jesus answering said unto them, Go your way, and tell John what things ye have seen and heard; how that the blind see, the lame walk, the lepers are cleansed, the deaf hear, the dead are raised, to the poor the gospel is preached.
>
> 23 And blessed is he, whosoever shall not be offended in me.

John dealt with his perplexity in the way people of faith deal with their doubts and questions. He addressed his question to Jesus. The Lord's answer was to tell John's disciples to report to John what Jesus was doing. Jesus was performing the kind of ministry predicted of the Servant in Isaiah. He had not come to bring final judgment but to make salvation possible.

When Jesus spoke in the synagogue in Nazareth, He read Isaiah 61:1–2 (see Luke 4:18–19). Using almost the same words, Jesus reminded John of His ministry of helping, healing, and preaching good news to the poor. John knew the Scriptures; Jesus expected John to recognize His actions as fulfillment of Scripture. John was not the only one close to Jesus who misunderstood His mission. Even the disciples of Jesus did not understand until after the Crucifixion and Resurrection.

3. Jesus' commendation of John (7:24–30)

Jesus used the occasion to commend John before the people. He did not want anyone to think He was being critical of John. Jesus reminded the people that they had not gone to the wilderness to see a timid person, like a reed blown about by the wind (v. 24). They had not gone to see pampered, well-dressed royalty (v. 25). Instead they had gone to see a man who was a prophet, indeed more than a prophet (v. 26). John was the messenger of the Lord foretold in Malachi 3:1 (v. 27). Jesus spoke the enigmatic words of verse 28 about none being greater than John, but the least in the kingdom being greater than he (v. 28). John was the last and greatest of the prophets, but he did not live to see the fulfillment of Christ's mission. Those who had listened to John praised God (v. 29), but the religious leaders rejected what God was doing through John and Jesus (v. 30).

APPLYING THE BIBLE

1. Sam Houston's baptism. Sam Houston played a key role in Texas's fight for independence from Mexico. He was the first president of the Republic of Texas. After Texas joined the Union, he served as governor and United States Senator.

When Lyndon B. Johnson was president, there hung on his wall a framed letter from Houston to Johnson's great-grandfather preacher who had led Houston to Christ. When Houston was converted he was a changed man. On the day he was baptized; he was reminded that his wallet was in his pocket. His reply was he wanted that baptized too!

A great many converts have been baptized; but, apparently, they left their purses high and dry as attested to by their giving records!

2. A great baptismal service. Were you baptized out-of-doors in a creek or a lake? Many have witnessed such moving services with the crowd lining the banks and the new converts making a long line down to the water, waiting their turn to follow the Lord in baptism.

John's baptism was a great one as multitudes came from all over Judea to be baptized in the Jordan River. Indeed, it was a happy day (Mark 1:5).

3. John's preaching. John's preaching included both a warning and a proclamation. He warned sinners to repent and confess their sins for the remission of sins (Mark 1:4), and demonstrate their change of heart by baptism (v.5). The joyous proclamation was that One was coming who would baptize them in the Holy Spirit (vv.7–8). In his desert preaching, John was preparing the way for Jesus to begin His public ministry.

Preaching today must also emphasize these same elements: repentance from sin, confession of sin, baptism, and the good news that Christ can change lives.

4. True humility. Abraham Lincoln was truly a humble man. But aren't the truly great men and women of history marked by this characteristic?

On one occasion, Lincoln called at General McClellan's house but was told the general had gone to a reception. Lincoln waited and waited, and finally the general returned home. Although he was told the president was waiting, McClellan ascended the stairs and went to bed. When the message was given to Lincoln, he quietly left. Later, Lincoln appointed McClellan as head of the Union Army. When Lincoln was asked by friends why he tolerated McClellan's insolence, the President replied: "Why, I would be willing to hold McClellan's horse, if only he will give victory to our army."

True humility was also one of John's chief virtues. He told his hearers that the One coming was mightier than he; that he was not worthy to stoop down and unlatch Jesus' sandals; that he must decrease but that Jesus must increase; and that he needed to be baptized of Jesus rather than baptize Jesus himself.

Unlike many of us who are offended at the least affront, there was none of this in John. He gave himself away in order to serve his Lord.

5. Satan's choice tool. Perhaps doubt is Satan's favorite tool. If he can get us to doubt our salvation or the goodness of God, he can destroy our Christian usefulness.

John the Baptist, suffering in prison, was plagued by deep doubts about the authenticity of Jesus (Luke 7:19–20). Jesus gave John the answer he needed for assurance (vv. 22–23). Satan is the author of doubt! Doubt no more about your relationship to Jesus. Do what John did: take it to Jesus and leave it there!

TEACHING THE BIBLE

- *Main Idea:* When we have doubts about Jesus, we should take them directly to Him.
- *Suggested Teaching Aim:* To lead adults to express their doubts to Jesus.

A TEACHING OUTLINE

1. Use a unit poster and an illustration to introduce the Bible study.

2. Use an advanced assignment to involve a member and enhance the lesson.

3. Use a poster and group discussion to guide Bible study.

4. Use group discussion to give the truth a personal focus.

Introduce the Bible Study

Prepare and display the following unit poster for the next four Sundays. Mark the lesson being studied each week.

Persons in Jesus' Ministry

John the Baptizer (Mark 1:1–15; Luke 7:18–30)—January 5

Mary and Martha (Luke 10:38–42; John 12:1–8)—January 12

Peter (Matt. 4:18–20; 16:13–23)—January 19

Judas Iscariot (Matt. 26:14–16, 20–25, 47–50; 27:1–5)—January 26

Ask: Is it wrong to question God? Say: Most of the great characters of the Bible questioned God. The lesson today is about one of these. Point out the theme for the next four Sundays and highlight the lesson for today.

Search for Biblical Truth

IN ADVANCE, enlist a member to read about "John the Baptist," in the *Holman Bible Dictionary,* page 805, or that entry in some other Bible dictionary and present a two- to three-minute report. On a chalkboard or a large sheet of paper write, "The Gospel and John's Ministry." Ask a volunteer to read Mark 1:4–6. Use a map of Judea to point out the Jordan River near Jericho as a possible site for John's preaching and baptizing. Ask: In what two actions did John engage? (Preaching and baptizing.) Ask a volunteer to read Luke 3:7–14 as an example of John's preaching. Ask members to identify elements in John's preaching. (Turn from sins, do right, be baptized.) Use "Studying the Bible" to explain the source of his baptism.

Write "John and the One Mightier than He" on the chalkboard. Use "True Humility" from "Applying the Bible." Ask: How did John demonstrate his true humility? (Said he was not worthy even to untie the Messiah's shoes.) How did John say his baptism differed from Jesus' baptism? (John's was water baptism; Jesus' was Spirit baptism.)

Write "Baptism of Jesus" on the chalkboard. Ask: Why did Jesus ask John to baptize Him? (See "Studying the Bible" for answers.) How does this passage depict the Trinity? (Father—spoke; Spirit—descended like a dove; Son—baptized.)

Ask a volunteer to read 1:14–15. Summarize the material in Mark 6:14–29 to explain why John was put in prison. Ask: What was the basic content of Jesus' preaching? (See v. 15.) **IN ADVANCE,** write this sentence from "Studying the Bible" on a sheet of paper and place on the focal wall: "Repent means to turn from sin, and believe means to turn to the Lord."

Write "John's Question" on the chalkboard. Call for a volunteer to read Luke 7:18–20. Ask: Why do you think John questioned whether Jesus was the Messiah? (See "Studying the Bible" for possible answers.)

Write "Jesus' Answer" on the chalkboard. Ask: What do you think of Jesus' answer to John's question as to whether He was the Messiah? Did Jesus really answer John's question? Do you think this answer satisfied John?

Give the Truth a Personal Focus

Ask: What do you do when you have doubts about God? Ask members to identify the process John followed. (Questioned, expressed his questions, went to Jesus for answers.) Say: Doubts are only wrong when we fail to bring them to Jesus. Jesus may not always answer our questions in the direct way we want; but if we are honest in asking, He will be honest in responding. Encourage members to express their doubts to Jesus and to be willing to seek Jesus' answer.

Mary and Martha

Basic Passages: Luke 10:38–42; John 12:1–8
Focal Passages: Luke 10:38–42; John 12:1–8

Mary and Martha were among the larger group of Jesus' friends and followers. They did not follow Jesus on His travels as did the apostles and some other followers, including some women (Luke 8:1–3). Instead, they showed their loyalty by what they did in a home setting. Martha exercised the gift of hospitality, and Mary sat at Jesus' feet to learn. She also showed great love and understanding as Jesus neared the time of His death.

Study Aim: *To explain what the words and actions of Mary, Martha, and Jesus reveal about Mary and Martha*

STUDYING THE BIBLE

OUTLINE AND SUMMARY

I. Jesus in the Home of Mary and Martha (Luke 10:38–42)
- **1. Two sisters (10:38–39)**
- **2. Martha's complaint (10:40)**
- **3. Jesus' reply to Martha (10:41–42)**

II. Mary Anointing Jesus (John 12:1–8)
- **1. After the raising of Lazarus from the dead (12:1–2)**
- **2. Mary's actions (12:3)**
- **3. Judas's objections (12:4–6)**
- **4. Jesus' defense of Mary (12:7–8)**

Martha received Jesus into her home, and her sister Mary sat at His feet and heard His words (Luke 10:38–39). Martha asked Jesus if He didn't care that Mary had left her to do all the work; she also asked Jesus to tell Mary to help (Luke 10:40). Jesus told Martha that she was anxious about many things while Mary had chosen the one thing that is necessary (Luke 10:41–42). After Jesus had raised Lazarus (LAZ uh ruhs) from the dead, He went to a meal where Martha served and Lazarus was at the table (John 12:1–2). Mary anointed Jesus' feet with expensive ointment and wiped His feet with her hair (John 12:3). Judas, treasurer for Jesus and the twelve, asked why the money had not been used to help the poor; but his motive was not concern, but greed (John 12:5–6). After Jesus told Judas to leave Mary alone, He commended her for anointing Him for burial, adding that—in contrast to helping the poor—anointing His body was a unique opportunity (John 12:7–8).

I. Jesus in the Home of Mary and Martha (Luke 10:38–42)

1. Two sisters (10:38–39)

38 Now it came to pass, as they went, that he entered into a certain village: and a certain woman named Martha received him into her house.

39 And she had a sister called Mary, which also sat at Jesus' feet, and heard his word.

John tells us that Mary and Martha lived in the village of Bethany (BETH uh nih) with their brother Lazarus (John 11:1). Bethany was about two miles southeast of Jerusalem (John 11:18). The last part of verse 38 evidently means that Martha was the mistress of the house and probably the older sister.

Martha showed her hospitality by greeting Jesus and welcoming Him into her house. Mary showed her devotion by sitting at Jesus' feet to learn from Him. "Sitting at someone's feet" was a way of saying that the person was studying under that teacher. The tense of the verb "heard" shows that Mary was continuing to listen to Jesus. Since rabbis did not teach women, Jesus having Mary as a student was a revolutionary act for both Mary and Jesus.

2. Martha's complaint (10:40)

40 But Martha was cumbered about much serving, and came to him, and said, Lord, dost thou not care that my sister hath left me to serve alone? bid her therefore that she help me.

The word "cumbered" means to be drawn about in different directions. She was distracted by her many duties in preparing the meal for Jesus. Every hostess can sympathize with what Martha was feeling. She had more to do than she had time to do it unless Mary joined in the preparations, but Mary seemed blissfully unaware of Martha's frustration. Finally her frustration became so great that she said something about it. However, rather than speaking directly to her sister, Martha addressed her complaint to Jesus. She asked a question and she made a request.

The question shows that she was not only angry with Mary, but she also was peeved with Jesus. Martha asked Jesus if He didn't care that Mary had left her to do all the work alone. This was a bold and brash thing for a hostess to say to any guest, especially to a rabbi, and even more especially to Jesus. However, Martha was so frustrated by all she had to do that she spoke in the heat of the moment. Later, she probably regretted such rash words. Jesus always cares for people, even if it appears to us that He doesn't.

Martha also asked Jesus to tell Mary to help her sister prepare the meal for their guest. Martha probably felt that Mary would pay no attention to Martha if Martha asked her to help. However, if their respected guest asked Mary to help, Martha felt that her sister would obey.

3. Jesus' reply to Martha (10:41–42)

41 And Jesus answered and said unto her, Martha, Martha, thou art careful and troubled about many things:

42 But one thing is needful: and Mary hath chosen that good part, which shall not be taken away from her.

The word "care" in verse 40 and the word "careful" in verse 41 are different words. The word Jesus used in verse 41 is the same word He used in warning against worldly anxiety (see Matt. 6:25, 28, 31, 34; Luke 12:11, 22, 26). The word implies a division and distraction of one's thoughts and actions based on a concern for too many material things.

Martha was anxious and distracted about many things: about the many dishes she needed to prepare and having the table and room just right.

Jesus told Martha that only one thing is necessary in the long run—hearing and responding to the word of God. Mary had chosen to spend this precious time sitting at the feet of Jesus. By so choosing, she had chosen something that nothing would ever take away from her.

The words of Jesus should not be taken as diminishing the value of Christian hospitality. Feeding and caring for others in one's home is clearly taught in the Bible. Hebrews 13:2 calls for believers to show hospitality to strangers as well as friends, "for thereby some have entertained angels unawares." This verse had in mind the warm welcome given by Abraham and Sarah to the three men who came to their tent, three men who later turned out to be two angels and the Lord (Gen. 18). Thus Martha felt she was showing that kind of hospitality to Jesus.

Some of life's choices are between good and bad, but many choices are between good and best. Martha's hospitality was good, but she was missing the best: to sit at Jesus' feet. Jesus' words were repeating the teaching that "man shall not live by bread alone, but by every word of God" (Luke 4:4; see Deut. 8:3). He was also restating what He said in Matthew 6:25–34. After warning against anxiety about food and clothing, Jesus said, "Seek ye first the kingdom of God, and his righteousness; and all these things shall be added unto you" (Matt. 6:33). Martha was concerned about a lavish meal in which everything was just right. Jesus would have preferred simple fare that would have allowed Martha to spend more time with Him.

II. Mary Anointing Jesus (John 12:1–8)

1. After the raising of Lazarus from the dead (12:1–2)

1 Then Jesus six days before the passover came to Bethany, where Lazarus was which had been dead, whom he raised from the dead.

2 There they made him a supper; and Martha served: but Lazarus was one of them that sat at the table with him.

Review John 11 to see the dramatic account of Jesus raising Lazarus from the dead. After that great miracle, the enemies of Jesus decided that Jesus must be killed (John 11:53). In this atmosphere, Jesus came to Bethany only a few days before His death. Jesus was invited to a supper. Mark 14:3 and Matthew 26:6 say that the meal was served in the house of Simon the leper. Martha was in her usual role as the one who served the meal. Lazarus was one of those at the meal.

2. Mary's actions (12:3)

3 Then took Mary a pound of ointment of spikenard, very costly, and anointed the feet of Jesus, and wiped his feet with her hair: and the house was filled with the odour of the ointment.

Spikenard was an expensive ointment or perfume. The heads of kings were often anointed with something like this (1 Sam. 10:1). Mary anointed the feet of Jesus with an entire pound of this ointment. This was a very expensive gift. Judas later estimated the cost as being about three hundred pence or denarii. Since a denarius was what a laborer earned for a day's work (Matt. 20:2), three hundred denarii were about a year's salary of a laborer, a considerable amount of money.

The humblest parts of the body were the feet. The crowning glory of a woman was her long hair (1 Cor. 11:15). It was unthinkable for a woman of Mary's reputation to use her hair to wipe someone's feet. The act showed Mary's humility and great love and devotion for Jesus. The Lord Himself also saw it as an act that encouraged Him as He faced the cross (vv. 7–8).

3. Judas's objections (12:4–6)

> 4 Then saith one of his disciples, Judas Iscariot, Simon's son, which should betray him,
>
> 5 Why was not this ointment sold for three hundred pence, and given to the poor?
>
> 6 This he said, not that he cared for the poor; but because he was a thief, and had the bag, and bare what was put therein.

We are not told to whom Judas addressed his question. Everyone no doubt heard it, including Mary. His words were actually an accusation against Mary. He was saying that she was wasteful and callous toward the poor. If the expensive ointment had been sold, the money could have fed many poor people.

Because Judas served as treasurer for Jesus and the apostles, he apparently felt it was his place to lodge this objection. Looking back at the words of Judas, who later betrayed Jesus, John wrote that Judas did not speak because he cared for the poor. Instead he cared for himself. John tells us that Judas was a thief who took for himself some of the money of Jesus and the others.

4. Jesus' defense of Mary (12:7–8)

> 7 Then said Jesus, Let her alone: against the day of my burying hath she kept this.
>
> 8 For the poor always ye have with you; but me ye have not always.

Rather than agreeing with Judas, Jesus sharply rebuked him. Jesus knew that the words of Judas must have cut Mary to the quick. Therefore, as Judas had publicly questioned Mary's act, Jesus publicly told Judas to leave Mary alone. Then He said that her act showed an empathy about His coming death and burial. She anointed Him ahead of time.

Jesus was only a few days away from His death. He had tried to tell His followers about His coming rejection, suffering, death, and resurrection; however, most of them had not understood. For the Messiah to suffer was too different from what they expected Him to do. As the end drew near, two of His followers seem to have taken Jesus seriously about His coming death. One was Mary of Bethany, and the other was Judas. They responded very differently to their awareness of Jesus' coming death. Judas betrayed Him, but Mary anointed Him as if for burial. Her act meant much to Jesus because it showed that at least one of His friends empathized with what He was going through.

Verse 8 has sometimes been understood to teach a callous acceptance of the plight of the poor. That was not Jesus' point. We know that He cared for the poor because of His own actions and teachings (Matt. 25:34–40; Luke 14:13, 21). Under the leadership of the Spirit of the Lord, the early Christians often showed their love for the poor (Acts 4:34–35; Rom. 15:26; Gal. 2:10; James 1:27–2:6, 14–16; 1 John 3:16–18).

APPLYING THE BIBLE

1. The epitaph on David Livingstone's parents' tombstone. David Livingstone, a pioneer missionary to Africa, wrote the epitaph that appears on his parents' headstone at Blantyre, Scotland: "To show the resting place of Neil Livingstone and Agnes Hunter, his wife, and to express the thankfulness of their children . . . for poor and pious parents."

Whether they are rich or poor parents is immaterial. But blessed are the children who are reared by pious parents—though it may take a lifetime for the children to recognize it.

Martha and Mary were not poor by the standards of their day but they were pious, each expressing her love for Jesus in her own way (Luke 10:38–39).

2. Angry Martha. Frustrated with all she had to do, Martha blurted out her anger (v. 40). Martha was also peeved at Jesus because Mary was sitting at His feet and He seemed not to care that Martha had all the work to do (v. 40). Notice that she did not take her complaint directly to Mary but went around her to Jesus. That's no way to confront people with whom we have difficulties. They need to be confronted directly but kindly. Telling loved ones and friends about the problem only fans a small fire into a bigger one.

When the British attacked New Orleans during the War of 1812, Andrew Jackson, who later became the seventh President of the United States, stopped the British cannonballs with bales of cotton. The soft cotton, crushed into strong bales, was a good defense. Solomon says the same kind of defense will work with people who irritate or anger us: "A soft answer turneth away wrath: but grievous words stir up anger" (Prov. 15:1). Look at how gently Jesus handled Martha's anger (Luke 10:41–42). What an example for us to follow. Almost everyone will respond to kindness and a smile.

3. Each of us can serve Jesus. In one way or another, each of us can serve Jesus. There are no believers without talents to dedicate to the Lord. Sure, some have one talent while others have two or ten. But each of us is endowed with some gift of service and love to give the Master. Mary was quiet and introspective, while Martha was outgoing, outspoken, and an activist. Mary sat at His feet and listened (v. 39), while Martha worked and served (v. 40, John 12:2). Probably Mary was no cook, and Martha was too active to sit still. Mary chose the better part, Jesus said (Luke 10:42), and He told Martha she was too "careful and troubled about many things" (v. 41). But He didn't condemn Martha for doing what she could. It takes both the Marys and Marthas to do the work of God.

4. Lazarus at the table. How would you feel to sit down by and visit with someone who had died and come back? In the dinner that Mary and Martha gave, there were two outstanding attractions—Lazarus and Jesus (John 12:1–2). Either would have attracted a crowd: Lazarus who was raised from the dead (11:38–44); and Jesus who had raised Lazarus. What a day in Bethany!

5. Humble extravagance. On the humblest part of the body, the feet, Mary poured her most extravagant gift, the spikenard, and dried Jesus' feet with her long hair, her crowning glory. What humble extravagance. Jesus was worthy of the best Mary had.

What a moving thing it is to read about someone who is extremely wealthy giving millions of dollars to the Lord's work. But that kind of gift given out of one's wealth counts no more with Jesus—though it makes the headlines—than the sacrificial gift given out of one's poverty (Mark 12:41–44). Christ accepts and honors all gifts given to Him, but the sacrificial gift is honored more (Mark 12:43). It is the spirit of giving that counts most.

6. Greed. Money is not evil, but the love of money is (1 Tim. 6:10). Greed, not concern for the poor, was Judas's problem (John 12:4–6). An anonymous poet expressed Judas's greed like this:

Dug from the mountain side or washed in the glen,
Servant am I or the master of men.
Earn me, I bless you; steal me, I curse you.
Grasp me and hold me—a fiend shall possess you.
Lie for me, die for me; covet me; take me.
Angel or devil, I am what you make me.

TEACHING THE BIBLE

➧ *Main Idea:* We can only serve Jesus when we serve Him the way He wants to be served.

➧ *Suggested Teaching Aim:* To lead adults to determine a selfless act they will perform for Jesus.

A TEACHING OUTLINE

1. *Use a question to introduce the Bible study.*
2. *Enlist a member to read the Scripture.*
3. *Use a poster to identify Mary and Martha.*
4. *Use discussion questions to guide the Bible study.*
5. *Use discussion questions to apply the study.*

Introduce the Bible Study

Ask: What is the most selfless act you have seen performed? Allow responses. Ask: What is the most selfless act you have performed? (Do not allow responses.) Use the unit poster prepared last week to indicate the lesson for today and point out that Mary performed a loving, selfless act commended by Jesus.

Search for Biblical Truth

Use a map to locate Bethany about two miles southeast of Jerusalem. On a chalkboard or a large sheet of paper write *Martha* and *Mary* at the top of two columns. Ask members to share what they know about these two and write their responses under each heading.

IN ADVANCE, enlist a reader for all of the Scripture. Call for the reader to read Luke 10:38–40. Ask: Why do you think Martha was upset? Since Mary was doing something that only men did in the first century, do you think Martha was upset by Mary's boldness? Why do you think Mary did not help Martha? Which one of these two women can you identify with most? Have you ever been angry with Jesus?

Ask the reader to read Luke 10:41–42. Ask: Did Martha have a responsibility and a right as mistress of the house to be concerned about preparing the meal? Was Martha doing what Jesus wanted done or what she wanted to do for Jesus? How do you reconcile Jesus' words here with the command for Christian hospitality in Hebrews 13:2? What is the most important thing as far as Jesus was concerned? Have you ever done what you wanted to do for Jesus instead of what He wanted you to do for Him?

Call for the reader to read John 12:1–3. Ask: Do you think Martha approached this meal any differently than she did the earlier one? How about Mary? How long does it take you to learn lessons Jesus wants to teach?

Call for the reader to read John 12:4–3. Use "Studying the Bible" to explain Mary's act and its value. Say: One way of looking at the value of her gift is that working forty hours a week at $5.00 an hour for a year would be $10,400. Mary's gift was quite expensive. Ask: How do you think Jesus felt when Mary anointed His feet? How do you think Mary felt? Why do you think she did it? Do you think she had planned it?

Call for the reader to read John 12:4–8. Ask: If you had been present, how would you have felt when Mary anointed Jesus? What was Judas's concern? How did Jesus interpret her action? How do you think Judas felt when Jesus rebuked him? How do you feel when someone rebukes you in front of people whose opinions you value? How do you think Mary felt about Judas's comments? Why do you think Mary's act meant so much to Jesus? How do you feel when you do something out of love and someone interprets it differently?

Give the Truth a Personal Focus

Ask: Can Christians be wasteful when it comes to giving to Jesus? Without responding aloud, what have you done in a spontaneous way that demonstrated great love for Jesus? How did you feel? Have you felt like you should do something loving and spontaneous but refused? How did you feel?

Challenge members to think of one act of love they will perform for Jesus just because they love Him and for no other reason. Allow time for private prayer and thought. Then close in prayer that members will have the courage to follow through on their decisions.

January

19

1997

Peter

Basic Passages: Matthew 4:18–20; 16:13–23

Focal Passages: Matthew 4:18–20; 16:13–23

Many Christians can identify with Simon Peter. He had high moments when he said and did inspiring things. At other times, he said and did things that showed his frailty and humanity. The Bible passages for this lesson include both kinds of words by Peter.

Study Aim: *To explain Peter's confession and rebuke of Jesus and the response Jesus made to each*

STUDYING THE BIBLE

OUTLINE AND SUMMARY

I. Following Jesus (Matt. 4:18–20)

II. Confessing Jesus as the Messiah (Matt. 16:13–23)

1. Peter confesses Jesus as the Christ (16:13–16)

2. Jesus commends Peter (16:17–19)

3. Jesus predicts His own death (16:20–21)

4. Jesus rebukes Peter (16:22–23)

When Jesus called Peter to follow Him, Peter immediately did so (4:18–20). Although many thought of Jesus as a prophet, Peter confessed Him as the Messiah (16:13–16). Jesus blessed Peter and promised to build His church that death could not destroy (16:17–19). After warning Peter not to tell anyone He was the Messiah, Jesus predicted His death and resurrection (16:20–21). Peter rebuked Jesus for saying such a thing, and Jesus rebuked Peter for becoming an instrument of Satan (16:22–23).

I. Following Jesus (Matt. 4:18–20)

18 And Jesus, walking by the sea of Galilee [GAL ih lee], saw two brethren, Simon called Peter, and Andrew his brother, casting a net into the sea: for they were fishers.

19 And he saith unto them, Follow me, and I will make you fishers of men.

20 And they straightway left their nets, and followed him.

Peter and Andrew were fishers by trade. Jesus sought them out while they were at work. When Jesus used the words "follow me," He was calling people to make a commitment to Him that superseded other commitments (Luke 9:57–62). The follower was to be with Jesus, learn from Him, be loyal to Him, and help Him fulfill His mission. Thus Jesus called Peter and Andrew to become fishers of men. The words "follow me" were used by Jesus to call people to become His disciples. The word "disciples" is often used of the Twelve who became the closest followers of Jesus (Matt. 10:1); however, the word was also used to describe the larger group of followers (Matt. 8:21).

John 1:35–42 records an earlier encounter of Jesus with these two brothers. Andrew had been a disciple of John the Baptist. When John had pointed to Jesus as the Lamb of God, Andrew told Simon about Jesus. When Simon came to investigate, Jesus said, "Thou art Simon the son of Jona: thou shalt be called Cephas [SEE fuhs], which is by interpretation, A stone" (John 1:42). "Cephas" is the Aramaic (air uh MAY ick) word for "stone." Although Andrew first brought Peter to Jesus, Peter became more prominent. In the lists of the Twelve, Peter's name is listed first. In verse 18, Peter is listed before Andrew.

II. Confessing Jesus as the Messiah (Matt. 16:13–23)

1. Peter confesses Jesus as the Christ (16:13–16)

13 When Jesus came into the coasts of Caesarea [ses uh REE uh] Philippi [FIL uh pigh], he asked his disciples, saying Whom do men say that I the Son of man am?

14 And they said, Some say that thou art John the Baptist: some, Elias [ih LIGH uhs]; and others Jeremias [jer ih MIGHS uhs], or one of the prophets.

A very calm Sea of Galilee at dusk in northern Israel as viewed from the southwestern shoreline towards snow-capped Mt. Hermon to the northeast. Credit: *Biblical Illustrator*.

Caesarea Philippi was a town located about twenty-five miles north of the Sea of Galilee (GAL ih lee). Herod Philip had named it for himself and Tiberias (tigh BIR ih uhs) Caesar (SEE zur). The word "coasts" does not mean sea coast, but a region or part of the country.

Before asking His disciples their own opinion of Him, Jesus first asked them what others were saying about who He was. Jesus referred to Himself as Son of man, the title Jesus most often used of Himself. After John the Baptist had been executed, some people thought that Jesus was John the Baptist raised from the dead (Matt. 14:1–2). Because Malachi 4:5–6 predicted that Elijah would precede the coming of the Lord, some people thought Jesus was Elijah. Others thought Jesus was Jeremiah or one of the other prophets.

15 He saith unto them, But whom say ye that I am?

16 And Simon Peter answered and said, Thou art the Christ, the Son of the living God.

Jesus asked the disciples who they thought He was. Notice that "ye" is plural. He addressed His question to all the disciples; but as was often the case, Peter was the one who answered. He often served as spokesman for the group. At other times, he simply was the first to speak.

Peter used two titles to describe who he thought Jesus was. "Christ" is the Greek equivalent of "Messiah." Both words mean "anointed one." Since kings were often anointed, the word had come to mean "king." God had promised David that a descendant of his would reign over an everlasting kingdom (2 Sam. 7:13–16). For centuries, Jews had looked for the coming of this Messiah. Peter's confession shows that he believed that Jesus was the promised Messiah.

Peter also called Jesus "the Son of the living God." The angel Gabriel had used the same title to describe Jesus when Gabriel told the virgin Mary that she was to have a son, who would be conceived by the Holy Spirit (Luke 1:35). At the baptism of Jesus, God's voice from heaven had declared that Jesus was His beloved Son (Matt. 3:17).

2. Jesus commends Peter (16:17–19)

> 17 And Jesus answered and said unto him, Blessed art thou, Simon Bar-jona [bahr-JOH nuh]: for flesh and blood hath not revealed it unto thee, but my Father which is in heaven.

In pronouncing a blessing on Peter, Jesus said that this faith of Peter's was not a purely human achievement. Peter had not reasoned his way to this conclusion. God had used the words and acts of Jesus to reveal to Peter that Jesus was His Son and the promised Messiah.

> 18 And I say also unto thee, That thou art Peter, and upon this rock I will build my church; and the gates of hell shall not prevail against it.

Verse 18 has been one of the most controversial verses in Christian history. The controversy swirls about the meaning of the words "this rock." Various Bible students have identified the rock as Christ, as Peter, as Peter's confession of faith, or as a combination of the above. Christ Himself is surely the ultimate foundation of the church (1 Cor. 3:11). On the other hand, the apostles can also be referred to as the foundation of the church (Eph. 2:20; Rev. 21:14). The testimony of the apostles, the unique eyewitnesses of Jesus, in a sense forms the foundation for the church.

If Jesus was referring to Peter as the rock, He may have seen him as representing all the apostles, whose testimony would provide the church's foundation. If Jesus was speaking of Peter himself, He was thinking of Peter's leadership role among the disciples and in the early church. Only one group sees this verse as justification for claiming Peter as the first pope and the head of a worldwide organization, controlled by Peter's successors.

When Christ spoke of "my church," He was speaking of His people, not an organization. Most of the uses of the word "church" in the New Testament refer to local congregations of believers. See, for example, Matthew 18:17. However, in Matthew 16:18, He was referring to those who, like Peter, confess Him as Christ and Son of God. He calls such to follow Him and be His people.

The phrase "the gates of hell [*hades*]" was often used to mean "the power of death." Thus the promise is that the power of death will not be able to destroy Christ's church. Christ was soon to die, and many of His followers would be put to death; but death would not be able to overcome the church.

> 19 And I will give unto thee the keys of the kingdom of heaven: and whatsoever thou shalt bind on earth shall be bound in heaven: and whatsoever thou shalt loose on earth shall be loosed in heaven.

Those who see Peter as the first pope of a universal church organization interpret verse 19 as the church's power to forgive sins. Whatever Jesus meant, He later said similar words to the church (Matt. 18:18). Jesus' image of keys of the kingdom may refer to the church's responsibility to make entrance to the kingdom available to people by telling them of Christ. The Lord is the One who receives people into His kingdom, but He has entrusted to us the task of pointing people to the open door. When we fail in our task, we in essence close the door to the kingdom to those who need our witness.

3. Jesus predicts His death (16:20–21)

> 20 Then charged he his disciples that they should tell no man that he was Jesus the Christ.
>
> 21 From that time forth began Jesus to shew unto his disciples, how that he must go unto Jerusalem, and suffer many things of the elders and chief priests and scribes, and be killed, and be raised again the third day.

Why would Jesus commend Peter for confessing Him as Christ and then command Peter and the others not to tell anyone? A study of the Gospels shows that Jesus was reluctant to use the title Messiah of Himself. He knew that many Jews were looking for an earthly king who would lead Israel to defeat the Romans and to make the people prosper. After Jesus fed the five thousand, some tried to make Him their king; but He refused (John 6:15). Therefore, Jesus warned Peter and the others not yet to tell others that Jesus was the Messiah. After His death and resurrection, He would commission them to tell the whole world (Matt. 28:18–20).

Jesus knew that the disciples themselves shared the false expectations of the people about the Messiah. Therefore, after commending Peter for his confession, Jesus began to teach His followers the kind of Messiah He had come to be. He told them that He must go to Jerusalem, where He would suffer many things at the hands of the religious leaders. Jesus predicted that He would be killed, but be raised again on the third day.

It was as if Jesus said to Peter: "You are right about me being the Messiah, but let me explain to you the kind of Messiah I am. I am not going to lead an army or use my powers to build an earthly kingdom. To the contrary, I am going to be rejected, to suffer and die, and to be raised from the dead. Only in that way will I be able to save people from sin and death, and thus to fulfill my Father's mission for Me."

4. Jesus rebukes Peter (16:22–23)

> 22 Then Peter took him, and began to rebuke him, saying, Be it far from thee, Lord: this shall not be unto thee.

23 But he turned, and said unto Peter, Get thee behind me, Satan: thou art an offence unto me: for thou savorest not the things that be of God, but those that be of men.

One minute Peter was confessing Jesus as the Christ. The next minute Peter was rebuking Jesus for speaking of His suffering and death. Peter obviously shared the popular view of the Messiah. Although he had come to believe that Jesus was the promised Messiah, he never expected the Messiah to suffer and die. In the popular view, the Messiah was a warrior king like his forefather David. The last thing such a king would do would be to allow himself to suffer and be killed.

Just as Peter used forceful language to rebuke Jesus, so did Jesus in rebuking Peter. Earlier Peter had spoken what God had revealed to him. Now he spoke words that grew out of human understanding, not divine revelation. Jesus had just commended Peter as a rock, but now he was becoming a stumbling block ("offence"). Peter's words constituted a recurrence of the temptations of Satan for Jesus to find some other way than the cross to achieve His purpose (Matt. 4:1–11).

APPLYING THE BIBLE

1. Building up God's kingdom. How does God build His kingdom? By one poor, hungry beggar telling another where to find the Bread of Life.

As our lesson points out, Andrew had found the Messiah (John 1:35–42) and he introduced Peter, his brother, to Jesus. In his book *God's Psychiatry*, Charles Allen observes that in a year if one person brought another person to Jesus, at the end of the year there would be two believers. Following that same pattern, at the end of the second year there would be four believers. And now for the shocker! At the end of just thirty-one years, one winning one, there would be 2,147,483,648 believers! Since Jesus died for us nearly two thousand years ago, we have had enough time to win hundreds of worlds like ours. We haven't done it because we have not been faithful followers of Him whom we call Lord and Master.

2. Hand-picked fruit. John Bunyan, author of *Pilgrim's Progress,* was won to Jesus as he overheard three women talking about the joy they had in Christ. William Carey, the father of the modern missionary movement, was led to Christ by John Warr, by whose side Carey worked as a shoe cobbler. Charles Spurgeon was won by an uneducated "lay preacher." Add to this number millions of believers who were won by one. Simon Peter, won to Jesus by Andrew his brother, became the great preacher of Pentecost, when three thousand souls were saved (Acts 2:41). Have you found Jesus, the Bread of Life? Surely, then, there is someone with whom you can share the good news (John 3:16).

3. What others have said about Jesus. The early American patriot and unbeliever Thomas Paine said about Jesus, "The morality that He preached has not been exceeded by any." Thomas Jefferson, author of the Declaration of Independence, said: "Jesus Christ has given to us the most sublime and benevolent code of laws ever offered to man." Atheist

Colonel Robert Ingersoll called Jesus only "a man among men." Lew Wallace, author of *Ben Hur*, called Him "the Son of God." The Roman centurion at the cross said, "Truly this was the Son of God." And Judas Iscariot believed Jesus' worth was only thirty pieces of silver.

Before Jesus got personal with His question about His identity, He asked His disciples, "Whom do men say that I am?" (16:13–14). But the question was a personal question, and He pressed them for a personal answer. Peter responded for them all, "Thou art the Christ, the Son of the living God" (16:15–16).

What is your view of Jesus? Have you accepted Him as your Savior? You can if you will ask Him to come into your life right now and trust Him alone (Acts 16:31; Rom. 10:9–10).

4. The Great Confession. Peter confessed, "Thou art the Christ, the Son of the living God" (16:16). What Peter was saying from his heart was that he believed the man Jesus, whom he (Peter) had been following, was none other than the long-promised Messiah or Christ ("the Anointed One") promised by the prophets. What a magnificent leap of faith! Here was an uneducated fisherman, untrained in theology, who was convinced by the evidence he had seen. It is the same with us. Although we have not seen Him in the flesh, we who are His followers have been convinced by the evidence given in the Scriptures and witnessed to our hearts by the Holy Spirit, that Jesus is exactly who He claimed to be. Like Peter, not knowing all we would like to know, we received Him into our hearts as Savior and Lord by a childlike act of faith (Eph. 2:8–10).

5. The keys of the kingdom. Jesus told both Peter (v. 19) and the church (18:18) that the keys of the kingdom were given to them. Was he appointing Peter the pope of the church? No. He was placing in Peter's hands, and later into His church's hands, the keys—the gospel of salvation by grace through faith—that will open the gates to all who believe!

6. No other way. Two young boys were exploring when they came upon a cave in the side of the mountain. With their flashlights showing the way, they wandered deeply into the cave's interior. No light was visible from the outside, and they knew they must turn around and retrace their steps. By this time their flashlight had failed, and for hours they stumbled in the darkness trying to find the only way out. It was only when the boys heard the searchers calling their names that they were able to find the mouth of the cave and safety.

Jesus told His disciples that He must die and then be raised from the dead (16:21). Peter, not understanding the divine plan, rebuked Him (16:22). But Jesus told Peter that there was no other way for God to save a lost world (16:23). Jesus, alone, is the Light of the world.

TEACHING THE BIBLE

- *Main Idea:* We all must confess Jesus as the Messiah.
- *Suggested Teaching Aim:* To lead adults to confess Jesus as the Messiah.

A TEACHING OUTLINE

1. Use an illustration to begin the study.
2. Use a lesson outline poster and brief lectures to guide the Bible study.
4. Use discussion questions to apply the Scriptures.

Introduce the Bible Study

Use "What others have said about Jesus" from "Applying the Bible" to introduce the study. Say: Today's lesson examines what Peter said about Jesus.

Search for Biblical Truth

Point out the lesson on the unit poster used the past two weeks. Make and display the following lesson poster:

Peter	
Following Jesus	Matt. 4:18–20
Peter Confesses Jesus as the Christ	Matt. 16:13–16
Jesus Commends Peter	Matt. 16:17–19
Jesus Predicts His Death	Matt. 16:20–21
Jesus Rebukes Peter	Matt. 16:22–23

Either cover the points until you are ready to use them or write the headings on strips you can put up as you teach.

Uncover the first outline point ("Following Jesus"). Ask a volunteer to read Matthew 4:18–20. Use a map to locate the Sea of Galilee and the city of Capernaum (kuh PURR nay uhm) as possibly the place where this event occurred.

Lecture briefly covering the following points: (1) what "follow me" meant; (2) the meaning of "disciple;" (3) Jesus' previous contact with Peter; and (4) the meaning of "stone."

DISCUSS: If Jesus called you, what new name would He give you?

Uncover the second outline point ("Peter Confesses Jesus as the Christ"). Ask a volunteer to read 16:13–16. Locate Caesarea Philippi (about twenty-five miles north of the Sea of Galilee). Ask members to identify the names the disciples suggested people were calling Jesus. (John the Baptist, Elijah, Jeremiah, prophet.) Use "Studying the Bible" to explain why people suggested each of these titles.

DISCUSS: Based on the way you live, who do you say Jesus is? Do we really believe something if we do not act like it?

Uncover the third outline point ("Jesus Commends Peter"). Ask a volunteer to read 16:17–19. Using "Studying the Bible," lecture briefly, explaining: (1) the various meanings of the word "rock"; (2) the use of the word "church" in this context; (3) the meaning of "gates of hell"; and (4) the meaning of "keys of the kingdom." **IN ADVANCE,** enlist a member to read "Keys of the Kingdom," *Holman Bible Dictionary,* page 839, and prepare a two- to three-minute report to be presented at this time.

DISCUSS: What have you done with the keys to the kingdom God has given you?

Uncover the fourth outline point ("Jesus Predicts His Death"). Using "Studying the Bible," lecture briefly, explaining the following: (1) why Jesus warned His disciples not to tell who He was; (2) how Jesus taught His disciples the kind of Messiah He was.

DISCUSS: How do you try to make Christ into someone He is not?

Uncover the fifth outline point ("Jesus Rebukes Peter"). Using "Studying the Bible," lecture briefly, explaining the following: (1) what was Peter's idea of the Messiah; (2) Jesus' rebuke of Peter.

DISCUSS: How have your actions created a stumbling block for the cause of Christ?

Give the Truth a Personal Focus

Ask: Can you affirm beyond any shadow of doubt that Jesus is the Messiah of God? If so, what does that mean to you? Challenge members not to try to force Jesus to be something He is not just to fit their idea of who Jesus is.

January

26

1997

Judas Iscariot

Basic Passages: Matthew 26:14–16, 20–25, 47–50; 27:1–5
Focal Passages: Matthew 26:14–16, 20–25, 47–50; 27:1–5

The name "Judas" is one of the hated names of human history. He is like Benedict Arnold and Quisling in that he practiced betrayal for a price. Only a friend or insider can commit betrayal. Whereas Arnold and Quisling betrayed their country, Judas betrayed Jesus the Savior.

Study Aim: *To describe how Judas betrayed Jesus*

STUDYING THE BIBLE

OUTLINE AND SUMMARY

I. Judas Bargained to Betray Jesus (Matt. 26:14–16)
II. Jesus Predicted His Betrayal (Matt. 26:20–25)
III. Judas Betrayed Jesus (Matt. 26:47–50)
IV. Judas Reacted to Jesus' Condemnation (Matt. 27:1–5)

Judas made a bargain with the enemies of Jesus to betray the Lord (26:14–16). At the Last Supper, Jesus let Judas know that He was aware of what Judas intended to do (26:20–25). Judas betrayed Jesus with a kiss (26:47–50). After Jesus was condemned by the Sanhedrin, Judas expressed remorse, returned the blood money, and hanged himself (27:1–5).

I. Judas Bargained to Betray Jesus (Matt. 26:14–16)

14 Then one of the twelve, called Judas Iscariot, went unto the chief priests,

15 And said unto them, What will ye give me, and I will deliver him unto you? And they covenanted with him for thirty pieces of silver.

16 And from that time he sought opportunity to betray him.

Two facts lie in the background of Judas's actions: (1) As Passover approached, Jesus told His disciples that the time was near when He would be betrayed and crucified (Matt. 26:1–2). (2) The high priest and other religious leaders were plotting to have Jesus killed (Matt. 26:3–5). Judas knew of Jesus' prediction because he had heard it. He probably suspected that the leaders were plotting to kill Jesus.

Judas took the initiative. The high priest and the other plotters did not seek out Judas; instead, he sought them out. They probably were surprised that one of Jesus' disciples would offer to betray Him, but they quickly accepted Judas's offer. They made a deal with him for thirty pieces of silver. From that time on, Judas was alert for an opportunity to betray Jesus.

Why did the plotters welcome a betrayer? Because Jesus was popular with many of the people, the religious leaders knew they might start a riot if they tried to seize Jesus when He was surrounded by friends (Matt. 26:5). Therefore, a betrayer offered a way for the enemies of Jesus to seize Him when few friends were with Him. A betrayer was also helpful because Judas knew the places where Jesus was most likely to be found.

Why did Judas offer to betray Jesus? The New Testament never gives a clear answer to that question. Several theories have been proposed. Most of the theories agree about two things: (1) Judas wanted Jesus to set up an earthly kingdom. (2) Judas had become convinced that Jesus was not going to set up such a kingdom, but was determined to lay down His life.

Building on those facts, one theory says that Judas betrayed Jesus hoping to force Jesus to use His power and thus bring in an earthly kingdom. Another theory is that when Judas became convinced that Jesus was determined to throw away His life, Judas decided to salvage for himself what he could. This latter theory stresses the selfishness in Judas's question, "What will ye give me, and I will deliver him unto you?"

The Bible text gives two clear indications of the horror of Judas's bargain: (1) The words "one of the twelve" remind the reader that Judas was one of Jesus' closest associates and presumably loyal friends. (2) The "thirty pieces of silver" would have reminded faithful Jews of the price of a slave (Exod. 21:32). Judas sold out the Savior for the price of a slave!

II. Jesus Predicted His Betrayal (Matt. 26:20–25)

20 Now when the even was come, he sat down with the twelve.

21 And as they did eat, he said, Verily I say unto you, that one of you shall betray me.

22 And they were exceeding sorrowful, and began every one of them to say unto him, Lord, Is it I?

Earlier Jesus had spoken of His betrayal (Matt. 26:1–2). At the Last Supper, Jesus revealed to the Twelve that one of them would be the betrayer. This announcement upset the disciples. Each asked if he was the betrayer. The wording of the question in verse 22 expects a "no" answer. It was as if each asked, "Lord, it's not I, is it?" None of the others thought himself capable of such a terrible act, but none knew for sure that he might not become the betrayer.

23 And he answered and said, He that dippeth his hand with me in the dish, the same shall betray me.

24 The Son of man goeth as it is written of him: but woe unto that man by whom the Son of man is betrayed! it had been good for that man if he had not been born.

25 Then Judas, which betrayed him, answered and said, Master, is it I? He said unto him, Thou hast said.

They were not sitting at a table as we do when we eat. They were reclining on cushions in the shape of a *U* with food placed in the middle. One dish contained a gravy into which each dipped his bread. Thus verse 23 merely reemphasized that one of those eating with Jesus would betray Him. Jesus said that He had come to lay down His life according to the Scriptures. But Jesus pronounced a severe judgment on the one who betrayed Him.

Then Judas asked the same question the others had asked. The only difference was that the others called Jesus "Lord," but Judas called Him "Master" or "Rabbi." Judas also worded his question as if to receive a negative answer, but Jesus told Judas that he was the betrayer. Jesus apparently did this in such a way that most of the others didn't realize what Jesus meant. John 13:21–27 shows that John was aware of what Jesus meant, but he apparently did not tell the others. Soon after Jesus revealed to Judas that He knew of his evil plans, Judas went out into the night (John 13:27).

If Jesus knew that Judas was going to betray Him, why didn't Jesus take steps to stop the betrayer? Jesus came to offer Himself voluntarily. None of those who acted in taking His life could have taken the Son of God if Jesus had not allowed them to do so. When He was arrested, one of the disciples prepared to defend Jesus with a sword. Jesus told him to put away the sword. Then He asked, "Thinkest thou not that I cannot now pray to the Father, and he shall presently give me twelve legions of angels?" (Matt. 26:53).

III. Judas Betrayed Jesus (Matt. 26:47–50)

47 And while he yet spake, lo, Judas, one of the twelve, came, and with him a great multitude with swords and staves, from the chief priests and elders of the people.

48 Now he that betrayed him gave them a sign, saying, Whomsoever I shall kiss, that same is he: hold him fast.

49 And forthwith he came to Jesus, and said, Hail, master; and kissed him.

50 And Jesus said unto him, Friend, wherefore art thou come? Then came they, and laid hands on Jesus, and took him.

After leaving the last supper, Judas acted to fulfill his part in the bargain to betray Jesus. The religious leaders sent with Judas a large group armed with swords and clubs. Most were temple police and Roman soldiers (John 18:12). Judas led this group to Gethsemane. He promised to give them a sign so they would know whom to arrest. In the darkness, some kind of sign was necessary.

Judas told them that he would greet Jesus with a kiss. This was a common greeting at that time. Pupils often greeted their teachers with a kiss, as a sign of respect and affection. When Judas spotted Jesus, he went up to him, said, "Greetings, teacher," and kissed Jesus. The word for "kissed" in verse 49 is the strong form of the verb. This shows that Judas made a strong outward show of affection as he betrayed Jesus.

Jesus called Judas "friend" or "comrade." Some Bible versions translate the words of Jesus in verse 50 as a statement rather than a question. In other words, Jesus may have told Judas to do what he had come for. If Jesus asked him "wherefore art thou come?" it was not because Jesus was unaware of why Judas came. Jesus had already told Judas that He knew what Judas planned to do. The question of verse 50, therefore, was not an inquiry, but a rebuke.

As in Matthew 26:14, verse 47 reminds the reader that Judas was "one of the twelve." Once again, these words underscore the horror of what Judas was doing. We are not surprised when our enemies seek to do us harm. We are shocked and hurt when our friends aid our enemies.

IV. Judas Reacted to Jesus' Condemnation (Matt. 27:1–5)

1 When the morning was come, all the chief priests and elders of the people took counsel against Jesus to put him to death:

2 And when they had bound him, they led him away, and delivered him to Pontius [PAHN tih uhs] Pilate [PIGH luht] the governor.

The Sanhedrin (san HEE druhn) had already tried and condemned Jesus in an illegal night trial (Matt. 26:57–68). They met early the next morning to ratify their action. They also met to send Jesus to the Roman procurator. The Jewish court had authority to decide religious issues, but they lacked the authority to condemn a prisoner to death (John 18:31). Since Pilate had that power, they brought Jesus to Pilate for sentencing.

3 Then Judas, which had betrayed him, when he saw that he was condemned, repented himself, and brought the thirty pieces of silver to the chief priests and elders,

4 Saying, I have sinned in that I have betrayed the innocent blood. And they said, What is that to us? see thou to it.

5 And he cast down the pieces of silver in the temple, and departed, and went and hanged himself.

After the Sanhedrin condemned Jesus and sent Him to Pilate for sentencing, Judas recognized the horror of what he had done. He had betrayed an innocent man, who was now on His way to die. Judas realized that the blood of the innocent Jesus would be on his hands.

Why did Judas have this sudden change of heart? As noted earlier, some Bible students believe that Judas betrayed Jesus in order to force Jesus to use His power and thus help set up an earthly kingdom. According to this theory, Judas was upset because he never expected Jesus actually to allow Himself to be executed. The other possibility is that Judas acted selfishly in betraying Jesus. In his mind, Judas knew he was betraying Jesus to those who intended to kill Him. However, when this was actually about to happen, Judas had a moment of truth. His conscience, which had been inactive, now awoke enough to show him the evil that he had done.

By contrast, the religious leaders seem to have totally suppressed their consciences. They shared none of Judas's second thoughts. When he came and told them that he had sinned by betraying innocent blood, the enemies of Jesus said in essence, "What do we care? Keep your regrets to yourself."

The word "repented" in verse 3 is not the usual word for true repentance, which involves sorrow for sin, turning from sin, and turning to God in trust. The word in verse 3 stresses the regret and remorse that Judas felt. Although Judas used the words "I have sinned," he was not expressing true repentance and faith. He lacked the trust to cast himself on God's mercy. Instead of confessing to God, he went to the callous Sanhedrin.

After Peter denied Jesus, he "went out, and wept bitterly" (Matt. 26:75). After the resurrection of Jesus, Peter was forgiven and restored to service. Judas responded to his sense of guilt and regret by hanging himself.

APPLYING THE BIBLE

1. The slow growth of evil. Roy Angell tells about a country preacher who came upon a farmer plowing between some rows of corn. "What are you doing?" asked the preacher. "I am plowing under the grass and weeds," said the farmer. "But the field is almost bare between the corn," the preacher replied. But the farmer had the last word. "Preacher, you know as well as I do that grass and weed seeds lie dormant here, and with the first spring rain these rows will be filled with grass and weeds unless I plow them under."

Evil grows slowly. Each of us has a sinful nature; and unless Jesus takes care of our sin problem, it will grow like a monstrous master within us.

So it was with Judas. When Jesus called Judas to follow Him, Jesus saw a lot of potential in Judas, though Jesus knew from the beginning that Judas would betray Him (John 6:64). The evil in Judas's heart grew slowly, just as it will in our hearts if it is not countered by the grace of God in Christ.

2. Selling out to sin. An artist in Italy once painted Mary and the Christ child. Years later, he was painting another New Testament scene, some say the Last Supper; and he needed someone to pose as Judas. Searching the prisons, he finally found his character; and day after day he went to the prison to sketch the man. But the more the artist visited the man, the more familiar he seemed. "Did I ever paint you?" the artist asked. "Yes," the man said shamefully. "My mother told me that when I was just a child, I posed for you as you painted Jesus on Mary's bosom."

So it was with Judas. He started well, but the race is not marked by how well one starts but how well one finishes! Judas sold out Jesus because Judas first sold out to sin. It is a warning to each of us. I have known too many Christians who started well only to finish tragically.

3. The bitter betrayal. Our lesson points out that the most infamous names in history are the betrayers, and Judas heads the list. But wait a minute! What about the person who hears the gospel again and again but refuses to yield his heart to the Savior? Has he not denied and betrayed the Savior who died for him? He knows that Jesus died for his sins, and that the Holy Spirit is convicting him. But to it all he gives a steadfast "No!" Does his or her sin not fall into the same category as Judas's sin? Vehemently, we would say it doesn't. But does it? Think about it. Jesus said it would have been good if Judas had not been born, for he will spend eternity in hell (26:24). But where will the rejector of Jesus spend eternity? The Bible gives the answer: with Judas in hell (Rev. 20:15; 21:8)!

4. The burning kiss. Can you remember the first kiss you received from a boyfriend or girlfriend? Do you remember your mother's kisses when you returned home from school? What about the first time you kissed your babies and the first time they put their wet lips on your cheeks?

Judas had told the chief priests he would give them a sign: "Seize the man I kiss and hold Him fast." According to Greek scholar A. T. Robertson, this means that he "kissed him fervently"! What hypocrisy! He who had laid His tender hands on the heads of little children and blessed them, is betrayed by a "fervent kiss!"

But mark it down: our affection for Jesus can be just as hypocritical! To be a friend of Jesus, He tells us, we must do as He commands us: "Ye are my friends, if ye do whatsoever I command you" (John 15:14). Are you a friend of Jesus?

5. Judas's remorse. A guilty conscience is a heavy burden to bear. John Randolph (1773–1833) was both a United States Representative and Senator. He had a cruel, biting tongue and opposed many popular measures that came before those bodies. When he used insulting language in opposing Henry Clay as Secretary of State, Clay challenged Randolph to a duel; but no blood was spilled. When he lay dying in Philadelphia, Randolph kept repeating, "Remorse! Remorse!" He asked for a dictionary so he could study the word, and when none could be found he had his physician write on a paper, "Remorse!"

There we have a picture of Judas overwhelmed, not by genuine repentance, but by remorse (27:3–5). He who made such a good start had a terrible and tragic end. What a poignant warning to each of us!

TEACHING THE BIBLE

- *Main Idea:* Each of us is capable of betraying Jesus.
- *Suggested Teaching Aim:* To lead adults to identify ways they are capable of betraying Jesus and to discover steps they can take to prevent it.

A TEACHING OUTLINE

1. Use an illustration to introduce the Bible study.

2. Use the unit poster and a lesson outline poster to show progression in the unit and the lesson.

3. Use Scripture search, questions and answers, and group discussion to search for biblical truth.

4. Use a poster to apply Bible study.

Introduce the Bible Study

Use "The slow growth of evil" from "Applying the Bible" to introduce the Bible study. Say: The lesson will examine how Judas betrayed Jesus.

Search for Biblical Truth

IN ADVANCE, write the following on large strips of paper and fasten them to the backs of four chairs:

1. Judas Bargained to Betray Jesus (Matt. 26:14–16)
2. Jesus Predicted His Betrayal (Matt. 26:20–25)
3. Judas Betrayed Jesus (Matt. 26:47–50)
4. Judas Reacted to Jesus' Condemnation (Matt. 27:1–5)

Point out today's lesson on the unit poster. Ask the person with the first outline point to place it on the focal wall. Ask members to read Matthew 26:14–16 silently. Point out that the Bible does not specifically tell us why Judas betrayed Jesus. Use "Studying the Bible" to explain possible motives Judas had for betraying Jesus.

DISCUSS: Why do you think Judas betrayed Jesus?

Ask the person with the second outline point to place it on the wall. Ask members to read silently Matthew 26:20–25. Using "Studying the Bible," explain (1) the eating custom involved in the supper; (2) Judas's use of "Master" instead of "Lord"; (3) why Jesus did not stop Judas.

DISCUSS: What warning signs of betrayal do you look for in your own behavior?

Ask the person who has the third outline point to place it on the focal wall. Ask members to read Matthew 26:47–50. Use a map to locate the garden of Gethsemane in relation to Jerusalem. Ask: Who came with Judas to arrest Jesus? (Jewish temple police and likely some mob elements.) What was the sign Judas had chosen to identify Jesus? (A kiss.) Why was a signal necessary? (It was dark, they had only torches for lights, and they were in a garden.) What did Jesus call Judas even after Judas had betrayed Him? (Friend.)

DISCUSS: How do you feel when an enemy hurts you? How do you feel when a friend betrays you? What makes the friend's betrayal so hurtful?

Ask the person with the fourth outline strip to place it on the wall. Ask members to read Matthew 27:1–5 silently. Ask: Why do you think Judas did what he did in these verses? What made him sorry for his actions? Was his repentance real? How did Judas's actions differ from Peter's?

DISCUSS: What do you think would have happened if Judas had waited around for the resurrection?

Give the Truth a Personal Focus

On a chalkboard or a large sheet of paper, write **Betrayal** in one column and **Prevention** in another. Ask members to suggest ways we betray Jesus today. List these on the chalkboard under **Betrayal.** Ask: Are our actions as bad as Judas's? What makes our actions different from Judas's? Are we ever safe from betraying Jesus?

Ask members to suggest steps they can take to keep themselves from betraying Jesus. List these under **Prevention.**

Remind members that the only betrayal Jesus cannot forgive is that which is not confessed. Stress that we are also just one action away from betrayal, but with the Holy Spirit's help we can refuse to betray our Lord.

Barnabas

Basic Passages: Acts 4:32–37; 9:23–31; 11:19–30

Focal Passages: Acts 4:32, 36–37; 9:26–27; 11:22–30

This lesson begins a four-lesson unit on "Persons of the New Testament Church." None of the early believers had a more attractive personality than Barnabas (BAHR nuh buhs). He is pictured in the New Testament as one who encouraged and helped others in the Christian way.

Study Aim: *To list examples of Barnabas as an encourager*

STUDYING THE BIBLE

OUTLINE AND SUMMARY

I. **Barnabas Gave Generously (Acts 4:32–37)**
 1. **Oneness of the early church (4:32–35)**
 2. **Introduction of Barnabas (4:36–37)**

II. **Barnabas Welcomed Saul (Acts 9:23–31)**

III. **Barnabas Encouraged the Antioch Church (Acts 11:19–30)**
 1. **Helping a new church (11:19–24)**
 2. **Teaching new converts (11:25–26)**
 3. **Entrusted with a relief offering (11:27–30)**

One expression of the oneness of the Jerusalem church was their sharing of possessions with those in need (4:32–35). Barnabas, son of encouragement, sold a field and gave the money to be shared with the needy (4:36–37). When the apostles feared Saul and didn't believe him, Barnabas encouraged Saul by sponsoring him for membership in the Jerusalem church. (9:23–31). Barnabas encouraged the new church at Antioch (AN tih ahk), which had taken a new direction by including Gentiles (11:19–24). Barnabas and Saul encouraged the Antioch church by spending a year teaching (11:25–26). Barnabas encouraged the Jerusalem church by joining Saul in taking an offering from the Antioch church (11:27–30).

I. Barnabas Gave Generously (Acts 4:32–37)

1. Oneness of the early church (4:32–35)

32 And the multitude of them that believed were of one heart and of one soul: neither said any of them that aught of the things which he possessed was his own; but they had all things common.

The Bible says that the early believers were a *koinonia* (Acts 2:42). English translations often use the word "fellowship" to describe what *koinonia* means, but the word means more than what we usually mean by "fellowship." *Koinonia* refers to the common life that believers share because of their relationship with God through Jesus Christ (1 John 1:3).

One expression of this oneness in the Jerusalem church was the sharing of material possessions. This is mentioned in Acts 2:44–45 and 4:32–37. Because they were of one heart and one soul, they voluntarily shared with one another. They continued to reach out to nonbelievers as the apostles bore witness to the resurrection of the Lord Jesus (v. 33). They cared for one another as those that had possessions sold them and brought the money for distribution to the needy (vv. 34–35).

2. Introduction of Barnabas (4:36–37)

> 36 And Joses (JOH seez), who by the apostles was surnamed Barnabas, (which is, being interpreted, The son of consolation,) a Levite, and of the country of Cyprus,
>
> 37 Having land, sold it, and brought the money, and laid it at the apostles' feet.

Acts 4:36–37 introduces a personality of the early church who played a major role in later events. These verses tell about a man named Joseph (or Joses). He was originally from Cyprus, but was now living in Jerusalem. He was a Levite, a group originally set aside for temple service. Although Levites originally owned no land (Deut. 10:9; Num. 18:20, 24), this seems no longer to have been true; because Joseph was a land owner.

Joseph was an outstanding example of the practice described in verses 32–35. Joseph sold his land, brought the money, and laid it at the apostles' feet for distribution to needy members of the church. This action and his later actions led the apostles to give Joseph a nickname. They called him Barnabas, which means "son of encouragement." The word translated "consolation" has a broader meaning than what we usually mean by "consolation." Barnabas did more than console people in sorrow; he encouraged them in a variety of situations.

II. Barnabas Welcomed Saul (Acts 9:23–31)

After Saul's conversion, he continued as a bold witness in Damascus (duh MASS cuss; Acts 9:20–22). His preaching was so effective that his enemies plotted to kill him (v. 23). When Saul and his friends discovered that enemies were watching the gates day and night (v. 24), they lowered Saul over the wall of the city in a basket (v. 25).

> 26 And when Saul was come to Jerusalem, he assayed to join himself to the disciples: but they were all afraid of him, and believed not that he was a disciple.
>
> 27 But Barnabas took him, and brought him to the apostles, and declared unto them how he had seen the Lord in the way, and that he had spoken to him, and how he had preached boldly at Damascus in the name of Jesus.

The last time Saul was in Jerusalem, he was a relentless persecutor of believers in Jesus (Acts 8:1–3). He had gone to Damascus to continue his angry persecution (Acts 9:1–2). Therefore, when Saul returned to Jerusalem, the apostles' memories of him caused them to fear him. The apostles had probably heard what Saul was saying about his encounter with the Lord and of the Lord's commission to him (Acts 9:3–16). However, the apostles didn't believe Saul. They no doubt suspected that he was laying an elaborate trap to ensnare followers of Jesus.

At this point, Barnabas intervened on behalf of Saul. He brought Saul to the apostles. Barnabas then told them how the Lord had appeared to Saul and had spoken to him. Barnabas also told the apostles of Saul's bold testimony for Christ in Damascus. By doing this, Barnabas risked his reputation and perhaps his life as well. He had no way of knowing for sure that Saul was a true convert, but Barnabas was willing to take the risk. He stood up for Saul when no one else did.

As a result, Saul was accepted and began sharing church fellowship (v. 28) and bearing testimony for Christ in Jerusalem. Saul's preaching was so effective that his enemies were determined to kill him (v. 29). As a result, the brothers in Christ took Saul to Caesarea, where he sailed back to his native Tarsus (TAHR sus; v. 30). As a result of the conversion of this former persecutor and his bold preaching, churches throughout the entire region were strengthened (v. 31). Saul of Tarsus later became Paul the great missionary. His name overshadows the name of Barnabas in the Bible, but consider the key role that Barnabas played in Saul's life. He sponsored Saul at a crucial stage in the life of this new convert with so much promise.

III. Barnabas Encouraged the Antioch Church (Acts 11:19–30)

1. Helping a new church (11:19–24)

After the death of Stephen, believers were scattered from Jerusalem; and wherever they went, they preached the good news (Acts 8:4). Some of the believers went to the city of Antioch and preached Jesus to their fellow Jews (v. 19). Some of the Jewish believers, however, began to preach to Greeks (v. 20). Because God was with them in such bold witness, many believed and turned to the Lord (v. 21).

> 22 Then tidings of these things came unto the ears of the church which was in Jerusalem: and they sent forth Barnabas, that he should go as far as Antioch.
>
> 23 Who, when he came, and had seen the grace of God, was glad, and exhorted them all, that with purpose of heart they would cleave unto the Lord.
>
> 24 For he was a good man and full of the Holy Ghost and of faith: and much people was added unto the Lord.

Including Gentiles as well as Jews in the church was something new. It is true that Peter had been to Cornelius, but little had been done to follow up by the Jerusalem believers (Acts 10:1–11:18). The Jerusalem church expressed an interest in the new direction by sending Barnabas to see what was going on in Antioch. Barnabas was a good choice for such a delicate mission. He was a good man who was led by God's Spirit.

Barnabas saw what was happening in Antioch as evidence of God's grace at work. Rather than rebuking them for their inclusion of Gentiles in the church, Barnabas encouraged the Antioch believers to remain true to the Lord with all their hearts. As a result of such encouragement, the Lord was able to continue to add new converts to their number.

2. Teaching new converts (11:25–26)

25 Then departed Barnabas to Tarsus, for to seek Saul:

26 And when he had found him, he brought him unto Antioch. And it came to pass, that a whole year they assembled themselves with the church, and taught much people. And the disciples were called Christians first in Antioch.

Barnabas realized that the new converts needed to be taught. He decided to go and get Saul to help him. Thus Barnabas went to Tarsus and found Saul. Then they returned to Antioch and spent an entire year with the church. During that year these two choice leaders taught many people. Thus Barnabas the encourager helped both Saul and the believers at Antioch. Earlier, Barnabas had stood up for Saul when he wanted to join the Jerusalem church. Now Barnabas helped Saul by enlisting him in work that eventually launched Saul as a missionary (Acts 13:1–4). Barnabas continued his encouraging role as he and Saul taught the church.

The Antioch disciples were the first to be called Christians. They had been called disciples, brothers, or believers. The name "Christian" appears only two other times in the New Testament (Acts 26:28; 1 Pet. 4:16). Each reference suggests that the name was first used by nonbelievers to describe followers of Christ. The title means those belonging to or having been identified with Christ, and it may originally have been intended as a term of derision.

3. Entrusted with a relief offering (11:27–30)

27 And in these days came prophets from Jerusalem unto Antioch.

28 And there stood up one of them named Agabus [AG uh buhs], and signified by the spirit that there should be great dearth throughout all the world: which came to pass in the days of Claudius [KLAW dih uhs] Caesar [SEE zur].

29 Then the disciples, every man according to his ability, determined to send relief unto the brethren which dwelt in Judaea:

30 Which also they did, and sent it to the elders by the hands of Barnabas and Saul.

Among a group of prophets who came from Jerusalem was a prophet named Agabus. The same man appeared later to speak a prophecy concerning Paul (Acts 21:10–11). Agabus had the gift to foresee some future events. He told the Antioch church that a severe and widespread famine was coming. Luke adds that such a famine actually came during the reign of Claudius Caesar (A.D. 41–54).

The Antioch church responded to this prediction by deciding to send financial help to their brothers in Judea. We are not told why they concentrated on Judea. Perhaps Agabus indicated that the famine would be especially hard there. Perhaps since many of the Antioch believers had come from Jerusalem, they knew the large number of poor in the church and the growing hostility of unbelievers. Perhaps the Antioch church wanted to show their Jewish brothers that a Jew-Gentile church could demonstrate Christian love. Paul later asked for an offering from Gentile churches for these reasons (Rom. 15:25–27; 2 Cor. 8–9).

At any rate, the Antioch church followed the principle of voluntary giving according to one's ability. Then they asked Barnabas and Saul to carry the offering to Jerusalem. This shows how much the Antioch church trusted and respected these two choice leaders. Earlier, Barnabas had helped needy disciples in Jerusalem by giving his own money. Now he and Saul helped and encouraged the Jerusalem church with this love offering from their brothers and sisters in Antioch.

APPLYING THE BIBLE

1. William McKinley's philosophy. When William McKinley, the twenty-fifth president of the United States, was elected governor of Ohio, he considered appointing a bitter opponent to a high office in the state. When McKinley was challenged by one of his advisors, McKinley replied he felt the man was the best qualified for the job. Then, he added with a smile: "If we spend all our time getting even, we shall never get ahead."

The church at Jerusalem had its problems which later emerged; but at the outset it was interested in getting ahead, so the people had to be united and pull together (Acts 4:32–35). And the church did get ahead. According to New Testament scholar Henry Clarence Thiessen, by A.D. 65 the Jerusalem church may have had as many as twenty thousand members.[1] Any church that wants to get ahead and stay ahead must pull together. It's called *unity.*

2. A sacrificial church. A plaque in the Alamo reads: "It was here that a gallant few, the bravest of the brave, threw themselves between the enemy and the settlements, determined never to surrender nor retreat. They redeemed their pledge to Texas with the forfeit of their lives. They fell the chosen sacrifice to Texas freedom."

The Jerusalem church was a sacrificing church (4:32–35). They shared what they had—their lives, their all—with each other to protect the needy in their fellowship. Those able to do so "threw themselves between the enemy"—hunger and privation—and the less fortunate.

With the needs of our world so great, we ought to move out of our stingy giving to follow the example of "the mother church."

3. Barnabas leads the way. The New International Version translates the name of Barnabas as "Son of Encouragement" (4:36). He was devout and wealthy. Also, he was unselfish (4:37). Seeking no applause for himself, he sold his land, brought the proceeds, and laid them at the apostles' feet. What a marvelous and unselfish example he set! The church took note of it, and he is memorialized in Scripture for his generosity.

I grew up in Oklahoma, often hearing my father tell this story. He was helping take the offering one Sunday morning in our church. It was during the years of the Great Depression and the church was struggling financially. When he passed the plate to a certain doctor that morning, the doctor laid a folded bill in the plate, covering it with his hand as though he did not want his gift to be seen. When, later, the morning offering was counted, the bill was unfolded and found, to the shock of the money-counter, to be a $1,000 bill. My father treasured the story and appreciated the doctor for his sacrificial gift that made so much difference to a struggling church.

That's the Barnabas spirit!

4. "Mr. Encourager." We can call Barnabas "Mr. Encourager." Everywhere we see him in the Scriptures, Barnabas has his arm around someone saying, "You can make it" (Acts 9:26–27; 11:19–24; 25–26; 27–30)! And don't forget John Mark (15:36–41). Had it not been for Barnabas, Saul (Paul) would not have been received by the church (9:26–29). If it had not been for Barnabas, Paul might have stayed in Tarsus and been lost to the great missionary enterprise to the Gentiles (11:25–26). It is to Paul's discredit that he wanted to write young Mark off (15:36–39). But it is to Barnabas's credit that he took Mark in. Had it not been for Barnabas, we would not have the Gospel of Mark. What a Christian was Barnabas!

5. The thing everybody needs. Everybody needs encouragement! Young Fanny was blinded in 1826 when she was only six weeks old. But her grandmother became Fanny's eyes, telling her about the beauties of nature. When Fanny showed an interest in poetry, her grandmother encouraged her. The next time you sing Fanny Crosby's "Blessed Assurance, Jesus Is Mine" or "Jesus Keep Me Near the Cross," give thanks for a grandmother who encouraged a little blind girl.

Remember: Few need your criticism, but everybody needs your encouragement!

TEACHING THE BIBLE

- *Main Idea:* Encouraging others is a mark of a mature Christian.
- *Suggested Teaching Aim:* To lead members to identify how they can become encouragers.

A TEACHING OUTLINE

1. *Use an illustration to introduce the lesson.*
2. *Use member-created questions to examine the Bible.*
3. *Use listing to apply the Bible.*

Introduce the Bible Study

Prepare the following unit poster.

Persons of the New Testament Church		
Barnabas	Acts 4:32–37; 9:23–31; 11:19–30	February 2
Stephen	Acts 6:1–8:3	February 9
Priscilla and Aquila	Acts 18:1–4, 18–19, 24–26; Rom. 16:3–5a	February 16
Timothy	Acts 16:1–5; 1 Cor. 4:14–17; Phil. 2:19–24; 2 Tim. 1:3–7; 3:14–15	February 23

Use "Barnabas leads the way" in "Applying the Bible" to introduce the lesson. Locate the lesson on the unit poster.

Search for Biblical Truth

IN ADVANCE, write each of the following on a strip of paper. Fasten each strip to the wall as you teach.

Barnabas Encouraged Others by . . .	
1. Giving Generously	Acts 4:32,36–37
2. Supporting Saul	Acts 9:26–27
3. Helping a New Church	Acts 11:22–24
4. Teaching New Converts	Acts 11:25–26
5. Collecting an Offering	Acts 11:27–30

Place strips around the room at random. As you come to each point, place the proper strip on the focal wall.

Place the first strip on the focal wall. Tell members that you are going to play "Ask the Teacher." Ask members to read silently Acts 4:32, 36–37 and to compose one question each based on this passage to ask you. Be sure the following information is shared either in the form of answers or in a brief lecture (or use these for questions to ask members if they cannot come up with questions for you): (1) What is the meaning of the word *koinonia?* (2) Why did the believers in Jerusalem share with the needy? (3) What was Barnabas's tribal and national background? (4) What was Barnabas's act of generosity? (5) What was Barnabas's nickname?

Place the second strip on the focal wall. Ask members to read silently Acts 9:26–27 and to compose one question each based on this passage to ask you. Be sure the following information is shared: (1) What had happened to Saul since he had left Jerusalem? (2) Why were the Jerusalem disciples afraid of Saul? (3) How did Barnabas befriend Saul? (4) How would you have responded if you had been in Jerusalem?

Place the third strip on the focal wall. Ask members to read silently Acts 11:22–24 and to compose one question each based on this passage to ask you. Be sure the following information is shared: (1) Why was Barnabas sent to Antioch? (2) What was Barnabas's response to the situation in Antioch? (3) Why was Antioch so significant?

Place the fourth strip on the wall. Ask members to read silently Acts 11:25–26 and to compose one question each based on this passage to ask you. Be sure the following facts are shared: (1) Why do you think Barnabas went after Saul? (2) What did they do in Antioch to help the church?

Place the fifth strip on the focal wall. Ask members to read silently Acts 11:27–30 and to compose one question each based on this passage to ask you. Be sure the following information is shared: (1) Who prophesied that a famine was coming? (2) Why do you think the disciples chose Barnabas as one of the bearers of the offering to Jerusalem?

Give the Truth a Personal Focus

Review how Barnabas encouraged. Ask members to suggest ways they can be encouragers. List these on a chalkboard or a large sheet of paper. Ask them to choose at least one specific way they could be an encourager this week.

---

1. Henry Clarence Thiessen, *Introducing the New Testament* (Grand Rapids, Mich.: William B. Eerdmans Publishing Co., 1951), 136.

Stephen

February

9

1997

Basic Passage: Acts 6:1–8:3
Focal Passages: Acts 6:8–15; 7:54–60

Stephen is first mentioned as one of the seven chosen to serve tables, but he quickly became one of the boldest spokesmen for Christ. His testimony was so effective that the enemies of Christ put Stephen to death. The way he lived and the way he died are examples for later generations of believers.

Study Aim: *To show how Stephen was a bold witness for Christ by how he lived and how he died*

STUDYING THE BIBLE

OUTLINE AND SUMMARY

I. Selection of the Seven (Acts 6:1–7)

II. Reaction to Stephen's Words and Deeds (Acts 6:8–15)

1. Power of Stephen's words and deeds (6:8–10)

2. A campaign of lies (6:11–15)

III. Stephen's Speech to the Sanhedrin (Acts 7:1–53)

1. The patriarchs (7:1–16)

2. Moses (7:17–34)

3. History of rebellion (7:35–53)

IV. Stephen's Death (Acts 7:54–8:3)

1. Stephen's response to the mob's fury (7:54–56)

2. Stephen's dying prayers (7:57–60)

3. Aftermath (8:1–3)

Stephen was one of the seven chosen to oversee the distribution of food to widows (6:1–7). His words and deeds aroused opposition among Greek-speaking Jews (6:8–10). They mounted a campaign of lies that aroused the people and Sanhedrin (san HEE drun; 6:11–15). Stephen spoke to the Sanhedrin about Abraham, who never owned land in Canaan, and Joseph, who delivered his people by bringing them to Egypt (7:1–16). Moses was raised as an Egyptian, was rejected by his people, and received God's revelation at Mount Sinai (SIGH nay igh; 7:17–34). The Israelites had rebelled against God, rejected the prophets, and killed the Messiah (7:35–53). When the mob expressed its fury, Stephen spoke of seeing the Son of Man in heaven (7:54–56). As Stephen was stoned, he committed himself to the Lord and prayed for his executioners (7:57–60). As devout people buried Stephen, Saul launched a violent persecution of those who shared Stephen's faith (8:1–3).

I. Selection of the Seven (Acts 6:1–7)

The Greek-speaking widows in the Jerusalem church complained that they were being neglected in the daily distribution of food (v. 1). When the Twelve proposed that the church select seven men to oversee the distribution, Stephen was one of those selected (vv. 2–6). As a result, the word of God spread and the church grew (v. 7).

II. Reaction to Stephen's Words and Deeds (Acts 6:8–15)

1. Power of Stephen's words and deeds (6:8–10)

8 And Stephen, full of faith and power, did great wonders and miracles among the people.

9 Then there arose certain of the synagogue, which is called the synagogue of the Libertines [LIB ur teens], and Cyrenians [sigh REE nih uhns], and Alexandrians [al eg ZAN drih uhns], of them of Cilicia [sih LISH ih uh] and of Asia, disputing with Stephen.

10 And they were not able to resist the wisdom and the spirit by which he spake.

One of the qualifications for the seven was that they be "of honest report, full of the Holy Ghost and wisdom" (Acts 6:3). In the biblical list of the seven, Stephen's name is listed first; and he is described as "a man full of faith and of the Holy Ghost" (Acts 6:5). Stephen was selected because the church saw these qualities in him. Their choice was confirmed by what Stephen did after he was chosen. Stephen's actions clearly showed that he was "full of faith and power."

Stephen was not content to confine his service to overseeing the distribution of food to widows. He was the first person other than the apostles to be described as working miracles. Verse 10 shows that Stephen also spoke the word of God with effectiveness.

Such effective service soon aroused opposition. The groups named in verse 9 represent Jews who had lived outside the holy land. "Libertines" in this verse means "freedmen," apparently a synagogue of ex-slaves; but the other names are places outside Judea: Cyrene, Alexandria, Cilicia, and Asia (the Roman province, not the continent). Since Stephen's name was Greek, he too was probably one of the many Jews who had lived away from Judea. Thus the opposition to Stephen arose among the group from which he had come. They saw him as a traitor to them and their ways. They argued with Stephen, but his words showed such wisdom and spirit that his opponents lost the debate.

2. A campaign of lies (6:11–15)

11 Then they suborned men, which said, We have heard him speak blasphemous words against Moses, and against God.

12 And they stirred up the people, and the elders, and the scribes, and came upon him, and caught him, and brought him to the council,

After being unable to defeat Stephen in debate, his enemies resorted to a campaign of lies. They persuaded a number of men to participate in telling these lies throughout Jerusalem. The gist of the lies was that Stephen was guilty of blasphemy because he was speaking against Moses and God.

They were so successful at spreading these lies that they were able to stir up two crucial groups. For the first time in Acts, the people of the city were aroused against the cause of Christ. Prior to this time, the people had been favorably disposed or at least neutral (Acts 2:47; 3:11; 4:21; 5:26). Now they were aroused against Stephen by the campaign of lies.

The other group was the Jewish council or Sanhedrin, which consisted of the elders and the scribes. This was the group that had set out to kill Jesus. They had been divided about how to deal with the work of the apostles (Acts 5:33–40), but now they were aroused by the lies. Stephen's enemies acted quickly. They seized him and took him to the Sanhedrin.

> 13 And set up false witnesses, which said, This man ceaseth not to speak blasphemous words against this holy place, and the law:
>
> 14 For we have heard him say, that this Jesus of Nazareth shall destroy this place, and shall change the customs which Moses delivered us.

The campaign of lies continued during Stephen's hearing before the Sanhedrin. The witnesses claimed to have heard Stephen say that Jesus of Nazareth would destroy the holy temple and would change the traditions given by Moses. The two groups in the Sanhedrin were the priestly party or Sadducees (SAD joo sees) and the legal party or Pharisees (FER uh sees; see Matt. 15:1–9). The Sadducees were concerned about maintaining their control over the temple. The Pharisees were concerned about preserving their interpretations of the Mosaic law. The enemies of Stephen cleverly included both charges in order to mobilize both Sadducees and Pharisees against Stephen.

Throughout the account of Stephen's trial and death are numerous parallels to Jesus' trial and death. During the trial of Jesus, false witnesses claimed that He said He would destroy the temple (Matt. 26:60–61; Mark 14:57–58). A similar charge was made against Stephen. During His life, Jesus was often accused of departing from the Mosaic customs. What He departed from were the human traditions that had grown up and become sanctified by the Pharisees.

> 15 And all that sat in the council, looking stedfastly on him, saw his face as it had been the face of an angel.

During the trial, Stephen's face shone like that of an angel. Rather than faltering before this barrage of lies, Stephen shone with the light of truth. God gave this as a sign of His favor.

III. Stephen's Speech to the Sanhedrin (Acts 7:1–53)

1. The patriarchs (7:1–16)

Stephen's speech was a carefully crafted response to the false charges against him. Two themes run through the speech: (1) God has never been bound to one place. (2) Israel has repeatedly rejected the word of God. Abraham, for example, was a pilgrim of faith who never actually owned land in Canaan (vv. 1–8). Joseph, who was sold by the other patriarchs, became their deliverer, which involved moving to Egypt (vv. 9–16).

2. Moses (7:17–34)

Moses was raised as an Egyptian (vv. 17–22). When he tried to help the Hebrews, they rejected him (vv. 23–29). God revealed Himself to Moses at Mount Sinai (vv. 30–34).

3. History of rebellion (7:35–53)

The Israelites rebelled repeatedly in the wilderness (vv. 35–43). When Solomon built the temple, he acknowledged that God rules over the universe and does not dwell in one building (vv. 44–50). Directly addressing his accusers, Stephen accused them of killing the Messiah (vv. 51–53).

IV. Stephen's Death (Acts 7:54–8:3)

1. Stephen's response to the mob's fury (7:54–56)

54 When they heard these things, they were cut to the heart, and they gnashed on him with their teeth.

55 But he, being full of the Holy Ghost, looked up stedfastly into heaven, and saw the glory of God, and Jesus standing on the right hand of God,

56 And said, Behold, I see the heavens opened, and the Son of man standing on the right hand of God.

Those who had been listening to Stephen became infuriated at what he said. They were so angry that they gnashed their teeth. By contrast, Stephen was filled with the Spirit and saw a heavenly vision, which he described. During His ministry, Jesus repeatedly referred to Himself as the Son of man. Stephen's use of this title shows his understanding of Jesus' purpose and mission. God rewarded Stephen's faithfulness by opening heaven and allowing Stephen to see the Son of man. Stephen bore testimony to Christ by telling his enemies what he saw.

2. Stephen's dying prayers (7:57–60)

57 Then they cried out with a loud voice, and stopped their ears, and ran upon him with one accord,

58 And cast him out of the city, and stoned him: and the witnesses laid down their clothes at a young man's feet, whose name was Saul.

59 And they stoned Stephen, calling upon God, and saying, Lord Jesus, receive my spirit.

60 And he kneeled down, and cried with a loud voice, Lord, lay not this sin to their charge. And when he had said this, he fell asleep.

Because they had believed the lies about Stephen, most of his hearers had made up their minds about him much earlier. His speech only infuriated them, and his words about the Son of man in heaven were all they could stand. They stopped up their ears as a sign that Stephen was speaking blasphemy, rushed him out of the city, and proceeded to stone him. Luke mentioned in passing that those who stoned Stephen laid their clothes at the feet of Saul, who would become prominent later in the Book of Acts.

As Stephen was dying, he prayed two prayers that are similar to two of Jesus' prayers from the cross. As Jesus was being crucified, He prayed, "Father, forgive them; for they know not what they do" (Luke 23:34). As He died, He prayed, "Father, into thy hands I commend my spirit" (Luke 23:46). Stephen was the first Christian martyr. His dying, like his living, was a faithful reflection of the Lord in whom he believed and whom he served. What more can any believer hope for than to be as faithful in how we live and how we die (see Phil. 1:20)!

3. Aftermath (8:1–3)

Stephen's death was a watershed for the Christian movement. Stephen's life and death set the stage for the expansion of the gospel to all kinds of people. Saul's immediate reaction was to launch a persecution of all who shared Stephen's views (v. 1). As devout people mourned and buried Stephen, Saul launched a violent persecution (vv. 2–3).

APPLYING THE BIBLE

1. The "crowned one." Stephen's name means "crown," and what a marvelous spiritual crown he wore! Read the verses again in today's lesson and marvel at his spiritual character. This is the kind of people we need in our churches today: pious, godly, filled with the Holy Spirit, soul-winners, sacrificial. These qualities shine brightly against the backdrop of how many Christians behave themselves today—in church and out of church.

On his deathbed, Horace Greeley (1812–1872), founder and editor of *The New York Tribune,* said, "Fame is a vapor, popularity an accident, riches take wings; those who cheer today will curse tomorrow; only one thing endures—character."

Today, God give us Christian men and women of character like Stephen who will not blindly follow the masses.

2. The witnessing laymen. Stephen was not one of the Twelve officially called and set apart to preach, but preach he did (6:10; 7:1–53). And it resulted in his death (7:54–60).

Later, baptism and the Lord's Supper developed into "magical" rites with saving grace in them. This pagan idea demanded that these "magic" rites could only be preserved and administered by those who were trained and qualified to administer them. Thus the chasm developed between what today are called "the clergy" and the "the laity." "Clergy" means "those who have been called of God" and "laity" means "the people."[1] Certainly, God calls some to the sacred task of pastoring and preaching; but all, like Stephen, are to be evangelists—"good news tellers."

Our laity today find a good example in Brother Stephen.

3. The terrible power of a lie. Henry Ward Beecher said, "Even a liar tells a hundred truths to one lie; he has to, to make a lie good for anything." Even those from whose group Stephen had come (6:8–10) lied about what Stephen had said and done because they were unable "to resist the wisdom and the spirit by which he spoke" (v. 10). Like Jesus, his Lord, it appears that Stephen was sold out by his friends!

The lie spread like wildfire, as lies always do (vv. 11–14). More liars joined in and when Stephen was brought before the religious officials, he was condemned to death, not on the basis of truth, but of lies (vv. 13–14; 7:54–83).

Once a lie is out, it cannot be recalled. In spite of the liar's best efforts, it spreads like a raging fire (see James 3:1–12). A woman had been guilty of lying about her neighbor. Smitten by her conscience, she sought the counsel of her pastor. "Take a feather pillow," the pastor said, "shake out all the feathers, then go and gather each up and put it back in the pillow." "But that is impossible," the woman explained! "Exactly," said the pastor. "Your lies can never be recalled. They will go on and on hurting the neighbor against whom you spoke."

We ought to be very careful what we say about someone else. Even if we know it is true, we are under no obligation to pass it on.

4. The face of an angel. Devotional writer Virginia Ely tells of two brothers who were convicted of stealing sheep. As was the custom for sheep thieves in their country, the brothers were branded with the letters, "ST"—"sheep thief"—on their foreheads. One of the brothers was so ashamed that he moved to a far country and finally died in despair. The other stayed at home, lived an exemplary life, regained his character, and lived to be an old man. Many years later, a stranger to the area asked one who lived there the meaning of the letters. "I really don't know," the native replied, "it happened so many years ago. But I think it stands for saint!"

Stephen was branded and tried as a liar. But as he stood before the council "all that sat in the council . . . saw his face as it had been the face of an angel" (v. 15).

5. Stephen's homecoming welcome. After Christ's sufferings and resurrection, He ascended to heaven and sat down at the Father's right hand (Heb. 1:3). But Stephen, being stoned to death, saw Jesus "standing on the right hand of God" (7:56). Here is Jesus, pictured as arising from His throne, to welcome the first martyr home to glory! What a magnificent picture it is!

TEACHING THE BIBLE

- *Main Idea:* Christ calls us to be bold witnesses for Him.
- *Suggested Teaching Aim:* To lead adults to identify ways they can become bold witnesses for Christ.

A TEACHING OUTLINE

1. Use an illustration to introduce the lesson.

2. Use a chart to compare similarities between Stephen's and Jesus' death.

3. Use group discussion to search for biblical truth.

4. Use a thought question and brainstorming to give the truth a personal focus.

Introduce the Bible Study

Use "The witnessing layman" to introduce the lesson. Remind members that Stephen—a layman—was the first Christian martyr.

Search for Biblical Truth

Point out the lesson on the unit poster you made for February 2. On a chalkboard or a large sheet of paper write: **Similarities Between Jesus' and Stephen's Lives**. As you move through the lesson, list similarities as members mention them. (Some suggestions are made, but use members' ideas when possible.)

Read aloud Acts 6:8–10. Ask: Who was Stephen? To what office was he elected? How does the Bible describe him? What ministries did he perform? (*Chart*: Performed wonders and miracles.)

DISCUSS: Why do some people reject freedom and feel the need to control those who differ with them?

Read aloud 6:11–15. Ask: How did Stephen's enemies respond to his teaching? What lie did they tell? Who testified against him at his trial? With what crime was Stephen charged? (*Chart*: Arrested by a mob; testified against by false witnesses; charged with blasphemy.)

DISCUSS: What do you do when someone lies about you?

Summarize briefly the material in "III. Stephen's Speech to the Sanhedrin" in "Studying the Bible" to help members to understand the charges against Stephen and Stephen's defense.

Read aloud 7:54–8:3. Ask: Why do you think the council of the Sanhedrin reacted as they did to Stephen's defense? How did Stephen respond to their anger? How do you think this made his enemies feel? What was Stephen's response as he was being stoned? (*Chart*: Responded nonviolently; prayed as he died; forgave enemies.)

DISCUSS: What effect did Stephen's "turning the other cheek" have on his enemies? Is turning the other cheek always the best policy? Why doesn't turning the other cheek provide physical blessing for the person? Do you need to forgive someone who has wounded you?

Give the Truth a Personal Focus

Ask: If you had been present at Stephen's trial and stoning, which character would you have been: Stephen? his persecutor? uninterested bystander? part of the mob? Paul? those who buried Stephen? Ask members to respond.

Read the Teaching Aim: "To lead adults to identify ways they can become bold witnesses for Christ." Ask: What do you think enabled Stephen to bear such a bold witness for Christ? What steps can you take to become a bold witness for Christ? List members' suggestions on a chalkboard or a large sheet of paper. Ask members to choose those steps that would apply to their lives. Distribute paper and pencils and let them write how they will put these steps into practice. Let them keep the paper. Close in a time of commitment and prayer.

---

1. Robert A. Baker, *A Summary of Christian History*, revised by John M. Landers (Nashville: Broadman & Holman, 1994), 38.

February

16

1997

Priscilla and Aquila

Basic Passages: Acts 18:1–4,18–19, 24–26; Romans 16:3–5a

Focal Passages: Acts 18:1–4,18–19, 24–26; Romans 16:3–5a

Priscilla (prih SIL uh) and Aquila (uh KWIL uh) are always mentioned together. They showed their commitment in several ways: sharing their home and work with Paul, instructing Apollos (uh PAHL uhs), risking their lives for Paul, providing a meeting place for the church, and faithfully serving Christ wherever they moved.

Study Aim: *To identify ways Priscilla and Aquila showed commitment to Christ*

STUDYING THE BIBLE

OUTLINE AND SUMMARY

I. In Corinth (Acts 18:1–4)

II. In Ephesus (Acts 18:18–19, 24–26)

1. From Corinth to Ephesus (18:18–19)

2. Helping Apollos (18:24–26)

III. In Rome (Rom. 16:3–5a)

Priscilla and Aquila shared their home and work with Paul while he was in Corinth (KAWR inth; Acts 18:1–4). When Paul left Corinth, they moved to Ephesus (EF uh suhs; Acts 18:18–19). When Apollos came to Ephesus, they instructed him more completely in the Christian way (Acts 18:24–26). When Paul wrote to Rome, he greeted Priscilla and Aquila as helpers, thanked God that they had risked their lives for him, and greeted the church meeting in their house (Rom. 16:3–5a).

I. In Corinth (Acts 18:1–4)

1 After these things Paul departed from Athens, and came to Corinth;

2 And found a certain Jew named Aquila, born in Pontus [PAHN tuhs], lately come from Italy, with his wife Priscilla; (because that Claudius had commanded all Jews to depart from Rome:) and came unto them.

3 And because he was of the same craft, he abode with them, and wrought: for by their occupation they were tentmakers.

4 And he reasoned in the synagogue every sabbath, and persuaded the Jews and the Greeks.

Priscilla and Aquila are first mentioned during Paul's first visit to Corinth. This happened during Paul's second missionary journey. He came to Corinth from Athens (Acts 17:15–34). Corinth was a seaport town in Greece, the Roman province of Achaia (uh KAY yuh). The city was so well-known for its sexual immorality that a word meaning "to live like a Corinthian" meant to live immorally. Corinth is prominent in the New Testament because the New Testament contains not only the account of Paul's work in the Book of Acts but also two long letters from Paul to the Corinthian church.

Paul was alone when he arrived in Corinth. His two missionary associates—Silas (SIGH luhs) and Timothy—arrived only later (v. 5). Like all Jewish rabbis, Paul had a trade other than teaching; his was tentmaking. (Some Bible scholars think the word means "leatherworking.") Paul sought and found a tentmaker named Aquila in Corinth. Aquila invited Paul to stay with him and to work with him while he was in Corinth.

Luke tells us that Aquila was a Jew who had been born in Pontus, a region of Asia Minor. Before coming to Corinth, Aquila had lived in Italy. Aquila and his wife Priscilla were forced to leave Rome because Claudius Caesar expelled the Jews from Rome. Large groups of Jews lived throughout the Roman Empire, especially in the large cities. Since the expulsion of Jews by Claudius was between January 25, A.D. 49 and January 24, A.D. 50, we have a general idea of when Paul arrived in Corinth.

Acts 18:2–3 gives some basic facts about Aquila and Priscilla, but it doesn't answer all our questions. For example, "Was Priscilla also a Jew?" Some have theorized that she was a Roman who married the Jew Aquila. Although Jewish leaders frowned on such mixed marriages, we know that Timothy's mother married a Greek (Acts 16:3).

An even more important question is, "Were Aquila and Priscilla Christians before Paul met them?" The Book of Acts doesn't tell us, but there are reasons for thinking that they were already believers. For one thing, nothing is said of Paul witnessing to them as he did with Lydia (LID ih uh; Acts 16:14–15). Even more compelling is the reason given by a Roman historian for Claudius's expulsion order. The Jews were expelled because of a tumult instigated by one "Chrestus." Very likely, this means that the Jews were arguing about whether Jesus was the Christ. This shows that there were some Christians in Rome at an early date, and thus Acts 18:2 probably means that Aquila and Priscilla were among them.

If Aquila and Priscilla were already Christians, this explains why they so quickly opened their home and shared their work with Paul. It explains why Paul so quickly accepted their invitation. Using their home as a base and the tentmaking for financial support, Paul was able to launch his missionary campaign in Corinth. As usual, he began by going to the Jewish synagogue and preaching to Jews and God-fearing Gentiles.

II. In Ephesus (Acts 18:18–19, 24–26)

1. From Corinth to Ephesus (18:18–19)

18 And Paul after this tarried there yet a good while, and then took his leave of the brethren, and sailed thence into Syria, and with him Priscilla and Aquila; having shorn his head in Cenchrea [sen KREE uh]: for he had a vow.

19 And he came to Ephesus, and left them there: but he himself entered into the synagogue, and reasoned with the Jews.

The account of the rest of Paul's first visit to Corinth is in Acts 18:5–17. He endured many threats and had a vision that encouraged him to persevere. Paul left Corinth on his way eventually back to Syria, where the Antioch (AN tih ahk) church was. On the way, he stopped first at Cenchrea, near Corinth. Then he went to Ephesus for a short visit. From there he went to Caesarea, then to Jerusalem, and finally to Antioch (vv. 20–22).

When Paul was in Cenchrea, he cut off his hair as part of a Jewish vow. This was probably part of a vow that culminated in a visit to the temple when Paul was in Jerusalem. Acts 21:23–24 refers to a later visit to the temple to perform a vow. This shows that Paul considered himself a loyal Jew.

The first-century world was a mobile society. People moved about on the Roman system of roads and sailed on seas patrolled by Roman ships. One empire facilitated travel across provincial boundaries. We know that Paul spent much of his life on the road. Aquila and Priscilla provide another good example of mobility. Acts tells us that Aquila was from Pontus, that he and Priscilla lived in Rome, that they then moved to Corinth, and that they went with Paul to Ephesus. References in Paul's letters show that they remained for a while in Ephesus (1 Cor. 16:19), that later they were in Rome (Rom. 16:3–5), and that still later they returned to Ephesus (2 Tim. 4:19).

Like Abraham, this dedicated couple had a mobile faith. They did not confine their practice of the Christian faith to one locale. They took their faith with them. Wherever they lived was where they served the Lord.

2. Helping Apollos (18:24–26)

24 And a certain Jew named Apollos, born at Alexandria [al eg ZAN drih uh], an eloquent man, and mighty in the scriptures, came to Ephesus.

25 This man was instructed in the way of the Lord; and being fervent in the spirit, he spake and taught diligently the things of the Lord, knowing only the baptism of John.

26 And he began to speak boldly in the synagogue: whom when Aquila and Priscilla had heard, they took him unto them, and expounded unto him the way of God more perfectly.

Apollos was from Alexandria in Egypt. A large colony of Jews had lived there for centuries. Acts 18:24 shows that the Christian gospel had reached Alexandria by the middle of the first century. Apollos came from Alexandria to Ephesus and began to teach the things of the Lord. When he spoke in the synagogue, Aquila and Priscilla heard him. This shows that Jewish believers at this stage still worshiped with fellow Jews in the synagogue.

Aquila and Priscilla detected something lacking in what Apollos said. What was lacking? The description of Apollos before he met Aquila and Priscilla is impressive. He was eloquent and fervent. He knew the Scriptures and had been instructed in the way of the Lord. This enabled him to teach about Jesus. In spite of all these things, Apollos knew "only the baptism of John." This may mean that Apollos had not heard about the death and resurrection of Jesus. It may mean that he had not heard about Pentecost or experienced the fullness of the Spirit. It may mean that what Apollos taught about baptism was limited to John's baptism of repentance and did not include the picture of death and resurrection in Christian baptism.

Whatever it meant, Aquila and Priscilla were disturbed to hear a spokesman for Jesus not declare all that God had revealed. Under similar conditions, lesser people might have launched a campaign of criticism against Apollos. Instead, this dedicated couple quietly invited Apollos to meet with them, and they explained to him more completely the way of God. This took love, courage, and tact. Apollos accepted their instruction with openness, humility, and gratitude. As a result, Apollos went on to effective ministry (Acts 18:27–28; 1 Cor. 3:4–7).

III. In Rome (Rom. 16:3–5a)

3 Greet Priscilla and Aquila my helpers in Christ Jesus:

4 Who have for my life laid down their own necks: unto whom not only I give thanks, but also all the churches of the Gentiles.

5 Likewise greet the church that is in their house.

By the time Paul wrote to the church at Rome, Priscilla and Aquila were back in Rome. Paul paid tribute not only by calling them helpers in Christ Jesus but also by thanking God that they had risked their own lives for him. We don't know the circumstances when these friends risked their lives for Paul. Acts 19:28–41 describes a riot in Ephesus, in which Paul was in danger. Paul mentioned dangers in Ephesus in 1 Corinthians 15:32 and 16:9. Perhaps one of these was the occasion. Wherever it was, Paul clearly testified that Priscilla and Aquila had risked their own lives for him.

Paul greeted not only them but also the church in their house. According to 1 Corinthians 16:19, a church had also met in their house when they were in Ephesus. First-century churches did not have buildings of their own. They met in rented halls (Acts 19:9) and more often in private houses (Acts 2:46; 12:12; Philem. 2). One evidence of the commitment of Priscilla and Aquila is that they practiced their faith wherever they moved. This is evident because they opened their house as a meeting place for the churches in Ephesus and in Rome.

It is interesting to notice that all New Testament references to either Priscilla or Aquila always include both names. Also, the sequence of their names varies. Sometimes Aquila is listed first, and sometimes, Priscilla. (Her name is sometimes listed as Prisca, but most often as Priscilla.) These references show that this Christian couple not only shared life together but also participated jointly in their service to the Lord.

APPLYING THE BIBLE

1. Persecution spreads the gospel. God uses all things that befall us—both the good and the bad—to further His work. A case in point is the persecution of Aquila and Priscilla. They were Jews driven from their

PAUL'S THIRD MISSIONARY JOURNEY
MACEDONIA
Philippi
THRACE
Thessalonica
Berea
BITHYNIA and PONTUS
GALATIA
CAPPADOCIA
EPIRUS
Troas
Assos
LESBOS
Mitylene
Pergamum
Thyatira
Aegean Sea
ASIA
Sardis
Smyrna
Philadelphia
Ephesus
PHRYGIA
Pisidian Antioch
Iconium
ACHAIA
KIOS
Athens
Corinth
Samos
Laodicea
Miletus
Derbe
Tarsus
CILICIA
Patmos
PAMPHYLIA
LYCIA
Cos
COS
Patara
Rhodes
Antioch
CRETE
Paphos
CYPRUS
SYRIA
Sidon
PHOENICIA
Tyre
Ptolemais
MEDITERRANEAN SEA
Caesarea
PALESTINE
Jerusalem
ARABIA
Alternative route
Route of Egnation Way
Scale of Miles
0
50
100
150
200

home in Rome by Emperor Claudius. According to the *Holman Bible Dictionary,* Claudius drove the Jews out of Rome in about A.D. 49 "probably due to a conflict between Jews and Christians in Rome"[1] (see also Acts 18:2). Claudius was probably poisoned by his fourth wife Aquippina "in A.D. 54 and [she] took charge of the empire for her son Nero"[2] But in human affairs, God always has the last word. Persecution of the Jews only served to spread the gospel more rapidly, for Aquila and Priscilla were forced to move to Corinth, where they met Paul (Acts 18:1–4).

2. God uses common folks. God often uses common people who do His work in the background. The ministry of Billy Graham has been unique and powerful, but no more important to God than that work of a faithful pastor in a country church who gives his all to Jesus. Aquila and Priscilla were simple tentmakers (v. 3) or leather workers. They worked with their hands, but they used their hands for God's glory.

3. Paul finds a home. When Paul moved from Athens to Corinth, he found an open door to the home of Aquila and Priscilla. Verse 3 says, "And because he was of the same craft, he abode with them." They probably worked as tentmakers in their own home. At least they offered Paul accommodations in their home and he lived and worked with them. How marvelously God works to care for His own, not only in spiritual blessings but in material blessings as well.

4. Taking the faith "on the road." Notice how much Paul moved about and how many cities he visited. Observe, too, the movements of Aquila and Priscilla who, like Paul, "took their faith on the road."

But the point is that the good news is tailored for the road. We are not to lock our faith up in some isolated cloister or closet at home. It is to be taken with us, following the example of Aquila and Priscilla, and shared with those we meet daily.

5. Tentmakers teach the teacher. When Apollos came to Ephesus, he began to teach in the synagogue, but Aquila and Priscilla readily saw that something was lacking. As our lesson points out very clearly, they took him aside and "expounded unto him the way of God more perfectly" (18:26). They did not criticize or embarrass him publicly. What gracious people they were; and, no doubt, this ministry to Apollos was one of their greatest contributions to the Christian faith because of Apollos's unique qualifications (18:24).

TEACHING THE BIBLE

- *Main Idea:* Christ calls us to share our faith wherever we go.
- *Suggested Teaching Aim:* To lead adults to identify ways they can serve Christ as they go about their daily work.

A TEACHING OUTLINE

1. Use thought questions to introduce the study.
2. Use small groups to examine the Bible passage or use the material with the whole class.

3. Use discussion questions to examine how the Scripture applies to members' lives.

4. Use a listing of principles to help members apply the Bible study to their personal lives.

Introduce the Bible Study

Ask: What do you think about a person who witnesses on the job? Should that person have a right to do so? Do you like to shop in a store where you know the person is a Christian? Would you more likely buy from a Christian business if you had a choice?

Suggest that today's lesson is about a husband and wife team who used their business to spread the gospel.

Search for Biblical Truth

Display the unit poster and point out the lesson for today. On three separate sheets of paper write one of the following cities: *Corinth, Ephesus,* and *Rome.* Place these at three places around the room.

If your class works well in groups, form three groups and assign each of them one of the cities. (You need not have more than one person in a group.) Ask them to read the biblical material about Priscilla and Aquila that relates to that city: Corinth—Acts 18:1–4; Ephesus—Acts 18:18–19, 24–26; Rome—Romans 16:3–5a. Ask them to answer the following questions: (1) Who is the passage about? (2) What did the people do? (3) How did this help spread the gospel? (4) What principles for living in today's world can you find in your passage? Either write these questions on a chalkboard or a large sheet of paper so all can see or make a copy for each of the three groups.

If your class does not work well in small groups, use the above four questions and ask members to work as a whole. Whether you work in groups or as a whole class, use the following discussion questions to help apply the Scripture after you have examined the Bible passage for each city.

Corinth: How do you think Priscilla and Aquila used their business to further Christianity? How can you use your business or job to further the cause of Christ? What should you do? What should you be careful to avoid? List the principles for living in today's world on a chalkboard or a large sheet of paper.

Ephesus: As you travel on vacations or business, how can you share your faith? What are some actions you could take? What should you avoid? Do you know someone who is immature in the faith whom you can help? Use "Studying the Bible" to explain the three possible meanings of "knowing only the baptism of John." List the principles for living in today's world on a chalkboard or a large sheet of paper.

Rome: How can you use your home to further the gospel of Christ? How willing are you to risk your "neck" (Rom. 16:4) to help someone who has taken a stand for Christ? List the principles for living in today's world on a chalkboard or a large sheet of paper.

Give the Truth a Personal Focus

Read over the list of principles for living in today's world and ask members if they would like to add any others to the list. Ask members to evaluate these principles to see which ones would apply to their lives. Ask them to choose at least one principle they will commit to put into practice. Distribute paper and pencils. Ask them to write this principle on the paper and keep it in their Bibles to remind them of it. Close with a prayer of commitment that members will follow through on the decisions they made.

---

1. *Holman Bible Dictionary*, s.v. "Claudius."
2. Ibid. 268.

February

23

1997

Timothy

Basic Passages: Acts 16:1–5; 1 Corinthians 4:14–17; Philippians 2:19–24; 2 Timothy 1:3–7; 3:14–15

Focal Passages: Acts 16:1–5; 1 Corinthians 4:14–17; Philippians 2:19–22; 2 Timothy 1:4–7

Paul and Timothy served the Lord by serving each other and the churches. Paul was Timothy's father in the faith. He taught Timothy and gave him many opportunities for service. Timothy was Paul's helper, companion, and representative on many missions. The churches benefited from the work of these two partners in the gospel.

Study Aim: *To describe how Paul and Timothy helped each other and the churches*

STUDYING THE BIBLE

OUTLINE AND SUMMARY

I. Paul Invited Timothy to Go with Him (Acts 16:1–5)

II. Paul Sent Timothy on Special Missions (1 Cor. 4:14–17; Phil. 2:19–24)

1. **Mission to Corinth (1 Cor. 4:14–17)**
2. **Mission to Philippi (Phil. 2:19–24)**

III. Paul Challenged Timothy to Remain Faithful (2 Tim. 1:3–7; 3:14–15)

1. **Remembering how he was raised (2 Tim. 1:3–5; 3:14–15)**
2. **Stirring up the gift of God (2 Tim. 1:6–7)**

Paul chose Timothy, a disciple living in Lystra (LISS truh), well spoken of by the believers, to join him on his missionary journey (Acts 16:1–5). Paul sent Timothy, his beloved and faithful son in the Lord, to remind the Corinthians of Paul's teachings about the Christian life (1 Cor. 4:14–17). In writing of his plans to send Timothy to Philippi (FILL ih pigh), Paul commended Timothy as one who cared for the Philippians and put the work of the Lord above his own interests (Phil. 2:19–24). In his final letter, Paul thanked God for the sincere faith of Timothy, his grandmother, and mother (2 Tim. 1:3–5; 3:14–15). Paul challenged Timothy to rekindle God's gift and to live in the courage of His Spirit (2 Tim. 1:6–7).

I. Paul Invited Timothy to Go with Him (Acts 16:1–5)

1 Then came he to Derbe [DIR bih] and Lystra: and, behold, a certain disciple was there, named Timotheus [tih MOH thih uhs], the son of a certain woman, which was a Jewess, and believed; but his father was a Greek:

2 Which was well reported of by the brethren that were at Lystra and Iconium [igh KOH nih uhm].

3 Him would Paul have to go forth with him; and took and circumcised him because of the Jews which were in those quarters: for they knew all that his father was a Greek.

4 And as they went through the cities, they delivered them the decrees for to keep, that were ordained of the apostles and elders which were at Jerusalem.

5 And so were the churches established in the faith, and increased in number daily.

On Paul's first missionary journey, he had preached in the cities mentioned in Acts 16:1–5 (Acts 14). Now he was returning in order to encourage the believers and strengthen the churches. While he was there, Paul also reported on the decisions of the Jerusalem Conference (Acts 15). Verse 5 shows the successful results of this return visit by Paul.

While he was in Lystra, Paul noticed a young disciple named Timothy. This young man had a good reputation in Lystra and in the neighboring town of Iconium. Paul was so impressed by Timothy that he invited him to join Paul and Silas in their missionary work. Thus began an association between Paul and Timothy that lasted throughout the rest of Paul's life.

Timothy probably had become a Christian during Paul's first visit to Lystra. His mother was a believing Jew. His father was a Greek; therefore, Timothy had not been circumcised. Paul circumcised Timothy because he was a Jew. Paul defended the principle that a Gentile believer need not be circumcised in order to follow Jesus; however, he recognized that circumcision was still proper for a Jew. If Timothy was not circumcised, he and Paul would encounter resistance in future work with fellow Jews.

II. Paul Sent Timothy on Special Missions (1 Cor. 4:14–17; Phil. 2:19–24)

1. Mission to Corinth (1 Cor. 4:14–17)

14 I write not these things to shame you, but as my beloved sons I warn you.

15 For though ye have ten thousand instructors in Christ, yet have ye not many fathers: for in Christ Jesus I have begotten you through the gospel.

16 Wherefore I beseech you, be ye followers of me.

17 For this cause have I sent unto you Timotheus, who is my beloved son, and faithful in the Lord, who shall bring you into remembrance of my ways, which be in Christ, as I teach every where in every church.

In the early chapters of 1 Corinthians, Paul rebuked the church at Corinth for their selfish pride and disruptive dissension. Paul contrasted their selfishness with the sacrifices of the apostles (1 Cor. 4:10–13). He explained that his purpose was not to shame them but to admonish them as a father does his children. They might have many teachers in the Christian life, but they had only one spiritual father. Paul referred to himself as their father because he was the one who brought the gospel to them and first taught them how to live as Christians (Acts 18:1–17). He was not seeking to replace God as their Father. He and they had a distinctive relationship that enabled him to speak to them as a father.

Verse 16 is not evidence of Paul's arrogance. The ancient world was a sinful place. Most Gentiles had no background in the moral teachings of Judaism. They needed to learn how to live as Christians. The missionaries taught them by their words and by their own example.

Timothy had been with Paul during much of his initial work in Corinth (Acts 18:5). Paul sent Timothy on many special missions (Acts 17:14–15; 18:5; 19:22; 1 Thess. 3:2, 6). Paul sent Timothy to Corinth on just such a mission. Paul himself planned to come soon to deal with the situation in Corinth (1 Cor. 4:18–19). In the meanwhile, he sent Timothy.

Paul commended Timothy as his beloved son, probably referring to Paul's part in Timothy's conversion and certainly referring to Paul's role as teacher and mentor. Paul also commended Timothy's faithfulness in the Lord. Paul trusted Timothy to remind the Corinthians of what Paul taught in all the churches about how to live as Christians in a non-Christian world.

2. Mission to Philippi (Phil. 2:19–24)

> 19 But I trust in the Lord Jesus to send Timotheus shortly unto you, that I also may be of good comfort, when I know your state.
>
> 20 For I have no man likeminded, who will naturally care for your state.
>
> 21 For all seek their own, not the things which are Jesus Christ's.
>
> 22 But ye know the proof of him, that, as a son with the father, he hath served with me in the gospel.

Paul was under arrest in Rome when he wrote the Philippian church. He wrote to testify to his joy in the Lord and to express gratitude for their partnership in the gospel. Paul's letter also shows that he saw signs of the kind of selfish pride that led to disruptive dissension in Corinth (Phil. 2:14; 4:2). Thus he challenged them to practice the kind of self-giving love perfectly exemplified in Jesus Christ (2:1–11). Then Paul gave some human examples of unselfish commitment to Christ. He mentioned himself (2:14–18), Timothy (2:19–24), and Epaphroditus (ih PAF roh DIGH tuhs) (2:25–30). Thus although on the surface Philippians 2:19–24 reads like travel plans, Paul had a more serious purpose.

Paul's commendation of Timothy in these verses is unsurpassed. No person was so like-minded to Paul as Timothy. He had for the Philippians the same deep concern as Paul had. Timothy had been with Paul when he answered the Macedonian call and went to Philippi (Acts 16). The Philippians knew of Timothy's relation with Paul and of his untiring work on behalf of the cause of Christ. In a self-seeking world, a spirit that too often invades Christian ranks, Timothy stood out as one who sought not his own interests; instead he sought the things of the Lord.

Like a son with a father, Timothy had served with Paul as a partner in the gospel. They both claimed the title "slaves" of Christ. They served their Master by serving the churches. As they did, their effectiveness was enhanced by their service to each other. Paul planned to send Timothy to Philippi, but for the time being he needed Timothy with him (v. 23). Paul hoped eventually to be set free and to visit Philippi himself (v. 24).

III. Paul Challenged Timothy to Remain Faithful (2 Tim. 1:3–7; 3:14–15)

1. Remembering how he was raised (2 Tim. 1:3–5; 3:14–15)

4 Greatly desiring to see thee, being mindful of thy tears, that I may be filled with joy;

5 When I call to remembrance the unfeigned faith that is in thee, which dwelt first in thy grandmother Lois, and thy mother Eunice [YOO niss]; and I am persuaded that in thee also.

Paul's final letter was to Timothy. Paul thanked God that Timothy was in his thoughts day and night (1:3). Later in the letter, Paul urged Timothy to come to him quickly (4:9). Paul was in prison again and knew that his death was near (4:6–8).

Although he faced death unafraid, he wanted to see Timothy one last time. Paul knew of Timothy's deep concern for him, and he hoped for the joy of seeing him again.

Paul paid tribute to the genuine faith of Timothy, a faith without any insincerity or hypocrisy. Paul reminded Timothy that this was the kind of faith his grandmother and mother had. Paul was sure Timothy had the same kind of faith. Lois and Eunice had been loyal Jews who believed in God as revealed in the Old Testament Scriptures. We don't know at what point Lois and Eunice became believers in Christ. Paul said that they were believers before Timothy was. They certainly taught Timothy the Scriptures when he was a child (2 Tim. 3:14–15). This knowledge of the Bible was the foundation for Timothy's own faith.

2. Stirring up the gift of God (2 Tim. 1:6–7)

6 Wherefore I put thee in remembrance that thou stir up the gift of God, which is in thee by the putting on of my hands.

7 For God hath not given us the spirit of fear; but of power, and of love, and of a sound mind.

Paul reminded Timothy that God had endowed him with a gift. Paul himself had laid his hands on Timothy in prayerful dedication of Timothy to faithfully use the gift entrusted to him. The apostle challenged Timothy to rekindle the gift as one stirs the coals of fire to keep it burning.

Then Paul reminded Timothy that God's Spirit does not produce fear. Instead God's Spirit imparts power, love, and self-discipline (the likely meaning of the word translated "sound mind"). Do these reminders indicate that Paul recognized in Timothy a timid spirit that might falter in the face of the worst kind of persecution? The same question might be asked about verse 8, where Paul challenged Timothy not to be ashamed of the Lord or of Paul, His prisoner. Some Bible students think such timidity is implied by Paul's famous challenge to Timothy: "Let no man despise thy youth" (1 Tim. 4:12).

Another explanation for Paul's challenges is that every believer is human enough at times to be tempted to falter in the face of dangers and threats. Who is there who hasn't felt some fears about giving a bold testimony for Christ? Paul's words, therefore, may not imply any perceived weakness in Timothy other than what afflicts all believers. All of us need to be reminded to stir up the gift of God. All of us need to remember that God gave us a Spirit of power, not of fear.

APPLYING THE LESSON

1. No such thing as a bad boy. Some of us grew up knowing about Father Joseph Flanagan, who founded Boys Town in Omaha, Nebraska, in 1917. He took in boys brought before the courts and gave them a second chance. Flanagan's motto was, "There is no such thing as a bad boy." He is remembered for a picture of a boy about ten or eleven years old carrying a smaller boy on his back. Beneath the picture are the words: "He's not heavy; he's my brother."

Paul met a youth named Timothy who was reared in a godly home, took him under his wing, and taught him. God used Timothy mightily in His service. Paul carried Timothy in his heart and was the making of the young preacher (Acts 16:1–5; 2 Tim. 1:5–6).

2. The best time of life. Someone has said, "Youth is the best time of life." But Robert Browning wrote: "Grow old along with me! The best is yet to be." Really, today is the best time of life, for it is all of life we have! But a great deal can be said about the advantages of youth.

George Bernard Shaw once said that youth is so wonderful that "it's too bad to waste it on young people!" Timothy was young when he met Paul, and that was the turning point in life for Timothy. They first met on Paul's first missionary journey. The good seed had already been planted in Timothy's heart at home (1:3–5). Paul said Timothy was "my beloved son" in the gospel (1 Cor. 4:17). It was the combination of Lois, Eunice, and Paul's witness that brought the youth to Jesus. Now Timothy was ready for the Master's finishing touches which he would learn from Paul (1 Cor. 4:15–17; 2 Tim. 1:6–7).

The best time in life to come to the Savior is when we are young and have all our life to give Him (see Eccles. 12:1). Fortunately, that has been the experience of many of us.

3. Timid Timothy? I have always thought of Timothy, at least in his early ministry, as being timid and unsure of himself. Perhaps it came from the strong influence of his mother and grandmother, for nothing is said of his father except he was a Greek. Was Timothy's timidity the reason Paul wrote the words found in 2 Tim. 1:6–7? Paul knew what was in Timothy and he knew it needed to be "stirred up" and shared courageously.

Many failures come to us because we lack confidence. We fear being inferior. More failures result from our lack of confidence than from our lack of ability. Some of us have had to wrestle hard with this problem that, somehow, was rooted in our early years. But Paul helped Timothy work through it, and Paul was able to write about his young son in the ministry the glowing recommendation of Philippians 2:19–24.

4. Three indispensable elements for the ministry. In 1 Corinthians 13:13, Paul lists three indispensable virtues for effective Christian living. In 2 Timothy 1:6–7, he lists three "indispensables" for the Christian minister: power, love, and a sound mind.

(1) *Power.* The Greek word for power gives us our English word *dynamite.* Kenneth Wuest says this was the force of character Timothy needed which—since apparently not natural to Timothy—could be inspired by the consciousness of a divine call.

(2) *Love.* This is not softness. It is the Greek word *agape,* which describes divine love that bestows itself freely without any thought of return. It is the fruit of the Spirit (Gal. 5:22).

(3) *Sound mind.* Wuest describes this indispensable quality as self-discipline, which is opposed to all easy self-indulgence that produces laxity. These three indispensable qualities every young minister needs are leadership, love, and self-control. They go together. Without any one of them trouble lies ahead for the aspiring young preacher.

TEACHING THE BIBLE

- *Main Idea:* All of us have the ability to affirm those who have helped us in the faith.
- *Suggested Teaching Aim:* To express thanks to those who have been our spiritual teachers.

A TEACHING OUTLINE

1. *Use testimonies to introduce the Bible study.*
2. *Use brief lectures and group discussion to guide the Bible study.*
3. *Use letter writing to make the Bible study personal.*

Introduce the Bible Study

Ask members to describe the person who has helped them most in their spiritual lives. If you know of special relationships in the class where mature Christians have helped new believers, contact the new believers **IN ADVANCE** and ask them to be ready to express how the mature Christians helped them.

Point out the lesson title on the unit poster and suggest that Paul and Timothy had a special relationship that lasted as long as Paul lived.

Search for Biblical Truth

IN ADVANCE, ask a member to read aloud the Scripture passages as you study them. Call for the reader to read Acts 16:1–5. Use a brief lecture to cover the following points in "Studying the Bible": (1) Timothy's Jewish-Greek background; (2) why Paul invited Timothy to join with him and Silas; (3) why Paul circumcised Timothy; (4) what was the result of their ministry.

DISCUSS: How do we know when we are violating some eternal principle or are helping to further the gospel by compromising some of our beliefs?

Call for the reader to read 1 Corinthians 4:14–17. Use a brief lecture to cover the following points in "Studying the Bible": (1) the situation at Corinth; (2) Paul's relationship to the Corinthians; (3) what Paul hoped would happen in Corinth; (4) Paul's relationship with Timothy.

DISCUSS: How do we know either as parents or spiritual parents when to correct and when to let our offspring make their own mistakes?

Call for the reader to read Philippians 2:19–22. Use a brief lecture to cover the following points in "Studying the Bible": (1) where Paul was when he wrote this; (2) why Paul wrote Philippians; (3) Paul's high estimation of Timothy; (4) Paul and Timothy's father-son spiritual relationship.

DISCUSS: How does a spiritual relationship increase the depth of friendship?

Call for the reader to read 2 Timothy 1:4–5. Use a brief lecture to cover the following points in "Studying the Bible": (1) where Paul was when he wrote this letter; (2) Paul's great love for Timothy; (3) the influence of Timothy's home life on his spiritual life.

DISCUSS: What steps can parents take to assure the spiritual growth of their children? Or can they assure it?

Call for the reader to read 2 Timothy 1:6–7. Use a brief lecture to cover the following points in "Studying the Bible": (1) Paul's reminder that God had gifted Timothy; (2) Paul's challenge to Timothy to stir up his commitment to God; (3) Paul's emphasis on power, love, and self-discipline instead of fearfulness.

DISCUSS: What helps you to rekindle your faith when you grow cold spiritually? How have others helped you at this point?

If you choose not to lecture you can use these questions in at least two other ways. Form five small groups and give each group a set of the questions to answer or you can ask the questions as a group activity. In some cases, you may have to supply the information because members will not have the information you have.

Give the Truth a Personal Focus

Distribute paper, envelopes, and pencils and ask members to write a letter to someone who has helped them grow spiritually. Ask members to mail the letter this week.

Hope for the Future (1 and 2 Thessalonians, Revelation)

MARCH
APRIL
MAY
1997

INTRODUCTION

This quarter's studies focus on three New Testament books that have much to say about hope for the future.

Unit I, "Stand Fast in the Lord," has five lessons that cover selected passages in 1 and 2 Thessalonians. Paul reminded his readers of how he had proclaimed the gospel to them. He challenged them to lives of love and holiness. He commended their faithfulness and prayed for them. He challenged them to earn their own living. The Easter lesson combines Matthew 28:1–10 on the resurrection of Christ with 1 Thessalonians 4:13–18 on the resurrection of believers.

Unit II, "Letters to Churches," has an introductory lesson on Revelation 1, which contains Jesus' command for John to write to the seven churches of Asia. Then there are three lessons from Revelation 2–3, dealing with the Lord's messages to five of the seven churches.

Unit III, "A Message of Hope," centers on reasons for hope and encouragement for God's people presented in selected passages in Revelation. One lesson presents the Lamb of God as worthy of all praise. Another lesson pictures the redeemed people of God worshiping the Lamb who has delivered them through great sufferings. A third lesson depicts the victory over evil by Christ and the judgment based on the book of life. The final lesson points to the glories of the new heaven and new earth.

Proclaim the Gospel!

Basic Passage: 1 Thessalonians 2:1–13
Focal Passage: 1 Thessalonians 2:1–13

Paul's two letters to the believers at Thessalonica (THESS uh loh NIGH kuh) were the earliest of his New Testament letters. (Some date Galatians earlier.) He wrote 1 Thessalonians (thess uh LOH nih uhns) not long after his missionary work there (Acts 17:1–9). Paul wrote to encourage new converts and to deal with some issues that had arisen since his visit. One of his purposes was to counteract false perceptions of the proclamation of the gospel by Paul and his companions.

Study Aim: *To recognize how Paul dealt with perceptions of false motives and methods in proclaiming the gospel*

STUDYING THE BIBLE

OUTLINE AND SUMMARY

I. Motives and Methods for Proclaiming the Gospel (1 Thess. 2:1–12)
- **1. Courage in face of opposition (vv. 1–2)**
- **2. Not error, immorality, or guile (vv. 3–4)**
- **3. Not flattery, greed, or pride (vv. 5–6)**
- **4 Gentle and self-giving (vv. 7–8)**
- **5. Hardworking and morally blameless (vv. 9–10)**
- **6. Fatherly exhortation to worthy living (vv. 11–12)**

II. Welcoming the Word of God (1 Thess. 2:13)

In spite of being opposed in Philippi, Paul and his companions went on to Thessalonica, prepared to boldly face further contention (vv. 1–2). They did not practice false teaching, unclean living, or deceit, but were faithful stewards of the gospel (vv. 3–4). They did not practice flattery, nor were they motivated by desire for money or glory (vv. 5–6). They were gentle as a nursing mother and self-giving rather than self-serving (vv. 7–8). They worked to support themselves and practiced what they preached in godly living (vv. 9–10). Like a father does his children, they exhorted and encouraged each Thessalonian believer to live a life worthy of the God who called them (vv. 11–12). Paul thanked God that the Thessalonians had welcomed the missionaries' words as the word of God, not of men (v. 13).

I. Motives and Methods for Proclaiming the Gospel (1 Thess. 2:1–12)

1. Courage in face of opposition (vv. 1–2)

1 For yourselves, brethren, know our entrance in unto you, that it was not in vain.

2 But even after that we had suffered before, and were shamefully entreated, as ye know, at Philippi [FIL ih pigh], we were

bold in our God to speak unto you the gospel of God with much contention.

Verses 1–12 were written to defend Paul against certain false charges or perceptions. Acts 17:5–14 show that Paul had aroused strong opposition. It was strong enough to drive him out of town and even out of the next town. After he left, his enemies may have tried to undermine Paul by attributing certain false motives to him. Traveling religious teachers were common in the first-century world. Many of them were little more than con men using religion for their own selfish purposes. The apostle wanted to head off any comparison to these religious hucksters.

In chapter 1, Paul thanked God for the genuine faith of the Thessalonians (vv. 3–4). God's Spirit had used the missionaries' proclamation to lead many to follow the Lord (vv. 5–6). They had become examples throughout the entire region (vv. 7–10). Paul continued this theme in 1 Thessalonians 2:1. No one knew better than the Thessalonians that the work of Paul among them had not been in vain.

Then Paul reminded them of the opposition he and his companions had faced in order to preach in Thessalonica. Just before going there, Paul had been falsely accused, beaten, and imprisoned in Philippi. He was shamefully treated although he was a Roman citizen (Acts 16:12–40). When Paul reached Thessalonica, he and his friends were subject to further opposition and humiliation at the hands of enemies of the gospel.

Paul's point is that the missionaries were not defeated by such opposition. They persevered boldly in spite of it. A charlatan would never have faced what Paul boldly faced.

2. Not error, immorality, or guile (vv. 3–4)

3 For our exhortation was not of deceit, nor of uncleanness, nor in guile:

Verse 3 lists three charges or false perceptions: error, immorality, and guile. The word translated "deceit" is a word from which we get our word *planet.* Because ancient people thought of planets as wandering and erratic, the word carried the idea of "error." Paul flatly denied that he was guilty of false teachings. The word "uncleanness" referred to moral uncleanness. Sexual immorality was a plague in many cities of the Roman Empire. Traveling preachers were often guilty of either promoting sexual sins or secretly committing such sins. The word "guile" referred to the use of underhanded methods to gain followers. Itinerant religious preachers were skilled in the art of persuading people by using various tricks and manipulation.

4 But as we were allowed of God to be put in trust with the gospel, even so we speak; not as pleasing men, but God, which trieth out hearts.

Paul not only denied that he had used such methods, but he also stated the truth about his proclamation. The missionaries had been entrusted by God with the gospel. He had entrusted it to them because He had tested and proved them. The words "allowed" and "tried" translate the same word, which means "approved after passing the test." Because they viewed the gospel as entrusted to them by God, their goal was to please God, not to please people.

3. Not flattery, greed, or pride (vv. 5–6)

5 For neither at any time used we flattering words, as ye know, nor a cloak of covetousness; God is witness:

6 Nor of men sought we glory, neither of you, nor yet of others, when we might have been burdensome, as the apostles of Christ.

Verses 5–6 reflect three other charges or false perceptions. Paul denied that the missionaries had used flattery. This charge is closely related to the idea of using guile. Flattery is one of the tools of a con man. Paul reminded the Thessalonians that they themselves well knew that the missionaries didn't resort to flattery to gain a following.

Paul also denied that he and his associates were guilty of another besetting sin of traveling preachers: covetousness. Such religious hucksters used religion to make money for themselves. Paul said that God was witness to the fact that the missionaries were not in it for the money.

Religious leaders often gain a certain amount of praise from their followers. A worldly spirit feeds on such worldly praise. Some who proclaim the gospel successfully are tempted to forget what Jesus said about true greatness (Mark 10:35–45). Paul denied that he sought glory either from the Thessalonians or from others. The word translated "burdensome" means "weight." It can mean a burden or a weighty, important person. Thus Paul might have been saying that the apostles could have expected financial support, but Paul refused it from the Thessalonians. Or he could have been reminding them that the apostles could have expected praise and honor as weighty men, but chose to follow the Lord's example of humble service.

4. Gentle and self-giving (vv. 7–8)

7 But we were gentle among you, even as a nurse cherisheth her children:

8 So being affectionately desirous of you, we were willing to have imparted unto you, not the gospel of God only, but also our own souls, because ye were dear unto us.

Verses 7–8 stress the love of Paul and the others for the Thessalonians. Rather than being self-serving charlatans, they were self-giving servants. This theme is set forth in several ways. Verse 7 describes their love for the Thessalonians as being gentle, like that of a nurse or nursing mother. Some translators think the context and meaning of the word favor "nursing mother" rather than "nurse." In either case, the picture is one of gentleness, nurture, and love.

Verse 8 is filled with words of similar meaning. Paul spoke of affection for them. Because of such love, the missionaries shared the good news of God with them. However, they didn't stop with sharing the gospel; they also shared themselves because the Thessalonians were dear to them. The word "dear" is an adjective connected with the word *agape.*

5. Hardworking and morally blameless (vv. 9–10)

> 9 For ye remember, brethren, our labour and travail: for labouring night and day, because we would not be chargeable unto any of you, we preached unto you the gospel of God.

Paul refused to accept money from the people of Thessalonica. In Corinth, he followed a similar policy, which he explained in 1 Corinthians 9 (see also 2 Thess. 3:9). Paul claimed that preachers had a right to expect to be paid; however, Paul voluntarily refused pay at places where he thought accepting money could be used by his opponents to attack Paul and his message. Paul did accept money from the Philippians, some of it even when he was in Thessalonica (Phil. 4:10–19). However, Paul often worked, apparently at tentmaking (Acts 18:3), in order not to provide any grounds for criticism about money.

Paul reminded the Thessalonians of this fact in verse 9. He had worked night and day both earning his living and telling the good news of God. No one could accuse Paul of being greedy or lazy.

> 10 Ye are witnesses, and God also, how holily and justly and unblameably we behaved ourselves among you that believe:

Paul reminded his readers that the missionaries practiced what they preached. Nothing so undermines a preacher's credibility as committing the sins he condemns. Paul used three words to emphasize the godly example of the missionaries: holy, righteous, and blameless. They lived as people set apart by God and for God. They did what was right. Their lives were above reproach. No one could rightly accuse them of sinful living.

As in verse 5, Paul cited two witnesses of the truth of what he wrote. The believers in Thessalonica were witnesses, and God Himself was a witness on their behalf.

6. Fatherly exhortation to worthy living (vv. 11–12)

> 11 As ye know how we exhorted and comforted and charged every one of you, as a father doth his children,
>
> 12 That ye would walk worthy of God, who hath called you unto his kingdom and glory.

In verse 8, Paul had compared the missionaries' love to the gentle love of a mother for her children. In verse 11, he compared their love to the firm but encouraging love of a father for his children. Just as a father exhorts and encourages each of his children to live worthily of his name and upbringing, Paul exhorted the believers to walk worthily of the divine calling (see Eph. 4:1). Children of God are citizens of an eternal kingdom. We live in a world that is governed by worldly values, but we are expected to live worthily of God's kingdom.

II. Welcoming the Word of God (1 Thess. 2:13)

> 13 For this cause also thank we God without ceasing, because, when ye received the word of God which ye heard of us, ye received it not as the word of men, but as it is in truth, the word of God, which effectually worketh in you that believe.

The second word translated "received" carries the idea of welcoming the word of God. The Greek word is the usual one for the reception of a guest. Outwardly receiving the word is comparable to hearing it. Inwardly receiving it takes place when the hearer accepts and welcomes it. Paul expressed continual gratitude to God that the Thessalonians accepted the words of the missionaries as much more than the words of some traveling preachers. They welcomed the words as the word of God, which indeed it was. This same word continues its work in the lives of those who believe.

APPLYING THE BIBLE

1. The importance of encouragement. After the end of the Civil War, General Robert E. Lee was named president of Washington College in Virginia. In one of his classes there was a poor boy who worked for a farmer several miles away and walked to class each day. Lee noticed the tired look on the boy's face and knew he was working hard on the farm and staying up late at night to study. One day Lee asked the boy what he did between classes, and the boy replied that he looked for an empty classroom that was warm.

"Don't do that," said the general. "Come to my office and sit. It's warm and I am seldom there."

Lee helped the boy get a job as a schoolteacher when he graduated, and his lifelong ambition was to be as kind and encouraging to others as Lee had been to him.

Our lesson writer points out that Paul wrote the new converts at Thessalonica to encourage them in the faith. Encouragement is one thing everyone needs, and each of us can give it to others.

2. Courage needed. When a Virginia plantation owner named George Washington took command of 13,743 "rebels," they were a motley crew. They had old weapons and no training. They were farmers dressed in tattered clothing, but he molded them into the Continental Army that defended their homeland and freed America from Britain's tyranny. Washington and his army did it through sheer force of will and fierce courage.

Paul cites the courage he exerted amid strong, satanic opposition, and uses it to stir up the courage of his readers to live for Jesus where it was so costly (vv. 1–2).

3. Kindness pays off. In his book *A Dictionary of Illustrations*, James Hefley tells about a traveler from New Jersey who stopped one Sunday to attend the worship services of the Methodist Church in Andersonville, Georgia. He never forgot the kindness that was shown to a stranger. When that stranger, Robert B. Brown, died at ninety, he left his entire estate, $178,302, to the Andersonville church. Kindness always pays off!

Paul reminds the Thessalonians how kindly and gently, "even as a nurse," he had ministered to them (vv.7–8). Surely, his example was an encouragement to them to treat others in the church the same way.

4. "The world has yet to see . . ." Dwight L. Moody, the well-known evangelist of the last century, was visiting one day in England with a man named Henry Varley. In the course of their conversation, Varley said:

"Moody, the world has yet to see what God will do with a man fully consecrated to Him."

Moody later confessed to Varley that those words became the driving force in his life. Before his death, Moody preached to more than a million people in America and England; and God used him to bring thousands to Christ.

This was also the driving force in Paul's life; and, surely, he came as close to it as any person who has ever lived (vv. 9–12).

TEACHING THE BIBLE

Main Idea: Facing problems head-on is the best way to correct false accusations and charges.

Suggested Teaching Aim: To lead adults to use gentleness and self-giving—not such methods as flattery and greed—to proclaim the gospel.

A TEACHING OUTLINE

1. Use a thought question to introduce the lesson.
2. Use two readers to help you with the lesson.
3. Use a poster to identify Paul's motives and methods for proclaiming the gospel.
4. Use summarizing to apply the Scripture to life.

Introduce the Bible Study

Ask members what motives the world attributes to many of the television and radio evangelists. Ask: Why do they do that? What could be done to change this attitude?

Search for Biblical Truth

Write on a chalkboard or a large sheet of paper:

"Motives and Methods for Proclaiming the Gospel"	
Positive	Negative

IN ADVANCE, enlist a member to read aloud the Scripture passages. Also, enlist a reader to read the summary statements in the outline and summary that correspond to the appropriate Scripture. Call for 2:1–2 and the corresponding summary statements to be read.

On a map locate Thessalonica and Philippi. In a brief lecture make the following points: (1) Verses 1–12 were written to defend Paul against certain false charges; (2) briefly summarize Acts 16:12–40 and 17:5–14 to show Paul's treatment at Philippi and Thessalonica; (3) the missionaries were not defeated by such opposition; a charlatan would not have faced what Paul boldly faced; (4) the missionaries demonstrated courage in face of opposition. Under "Positive" on the poster write *Courage in face of opposition.*

Call for 2:3–6 and the corresponding summary statements to be read. Say: Apparently three charges had been made against Paul by the Jews in Thessalonica after the missionaries had been run out of town. Paul denied that his teachings had contained any of these. What were the three charges listed in verse 3? (Error, immorality, and guile.) Use "Studying the Bible" to explain the three words. Ask: Why had God allowed this persecution to happen to faithful missionaries? (To test them to see if they were worthy to be entrusted with the gospel.) Ask: What three further charges did Paul deny in verses 5–6? (Flattery, covetousness, glory.) Use "Studying the Bible" to explain these three terms. Under "Negative" on the poster write *not error, immorality, guile, flattery, greed, pride.*

Call for 2:7–10 and the corresponding summary statements to be read. Ask members to look at these verses and to identify the positive reasons Paul and the missionaries shared the gospel with the Thessalonians. (Gentle, self-giving, love, hardworking, morally blameless, holy, righteous, and blameless.) Write these under "Positive" on the poster. Ask: Who did Paul call as witnesses to the missionaries' proper motives and behavior? (The believers in Thessalonica and God Himself.)

Call for 2:11–12 and the corresponding summary statement to be read. Ask: What was the goal of Paul's preaching to the Thessalonians? (Urging them to worthy living.) Under "Positive" write *Worthy living.*

Call for 2:13 and the corresponding summary statement to be read. Ask members to look at this verse to determine how the Thessalonians received the gospel the missionaries had preached. (As word of God, not word of men.)

Give the Truth a Personal Focus

Briefly review the poster and the positive and negative reasons for proclaiming the gospel. Ask members to write a one-sentence statement that would summarize the meaning of this passage for today. Let members develop their own statement, but consider this: *When believers face opposition to the gospel, they should not use such methods as flattery and greed but gentleness and self-giving to counteract the opposition.* Close with a prayer that members will be able to put this lesson into practice this week.

Live in Love and Holiness

March
9
1997

Basic Passage: 1 Thessalonians 3:6–4:12
Focal Passage: 1 Thessalonians 3:12–4:12

Early Christian missionaries obeyed the Great Commission by teaching new converts the things Jesus had commanded (Matt. 28:18–20). The teachings stressed relationships and character. The new converts were taught how to love one another and all people. They were taught how to live as people set apart by God and for God. An example of this twofold emphasis is found in 1 Thessalonians 3:6–4:12.

Study Aim: *To state what Paul taught about expressing love and holiness*

STUDYING THE BIBLE

OUTLINE AND SUMMARY

I. Paul's Relations with the Thessalonians (1 Thess. 3:6–13)
- **1. Good news about the Thessalonians (vv. 6–10)**
- **2. Paul's prayer (vv. 11–13)**

II. Exhortations About Christian Living (1 Thess. 4:1–12)
- **1. Growth in Christian living (vv. 1–2)**
- **2. Set apart from sexual sins (vv. 3–8)**
- **3. Growth in love (vv. 9–10)**
- **4. Necessity for work (vv. 11–12)**

Paul rejoiced at the good news Timothy brought about the faith and love of the Thessalonians (3:6–10). He prayed that they might grow in love and holiness (3:11–13). He exhorted them to live according to the teachings of Jesus (4:1–2). He told them to abstain from sexual immorality because that was God's will, and he warned that committing such sins hurt people and would cause them to face God's wrath (4:3–8). Paul commended them for their love for one another and urged them to grow in such love (4:9–10). He repeated his earlier teachings to mind their own business and to do their own work (4:11–12).

I. Paul's Relations with the Thessalonians (1 Thess. 3:6–13)

1. Good news about the Thessalonians (vv. 6–10)

After leaving Thessalonica (THESS uh loh NIGH kuh), Paul was concerned about how well the church was enduring persecution (2:14). Therefore, he sent Timothy to bring him a report on the church (3:1–5). Paul rejoiced when Timothy brought good news about their faith and love (3:6). He was comforted by knowing they stood fast in the Lord (3:7–8). Paul could not thank God enough for his joy (3:9). He prayed continually that he might see them again and supply whatever was lacking in their faith (3:10).

2. Paul's prayer (vv. 11–13)

12 And the Lord make you to increase and abound in love one toward another, and toward all men, even as we do toward you:

13 To the end he may stablish your hearts unblameable in holiness before God, even our Father, at the coming of our Lord Jesus Christ with all his saints.

Paul asked God the Father and the Lord Jesus Christ to direct his way again to Thessalonica (v. 11). He also prayed that the Lord would cause them to grow in love—both to one another and to all people. Paul's prayer thus reflects the teaching of Jesus about love. Jesus stressed love for one another (John 13:34–35), but He also taught love for all people—neighbors and even enemies (Luke 10:25–37; Matt. 5:43–47).

Such abounding love would lead to inner stability with the final result that they would fulfill the purpose of being set apart by God. Several English words are translations of words from the same root word in Greek. The basic word means to be set apart by God and for God. The word "holy" describes those who have been set apart. So does the word "saints," which literally means "holy ones." "Sanctified" means "set apart." "Sanctification" is the process that results from being set apart. "Holiness" is the state resulting from being set apart. Believers are set apart at conversion and are called and empowered for a life that pleases God—one characterized by righteousness and purity.

Paul prayed that they would stand blameless before the Lord at His coming. They would stand in that holiness which was the result of God's work in their lives.

II. Exhortations About Christian Living (1 Thess. 4:1–12)

The first three chapters dealt with a review of Paul's relations with the Thessalonians. Then Paul turned to a variety of issues about Christian living and doctrine. Some of the issues are more specific than others. Some issues may have been matters of concern about the Thessalonian church that Timothy reported to Paul. Some may simply have been teachings needed by all new converts in the first-century world.

1. Growth in Christian living (vv. 1–2)

1 Furthermore then we beseech you, brethren, and exhort you by the Lord Jesus, that as ye have received of us how ye ought to walk and to please God, so ye would abound more and more.

2 For ye know what commandments we gave you by the Lord Jesus.

Verse 1 begins a new section of Paul's letter. Paul began with a general exhortation to walk or live in accordance with what they had been taught by the missionaries. These teachings in turn had come from Jesus Himself. No doubt the life and teachings of Jesus formed the crux of what the apostles taught to new converts, just as the Cross and Resurrection formed the heart of the good news they preached to unbelievers (see

1 Cor. 7:10; 15:1–4). Paul acknowledged that they were already doing this, but he urged them to do so more and more.

2. Set apart from sexual sins (vv. 3–8)

> 3 For this is the will of God, even your sanctification, that ye should abstain from fornication:

Some areas of God's will must be sought diligently, but other areas are crystal clear. One such area is God's clear will that His children be set apart by God and for God. In verse 3, Paul focused on one specific aspect of holy living. Christians are to abstain from sexual immorality. The word "fornication" includes not only adultery but also sexual relations with anyone who is not one's spouse.

Was Paul aware of some specific problem in Thessalonica, as he was at Corinth (1 Cor. 5–6)? More likely, Paul was writing because he knew that the ancient world was riddled with sexual immorality. All kinds of sexual sins were widely practiced and condoned; some were even advocated as part of some religion. Also remember that Paul was writing from Corinth, which was noted as a sexual wilderness. Paul knew that many Gentile converts came from and still lived in such an environment. He wanted believers to know what the Lord expected in this key area of life.

> 4 That every one of you should know how to possess his vessel in sanctification and honour;
>
> 5 Not in the lust of concupiscence, even as the Gentiles which know not God:

Bible scholars debate the meaning of the word "vessel." Some believe that Paul was referring to the "body"; while others think Paul meant "wife." Those who think he meant "wife" also translate "possess" as "acquire." Thus the idea would be that Christian marriage makes far higher demands on men than the pagan double standard of sexual freedom for men. God demands lifetime loyalty to one woman in the one-flesh union of marriage.

If "vessel" meant "body," Paul was saying much the same thing as in 1 Corinthians 6:12–20. One's body is not for sexual immorality but is the temple of the Holy Spirit. For some, like Paul, this means to remain single; but for most it means Christian marriage (1 Cor. 7). Such marriage is only in the Lord (1 Cor. 7:39–40). It involves a mutual respect for each other within the one-flesh union of marriage (Gen. 2:24; 1 Cor. 7:2–5; Eph. 5:22–33).

The Bible teaches and the early missionaries stressed a Christian view of sex and marriage that ran counter to pagan practice. The practice of the non-Christian Gentile world is set forth in Romans 1:21–32. Christ calls for abstinence from sex before marriage and absolute faithfulness after marriage (see Matt. 19:1–12).

> 6 That no man go beyond and defraud his brother in any matter: because that the Lord is the avenger of all such, as we also have forewarned you and testified.
>
> 7 For God hath not called us unto uncleanness, but unto holiness.

8 He therefore that despiseth, despiseth not man, but God, who hath also given unto us his holy Spirit.

Many people today do not regard sexual immorality as sinful. Paul gave two reasons why it is. For one thing, sexual sin hurts people. Paul warned that it transgressed and defrauded one's brother. He probably used "brother" here more broadly than a man whose wife has been seduced into committing adultery. Paul surely included such an evil result; but he also included the harm done to the woman, her children, and many others touched by the sin. People sometimes try to excuse their sin by saying, "I'm hurting no one but myself." This is never true of sexual sins.

The second reason why sex outside marriage is wrong is because it ultimately is a sin against God. When David confessed his great sins, he prayed, "Against thee, thee only have I sinned, and done this evil in thy sight" (Ps. 51:4). David was not discounting the terrible harm of his sin to Uriah (yoo RIGH uh), Bathsheba (bath SHEE buh), and many others; but he was aware that the worst thing was that he had sinned against God. Paul warned that those who commit such sins place themselves under the wrath of God. They may or may not taste evil consequences during life; however, after death they surely must answer to God.

3. Growth in love (vv. 9–10)

9 But as touching brotherly love ye need not that I write unto you: for ye yourselves are taught of God to love one another.

10 And indeed ye do it toward all the brethren which are in all Macedonia: but we beseech you, brethren, that ye increase more and more;

God Himself by His Spirit had impressed on the Thessalonians the importance of loving one another. Paul commended them for their faithfulness in doing this. Their love was known throughout the province of Macedonia (mass uh DOH nih uh). Paul had visited two other Macedonian cities, Philippi (FILL ih pigh) and Berea (buh REE uh; Acts 16:11—17:15). People traveled back and forth. Thus their reputation spread. Later when Paul wrote 2 Corinthians 8:1–5, he commended the churches of Macedonia for their sacrificial giving to help believers in faraway Judea.

Paul urged them to continue to grow as they expressed such love. A loving Christian fellowship ought not to be taken for granted. Dangers and temptations constantly threaten believers' love for one another.

4. Necessity for work (vv. 11–12)

11 And that ye study to be quiet, and to do your own business, and to work with your own hands, as we commanded you;

12 That ye may walk honestly toward them that are without, and that ye may have lack of nothing.

When Paul was with the Thessalonians, he taught them to mind their own business and work with their hands. He reemphasized this in verse 11. In 2 Thessalonians 3:6–13, the apostle gave even more emphasis to hard work and minding one's own business. He warned against being lazy busybodies. This seems to have been a special problem among Thessalonian believers.

Because both letters to Thessalonica deal with Paul's teachings about the Lord's coming (1 Thess. 4:13–5:11; 2 Thess. 2), some Bible students think some people there had quit their work because they expected the Lord to come right away. The Bible emphasizes that the way to be ready for the Lord's coming is to be faithfully at work for the Lord, not standing idly looking into heaven (Matt. 24:42–25:46; Acts 1:7–11).

By minding their own business and doing hard, honest work, Christians provide a good testimony before an unbelieving world as well as support themselves.

APPLYING THE BIBLE

1. Hudson Taylor's motto. Hudson Taylor (1832–1905), a pioneer missionary to China, once told a congregation that his life's motto was "Have faith in God" (Mark 11:22). Taylor said that to him the verse meant, "Reckon on God's faith to you."

Hudson Taylor's life was lived daily depending on God's faithfulness. One time, while he was ministering in China, Taylor was asked to come and pray for a man's wife who was near death. Upon arriving at the man's home, Taylor found a room full of sick, starving children. Telling the family how much God loved them, Taylor took out his last coin and gave it to the man. Later in the day, Hudson received a package with money in it for more than he had given the man.

Paul has received good news about the family of the believers at Thessalonica. In verses 6–10 he commended them for it and encouraged them to stand firm in their faith. "Have faith in God' is a good motto for us to follow today.

2. The wonder of love. After Andrew Jackson had retired from military and political life, visitors who entered his room at the Hermitage would find "Old Hickory" sitting before the fire with a Bible in one hand and a picture of his beloved Rachel in the other hand. Her epitaph, which Jackson himself wrote, is carved on her headstone at the Hermitage near Nashville, Tennessee: "Age 61 years. Her face was fair, her person pleasing, her temper amiable, her heart kind. A being so gentle and so virtuous, slander might wound her but could not dishonor. Even death, when he bore her from the arms of her husband, could but transport her to the bosom of her God."

All who read about Jackson know how much he loved his dear Rachel. Paul encouraged the Thessalonian saints to have a deep, abiding love toward each other and all others (vv. 11–13).

3. Sexual immorality. A student on the campus of a leading university responded to a reporter's question about premarital sex in this way: "Why hide it? I have sex with boys. The only difference between me and a lot of other girls on this campus is that I admit it." She is from a small, rural town. She makes good grades and attends church regularly. She dates regularly but says she has had sex with "only seven or eight boys" in her two years at the university.

This is not an isolated case. But God has something to say about sexual immorality, and Paul addresses this sin very strongly in verses 3–8. Each believer must practice the Holy Spirit's command in verse 7: "For God has not called us unto uncleanness, but unto holiness."

4. The worth of work. The great achievers of history have been diligent workers.

- Michelangelo frequently slept in his clothes in order to get back to his work without delay. Often he took a block of marble to his bedroom so that he could work on it when sleep eluded him.
- John James Audubon apologized for some trifling bit of carelessness in his famous drawing of mockingbirds being attacked by a snake. He explained the sketch was made in Louisiana where the heat was so intense he had to stop after only sixteen hours!
- Sir Walter Scott, goaded on by the determination to pay his debts and clear his good name, wrote the "Waverly" novels at the rate of one a month.
- President Ulysses S. Grant wrote his memoirs, though he was dying from cancer, in order to leave his family enough money to carry on with their lives.

Almost without exception, men and women in every walk of life have earned success by diligent, hard work. Paul addresses the worth of work in verses 11–12. Laziness is out of character for a Christian.

TEACHING THE BIBLE

- *Main Idea:* Christians should live in love and holiness.
- *Suggested Teaching Aim:* To lead adults to correct aspects of their lives so they may live in love and holiness.

A TEACHING OUTLINE

1. Use articles you have clipped from newspapers and magazines to create interest.
2. Use a poster you have made to explain "set apart."
3. Use a lesson poster to guide the Bible study.
4. Issue a challenge to members to live holy and pure lives.

Introduce the Bible Study

Cut articles from newspapers and magazines that relate to sexual sins (for example: rape, child abuse, abortion) and place them on a chalkboard or a large sheet of paper. Mount these on a focal wall. **IN ADVANCE,** copy the "Main Idea" on a strip of paper. After mentioning some of the articles, place the strip of paper across the articles and point out that God demands that believers live in love and holiness.

Search for Biblical Truth

On a large map locate Thessalonica. Locate Corinth and indicate that this is where Paul was when he wrote the Thessalonians. Ask members to open their Bibles to 3:11–13 and answer the following questions: What was Paul's attitude toward the Thessalonians? (Loved them—v. 12.) What did Paul want God to do for them? (Make them blameless and holy—v. 13.)

Point out the following you have prepared **IN ADVANCE** and ask members to look for these words as they study. Point out that these words apply to all believers.

Set Apart		
Holy	=	those who have been set apart
Saints	=	holy ones
Sanctified	=	process that results from being set apart
Holiness	=	state resulting from being set apart

On a chalkboard or a large sheet of paper make a poster by writing *How to live.* Under it write, *1. Growth in Christian living.* Ask members to read silently 4:1–2. Ask: What instructions do you think Paul had given the Thessalonians when he first preached to them? (Probably the life and teachings of Jesus.) How well were the Thessalonians living up to these teachings? (Well, but Paul encouraged them to continue onward and upward.)

Write, *2. Set apart from sexual sins* on the poster. Ask: What is God's will for believers in the sexual area? Why was this so important in the first century? Is it any less important today?

Use "Studying the Bible" to explain the possible meanings of "vessel" (4:4). Ask members to read this verse in different translations of the Bible.

DISCUSS: How do you react to this statement: Those who have sex outside of marriage are only hurting themselves.

Write, *3. Growth in love* on the poster. Ask: How well were the Thessalonians doing in this area? (Well; the whole province knew of their love for other believers.) How did they show this love? (Likely through gifts for the poor.)

Write, *4. Necessity for work* on the poster. Ask members to read silently 4:11–12. Using "Studying the Bible," explain why Paul likely included this statement on the need to work.

Give the Truth a Personal Focus

Ask: What does it mean to you to live in love and holiness? Briefly review Paul's four statements on the poster. Ask members to suggest other areas they feel should be included in holiness and love. Ask: What aspects of your life do you need to correct so you may live in love and holiness? Do you need to change some aspects of your life drastically? Do you need to continue in the way you are going? Close in prayer for strength for your members to live in holiness and love.

March
16
1997

Pray for Others!

Basic Passage: 2 Thessalonians 1:1–12
Focal Passage: 2 Thessalonians 1:1–12

Many of Paul's letters mention prayers for his readers. For example, 1 Thessalonians 3:11–13 describes Paul's prayer for the church at Thessalonica (THESS uh loh NIGH kuh). Near the end of the same letter, he wrote, "Brethren, pray for us" (1 Thess. 5:25). In a similar spirit, Paul began 2 Thessalonians with thanks for his readers and a prayer for them.

Study Aim: *To describe Paul's prayer of thanksgiving and intercession for the Thessalonians*

STUDYING THE BIBLE

OUTLINE AND SUMMARY

I. Greeting (2 Thess. 1:1–2)

II. Thanksgiving and Prayer (2 Thess. 1:3–12)

1. Thanksgiving for the Thessalonians (vv. 3–4)

2. The righteous judgment of God (vv. 5–10)

3. Prayer for the Thessalonians (vv. 11–12)

Paul sent greetings to the church at Thessalonica (vv. 1–2). He was fully justified in thanking God for their growing love and faith in the face of persecution (vv. 3–4). The evidence of God's righteous judgment was twofold: the preparation of God's people for the coming kingdom and the justice meted out to unbelievers when Christ comes (vv. 5–10). Paul prayed that God would fulfill His calling in His people and hasten the time when Christ would be glorified in and with His people (vv. 11–12).

I. Greeting (2 Thess. 1:1–2)

1 Paul, and Silvanus [sihl VAY nuhs], and Timotheus [tih MOH thih uhs], unto the church of the Thessalonians in God our Father and the Lord Jesus Christ:

2 Grace unto you, and peace, from God our Father and the Lord Jesus Christ.

Ancient letters began with the writer's name. This is one of the thirteen New Testament letters that begins with the name "Paul." In his two letters to Thessalonica, Paul included his two fellow missionaries in the greeting. Paul was clearly the writer, but all three shared in greetings, prayers, and concern for the church. Silas ("Silvanus" was another form of the same name) and Timothy (or "Timotheus") had been with Paul on his visit to Thessalonica (Acts 17:14), and Paul sent Timothy back on a special mission (1 Thess. 3:2, 6).

The church's geographic location was in Thessalonica, but its spiritual state was "in God our Father and the Lord Jesus Christ." Paul, who shared the same spiritual state, sent the twofold greeting of grace and peace. This greeting is found in most of Paul's letters. It uses the typical

Jewish greeting of "peace." Instead of the usual Greek greeting "hail" (*charein*), Paul used the word "grace" (*charis).*

Second Thessalonians was written only a few months after 1 Thessalonians. Paul probably had received some information about how the church was faring. His second letter focused on three issues: persecution (2 Thess. 1), the second coming (2 Thess. 2), and work (2 Thess. 3). He had written about these three subjects in his first letter, but Paul felt that the church needed continued help in these areas.

II. Thanksgiving and Prayer (2 Thess. 1:3–12)

1. Thanksgiving for the Thessalonians (vv. 3–4)

3 We are bound to thank God always for you, brethren, as it is meet, because that your faith groweth exceedingly, and the charity of every one of you all toward each other aboundeth;

4 So that we ourselves glory in you in the churches of God for your patience and faith in all your persecutions and tribulations that ye endure:

Most of Paul's letters begin with a word of gratitude for his readers. Paul thanked God for their growth in faith and in love for one another. In his first letter, Paul had expressed the desire to help perfect what was lacking in their faith (3:10); and he prayed that their love for one another might grow (3:12). Verse 3 of the second letter shows that Paul's desire and prayer had been answered. Their faith had grown exceedingly, and their love for one another abounded.

The words "bound" and "meet" indicate that Paul felt that such thanks for them were fully justified. Paul had commended them for their faith, love, and hope in 1 Thessalonians 1:3. Perhaps some of them had said that Paul had overstated their virtues. Second Thessalonians 1:3 may have been Paul's way of replying that such thanks were not only justified but also needed. (Although he did not mention the word "hope," he wrote of their steadfastness in v. 4.)

Paul said that he praised the Thessalonians as he went to other churches. He praised them specifically for their perseverance and trust amid persecution and afflictions. During Paul's visit, enemies in the synagogue had run him out of town and even pursued him to a neighboring town (Acts 17:1–13). In his first letter, Paul wrote of persecution of the Thessalonians from fellow countrymen (1 Thess. 2:14). The Thessalonian believers had persevered through such times because of their faith in God.

The word "patience" referred not to passive waiting but active perseverance and endurance of trouble. The word "faith" referred here to the trust in God that sustains believers during times of trouble. Although times of trouble tempt believers to doubt that God knows and cares, faith keeps us in touch with God's goodness and power.

2. The righteous judgment of God (vv. 5–10)

5 Which is a manifest token of the righteous judgment of God, that ye may be counted worthy of the kingdom of God, for which ye also suffer:

> 6 Seeing it is a righteous thing with God to recompense tribulation to them that trouble you;

In times of persecution, believers sometimes doubt that God is just. God's people suffer while their persecutors prosper. Paul cited two evidences of the righteous judgment of God: (1) God would use their faith amid suffering to prepare His people for the coming kingdom. (2) God would mete out justice to those who persecute others.

The New Testament teaches that perseverance through troubles can enable believers to grow in faith, love, and hope (see Matt. 5:10–12; Rom. 5:3–5; 1 Pet. 1:6–8; James 1:2–3). This teaching lies back of verses 4–5. The persecuted believers needed to take the long look. At the time, all they could see were the power and brutality of their persecutors. But Christian hope promised that their perseverance was helping prepare them to be counted worthy of the kingdom of God.

To be counted worthy of the kingdom does not imply that they would earn their entrance into God's kingdom. When we believe, God's grace counts us worthy although we are unworthy. But His grace continues to work in us to show how God can prepare His people for His coming kingdom.

God's righteousness will also be shown in how He renders righteous judgment on those who have persecuted His people. In a world filled with injustice, many people echo the sentiment in the popular saying, "There ain't no justice." However, a just God rules this universe. In the end, accounts will be set right. Justice will finally prevail.

> 7 And to you who are troubled rest with us, when the Lord Jesus shall be revealed from heaven with his mighty angels,

"Rest" is one of the Bible words to describe the future state of the blessed (see Heb. 4:9). Just as God promised to lead Israel into a land of rest, so He promises a place of eternal rest for His people. Revelation 21:4 promises a new heaven and new earth in which there will be no more pain, sorrow, and death. Revelation 14:13 describes those in Christ as resting from their labors.

The future coming of Christ was a key theme in both letters to Thessalonica (1 Thess. 4:13–5:11; 2 Thess. 2). Verse 7 refers to Christ's coming as a revelation. Christians have already responded to God's revelation through faith. At His future coming, Christ will be revealed so that all can see Him.

> 8 In flaming fire taking vengeance on them that know not God, and that obey not the gospel of our Lord Jesus Christ:
>
> 9 Who shall be punished with everlasting destruction from the presence of the Lord, and from the glory of his power;

When Christ is revealed at His coming, He will be revealed in judgment on those who have rejected the good news. The word "vengeance" has none of the vindictiveness associated with human revenge. It is a compound word based on the same root as the word "righteous" in verses 5 and 6. God's judgment will be the application of unwavering justice by the Judge of the universe.

Those judged will be those who know not God and disobey the gospel of Christ. Both descriptions refer to people who have had opportunities to know God or to respond to the gospel, but they have chosen not to know God or to obey the message of Christ. God's wrath abides on those who could have known God but deliberately rejected Him (Rom. 1:18–32).

Their fate will be eternal separation from God's presence and glory. They will reap what they have sown. They rejected God. They thus chose a destiny deprived of the presence of God.

> 10 When he shall come to be glorified in his saints, and to be admired in all them that believe (because our testimony among you was believed) in that day.

Verse 10, like verses 5–6a, focuses on the positive aspects of the Lord's coming. Christ will be glorified not only by His saints but in His saints. That is, the saving and transforming work of Christ shall be evident in the lives of the redeemed people of God. The redeemed will join the heavenly chorus in glorifying the Redeemer (see Rev. 5). Paul reminded the Thessalonians that this salvation began for them when they believed the testimonies of the missionaries.

3. Prayer for the Thessalonians (vv. 11–12)

> 11 Wherefore also we pray always for you, that our God would count you worthy of this calling, and fulfil all the good pleasure of his goodness, and the work of faith with power:
>
> 12 That the name of our Lord Jesus Christ may be glorified in you, and ye in him, according to the grace of our God and the Lord Jesus Christ.

Paul prayed that what he had just described would come to pass. He was looking toward the coming of Christ and was praying that the Thessalonians might arrive at the point unto which God was leading them. As noted in comments on verse 5, being counted worthy of the kingdom does not imply that they were to earn entrance into the kingdom. It referred to the completion of God's work of grace in them, which would be revealed at the Lord's future coming.

God places within believers a desire for goodness and for faithful service. Paul prayed that God would fulfill these God-given impulses in the Thessalonians.

Verse 12 links with verse 10. Verse 10 predicted the future glorification of Christ in His people. Verse 12 prayed for that day to come. When Christ is glorified, so will His people be glorified in Him. Back of it all is the grace of God and the Lord Jesus Christ. All praise to Him!

APPLYING THE BIBLE

1. Grace is free. Then-colonel Theodore Roosevelt wanted to buy some delicacies for wounded troops in Cuba during the Spanish American War. He approached Clara Barton, founder of the Red Cross. When his offer was refused, he was troubled and asked what he might do to get the food he wanted. "Just ask for it," Roosevelt was told. "Oh," Roosevelt said, breaking into a big smile. "Then I do ask for it."

God's grace is free to each of us. Although it cost Him everything, even His only begotten Son, it is free to us for the taking.

Paul's greeting to the Thessalonian saints is that they might have "grace and peace" (v. 2). God has nothing better to give.

2. Thanksgiving for others. Here is a good spiritual exercise in which to engage: One day recently when I was reading my Bible and praying, I tried to remember the names of people who had made a significant contribution to my Christian life and thank God for them. I began with my parents who, early in my life, put beneath me a strong Christian foundation. I then thanked God for the Sunday School teachers who had first taught me the Scriptures. I then moved on to thank God for college professors, seminary professors, and people I served as pastor who impacted my life for good. I was amazed at how many have contributed to my life in Christ.

In verses 3–4, Paul gave thanks to God for the Thessalonian believers whom he clearly loved. He thanked God for their steadfast, growing faith and their abounding love for each other. Indeed, "It is a good thing to give thanks unto the Lord" (Ps. 92:1).

3. Which? According to one story, the theologian Augustine (A.D. 354–430) was annoyed by his neighbor. "O Lord," he prayed, "take away this wicked person." And God answered, "Which?" (Augustine or the neighbor!)

The Thessalonian Christians were suffering for their faith, and Paul wrote to comfort them (v. 5), assuring them that the day will come when the scales will be balanced. Our lesson writer says, "Paul cited two evidences of the righteous judgment of God: (1) God would use their faith amid suffering to prepare His people for the coming kingdom; and (2) God would mete out justice to those who persecute others."

God knows which will be rewarded and which will be punished. The Judgment Day will reveal the *which.*

4. Talk to the Shepherd. An elderly woman who had seen a great deal of trouble, but never complained, was much beloved in her community. One day as her pastor was visiting in her home, he asked, "Do you have any trouble sleeping?"

"Not much," answered the aged saint. "When I can't sleep I don't count sheep. I talk to the Shepherd!" Good advice.

Paul talks to the Great Shepherd about His sheep in Thessalonica. He prays that they will live in such a manner that Jesus will be glorified (vv. 11–12).

TEACHING THE BIBLE

- *Main Idea:* Christians should pray for others who are experiencing tragedy in their lives.
- *Suggested Teaching Aim:* To lead adults to commit to pray for someone who is experiencing tragedy.

A TEACHING OUTLINE

1. Use thought questions to relate to members' lives.
2. Use a lesson outline poster to guide the Bible study.
3. Use a commitment card to encourage members to pray for someone experiencing tragedy.

Introduce the Bible Study

Read the following statements: "Why did God allow this to happen?" "All suffering is the result of sin." "Why do evil people prosper when good people suffer?" Ask members to share their reactions to these questions. Point out that the lesson seeks to answer some of the questions we have about suffering and to encourage us to pray for those suffering.

Search for Biblical Truth

Ask a volunteer to read aloud 2 Thessalonians 1:1. Ask members to identify (1) who wrote the letter (Paul, Silas and Timothy), (2) to whom it was written (Thessalonian church), and (3) where the church was located (in Thessalonica geographically but in God spiritually). Ask all members to turn to 1 Thessalonians 1:1. Ask a member to read aloud 2 Thessalonians 1:1 as members look at 1 Thessalonians. Ask: What is the difference in the first part of the verse? (No difference.)

On a chalkboard or a large sheet of paper make a lesson outline poster by writing, *Thanksgiving and Prayer.* Under the heading write, *1. Thanksgiving for the Thessalonians.* Ask a volunteer to read 1:3–4. Ask: For what did Paul express gratitude to the Thessalonians? (Growth in faith and love for one another.) Use "Studying the Bible" to explain Paul's use of "patience" and "faith" (v. 4).

On the poster write, *2. The righteous judgment of God.* Ask a volunteer to read verses 5–10. Using "Studying the Bible," present a brief lecture in which you cover the following points: (1) the two evidences Paul cited of God's righteous judgment; (2) the New Testament teaching that perseverance through troubles can enable believers to grow in faith, love, and hope; (3) what "counted worthy" (v. 5) means and does not mean; (4) what God's promise of rest (v. 7) means to believers; (5) the meaning of "vengeance" (v. 9); (6) how Christ will be glorified (v. 10).

On the poster write, *3. Prayer for the Thessalonians.* Ask a volunteer to read aloud verses 11–12. Say: "Wherefore" (v. 11) can be interpreted, "With all this in mind"—referring to verses 5–10. Paul prayed that what he had just described would come to pass.

DISCUSS: What can we do to be counted worthy of God's calling? How does our praying for others help them in time of trouble? What should be the purpose of our praying?

Give the Truth a Personal Focus

Ask: How do you feel when Christians suffer and evil people prosper? Why does God allow this to happen? What can we do to help people to whom it is happening?

Suggest that one action they can take is to support these people in prayer. Distribute a small piece of paper to all members and ask them to write the name of a person they know who is experiencing tragedy. Then ask them to write below the name, "I will pray for daily this week" and to sign their name. Challenge members to take seriously this commitment to prayer. At the end of the week, suggest that they drop the person a note to share their prayer support. Close in prayer for both them and the people for whom they will be praying.

Do What Is Right!

Basic Passage: 2 Thessalonians 3:1–18

Focal Passage: 2 Thessalonians 3:1–16

The final part of most of Paul's letters contains challenge and encouragement about various aspects of Christian living. Second Thessalonians 3 is such a section. The heart of the chapter deals with the sin of idleness and the need for work.

Study Aim: *To compare what Paul said to do with what he said not to do*

STUDYING THE BIBLE

Outline and Summary

I. Words About Prayer (2 Thess. 3:1–5)
- **1. A personal request for prayer (vv. 1–2)**
- **2. Confidence and prayer (vv. 3–5)**

II. Words About Work (2 Thess. 3:6–15)
- **1. Follow Paul's example and teaching (vv. 6–10)**
- **2. Avoid being idle busybodies (vv. 11–12)**
- **3. Keep doing right (v. 13)**
- **4. Discipline disobedient brothers (vv. 14–15)**

III. Concluding Words (2 Thess. 3:16–18)

Paul asked the Thessalonians to pray for the swift advance of the word of God (vv. 1–2). He expressed confidence in his readers based on the faithfulness of the Lord, and he prayed that they would grow in God's love and Christ's endurance (vv. 3–5). He reminded them of his example and teaching concerning work (vv. 6–10). He commanded idle busybodies to settle down and earn their own living (vv. 11–12). Paul encouraged all not to be weary in doing good (v. 13). He told the church to discipline any member who disobeyed Paul's letter (vv. 14–15). Paul closed with a benediction of peace and grace (vv. 16–18).

I. Words About Prayer (2 Thess. 3:1–5)

1. A personal request for prayer (vv. 1–2)

1 Finally, brethren, pray for us, that the word of the Lord may have free course, and be glorified, even as it is with you:

2 And that we may be delivered from unreasonable and wicked men: for all men have not faith.

Paul made two specific requests for prayer. His primary concern was for the advance of the good news; therefore, he asked them to pray that the word of the Lord might spread rapidly and be glorified. The word translated "have free course" means "run." Paul sometimes used it in comparing the Christian life to a race (1 Cor. 9:24, 26). Psalm 147:15 says, "His word runneth very swiftly." Paul asked them to pray that God's word would swiftly advance like a runner in a race. Paul was not thinking of one spurt of growth but of continued rapid advance for God's word.

The apostle also asked that they pray for his deliverance from perverse and wicked men. On the surface, verse 2 may appear to be a selfish request; however, Paul was concerned for his deliverance in order that he might do his part in the continued advance of the word of God.

2. Confidence and prayer (vv. 3–5)

> 3 But the Lord is faithful, who shall stablish you, and keep you from evil.
>
> 4 And we have confidence in the Lord touching you, that ye both do and will do the things which we command you.
>
> 5 And the Lord direct your hearts into the love of God, and into the patient waiting for Christ.

In verses 3–5, Paul expressed his confidence in the Lord and in the Thessalonians; then he prayed for the believers.

In the original language, the final word in verse 2 is "faith" *(pistis)*, and the first word in verse 3 is "faithful" *(pistos)*. Paul contrasted unbelievers' lack of faith with the faithfulness of the Lord. Because the Lord is faithful, Paul trusted Him to provide a solid foundation for the faith and life of the Thessalonians. Paul was also confident that the Lord would keep them from evil and the evil one. Paul may have been thinking of Matthew 6:10, which uses the same words. Since both verses use "the" with "evil," Jesus and Paul probably meant not just evil in general but the evil one who is the source of evil.

Paul's confidence in the Lord gave him confidence about God's people. Thus Paul expressed confidence that the Thessalonians were doing and would continue to do what Paul had commanded. Paul probably had in mind the subject he dealt with in verses 6–15, but it also included other things. Thus before Paul rebuked some of them for their sins, he expressed confidence that with the Lord's help, they would obey what they had been taught.

Paul prayed that the Lord would provide an open path for their hearts into the love of God and the perseverance of Christ. They would be strengthened by a growing assurance of God's love for them. They would be challenged by the example of the One who steadfastly endured so much for others (compare Heb. 12:1–4).

II. Words About Work (2 Thess. 3:6–15)

1. Follow Paul's example and teaching (vv. 6–10)

> 6 Now we command you, brethren, in the name of our Lord Jesus Christ, that ye withdraw yourselves from every brother that walketh disorderly, and not after the tradition which he received of us.

Verse 6 introduces the central issue in 2 Thessalonians 3. Apparently the problem he addressed in his first letter had become more serious (1 Thess. 4:11–12). The key word "disorderly" occurs several times in one form or another throughout Paul's discussion (vv. 7, 11; see also 1 Thess. 5:14). Originally the word meant soldiers who broke ranks and thus created disorder. In Paul's day, the word was used of an apprentice who avoided doing assigned work. Later verses confirm that deliberate idleness was the problem Paul had in mind.

He commanded other Christians to avoid close fellowship with a brother guilty of this sin. The word "withdraw" meant to "shorten sail," thus to sail around or give a wide berth to such people. Paul elaborated on this in verses 14–15.

> 7 For yourselves know how ye ought to follow us: for we behaved not ourselves disorderly among you;
>
> 8 Neither did we eat any man's bread for nought; but wrought with labour and travail night and day, that we might not be chargeable to any of you:
>
> 9 Not because we have not power, but to make ourselves an ensample unto you to follow us.

Paul reminded his readers how he, Silas, and Timothy had behaved when they were in Thessalonica. Although they had the right to expect financial support from the church, they had not accepted such support (compare 1 Cor. 9:1–18). Instead they had worked night and day to earn their own living and to preach the gospel. In 1 Thessalonians 2:9, Paul used similar words in refuting the perception that the missionaries were preaching for money. Paul's point in 2 Thessalonians 3:7–9 is that the hard work of the missionaries set an example for the church to follow.

> 10 For even when we were with you, this we commanded you, that if any would not work, neither should he eat.

When Paul was in Thessalonica, he not only set an example by earning his own living; but he also taught the dignity and necessity of work. The Greeks had a low opinion of work, especially manual labor. Paul shared the biblical view of work as a gift and trust from God.

Part of God's original plan for Adam was to tend the garden of Eden (Gen. 2:15). Part of sin's curse is that it changed fulfilling work into grinding toil (Gen. 3:17–19). The Bible's emphasis on honest work shows that people of faith are expected to seek to fulfill God's original purpose. The Book of Proverbs condemns laziness and commends work (Prov. 6:6–11; 18:9). Jesus said, "My Father worketh hitherto, and I work" (John 5:17). Paul's words in 2 Thessalonians 3:10 contain one of the key Bible commands about work.

One word of caution is in order. Paul did not intend to overlook legitimate needs for help from those who were able to work. In fact, Ephesians 4:28 is probably Paul's most complete statement about work: "Let him that stole steal no more: but rather let him labour, working with his hands the thing that is good, that he may have to give to him that needeth." Christians are not to engage in any form of dishonesty or theft. Instead they are to work with their hands to produce what is good. This work is not only to provide support for themselves but also to provide money with which to help the needy.

Paul was writing about those who deliberately avoided opportunities for work. Such people shouldn't expect to be cared for by the hardworking members of the fellowship.

3. Avoid being idle busybodies (vv. 11–12)

> 11 For we hear that there are some which walk among you disorderly, working not at all, but are busybodies.

Paul had heard that some believers had quit their jobs and were thus causing a problem in the fellowship. These idlers were probably the same group mentioned in 2 Thessalonians 2:1–2. Some church members were unsettled and alarmed at the teaching that the coming of Christ was at hand. The problem of 2 Thessalonians 3:11 probably grew out of such confusion about the second coming. Paul taught that the Lord was coming and that Christians should live in light of that hope (1 Thess. 4:13–5:11; Phil. 3:21; 4:5). He followed Jesus in teaching that we don't know when the Lord is coming and that the way to be ready is to continue to be faithful in service (Matt. 24:36–25:46).

Throughout history, some groups have quit their jobs in expectation of the Lord's immediate coming. This was probably what was going on in Thessalonica. We cannot know for sure their excuses for not working; we do know that they were not working and that they had become busybodies. In Greek, the two words are from the same root. Thus Paul said that they were "not busy, but busybodies." Not only were they a financial burden for the church but they also created confusion and discord. They may have been spreading false ideas about the second coming, or they may have simply become people whose idleness led to gossiping and butting into the lives of others.

> 12 Now them that are such we command and exhort by our Lord Jesus Christ, that with quietness they work, and eat their own bread.

Paul expected his letter to be read to the congregation. Thus he wrote directly to the idle busybodies. He commanded and exhorted them in the Lord's name. They were to settle down and do their own work. In this way, they were to earn their own living. This seems to be the meaning of the words "eat their own bread."

3. Keep doing good (v. 13)

> 13 But ye, brethren, be not weary in well-doing.

Verse 13 was addressed to the members of the church who were already working hard. Paul knew that they might be tempted to grow frustrated and slack off in their own faithfulness. This is a constant temptation to those in any church who constantly bear the burdens of others. Paul wrote a similar encouragement in Galatians 5:9. His words follow the command about fulfilling one's own job and bearing one another's burdens (Gal. 5:2, 5).

4. Discipline disobedient brothers (vv. 14–15)

> 14 And if any man obey not our word by this epistle, note that man, and have no company with him, that he may be ashamed.
>
> 15 Yet count him not as an enemy, but admonish him as a brother.

Paul instructed the church to discipline any member who disobeyed what the apostle commanded. Exactly what he meant is not clear, but Paul told them not to associate with such a one. Paul was careful to remind them that the member was still a brother in Christ and that the purpose of discipline was to make the disobedient brother ashamed. Such shame hopefully would lead him to repent and obey the Lord's word.

III. Concluding Words (2 Thess. 3:16–18)

16 Now the Lord of peace himself give you peace always by all means. The Lord be with you all.

Paul authenticated the letter by writing the closing words with his own hand (v. 15; Rom. 16:22 shows that Paul ordinarily dictated and someone else penned the words). As Paul began with a greeting of grace and peace (2 Thess. 1:2), he closed with a benediction of grace and peace (vv. 16,18). The source of all true grace and peace is the Lord Himself. Thus Paul prayed that the Lord would be with them.

APPLYING THE BIBLE

1. "On your knees, man!" George Adam Smith (1856–1942), English minister and theologian, tells of climbing the 14,804 foot Weisshorn mountain of Switzerland. When he was near the summit, he started in his enthusiasm to stand up to view the majestic scenery below. His guide seized him, pulled him down, and shouted above the roar of the wind, "On your knees, man! In a place like this, you must stay on your knees!"

What a word for the church today. The church must be a praying church in order to have victory in its work for the kingdom of God.

In verses 1–5, Paul pleads for the prayers of the church to strengthen him and expresses his confidence that their prayers will assure victory in their ministry for Jesus.

2. Our best work. Bertel Thorvaldsen (1770–1844) was Denmark's greatest sculptor. On one occasion he was asked, "Which is your greatest statue?" Promptly he replied, "My next one!"

Any work we do with our hands or our minds, from cleaning house to running a great corporation, ought to be work done for God's glory. Remembering that our hands and minds are the hands and mind of Christ ministering to our hurting world, our work ought to be done to the best of our ability. In verses 6–10, Paul encourages the Thessalonian saints to stay busy with their work for God's glory.

3. Busybodies. American writer Washington Irving, some of whose stories contained such personalities as Rip Van Winkle and Ichabod Crane, said that a sharp tongue is the only tool whose edge grows small with constant use. English pastor Charles H. Spurgeon lamented that some people's tongues are sharper than their teeth. Each of us knows that many a blunt word has a sharp edge!

When Colonel Risner was a prisoner during the Vietnam War, he gargled with lye water, hoping that it would so sear his vocal chords that he would be unable to broadcast propaganda when forced to by the enemy.

Paul warns the Thessalonians not to be busybodies. Apparently some members of that church were not content with being miserable; they wanted to make everybody else miserable by spreading gossip that hurt their fellow believers. Paul tells them to stop it (v. 11).

If we will occupy ourselves with the tasks God has assigned to us, we won't have time to "nose in" on the business of others.

4. The worth of work. Paul has a good bit to say in his epistles about the worth of work. There is a godlike quality about honest work. As God worked in creation, so we are to dedicate ourselves to honorable work.

One such person who magnified the worth of work was John Milton (1608–1674). This English author distinguished himself at Cambridge as a scholar. He had a full life serving others in public service. But consider him in his later years. He had grown old. Pain and ill health were his constant companions. Imagine his hands, knotted and gnarled by arthritis. He suffered the torture of gout. In addition, he was blind. What was he to do? Give up? No, in his blindness and beset by other afflictions, he produced *Paradise Lost* and *Paradise Regained* as well as other noted works of literature.

Paul tells the saints at Thessalonica to give themselves to their work. He commands the idle busybodies in the church to work with quietness "and eat their own bread."

TEACHING THE BIBLE

- *Main Idea:* True believers will pray and work so that neither aspect is neglected.
- *Suggested Teaching Aim:* To lead members to identify aspects of their prayer and work life that need to be improved.

A TEACHING OUTLINE

1. Use a thought question to introduce the Bible study.

2. Use a lesson outline poster to guide the Bible study.

3. Use questions-answers and group discussion to explain the Scripture.

4. Use thought question and listing to give the truth a personal focus.

Introduce the Bible Study

On a chalkboard or a large sheet of paper, **IN ADVANCE** write: "Who do you know who is so heavenly minded that he or she is of no earthly use?" Without letting them name names, ask: How do you feel about persons like this? Are they beneficial to the kingdom of God? Say, Paul addressed a similar problem in Thessalonica.

Search for Biblical Truth

Ask members to open their Bibles to 2 Thessalonians 3:1. **IN ADVANCE,** prepare the following strip posters or write the statements on a chalkboard or a large sheet of paper:

Do What Is Right

I. Words About Prayer (2 Thess. 3:1–5)

II. Words About Work (2 Thess. 3:6–15)

Place the title and the first point on the focal wall before the class. Ask a volunteer to read 2 Thessalonians 3:1–5. Use the following questions to guide the study. Ask: What were Paul's two specific requests for prayer in 3:1–2? (That the word of the Lord might spread swiftly; that Paul might be delivered from wicked people.) How did Paul contrast wicked men in verse 2b and the Lord in verse 3a? (Wicked do not have faith; the Lord is faithful.) What was Paul's attitude toward the Thessalonians' response to his instructions? (Believed they would fulfill them.)

Place the second poster strip on the wall beneath the first outline point. Ask a volunteer to read 3:6–15. Use "Studying the Bible" to explain "walketh disorderly" and how Paul suggested that the Thessalonians respond to those who would not work. Suggest that apparently some of the people were so wrapped up in anticipating Christ's second coming that they had quit their jobs and were having to be supported by the rest of the church. Ask members to search these verses and find Paul's statement concerning how they were to treat these people. (Verse 10b.)

Say: Apparently the Thessalonians had moved from not working to sitting around gossiping. Use "Studying the Bible" to show the relation between "busy" and "busybodies."

DISCUSS: What right do people who want to be religious have to expect others to support them? Does this mean that churches should not support church staffs?

Ask: What did Paul say we are to do to those who are acting "disorderly"? (Discipline them.) How are we to treat such people? (As friends.)

DISCUSS: Is church discipline outdated? Should churches practice it today? Under what circumstances?

Give the Truth a Personal Focus

Ask: What should be the balance between spending time in religious activities and working to earn a living? How can we tell when one area is interfering with the other? Which is worse, to be so heavenly minded that we are of no earthly use or to be so earthly minded that we are of no heavenly use?

Distribute paper and pencils to members and ask them to list areas of their work or prayer life that need to be improved. Point out that an imbalance in either area is not in keeping with God's plan for His people. Encourage members to bring the two areas into balance.

The Resurrection Hope

Basic Passages: Matthew 28:1–10; 1 Thessalonians 4:13–18
Focal Passages: Matthew 28:1–10; 1 Thessalonians 4:13–18

The Christian hope of victory over death is based on the death and resurrection of Christ. This study combines two passages: one focuses on the resurrection of the Lord, and the other points to the future resurrection of believers.

➧**Study Aim:** *To testify to the Christian hope of victory over death based on the resurrection of Christ*

STUDYING THE BIBLE

OUTLINE AND SUMMARY

I. The Resurrection of Christ (Matt. 28:1–10)
1. **The empty tomb (vv. 1–4)**
2. **The angel's message (vv. 5–7)**
3. **The risen Lord (vv. 8–10)**

II. The Resurrection of Believers (1 Thess. 4:13–18)
1. **The basis for Christian hope (vv. 13–14)**
2. **Hope for living and dead believers (vv. 15–17)**
3. **Comfort one another (v. 18)**

An angel rolled away the stone from the tomb (Matt. 28:1–4). The angel told the women that Jesus had been raised from the dead (Matt. 28:5–7). Jesus Himself appeared to the women (Matt. 28:8–10). The death and resurrection of Jesus provide the basis for confident hope of victory over death (1 Thess. 4:13–14). When Christ comes, the dead in Christ will rise and be gathered up together with living believers to meet the Lord (1 Thess. 4:15–17). Christians should comfort one another with these words (1 Thess. 4:18).

I. The Resurrection of Christ (Matt. 28:1–10)

1. The empty tomb (vv. 1–4)

1 In the end of the sabbath, as it began to dawn toward the first day of the week, came Mary Magdalene [MAG duh lene] and the other Mary to see the sepulchre.

2 And, behold, there was a great earthquake: for the angel of the Lord descended from heaven, and came and rolled back the stone from the door, and sat upon it.

3 His countenance was like lightning, and his raiment white as snow:

4 And for fear of him the keepers did shake, and became as dead men.

Mary Magdalene and another Mary came to the tomb of Jesus about dawn on the first day of the week. Mark 16:1 identifies the other Mary as "the mother of James" and says they came to anoint the body of Jesus.

After Jesus was buried, these two women had been there when a great stone was rolled across the door (Matt. 27:60–61).

Verse 2 describes a great earthquake and the angel of the Lord coming from heaven, rolling away the stone, and sitting on it. These were signs that God had raised Jesus from the dead.

The enemies of Jesus had stationed guards at the tomb to keep anyone from stealing the body (Matt. 27:62–66). When the events of Sunday morning took place, the guards were terrified and fell to the ground as if they were dead.

2. The angel's message (vv. 5–7)

> 5 And the angel answered and said unto the women, Fear not ye: for I know that ye seek Jesus, which was crucified.
>
> 6 He is not here: for he is risen, as he said. Come, see the place where the Lord lay.
>
> 7 And go quickly, and tell his disciples that he is risen from the dead; and, behold, he goeth before you into Galilee [GAL ih lee]; there shall ye see him: lo, I have told you.

The angel spoke to the women, telling them not to be afraid. Then he made the joyful announcement that Jesus was no longer in the tomb because He had been raised from the dead. The angel reminded them that Jesus had predicted His resurrection. As confirmation of his message, the angel told the women to look into the tomb. As someone has observed, the stone was not rolled away to let Jesus out but to let in those who came to the tomb.

Then the angel told them to go quickly to the disciples and tell them that Jesus had been raised from the dead. The women also were to tell the disciples that the Lord Himself was going before them into Galilee, where they would see Him for themselves. The disciples were to be reminded that all of this was just as Jesus had earlier predicted (see Matt. 26:32).

3. The risen Lord (vv. 8–10)

> 8 And they departed quickly from the sepulchre with fear and great joy; and did run to bring his disciples word.
>
> 9 And as they went to tell his disciples, behold, Jesus met them, saying, All hail. And they came and held him by the feet, and worshipped him.
>
> 10 Then said Jesus unto them, Be not afraid: go tell my brethren that they go into Galilee, and there shall they see me.

The women obeyed the angel and ran quickly to spread the word. Because of what they had seen and heard, the women felt a mixture of fear and joy. As they ran, they met Jesus Himself. When He greeted them, they grabbed His feet and worshiped Him. Because they were still afraid, Jesus tried to calm their fears. He told them to deliver the same message that the angel earlier had given them.

The disciples were to go to Galilee, where they would see Jesus. Matthew's account does not rule out the appearances in Judea (joo DEE uh) recorded in Luke 24 and John 20, but does prepare the way for Jesus' later appearances back in Galilee, where most of His ministry had taken place (John 21; Matt. 28:16–20).

II. The Resurrection of Believers (1 Thess. 4:13–18)

1. The basis for Christian hope (vv. 13–14)

13 But I would not have you to be ignorant, brethren, concerning them which are asleep, that ye sorrow not, even as others which have no hope.

14 For if we believe that Jesus died and rose again, even so them also which sleep in Jesus will God bring with him.

Paul seems to have placed special emphasis on the future coming of Christ when he first preached to the Thessalonians. The doctrine is mentioned throughout his letters to them. After his visit, a question arose in the minds of the believers. Paul received word, probably from Timothy (3:1–6), that they had questions about the dead in Christ. Apparently they had expected Christ to come while all of them were still alive. After some died before His coming, the survivors wondered if the dead would share fully in the Lord's coming and glory.

The dead are referred to as "asleep" (see also v. 15). This was a normal way of speaking of the dead in ancient society. In fact, our word *cemetery* comes from the word translated "asleep." Unbelievers used the word to describe the appearance of the dead, who look as if they are asleep. Most people of the first century had no hope of life after death; therefore, they did not expect anyone to awake from this final sleep.

Christians used the word, but always with the expectation that the dead would awaken (compare Luke 8:49–56; John 11:11–15, 25–26, 43–44). Thus Paul referred to those who "sleep in Jesus" as having victory over death because of the death and resurrection of Jesus Christ.

"Those who have no hope" were the people who did not know Christ. Elsewhere Paul described them as "having no hope, and without God in the world" (Eph. 2:20). This does not mean that they didn't have various human and religious hopes. Some—although only a few—even claimed to believe in some kind of existence beyond death. However, whatever their hopes, they had no real hope because they did not know God and the crucified and risen Lord Jesus Christ.

Thus they grieved in hopeless despair when loved ones died. Christians also grieve when their loved ones die, but our human feelings of grief are comforted by the sure hope of victory over death for us and all who know the Lord. The basis for our confident hope is spelled out in verse 14. The word "if" should be translated "since." Neither Paul nor his readers questioned that Jesus had died and been raised from the dead. Paul assured them that this was the basis for assurance that those who sleep in Jesus will share the coming glory.

2. Hope for living and dead believers (vv. 15–17)

15 For this we say unto you by the word of the Lord, that we which are alive and remain unto the coming of the Lord shall not prevent them which are asleep.

Paul cited the Lord as authority for what he wrote in verse 15. Since this saying is not in the Gospels, it may have been a special revelation of Christ to Paul. Or it could have been a saying of Jesus that was not recorded in the Gospels (for example, see Acts 20:35; John 20:30; 21:25).

The word of the Lord makes this promise: believers who are alive when Christ comes will not precede the dead in Christ. The meaning of the word "prevent" has changed. When the translation known as the King James Version was made, the word meant "precede" or "go before," which is the meaning of the Greek word it translates.

> 16 For the Lord himself shall descend from heaven with a shout, with the voice of the archangel, and with the trump of God: and the dead in Christ shall rise first.
>
> 17 Then we which are alive and remain shall be caught up together with them in the clouds, to meet the Lord in the air: and so shall we ever be with the Lord.

Christ's coming will be accompanied by a shout, a voice of an archangel, and a trumpet blast (compare Matt. 24:31; 1 Cor. 15:52). When Christ comes, the dead in Christ will rise first. Verse 15 assured the Thessalonians that when Christ comes, living believers will not go before the dead in Christ. Verse 16 states the same truth in a different way. Before the living are caught up to glory, something happens first. The dead in Christ are raised. Then after the dead in Christ are resurrected, they will join living believers; and both groups will be caught up together to meet the Lord in the air.

Paul stuck to the main issue with the Thessalonians, and thus he did not answer all our questions about the coming of Christ and the resurrection of believers. Other passages deal with some of the questions. For example, 1 Corinthians 15 contains Paul's description of the resurrection body.

One of the first questions asked by modern readers about 1 Thessalonians 4:13–18 is, "What about the state of the dead in Christ before the final resurrection?" Paul believed that the dead in Christ go immediately to be with the Lord. This is implied in the last part of verse 14. God will bring with Him the dead in Jesus. This suggests that the dead in Christ are in some way already with Him, not unconsciously sleeping in the grave. First Thessalonians 5:10 is clearer: Christ "who died for us, that, whether we wake or sleep, we should live together with him." Clearest still is Paul's testimony in Philippians 1:23, where he wrote of his desire "to depart, and to be with Christ."

When such passages are placed alongside passages about the future resurrection, we are reminded that even the dead in Christ look forward to the coming of Christ and the resurrection. They are already with the Lord, but all God's people are not yet there and all God's purposes are not yet fulfilled. Paul did not get into all the questions and details in 1 Thessalonians 4:13–18. He summed up the final outcome of Christ's victory over death with these joyful words: "So shall we ever be with the Lord."

3. Comfort one another (v. 18)

18 Wherefore comfort one another with these words.

Paul wrote to comfort and encourage those who were worried and confused about the dead in Christ. Paul had assured them of victory over death for all believers: dead and living. He had assured them of reunion of living and dead believers when God's purpose is fulfilled. He told them to comfort one another with these words of assurance and hope. Believers in countless generations have found comfort for themselves and others in these inspired words.

APPLYING THE BIBLE

1. The ministry of angels. I suppose more has been said and written about angels in the last decade than ever before. Books about angels have flooded the market. It is interesting to observe that the Bible has more to say about angels than it says about the devil and demons.

In his book *Angels, Angels, Angels,* Billy Graham says that "angels minister to us personally" (Heb. 1:13–14). The New Testament shows how angels personally ministered to Jesus. They announced His birth (Matt. 1:20, 24); named Him (Luke 2:21); protected Him from Herod (Matt. 2:13); and ministered to Him in His temptations (Matt. 1:13). Jesus taught about angels (Matt. 18:10). Angels were available to rescue Him from the cross (Matt. 26:53); opened and guarded His tomb (Matt. 28:2); witnessed His ascension (Acts 1:10–11); and shall return with Him (Matt. 25:31).

Our lessons today focuses on the angel of the Lord who rolled back the stone to open His tomb. This was not done so Jesus could come out but so the unbelieving world could come in!

2. The resurrection of Jesus. The resurrection of Jesus is a well-attested fact of history. Angels saw Him (Matt. 28:5–6); Mary Magdalene and "the other Mary" saw Him (Matt. 28:9–10); the apostles saw Him (1 Cor. 15:6); Paul saw him (1 Cor. 15:8); the Emmaus disciples saw Him (Luke 24:13–32); the seven saw Him (John 21:1–23).

Beyond question, the early Christians believed that Jesus had been raised from the dead. But in spite of the evidence, various theories have been advanced to deny the resurrection of Jesus' body:

- The stolen body theory teaches that the disciples stole His body;
- The swoon theory teaches that Jesus did not die but only fainted on the cross;
- The telegram theory teaches that the spirit of Jesus communicated with the disciples to let them know that He was alive in heaven;
- The legend theory teaches that the resurrection was a myth that originated among early Christians;
- The hyperbolic theory teaches that Jesus was never raised but that the disciples used such strong language in describing His continuing life that the early church misunderstood what the disciples were saying.[1]

3. The significance of the resurrection. The resurrection declares Jesus to be the Son of God (Rom. 1:4); provides salvation (Rom. 4:25; 1 Cor. 15:17); proves that death is not the end (John 11:25–26); and promises our own resurrection (1 Cor. 15:20). The resurrection is the crowning of Jesus (Phil. 2:8–9).

4. Our resurrection body. Our resurrection body will not be the same as the one laid in the grave (1 Cor. 15:35–38); will not be flesh and blood (1 Cor. 15:50–58); will not be just spirit but will have flesh and bones (Luke 24:39); will be incorruptible (1 Cor. 15:42); will be glorious (1 Cor. 15:43); will be powerful (1 Cor. 15:43); will be heavenly (1 Cor. 15:47–49); will be like the resurrected body of Jesus (1 Cor. 15:49); will be shining and bright as the body of Jesus (Matt. 17:2—because we shall be like Him); and our resurrection shall be the consummation of our redemption (Rom. 8:23).

5. We will look fine. A newspaper correspondent visited former-president Dwight Eisenhower. He was showing his age. Although Eisenhower looked pale and frail, the reporter told the old general that he was looking well. Eisenhower replied, "Well, you know that a man has three ages. There is youth, then middle age, and then the time when everybody says, 'My, how fine you are looking!'"[2]

Our bodies grow old and weak, but the day is coming for each believer when his or her body will be and look just fine!

TEACHING THE BIBLE

- *Main Idea:* The resurrection of Christ and believers should influence the way we live daily.
- *Suggested Teaching Aim:* To lead adults to identify ways Christ's resurrection and their resurrection affects the way they live.

A TEACHING OUTLINE

1. Use a thought question to relate the Bible study to members' lives.

2. Guide members in developing two facts sheets to help in their search for biblical truths.

3. Use a question and listing to apply the study.

Introduce the Bible Study

Ask: What difference does Easter make in the life of the average nonbeliever? What difference does it make in your life? What difference has it made this past year? Allow members to respond. Suggest that one way Easter and Jesus' resurrection affect us is to give us hope.

Search for Biblical Truth

IN ADVANCE, provide two small sheets of paper (an 8 1/2-by-11-inch sheet cut in half) for each member. At the top of one write, *Facts Sheet About Christ's Resurrection.* At the top of the other write, *Facts Sheet About the Resurrection of Believers.* Have a large sheet of paper or a chalkboard divided into two columns. Label each column with one of the above headings.

Ask members to open their Bibles to Matthew 28:1–10. Ask members to help you compose a "Facts Sheet About Christ's Resurrection." Let them search these verses and list facts about Jesus' resurrection. Their list will likely differ from the following, but should include these:

- It occurred on Sunday morning.
- The first people to know that Jesus had been raised were women.
- An angel rolled away the stone.
- The purpose of rolling away the stone was not to let Jesus out but to let others see in.
- Jesus had predicted His resurrection.
- Those who had seen that He was risen were to tell others.
- Jesus arranged a meeting with His disciples to assure them of His resurrection.

DISCUSS: What difference does it make to you personally that Jesus has risen from the dead? What difference did it make this past week?

Ask members to open their Bibles to 1 Thessalonians 4:13–18. Ask members to help you compose a "Facts Sheet About the Resurrection of Believers." Let them search these verses and list facts about how Paul said the resurrection of believers would take place. Their list will likely differ from the following, but should include these:

- Our resurrection is based on Jesus' resurrection.
- Christ's coming will be accompanied by a shout, an archangel's voice, and a trumpet blast.
- Believers who have died are already with Christ in some form.
- Christ will raise those believers who have died first.
- Christ will then bring those raised believers and come for those who are living.
- Believers living on earth will meet this group in the air.
- All believers will be with the Lord forever.
- We should comfort each other with these facts.

DISCUSS: What about the state of the dead in Christ before the final resurrection? How does your resurrection affect the way you live in the world?

Give the Truth a Personal Focus

On the facts sheets you have written on the chalkboard or large sheet of paper, write in large letters: SO WHAT?? Ask members to write one way Christ's resurrection will affect the way they live and one way the facts about the resurrection of believers will affect the way they will live. Close in prayer.

---

1. Ray Summers, *The Life Beyond* (Nashville: Broadman Press, 1959), 34–36.
2. Benjamin P. Browne, *Illustrations for Preaching* (Nashville: Broadman Press, 1977), 95.

Commanded to Write

April
6
1997

Basic Passage: Revelation 1:1–20
Focal Passage: Revelation 1:4–15

The Book of Revelation has challenged Christian readers for many centuries. The next eight weeks will be devoted to studying portions of this fascinating book. The first study concerns the introductory words of the writer and his account of the first vision of the book.

Study Aim: *To describe how John was called to write the Book of Revelation*

STUDYING THE BIBLE

OUTLINE AND SUMMARY

I. The Revelation of Jesus Christ (Rev. 1:1–8)
- **1. Title and blessing (vv. 1–3)**
- **2. Greeting (vv. 4–5a)**
- **3. Doxology (vv. 5b–8)**

II. John's Call and Vision of the Son of Man (Rev. 1:9–20)
- **1. John, a persecuted exile (v. 9)**
- **2. John's commission to write (vv. 10–11)**
- **3. Vision of the Son of man (vv. 12–16)**
- **4. Message of the crucified, risen Lord (vv. 17–20)**

The book is the revelation of Jesus Christ sent and signified to John (vv. 1–3). John greeted the seven churches of Asia in the name of the triune God (vv. 4–5a). John praised Christ, and God declared His future coming (vv. 5b–8). John wrote from the island of Patmos to others who also were being persecuted (v. 9). John heard a voice telling him to write to the seven churches (vv. 10–11). Turning, John saw the Son of man standing in the midst of seven golden lampstands (vv. 12–16). The crucified, risen Lord touched John and confirmed the call to write (vv. 17–20).

I. The Revelation of Jesus Christ (Rev. 1:1–8)

1. Title and blessing (vv. 1–3)

Although the book is often called the Revelation of John, after its human author, the book itself is "the Revelation of Jesus Christ" (v. 1). The divine revelation came to John, who bore witness to what he saw (v. 2). A blessing is pronounced on those who read and obey what is written (v. 3).

2. Greeting (vv. 4–5a)

4 John to the seven churches which are in Asia: Grace be unto you, and peace, from him which is, and which was, and which is to come; and from the seven Spirits which are before his throne;

5 And from Jesus Christ, who is the faithful witness, and the first begotten of the dead, and the prince of the kings of the earth.

The first line of verse 4 reads like the greeting in most of the letters of the New Testament. John identified himself by name. He apparently was so well known in the Roman province of Asia that they knew which John this was. This was especially true in light of later information about him in verse 9. Early tradition identified the apostle John as living in Ephesus, the chief city of Asia, and thus as the author of the Book of Revelation. "Asia" referred to the Roman province located at the western end of Asia Minor, not to what we know as the continent of Asia. The seven churches are identified in verse 11.

The source of the grace and peace is the triune God. The eternal Creator, God the Father is called the One "which is, and which was, and which is to come." This is reminiscent of His revelation to Moses as the great "I AM" (Exod. 3:14). He had no beginning. He is always at work. He will continue forever.

Although the first line of verse 4 is a familiar style of greeting in New Testament letters, the rest of verse 4 shows that the style of this book will be different from the style of letters. This is especially true of the description of seven Spirits before the throne. The Book of Revelation was written in a style called apocalyptic (uh pahk uh LIP tik), which used symbolic numbers and vivid, sometimes bizarre visions. Many Bible students consider the seven Spirits to represent the Holy Spirit. Seven was considered a number of completion or perfection.

Mentioning the seven spirits between the eternal God and Jesus Christ adds weight to the conclusion that John was referring to the Holy Spirit.

Jesus is described in three ways. He was not a martyr, but He was faithful unto death (Heb. 12:1–4). He was the firstborn from the dead because His victory over death assures victory over death for those who follow Him (1 Cor. 15:20–21). In contrast to the puny Roman emperor who threatened the Christians, Jesus Christ is King of kings and Lord of lords (Rev. 19:16).

3. Doxology (vv. 5b–8)

> 5 Unto him that loved us, and washed us from our sins in his own blood,
>
> 6 And hath made us kings and priests unto God and his Father; to him be glory and dominion for ever and ever.
>
> Amen.

Mentioning the person and work of Christ inspired John to burst forth into praise. The word translated "loved" is in the present tense and means "loves." The word translated "washed" means "loosed" or "freed from." Because Christ loves us, He set us free from our sins through giving His life and shedding His own blood.

The word translated "kings" means "kingdom." Christ made us a kingdom of priests. When God made the covenant with Israel at Mount Sinai, God said, "ye shall be unto me a kingdom of priests" (Exod. 19:6). Peter had the Exodus passage in mind when he wrote that Christians are "a chosen generation, a royal priesthood, an holy nation" (1 Pet. 2:9). John also believed that the ultimate fulfillment of the Exodus promise is all those who know Christ. When we are brought into God's kingdom,

THE SEVEN CHURCHES OF ASIA

One of the Seven Churches (Cities) of Revelation 1–3

no special group serves as priests. All are priests who offer themselves to God and for one another, and who represent the Lord before the world.

John praised such a wonderful Savior, to whom is given glory and power forever.

> 7 Behold, he cometh with clouds; and every eye shall see him, and they also which pierced him: and all kindreds of the earth shall wail because of him. Even so, Amen.

The glory and power of Christ will be fully revealed to all people at His coming. Now only believers live in light of His kingdom and coming. When Christ comes, every eye shall see Him. This will include those responsible for His death, as well as all the people of the earth. Believers shall greet His coming with joy, but others will wail because they recognize that they stand under His judgment.

> 8 I am Alpha [AL fuh] and Omega [oh MEG uh], the beginning and the ending, saith the Lord, which is, and which was, and which is to come, the Almighty.

The One who spoke this prophecy of Christ's coming identified Himself in verse 8. He was none other than Almighty God. He is Alpha and Omega. These are the first and last letters of the Greek alphabet. This means that He is the beginning and the end. God also identified Himself again as the One who is, was, and is coming (as in v. 4). Thus verse 8 is like a divine signature verifying the source of the revelation given to John.

II. John's Call and Vision of the Son of Man (Rev. 1:9–20)

1. John, a persecuted exile (v. 9)

> 9 I John, who also am your brother, and companion in tribulation, and in the kingdom and patience of Jesus Christ, was in the isle that is called Patmos [PAT muhs], for the word of God, and for the testimony of Jesus Christ.

John identified himself as a brother in Christ and as one who shared with his readers in tribulation, kingdom, and perseverance in Jesus. The word translated "patience" means more than patient waiting; it means actively bearing up under trials. When John received his commission to write, he was on the island of Patmos. This small island off the coast of Asia Minor was used by the Romans as a place of exile for persons guilty of certain crimes. John's "crimes" were his faithful testimony to God's Word and Jesus Christ.

This verse and many others show that the Book of Revelation was written to persecuted believers. Emperor Domitian (doe MISH un), who reigned from A.D. 81 to 96, sought to enforce emperor worship throughout the Roman Empire. The cult of emperor worship had been around for a long time, but most earlier emperors had not taken it too seriously. Domitian was determined that everyone worship the emperor.

For most people of that day, adding one more god to their many gods posed no problem. However, Christians faced a serious dilemma. They were loyal citizens; but their total commitment to Christ would not allow them to say, "Caesar is lord." Instead, they declared, "Jesus is Lord." Their refusal to worship the emperor resulted in various kinds of persecution, including exile in John's case. One key to understanding the Book of Revelation is to read it from the perspective of the persecuted people for whom it was originally written.

2. John's commission to write (vv. 10–11)

10 I was in the Spirit on the Lord's day, and heard behind me a great voice, as of a trumpet,

11 Saying, I am Alpha and Omega, the first and the last: and, What thou seest, write in a book, and send it unto the seven churches which are in Asia; unto Ephesus [EF uh suhs], and unto Smyrna [SMUR nuh], and unto Pergamos [PUR guh muhs], and unto Thyatira [thigh uh TIGH ruh], and unto Sardis [SAHR diss], and unto Philadelphia [fil uh DEL fih uh], and unto Laodicea [lay ahd ih SEE uh].

While John was caught up in the Spirit on one Lord's Day, he heard a voice that sounded like a trumpet. The Speaker identified Himself, using the language of verse 8. This shows that both God the Father and God the Son were called the Alpha and the Omega. The voice told John to write to seven churches in the Roman province of Asia. The seven churches were named. Revelation 2–3 contain letters addressed to each of the seven churches.

3. Vision of the Son of man (vv. 12–16)

12 And I turned to see the voice that spake with me. And being turned, I saw seven golden candlesticks;

13 And in the midst of the seven golden candlesticks one like unto the Son of man, clothed with a garment down to the foot, and girt about the paps with a golden girdle.

14 His head and his hairs were white like wool, as white as snow; and his eyes were as a flame of fire;

15 And his feet like unto fine brass, as if they burned in a furnace; and his voice as the sound of many waters.

When John turned around, he saw a vision of the exalted Son of man standing among seven golden lampstands. Later Christ identified the lampstands as the seven churches (v. 20). The name "Son of man" and the description of Him clearly show that this was none other than the Lord Jesus Christ. The details of His appearance in verses 13–15 emphasize His purity and His power. This is further seen in verse 16, where He is said to hold seven stars in His right hand, to have a two-edged sword coming out of His mouth, and to have a face that shone like the sun.

The impact of the message was to remind the persecuted believers that Jesus was Lord, not Caesar. They may have wondered whether the Lord knew or cared about their plight. The vision assured them that He was standing with them in the midst of the persecuted churches. This is the central message of the Book of Revelation: The final victory will be Christ's. Meanwhile, believers must remain faithful unto death.

4. Message of the crucified, risen Lord (vv. 17–20)

When John fell down terrified, the Lord laid His right hand on him and told him not to be afraid (v. 17). The Lord said that He had died and was now alive forever, and that He held the keys to death and the grave (v. 18). He told John to write what he had seen, what is, and what will take place later (v. 19). He explained that the seven stars were the angels (or messengers) of the seven churches, and the seven lampstands were the seven churches (v. 20).

APPLYING THE BIBLE

1. Christ's picture in Franklin's room. The religion of Benjamin Franklin was much different from that of the evangelical church. He was a deist who saw God in the world, but that was about all. However, when Franklin was dying he asked for a crucifix, or a picture of Christ on the cross, to be placed in his bedroom so that Franklin could look, as he said, "upon the form of the Silent Sufferer."

John's vision of Christ on Patmos was neither a crucifix nor a picture. John saw the resurrected Christ in all His heavenly glory, and Jesus was real and alive!

2. Christ preeminent. One of Leonardo da Vinci's greatest accomplishments was his painting "The Last Supper." Taking an artist friend along to get his opinion, da Vinci asked his friend what he thought about it. Looking at it carefully, the friend said: "The chalice on the table is remarkably beautiful. In fact, it is the most beautiful thing in the painting." Quickly and deliberately, da Vinci picked up his brush and palette and removed the beautiful chalice. Stunned, the friend asked da Vinci why he had done such a thing. "It is Christ who must be preeminently seen as the center of my painting" da Vinci replied.

Christ is the preeminent person in the Revelation and in all history as well. Look at verses 5, 7–8, 11, 13–18.

3. Christ in history. The massive *Encyclopaedia Britannica* lists the biographies of many great men and women of history. But more words—20,000 words—are used to tell about Jesus than are used for the biographies of Aristotle, Alexander the Great, Cicero, Julius Caesar, or Napoleon Bonaparte. H. G. Wells, the British author of many books, blasphemed and ridiculed Jesus; but when he wrote his famous *Outline of History,* Wells never questioned that Jesus lived and used ten pages to discuss His life.

Christ is in history and Christ is history. He is the Alpha ("A") and Omega ("Z") of all history (v. 11).

4. What Jesus does for sinners. Jesus loves us in our sins (v. 5); He looses us from our sins (v. 5); He lifts us out of our sins (v. 6).

A shepherd who lived in the mountains of Montana had as his only companions a radio, the wild animals and birds, his sheep, his faithful sheepdog, and his beloved fiddle. When his day's work was done, he entertained himself by listening to the radio and playing his fiddle. One day his fiddle got out of tune, and the music went sour. He hit on the idea of writing to the radio station and asking them to sound "A" over the radio at a certain time on a specific day. When the day came, the shepherd was listening carefully, and as the station sounded "A" he tuned his fiddle.

All who tune their lives to the Master bring their lives into harmony with Him as He forgives their sins and lifts them to a higher level of life.

5. To see God walk down the street. Plato, the ancient Greek philosopher, said that he longed to see God walk down the streets of Athens. That is exactly what God did at Bethlehem in Jesus Christ. In the incarnation, God walked down the staircase of heaven to reveal Himself to mankind. We now know what God is like because we have seen Him in Jesus Christ (1 Cor. 1:15). This is what John experienced on Patmos.

TEACHING THE BIBLE

- *Main Idea:* Jesus reveals His concern for His people.
- *Suggested Teaching Aim:* To lead adults to describe how Jesus revealed His concern for His people to John.

A TEACHING OUTLINE

1. Use a word association test to introduce the Bible study.
2. Use an illustrated lecture to search for biblical truth.
3. Use recall and listing to make the study personal.

Introduce the Bible Study

Give a sheet of paper and pencil to all present. Ask members to number from 1 to 6. Read the following and ask them to write down the first book of the Bible that comes to mind when the word is mentioned: (1) Pastoral instructions, (2) Letter, (3) 666, (4) Beatitudes, (5) Millennium, (6) Antichrist. Allow members to respond and point out that all of the statements except (6) Antichrist are true about the Book of Revelation. In all likelihood, most people chose Revelation for (3), (5), and (6). However, the number *666* and the word "millennium" appear only once in the whole book and the word "Antichrist" doesn't appear at all. It appears only in 1 John and 2 John. Point out that we have let the extraordinary elements of the book overshadow the real meaning. The next eight weeks will help us to discover the real meaning of this book.

Search for Biblical Truth

IN ADVANCE, make a unit poster for the study of Revelation by writing the titles of the lessons, the Scriptures being studied, and the dates on a large poster. Cut out a colored arrow and place this beside the lesson being studied each week.

One of the times when lecture is appropriate is when you have information your members do not have and cannot discover easily. This applies to the lesson this week. **IN ADVANCE,** write the outline on page 237 on poster strips and place them on the wall as you lecture. Place "I. The Revelation of Jesus Christ" and "1. Title and blessing" on the wall. In your lecture point out: the title of the book from 1:1 and the blessing contained in 1:3.

Place "2. Greeting" on the wall. In your lecture: (1) explain who "John" was; (2) locate Asia Minor and the seven churches on a map; (3) explain the source of the grace and peace; (4) define "apocalyptic"; (5) explain the similarities and dissimilarities of the book with other letters; (6) identify the seven spirits; (7) point out the descriptions of Jesus.

Place "3. Doxology" on the wall. Explain: (1) "loved," "washed," and "kings"; (2) that Christ's glory will be revealed when He comes; (3) meaning and purpose of "Alpha and Omega."

DISCUSS: How do I practice my priesthood?

Place "II. John's Call and Vision of the Son of Man" and "1. John, a persecuted exile" on the wall. Then do the following: (1) explain "patience" and locate Patmos on a map; (2) identify Domitian and explain his practice of emperor worship; (3) point out that Revelation was written for people of the first century who were being persecuted.

Place "2. John's commission to write" on the wall. Explain: (1) how and when John received his revelation; (2) who made the revelation; (3) where the seven churches are located on a map.

Place "3. Vision of the Son of man" on the wall. Explain: (1) the lampstands; (2) that Christ's appearance emphasizes His purity and power; (3) that the purpose of the message was to remind believers that Jesus—not Caesar—was in control; (4) that Jesus standing in the midst of the persecuted Christians is the central message of Revelation.

Place "4. Message of the crucified, risen Lord" on the wall. Point out: (1) Jesus is alive; (2) He has the keys to death and hell; (3) the symbols used for the churches.

Give the Truth a Personal Focus

Ask: How does the picture of Jesus revealed in these verses describe His concern for His people? On a chalkboard or a large sheet of paper write members' suggestions. (Possible answers: Jesus stands in the midst of lampstands; Jesus comes to John; Jesus tells John to write this down so others can read it; Jesus' certain victory and return.) Ask: Which of these helps you the most in today's world? Why?

To Smyrna and Pergamum

April

13

1997

Basic Passage: Revelation 2:8–17
Focal Passage: Revelation 2:8–17

Revelation 2–3 contain letters to the seven churches of Asia from the Son of man of the vision of Revelation 1:12–20. This lesson focuses on the letters to Smyrna (SMUR nuh) and Pergamum (PUR guh muhm), which is the usual spelling of Pergamos (PUR guh muhs). The main theme of these two letters and of the Book of Revelation as a whole is the call for God's people to remain faithful unto death in the face of persecution.

Study Aim: *To state what the letters to Smyrna and Pergamum teach about being faithful to the Lord*

STUDYING THE BIBLE

OUTLINE AND SUMMARY

I. Letter to Smyrna (Rev. 2:8–11)
- **1. Greeting (v. 8)**
- **2. Commendation (v. 9)**
- **3. Challenge (v. 10)**
- **4. Promise (v. 11)**

II. Letter to Pergamum (Rev. 2:12–17)
- **1. Greeting (v. 12)**
- **2. Commendation (v. 13)**
- **3. Warning (vv. 14–15)**
- **4. Challenge (v. 16)**
- **5. Promise (v. 17)**

The crucified, risen Lord greeted the messenger of the church in Smyrna (v. 8). He commended church members for their faithful works and perseverance during persecution and poverty (v. 9). He challenged them to fear not and to remain faithful unto death (v. 10). He promised to those who heeded His word that they would not taste the second death (v. 11). The Lord with the sword coming out of His mouth greeted the church at Pergamum (v. 12). He commended them for faithfulness, even when one of them was killed (v. 13). He warned against the double sin of idolatry and immorality (vv. 14–15). He challenged them to repent (v. 16). He promised them acceptance into God's eternal kingdom (v. 17).

I. Letter to Smyrna (Rev. 2:8–11)

1. Greeting (v. 8)

8 And unto the angel of the church in Smyrna write; These things saith the first and last, which was dead, and is alive.

Each of the seven letters begins with a greeting to the angel of that church. Since the word "angel" means "messenger," many people think

Christ had in mind either the messenger carrying the letter or the pastor of the church. Others think that the "angel" was the guardian angel of the church. In either case, each letter was intended to be read and obeyed by all members of the church.

The sequence of the seven churches in Revelation 2–3 follows a circular route starting north from Ephesus and circling back to Ephesus. Smyrna, which was located on the coast about thirty-five miles north of Ephesus, contained temples to many of the Greek gods.

In most of the seven letters, Christ identified Himself by using descriptions from the vision of Revelation 1:12–20. Thus in verse 8, the exalted Lord used language from Revelation 1:17–18. They were greeted by the One who was crucified and was now alive forever as eternal Lord.

2. Commendation (v. 9)

> 9 I know thy works, and tribulation, and poverty, (but thou art rich) and I know the blasphemy of them which say they are Jews, and are not, but are the synagogue of Satan.

Persecuted Christians are tempted to doubt that Christ knows or cares about them. Thus the Lord assured the Christians in Smyrna that He knew their tribulation and poverty. He also assured them that He knew of their faithful good works in spite of their troubles. When property is confiscated and jobs are denied to believers, poverty becomes one of the results of persecution. Christ assured them that although they were economically poor, they actually were rich in God's sight (Matt. 6:19–21; James 1:9).

Taking the lead in the persecution in Smyrna were some Jews from the synagogue. Keep in mind that John himself was a Jew, as were all the apostles, and many of the early Christians. Thus this was no indictment of Jews in general, but of those who allowed themselves to become instruments of Satan in trying to destroy those who believed that Jesus is the Son of God. The word "blasphemy," when used against people, means "slander." Thus their opponents stirred up others against Christians by spreading lies about them.

3. Challenge (v. 10)

> 10 Fear none of those things which thou shalt suffer: behold, the devil shall cast some of you into prison, that ye may be tried; and ye shall have tribulation ten days: be thou faithful unto death, and I will give thee a crown of life.

Although this challenge was addressed to the church in Smyrna, it is repeated in various ways throughout the Book of Revelation. The challenge was twofold: not to be afraid, instead to be faithful unto death. Three reasons were given for being faithful: (1) Regardless of who the human persecutors were, the devil was back of what they did. (2) Although the devil intended persecution to break their faith, God allowed it in order that their faith might be tested and strengthened. (3) Their tribulations would be only for a limited time, but their reward was an eternal crown of life.

4. Promise (v. 11)

11 He that hath an ear, let him hear what the Spirit saith unto the churches; He that overcometh shall not be hurt of the second death.

The first part of verse 11 is found at or near the end of each of the seven letters. The words are similar to the words that Jesus often spoke after saying something that He especially wanted His followers to remember and obey. For example, after telling the parable of the soils, Jesus said, "Who hath ears to hear, let him hear" (Matt. 13:9). The point is that no one has really heard God's word unless hearing leads to obeying. The use of the word "Spirit" in verse 11 shows that the words of the living Christ can be spoken of as the words of the Spirit.

The promise was that those who overcame would never taste the second death. Christ promised no exemption from physical death. In fact, He assured them that remaining faithful could lead to their death as martyrs. His promise was that as believers, they would never face final separation from God, which is the second death (Rev. 20:6,14).

II. Letter to Pergamum (Rev. 2:12–17)

1. Greeting (v. 12)

12 And to the angel of the church in Pergamos write;

These things saith he which hath the sharp sword with two edges.

Pergamum was about fifty-five miles northeast of Smyrna and the northernmost of the seven cities. Not only did it contain temples to Zeus (ZUHS) and other Greek gods, but it also was the site of a great temple dedicated to Rome and Augustus (aw GUHS tuhs) in 29 B.C. This made Pergamum the greatest center of emperor worship in the eastern part of the empire.

The Lord identified Himself using the words of Revelation 1:16. A two-edged sword was a sharp instrument of warfare. In John's vision, Christ had such a sword coming out of His mouth. This signified the power of His word. Hebrews 4:12 uses a similar analogy to describe the power of God's word. Revelation 19:21 pictures Christ doing battle with His evil enemies and slaying them with a sword out of His mouth.

2. Commendation (v. 13)

13 I know thy works and where thou dwellest, even where Satan's seat is: and thou holdest fast my name, and hast not denied my faith, even in those days wherein Antipas [AN tih puhs] was my faithful martyr, who was slain among you, where Satan dwellest.

Christ assured the church in Pergamum that He knew of their faithfulness in the face of persecution. Satan's throne probably referred to Pergamum being the center for emperor worship. The Roman officials in Pergamum took seriously the task of enforcing emperor worship. At least one Christian, Antipas, had lost his life as a result of his faithfulness. Christ commended the church for standing firm during that time.

3. Warning (vv. 14–15)

14 But I have a few things against thee, because thou hast there them that hold the doctrine of Balaam [BAY luhm], who taught Balac [BAY lak] to cast a stumblingblock before the children of Israel, to eat things sacrificed unto idols, and to commit fornication.

15 So hast thou also them that hold the doctrine of the Nicolaitans [nik oh LAY uh tuhns], which thing I hate.

Most of the seven letters include not only commendation but also warning. Although no word of warning was given to the church at Smyrna, Christ warned the church at Pergamum of a serious danger. Although they had overcome the outward pressure of persecution, they were in danger of corruption from within. Verse 14 identifies this as the doctrine of Balaam, and verse 15 calls it the doctrine of the Nicolaitans. Likely, these were two names for the same problem.

Verse 14 identifies the sin as eating things sacrificed to idols and committing sexual immorality. The practice is similar to the snare into which Balaam lured Israel during the period of wilderness wanderings. Balaam was a prophet who was hired to curse Israel by Balak, king of Moab (MOH ab). God restrained Balaam from cursing Israel and led him to speak blessings instead (see Num. 22–24). Numbers 25:1–5 describes how the Israelites offered sacrifices to Moabite gods and committed sexual immorality with Moabite women. Numbers 31:16 shows that Balaam had advised the Moabites to lure the Israelites into these sins (see also 2 Pet. 2:15; Jude 11).

In the ancient world, many religions incorporated sexual immorality as part of their worship. Just as the Israelites often were lured into this double sin of idolatry and immorality, so were Christians tempted to do the same in their day. We don't know exactly the form this took in Pergamum, but verses 14–15 show that the church was condoning and in some cases participating in such sins. The Lord hated such deadly sins.

4. Challenge (v. 16)

16 Repent; or else I will come unto thee quickly, and will fight against them with the sword of my mouth.

Christ's will in such a situation is clear: Repent. He warned the church that unless they repented, He would take direct action against those who practiced, promoted, or condoned these evils. As elsewhere, He said He would go into battle with the sword of His mouth. Verse 16 may have meant that Christ would speak and implement words of judgment against the evildoers. Revelation 19:21 shows that this weapon can destroy all the forces of evil.

5. Promise (v. 17)

17 He that hath an ear, let him hear what the Spirit saith unto the churches; To him that overcometh will I give to eat of the hidden manna, and will give him a white stone, and in the stone a new name written, which no man knoweth saving he that receiveth it.

Many Jews expected the coming of the Messiah to be accompanied by God again providing manna as He had in the wilderness. During His ministry, Jesus claimed to be the Bread of Life (John 6:31–35). The exalted Lord promised to provide satisfying nourishment for His faithful people. They were tempted to join the pagan idol feasts; but if they were faithful, Christ promised that they would eat the hidden heavenly manna.

Victorious athletes were sometimes given a white stone as a ticket of admission to a victory feast and celebration. This may be the meaning of the symbol in verse 17. Faithful Christians were assured of welcome at the heavenly banquet. In some way, each ticket of admission will be personalized. Perhaps this is another sign to teach the same idea as the sign of having one's name written in the book of life (Rev. 20:12).

APPLYING THE BIBLE

1. "Quo vadis, Domine?" There is no statement in the New Testament that Peter was ever in Rome. But Christian writers of the second century developed the tradition that the church in Rome was founded by Peter and Paul. This is wrong, for Paul wrote his epistle to the church in Rome, a church that already existed but which he had never seen (Romans 1:7,11). Also, tradition says that Peter died a martyr's death in Rome, although there is no scriptural evidence to prove or disprove it. According to the tradition, Peter who had been in Rome, was fleeing from the persecution that had broken out within the city. On the road he met a stranger coming into the city. Recognizing that it was Christ, Peter asked, "Quo vadis, Domine?"—"Where are you going Lord?" Jesus answered, "I go to Rome to suffer in your place." Overcoming his fear, tradition relates that Peter turned and went back to Rome, where he suffered a martyr's death.

John's meeting with Jesus on Patmos is fact, not tradition. And Jesus gave John a message to share with the saints who were being persecuted in the seven churches of Asia Minor.

2. Overcoming fear. Dwight L. Moody (1837–1899) was an outstanding evangelist. His favorite verse was Isaiah 12:2: "I will trust and not be afraid." Moody used to say: "You can travel to heaven first-class or second-class. Second-class is, "What time I am afraid, I will trust." First-class is, "I will trust and not be afraid."

John tells these believers that persecution for Jesus' sake will increase but that they should fear none of the things that will befall them, for God always has the last word.

3. Keeping the faith. Eisleben, Germany, is a small inconspicuous town, but an important one nonetheless. At an inn on one end of the town, Martin Luther was born on a night in 1483. At the other end of the town is the house in which he died in 1546. On the night of February 18, 1546, the great reformer awoke in great pain and then sank into a coma. A friend roused Luther and asked, "Reverend father, do you stand firm by Christ and the doctrine you have preached?" In a child's whisper Luther answered, "Yes!"

John writes the suffering believers in the churches to stand by their faith in Christ although it may cost them their lives (v. 10).

4. Repentance required. Theologian Augustus Strong defines repentance as "that voluntary change in the mind of the sinner in which he turns from sin." In all the Bible, repentance is required of all sinners who would be saved.

A man traveling by foot asked a boy along the road how far it was to a certain community. The boy replied: "Mister, if you keep walking the way you are going it is about twenty-five thousand miles. But if you turn around it is about three miles!"

Repentance involves a turning, a change of mind and attitude. The risen Lord, through John, commands the saints at Pergamum to repent. Although they are suffering persecution for Christ's sake, repentance is still required (vv. 14–16). We never arrive at such a high state of holiness that we do not need to repent.

5. Reward waiting. A young man arrived in London and carried his bags down to "the tube" (underground subway) where he was to catch the train to his destination. He boarded the tube, picked up two bags, and was turning around to pick up the other two when suddenly the doors closed and the train sped away. Quickly, he shouted to a man nearby, "Put them out at the Mansion House, please." Then at the next stop, he caught a train back to where his bags were waiting and caught the next train to Mansion House. Sure enough, when he got off the train his two bags were on the platform waiting for him.

What we put in at the cross of Jesus will be waiting for us when we arrive at the Father's mansion house! To the suffering saints at Pergamum, John writes to tell them to be faithful to Jesus, for their reward will be waiting for them when they arrive in heaven (v. 19).

TEACHING THE BIBLE

- *Main Idea:* Jesus is with His suffering people.
- *Suggested Teaching Aim:* To lead adults to identify ways Jesus has supported them in their suffering.

A TEACHING OUTLINE

1. Use an illustration to introduce the Bible study.
2. Use a chart to guide the search for biblical truth.
3. Use discussion questions to give the truth a personal focus.

Introduce the Bible Study

Share the following illustration: Bill Wallace was a Southern Baptist medical missionary to China before the Communist takeover. He was captured and tortured physically and psychologically. His only crime was having committed his life to heal people physically and spiritually. At night his Communist guards stuck long poles through the bars of his cell and jabbed the doctor into unconsciousness. But something went wrong one night, and the battle was over. "Bill Wallace was dead to the world, but was alive forever with God."[1] Say: Many believers have died for their faith. Today's lesson tells of one of the earliest ones. But more than that, it tells us of Christ's presence in the midst of suffering.

Search for Biblical Truth

IN ADVANCE, make a chart on a large sheet of paper. The chart should have eight columns, and you will use it for the rest of April. Label the columns (1) Church; (2) Attribute of Christ; (3) Condition of the Church; (4) Exhortation; (5) Warning or Commendation; (6) Solemn Refrain; (7) Reward Promised; (8) Title. Leave space beneath to write.

IN ADVANCE, enlist a reader to read all of the Scripture reference. Call for Revelation 2:8–11 to be read at this time. Ask members to fill in (1) the Name of the Church. (Smyrna) and (2) the Attribute from Revelation 1:12–20. ("First and last.") Use a map to locate Ephesus (which will not be covered in this study), Smyrna, and the other five churches (Sardis will not be studied, either).

Ask members to identify (3) the Condition of the Church (v. 9). Use "Studying the Bible" to explain "synagogue of Satan" and "blasphemy." Ask: What assurance does this verse give that Jesus knows and cares about us when we suffer for Him?

Ask members to identify (4) the Exhortation ("Do not fear"); (5) the Warning or Commendation ("Be faithful"); (6) Solemn Refrain (v. 11); and (7) Reward (not hurt by second death). Ask: What three reasons are given for remaining faithful? (See "Studying the Bible.")

Ask members to suggest a title (8). It should be something like *persecuted.*

Call for the reader to read Revelation 2:12–17. Identify Pergamum on the map. Move through the verses and let members fill in the chart. Where appropriate, use "Studying the Bible" to explain the passage.

DISCUSS: What in these verses do you find helpful today? How can you know that Jesus cares about you in your hurt and suffering? What reward do you deserve for your faithfulness?

Give the Truth a Personal Focus

Remind members of Bill Wallace's suffering and death. Point out that although we may not be martyrs for our faith, Jesus is with us when we suffer for Him. Ask: How do we suffer today? (List responses on a chalkboard or a large sheet of paper.) How does Jesus help us today? (List responses.) Why should we be faithful today? (Same three reasons the Smyrna Christians were to be faithful; God has not changed.) Close with a prayer that all will be faithful in the situations in which they find themselves this week.

---

1. Jesse C. Fletcher, *Bill Wallace of China* (Nashville: Broadman Press, 1963, reprint, Broadman & Holman, 1996), 207.

To Thyatira

Basic Passage: Revelation 2:18–29
Focal Passage: Revelation 2:18–29

The longest of the seven letters was sent to the church in Thyatira (thigh uh TIGH ruh), the smallest of the seven cities of Asia. The letter to Thyatira is noted for its words of high praise and stern warning.

➧ **Study Aim:** *To explain why Christ spoke words of such high praise and stern warning to the church in Thyatira*

STUDYING THE BIBLE

OUTLINE AND SUMMARY

1. **Greeting (v. 18)**
2. **Commendation (v. 19)**
3. **Warning (vv. 20–23)**
4. **Challenge (vv. 24–25)**
5. **Promise (vv. 26–29)**

Christ greeted the church at Thyatira as the Son of God and Judge (v. 18). He commended them for their works, love, faith, service, and perseverance (v. 19). He warned of an evil "Jezebel" who was seducing them to idolatry and immorality (vv. 20–23). He challenged the faithful ones to hold fast until He comes (vv. 24–25). He promised the faithful that they would share in His reign and presence (vv. 26–29).

1. Greeting (v. 18)

> 18 And unto the angel of the church in Thyatira write; These things saith the Son of God, who hath his eyes like unto a flame of fire, and his feet are like fine brass.

Thyatira was located about forty miles southeast of Pergamum. It was known for its trade guilds. Lydia, whom Paul met in Philippi, had come from Thyatira and was a seller of purple (Acts 16:14). Purple dye was expensive. One of its sources was a root that was plentiful around Thyatira.

The exalted Christ spoke to Thyatira with the deity and authority of the Son of God. He used two descriptions of Himself taken from the vision of Revelation 1:14–15. Both descriptions stress His authority as Judge. Eyes like flames of fire penetrate and consume those guilty of sin. Feet of brass represent the strength and firmness of His judgment.

2. Commendation (v. 19)

> 19 I know thy works, and charity, and service, and faith, and thy patience, and thy works; and the last to be more than the first.

The word "know" plays a big role in the letters of Revelation 2–3. Christ used this word in each of His commendations (2:2, 9, 13, 19; 3:8) and in two of His warnings (3:1, 15). During times of trouble, Christians are tempted to think that Christ either doesn't know or doesn't care about them. The Lord reminded the believers in the seven churches of Asia that He was among them, that He knew, and that He cared.

The believers at Thyatira were noted for their "works." These were not things they did in order to earn salvation. They were the fruits of a saving knowledge of Jesus Christ. The Son of God used these same words, "I know thy works," to commend some of the other churches, but none received higher praise than Thyatira. Only of them did Jesus say that their last works exceeded their first works. In other words, they had grown in their good deeds and practice of the Christian faith.

The Lord also used other impressive words to describe their growth in good works. For example, their works grew out of self-giving love. "Charity" translates *agape,* the word used for God's love for us and our love as a response to His love. The church at Ephesus had been commended for its works, but the same church was rebuked for having lost its first love (Rev. 2:2–4). The works at Thyatira were rooted in love. Their works also showed their "faith," a word that means trust in God and faithfulness to God. Their works led to acts of service. The word translated "labour" means "service." It refers to acts of love done for others in Christ's name. Christ also commended their perseverance, the meaning of the word translated "patience."

3. Warning (vv. 20–23)

> 20 Notwithstanding I have a few things against thee, because thou sufferest that woman Jezebel [JEZ uh bel], which calleth herself a prophetess, to teach and to seduce my servants to commit fornication, and to eat things sacrificed unto idols.

The warning to the church at Thyatira was similar to the warning to the church at Pergamum. Both were warned against committing sexual immorality and eating things sacrificed to idols (v. 14). Both warnings used the names of villains from the Old Testament. Pergamum was warned against following people who held the teachings of Balaam, infamous for advising the Moabites to lure Israelites to worship idols and commit sexual immorality (Num. 25:1–4; 31:16). Thyatira was warned against a woman, whom Jesus called "Jezebel." This was probably not the actual name of the dangerous woman in Thyatira, but Christ was saying that she was doing the same things that evil Jezebel had done in her day.

Jezebel was a Sidonian princess who married Ahab, king of Israel. She practiced Baal worship, a fertility religion that combined sexual immorality with its worship. Not content to practice her religion privately, she corrupted Ahab and sought to enforce Baal worship throughout the land of Israel (1 Kings 16:29–33; 18:1–15). Elijah (ih LIGH juh) recognized the deadly danger of Baal worship and challenged Jezebel's prophets to a dramatic contest on Mount Carmel (KAHR mil; 1 Kings 18:16–46).

The exalted Lord warned the church at Thyatira of a woman who was as dangerous to them as Jezebel had been to Israel. The woman claimed to be a prophetess. The Bible mentions other women who were legitimate prophetesses (Exod. 15:20; Judg. 4:4; 2 Chron. 34:22; Luke 2:36; Acts 21:9). This "Jezebel" only claimed to be a prophetess. If the people of Thyatira applied to her the basic tests of a prophet, they would know she was a false prophet. Deuteronomy 13:1–5 warns against any prophet, regardless of his miracles, who tells people to follow other gods. This woman was claiming special inspiration and authority for her teachings, but her words and deeds showed her to be an instrument of evil.

Some people think that "Jezebel" was an evil woman outside the church, but her claim to be a prophetess and the use of the word "seduce" strongly suggest that she was a member of the church. The church was tolerating her, and some church members were being seduced into following her false teachings and evil practices.

We don't know for sure what she said, but we do know that her advice included idolatry and immorality. Such seduction was probably cloaked in seemingly harmless words. Some Bible students think that the setting was among the many trade guilds in Thyatira. These associations of merchants and workers conducted social gatherings and feasts. Since most people worshiped pagan gods, prayers and sacrifices to pagan gods were included as part of the occasions. Sometimes the celebrations got out of hand and became orgies. Perhaps the so-called prophetess was saying that Christians should participate freely in these celebrations. After all, such participation was good for business and for good relations with the rest of the population.

Very likely, her teaching was an early form of what later was called gnosticism (NAHS tih siz uhm), from the Greek word meaning "know." The Gnostics (NAHS tiks) claimed to have special knowledge withheld from the rank-and-file. Their basic assumption was that anything physical is evil. This led some of them to deny that the Son of God ever truly became flesh. In actions, some Gnostics became ascetics, who tried to deny to themselves any physical pleasures; and others became libertines, who indulged every fleshly appetite.

The latter group reasoned that if the soul is saved, what one does with the flesh doesn't matter. Some Gnostics boasted of their excesses as proof of their great spirituality. Such a view may be implied by the words of verse 24 about knowing "the depths of Satan." This sounds like the boast of someone who claimed that the only way to understand sin is to experience it in every way.

> 21 And I gave her space to repent of her fornication; and she repented not.
>
> 22 Behold, I will cast her into a bed, and them that commit adultery with her into great tribulation, except they repent of their deeds.
>
> 23 And I will kill her children with death; and all the churches shall know that I am he which searcheth the reins and hearts: and I will give unto every one of you according to your works.

The Lord had given the woman plenty of opportunities to repent, but she had continued in her evil ways. Now the Lord announced that judgment was at hand. She had sinned in beds of adultery; the Lord was about to cast her into a bed of judgment. The Lord warned all who committed adultery with her. This need not mean that she personally had committed adultery with each of them. It probably means that they followed her example of idolatry and sexual immorality. He warned that they would suffer intensely unless they repented.

Some think that "her children" mentioned in verse 23 referred to children born of her acts of adultery. More likely, "her children" were those who followed her and imitated her actions. Death would be their judgment. These terrible judgments would show not just Thyatira but all the churches that the Lord knows each person's emotions and thoughts as well as actions. More important, it would show that His piercing insight leads to sure judgment on those who think they can get by with sin.

4. Challenge (vv. 24–25)

> 24 But unto you I say, and unto the rest in Thyatira, as many as have not this doctrine, and which have not known the depths of Satan, as they speak; I will put upon you none other burden.
>
> 25 But that which ye have already hold fast till I come.

Verse 24 shows that although some church members in Thyatira had followed "Jezebel," others had not. The commendation of verse 19 and the challenge of verses 24–25 were addressed to the faithful ones in the church. Verse 19 describes them in terms of what they did; verse 24 describes them in terms of what they did not do. They did not follow the teachings of "Jezebel," nor did they participate in her evil deeds. As noted earlier, the evil is described here in language used by the sinners themselves. They boasted of experiencing the "depths of Satan."

Christ had no new challenge for the faithful members of the church. He merely reminded them of what they already knew and were doing. They knew Christ was coming. They knew He had told His people to prepare for His coming by remaining faithful to Him. Thus He reinforced this call to hold fast until He comes.

5. Promise (vv. 26–29)

> 26 And he that overcometh, and keepeth my works unto the end, to him will I give power over the nations:
>
> 27 And he shall rule them with a rod of iron; as the vessels of a potter shall they be broken to shivers: even as I received of my Father.

Christ used Psalm 2:9 as the basis of His first promise to the faithful. This verse is quoted in the New Testament as referring to Christ's coming rule over the nations (Rev. 19:15). Verses 26–27 promise that Christ's people will share in that reign.

The rod of iron was an iron-tipped rod used by a shepherd to guard his sheep. Here it is a sign of the rule of the Shepherd-King and His faithful people. The smashing of earthen pots is another sign of universal sovereignty. Ancient kings often showed their power by smashing clay vessels on which were written the names of subject kings and nations.

> 28 And I will give him the morning star.
>
> 29 He that hath an ear, let him hear what the Spirit saith unto the churches.

Revelation 22:16 refers to Jesus as "the bright and morning star." Like the morning star, Christ provides hope and guidance. Christ thus promised to give them His Spirit as a sign of hope and eventually at His coming to fulfill that hope by His appearing.

APPLYING THE BIBLE

1. "Good-bye, God!" Aaron Burr was vice-president of the United States from 1801 to 1805 under President Thomas Jefferson. Both men were running for the presidency in 1800, but Jefferson won only after the U.S. House of Representatives took thirty-six ballots. On July 11, 1804 Aaron Burr fatally wounded Alexander Hamilton in a duel at Weehawken, New Jersey, and a coroner's inquest found Burr guilty of "willful murder." He was acquitted but his political career was ruined.

A religious revival stirred Princeton University when Aaron Burr was a student. According to a campus tradition, Burr resisted, saying that before the night was over he would decide his relationship with God. Later that night, his fellow students heard Burr fling open the shutters on his window and exclaim loudly, "Good-bye, God!"

There are times we rule God out of our lives, thinking that He doesn't know us and our needs, and if He does know He doesn't care. John reminds the church at Thyatira that God knows all about them and holds them responsible (v. 19).

2. Playing with sin. Several years ago, a newspaper carried the story of Kathy Cramer, of El Toro, California, who was attacked by her "pet" python snake. When she called Monte, the python, to his lunch, it crawled out from under the bed and clamped its jaws on the back of Cramer's neck. She called for her boyfriend, Richard Hull, to help her but by this time the snake had coiled around Cramer's head and neck. Hull couldn't loosen the snake's grip; so, in desperation, he cut off its head. After having been treated for bites from the nonpoisonous snake Cramer said: "I'm really sorry we had to kill him because he was a beautiful snake!"

Jesus warns the church about the Jezebel in their midst. Like the Jezebel of the Old Testament who combined worship with sexual immorality, this woman at Thyatira, who claimed to be a prophetess, was teaching things the Lord could not tolerate. The Lord had given her plenty of opportunities to repent, but she refused (vv. 20–23). The occasion served for the risen Lord to warn the church about playing with sin because its consequences are deadly and eternal.

3. A call to faithfulness. One author has written that more believers have died for their faith in the last fifty years than in all recorded history. Although it was difficult to be a Christian in Thyatira, Jesus calls on the saints there "to hold fast till I come."

A strong example of this kind of faithfulness is seen in the life and death of John the Baptist. One of Auguste Rodin's (1840–1917) sculptures is his head of John the Baptist. The head rests on a platter with the hair flowing down nearly covering the ugly scar of the sword. But his mouth is open and his facial muscles are taut as though John were, in death, faithful to his mission, declaring, "I am the voice of one crying" (John 1:23).

Faithfulness is commanded of each of us regardless of the consequences (v. 25).

TEACHING THE BIBLE

- *Main Idea:* Believers must do good works and avoid false doctrine.
- *Suggested Teaching Aim:* To lead adults to identify good works they will perform.

A TEACHING OUTLINE

1. Use a group writing experience to introduce the Bible study.
2. Use a map to help members locate Thyatira in relation to the other seven cities.
3. Continue to use a chart (see April 13 lesson) to guide the search for biblical truth.
4. Use discussion questions to help apply the Scripture passage.
5. Identify actions members can perform individually or as a group.

Introduce the Bible Study

Place a large sheet of paper on a wall. As members enter ask them to write the name of the Christian they think of first when someone mentions doing helpful things. Begin class by referring to the list and then point out that Jesus highly commended the church at Thyatira for its good works.

Search for Biblical Truth

On a map, locate Thyatira. Ask if anyone can remember someone who came from Thyatira. (Lydia, a seller of purple cloth—Acts 16:14.) Ask members to read silently Revelation 2:18–29. Using the chart started last week, fill in (1) the name of the church and (2) the attribute of Christ from 1:14–15.

DISCUSS: What do you think the reference to Christ's eyes means today?

Ask members to identify (3) the condition of the church. (v. 19.) Point out the importance of the word "know" in these letters. Explain the "works" of the Thyatirans. Point out that works are the fruit of a saving knowledge of Jesus and not a way to earn salvation. Ask: What four words did Jesus use to describe their works? (Love, service, faithfulness, and perseverance.) Point out that Jesus condemns the church as well as commending it. Ask: Why does Jesus condemn Thyatira? (Tolerated Jezebel.) **IN ADVANCE,** enlist a member to read "Jezebel," in the *Holman Bible Dictionary*, page 795, or some other Bible dictionary and give a brief report on Jezebel. Use "Studying the Bible" to explain the possible uses of Jezebel in this letter.

Ask members to fill in (4) exhortation (v. 21), (5) warning or commendation ("cast . . . kill . . . give"—vv. 22–23). Point out the Lord's promise of not putting any other burden on the believers (vv. 24–25).

DISCUSS: Do you believe that God does not put burdens on us that we cannot bear?

Ask members to fill in (6) reward promised (vv. 26–28). Use "Studying the Bible" to explain the promised reward: "rod of iron" and "morning star."

DISCUSS: What meaning do these images have for believers today?

Ask members to fill in (7) solemn refrain (v. 29) and (8) title. A suggested title is *Compromising Church* although members may suggest another title.

DISCUSS: Is compromise always bad? How can we know when to compromise and when to remain firm in our position?

Give the Truth a Personal Focus

Ask members to refer to the names they wrote on the poster at the beginning of class. Ask: What kind of good works did these people perform that you and others found so helpful? What type of good works can you do that would help someone? What criterion for judging our works do you think Christ uses?

Let members suggest actions they can take as individuals and/or as a class. If you choose a class project, select people to help you follow through on the project.

To Philadelphia and Laodicea

Basic Passage: Revelation 3:7–22

Focal Passage: Revelation 3:7–10, 15–21

The letter to the church at Philadelphia (fil uh DEL fih uh) has a warm commendation, but no warning. The letter to the church at Laodicea (lay ahd ih SEE uh) has no commendation, but a strong warning. One thing the letters have in common is Christ's use of "door" as a symbol.

Study Aim: *To explain Christ's use of "door" in the letters to Philadelphia and Laodicea*

STUDYING THE BIBLE

OUTLINE AND SUMMARY

I. Letter to Philadelphia (Rev. 3:7–13)

1. **Greeting (v. 7)**
2. **Commendation (vv. 8–10)**
3. **Challenge (v. 11)**
4. **Promise (vv. 12–13)**

II. Letter to Laodicea (Rev. 3:14–22)

1. **Greeting (v. 14)**
2. **Warning (vv. 15–17)**
3. **Challenge (vv. 18–20)**
4. **Promise (vv. 21–22)**

Christ greeted the church at Philadelphia as the holy and true One who alone holds the key to the eternal kingdom (v. 7). He commended the church for its faithfulness and reminded it of the open door set before it (vv. 8–10). Christ challenged the church members to hold fast until His coming (v. 11). He promised to make them pillars in God's temple (vv. 12–13). Christ greeted the church at Laodicea as the Amen, the faithful and true witness, and the source of creation (v. 14). He warned of lukewarmness, pride, and self-sufficiency (vv. 15–17). He challenged them to seek true wealth, righteousness, and insight by repenting and receiving Christ into their hearts (vv. 18–20). He promised that those who overcame would reign with Him (vv. 21–22).

I. Letter to Philadelphia (Rev. 3:7–13)

1. Greeting (v. 7)

7 And to the angel of the church in Philadelphia write;

These things saith he that is holy, he that is true, he that hath the key of David, he that openeth, and no man shutteth; and shutteth, and no man openeth.

Sardis (SAHR diss; Rev. 3:1–6) was about thirty-three miles southeast of Thyatira (thigh uh TIGH ruh), and Philadelphia was about twenty-eight miles southeast of Sardis. Philadelphia was founded in order to spread Greek language and culture to the barbaric tribes beyond it.

Christ addressed the church as the holy and true One. Christ is also the holder of the key of David. Christ came to fulfill God's promise to David of an everlasting kingdom. Jesus Christ and He alone holds the key to entering that eternal kingdom.

2. Commendation (vv. 8–10)

> 8 I know thy works: behold, I have set before thee an open door, and no man can shut it: for thou hast a little strength, and hast kept my word, and hast not denied my name.

An open door symbolized a God-given opportunity. To what God-given opportunity was Christ referring in verse 8? Some Bible scholars think that He was reinforcing the point He had just made about holding the key of David. In other words, Christ was assuring them of their inclusion in God's eternal kingdom. Because Christ had opened the door and alone had the key, no one could close it.

Many Bible scholars think that Christ was using the open door as a symbol of the missionary opportunity of the church at Philadelphia. Just as the city was founded to spread Greek culture, Christ wanted them to spread the Christian gospel. An "open door" is used several times in the New Testament to describe an opportunity for sharing the gospel (1 Cor. 16:9; 2 Cor. 2:12; Col. 4:3).

The last part of verse 8 speaks of the weakness of the church, but also of their faithfulness in keeping Christ's word and not denying His name. This suggests that they were few in number and had no wealth or prestige. Not many of the early Christians were people of wealth or worldly influence (1 Cor. 1:26–31). Yet their weakness became their strength because it encouraged them to rely solely on the Lord (2 Cor. 12:10).

> 9 Behold, I will make them of the synagogue of Satan, which say they are Jews, and are not, but do lie; behold, I will make them to come and worship before thy feet, and to know that I have loved thee.

Verse 9 is similar to the words of Revelation 2:9. Although John and most of the original believers were Jews, they and the early Gentile believers faced strong opposition in Asia from some Jews who rejected Jesus as Son of God. John charged that these persecutors were actually instruments of Satan, not of God. The Jews laid exclusive claim to a special covenant of God with Israel. Christ disputed this claim. The true Jews are not those who can trace their ancestry back to Jacob, but people who have faith in the Savior whom God sent for Israel and the whole world (see Matt. 3:9; Rom. 2:28–29; 4:16; Gal. 3:6–7, 28–29).

> 10 Because thou hast kept the word of my patience, I also will keep thee from the hour of temptation, which shall come upon all the world, to try them that dwell upon the earth.

Because of their faithfulness, Christ promised deliverance from the hour of trial that was coming on the world. Bible students debate whether Christ meant deliverance by providing strength to pass through trials, or deliverance from having to go through trials. Many believers, however would agree with these two biblical principles: (1) Christ did not exempt His followers from many of the trials of life, especially the test that comes by being persecuted. However, He did promise to be with them and enable them to be faithful unto death. For example, He said, "In the world ye shall have tribulation: but be of good cheer; I have overcome the world" (John 16:33). Many passages in Revelation and elsewhere speak of Christians going through the trial of persecution.

(2) Christ will punish an unbelieving world. Christians will be exempt from the punishment that God's wrath pours out on a godless world. This seems to be the kind of trial that Christ had in mind in verse 10. This trial is coming on "them that dwell on the earth," a phrase used throughout Revelation to refer to an unbelieving world (Rev. 6:10; 8:13; 11:10; 13:8, 14; 17:8).

3. Challenge (v. 11)

In light of Christ's imminent coming, believers should hold fast what they have.

4. Promise (vv. 12–13)

Christ promised to those who overcame that He would make them pillars in the temple of God, on which would be written the names of God, of the new Jerusalem, and of Christ.

II. Letter to Laodicea (Rev. 3:14–22)

1. Greeting (v. 14)

Christ greeted the church at Laodicea as the Amen, the faithful and true witness, and the source of divine creation.

2. Warning (vv. 15–17)

> 15 I know thy works, that thou art neither cold nor hot: I would thou wert cold or hot.
>
> 16 So then because thou art lukewarm, and neither cold nor hot, I will spue thee out of my mouth.

Christ used the words "I know thy works" to introduce commendations of five churches (2:2, 9, 13, 19; 3:8) and warnings to two churches (3:1, 15). The living Lord walked among His churches and knew what was happening. He knew the faithfulness of some and the unfaithfulness of others. He knew that Laodicea was a lukewarm church. This vivid condemnation communicates to people in every generation. People like some drinks hot and other drinks cold, but no one likes a lukewarm drink. Thus Jesus used a normal human experience to picture the spiritual plight of the church. Just as a person might spit out a tepid, lukewarm drink, so Christ would spit out the lukewarm Laodiceans.

He preferred that they be hot or cold rather than lukewarm. He had rather someone be hot with true zeal than lukewarm spiritually. He would even rather they be cold, like people who have never heard the gospel, than to have heard it and only become lukewarm. People who have not heard might hear and respond with genuine warmth and zeal.

The spiritual meaning of lukewarm is clear. This is a person who has been exposed to the white-hot glow of divine holiness and salvation but has only made a halfhearted response. Such people don't want to run the risks of not being professing Christians and church members, but they don't want to take their faith so seriously that it inconveniences them.

> 17 Because thou sayest, I am rich, and increased with goods, and have need of nothing; and knowest not that thou art wretched, and miserable, and poor, and blind, and naked:

Prosperity is often a greater test of faith than affliction. God warned Israel about the dangers of wealth, pride, and self-sufficiency after they settled in Canaan (Deut. 8). Laodicea was known for its wealth. Although most of the early Christians elsewhere were poor, this was not the case in Laodicea. Their wealth led them to feelings of pride and self-sufficiency, which are the opposite of feelings of trust and dependence on God.

Jesus had commended the church at Smyrna (SMUR nuh) for being rich although they were poor (Rev. 2:9). He condemned the Laodiceans for being poor although they were rich. They thought they were rich and needed nothing. Christ exhausted the dictionary in using words that described their true plight: wretched, miserable, poor, blind, naked.

3. Challenge (vv. 18–20)

> 18 I counsel thee to buy of me gold tried in the fire, that thou mayest be rich; and white raiment, that thou mayest be clothed, and that the shame of thy nakedness do not appear; and anoint thine eyes with eye-salve, that thou mayest see.

Laodicea was a banking center, a manufacturing center noted for its spun black wool and a medical center noted for its eye-salve. Christ used these facts to challenge them in three areas of their spiritual lives. They needed a faith that was tested and proved; such would be more precious than gold (1 Pet. 1:7). They needed divine cleansing and righteousness, which was like being clothed in white. They needed real healing and insight, which could only come from total commitment to the Lord.

> 19 As many as I love, I rebuke and chasten: be zealous therefore, and repent.
>
> Christ made clear that whatever chastening they received was done because He loved them (see Heb. 12:5–11). The Lord's goal was to lead them to repent of their pride, self-sufficiency, and lukewarmness.
>
> 20 Behold, I stand at the door, and knock: if any man hear my voice, and open the door, I will come in to him, and will sup with him, and he with me.

This is one of the most familiar verses in the Book of Revelation, and rightly so. It shows that the Lord is not so far away that He must be persuaded to hear us. Instead, He is as near as the entrance to our heart. All we need to do is to hear His voice and open our hearts to Him. Then He will come into our lives and bless us with His presence.

In context, this promise reinforced the call to repent in verse 19. If they repented, Christ would restore full fellowship with them. Thus the promise can apply to those who have drifted from the Lord. But it can also apply to those who have never known the Lord, which could have been the real problem of some in Laodicea.

4. Promise (vv. 21–22)

21 To him that overcometh will I grant to sit with me in my throne, even as I also overcame, and am set down with my Father in his throne.

This verse repeats the promise of Revelation 2:26–27 that believers who overcome will share in Christ's reign. Verse 22 closes this seventh letter with the same admonition found at the end of all the letters.

APPLYING THE BIBLE

1. The narrow way. John Glenn was the first American to orbit the earth in space. In his spacecraft, *Friendship 7*, he circled the earth three times in five hours on February 20, 1962. But reentry into earth's atmosphere to bring Glenn and his spacecraft back to earth was a very critical thing. *Friendship 7* had to reenter through a "corridor" in the earth's atmosphere only seven miles wide. As Glenn reentered, his spacecraft encountered tremendous temperature that began peeling all the "skin" off the spacecraft. If the corridor had been missed, the forces of heat and gravity would have consumed the spacecraft.

Jesus said "strait is the gate, and narrow is the way, which leadeth unto life, and few there be that find it" (Matt. 7:14). To the church at Philadelphia, John identified Jesus as the only One who can open the door to eternal life, for He has the key of David (the kingdom of God—vv. 7–8).

2. Called to be faithful. Roy Angell tells about a spindly boy who was sent in by the coach to represent his school in the mile run. All the other runners came in far ahead of the boy. When the last of the better runners crossed the line, the boy was half a lap behind. Finally, he crossed the line and fell exhausted to the track. The judges rushed out and asked the boy why he didn't quit since he was so far behind. The boy answered: "The coach didn't send me out here to quit, and he didn't send me to win. He sent me to run and I gave it my best!"

Christ doesn't call us to win; He calls us to be faithful (v. 8). We must give Him our best and leave the results up to Him.

3. Love expresses itself. Love is more than a four-letter word. Love works and expresses itself. A promising young doctor graduated from medical school and could have set up a lucrative practice in a large city. Instead, he went to a mountain community where people were poor and the needs were great. Day and night he rode his horse to the homes of the sick and needy. The years and hard work took their toll, and when he died the people gathered to place stones around his grave. Someone remembered his sign which hung at the drugstore. Retrieving the sign, which read, "Office Upstairs," they placed it at the head of his grave. His last act of kindness was to write across each page of his ledger of the people who owed him money, "Paid in full!"

Jesus tells the Philadelphian church, "I have loved thee" (v. 9). That love expressed itself in action at the cross.

4. Backsliders. A minister's little daughter and her friend were talking one day. The little friend, remembering that her pastor had preached on backsliding, asked, "What is a backslider?" The minister's daughter explained that "backsliders don't love Jesus as much as they once did." Continuing, she said, "Once they used to sit up front in church. Then they slide back a row, and they keep sliding until they are on the back row. Soon they don't even come to church at all!"

That's a pretty simple definition of a backslider, but many of us have been guilty of it. The church at Laodica was rebuked by the risen Lord: "I know thy works, that thou are neither cold or hot: I would thou wert cold or hot. . . . I will spew thee out of my mouth" (vv. 15–16).

5. Christ at the door. Revelation 3:20 is one of the best-known verses in Revelation. It is graphically pictured by Holman Hunt's 1854 painting, "Christ as the Light of the World." There stands Christ, knocking on the vine-covered door, waiting to be admitted. But there is no handle on the outside of the door. It represents the human heart that must be opened from within.

Verse 20 shows Christ knocking on the door of the Laodicean church which has, in its lukewarmness, shut Him out. Christ's promise is that if they will repent and open the door to Him, He will come in and fellowship with them.

What a tragedy it is for Christ to be shut out of His church!

TEACHING THE BIBLE

- *Main Idea:* God has set before all of us an open door of opportunity.
- *Suggested Teaching Aim:* To lead adults to identify opportunities they have as a church and as individuals.

A TEACHING OUTLINE

1. Use a question to introduce the Bible study.

2. Continue to use the chart you started on April 13.

3. Use a poster to help identify opportunities members have as a church and as individuals.

Introduce the Bible Study

Ask: What can doors be used for? Let members suggest ways doors can be used. Say, Jesus referred to doors in His letter to the two churches we study about today. In one, the door is an open door of opportunity; in the other, it is a closed door—one through which Jesus cannot even get in.

Search for Biblical Truth

On a map, locate Philadelphia and Laodicea. Ask members to read silently 3:7–10. Using the chart started April 13, fill in (1) the name of the church and (2) the attribute of Christ from 1:12–18 (key of David).

DISCUSS: What do you think the term "key of David" means?

Fill in the chart for (3) condition of the church ("know thy works . . . not denied my name") and (4) exhortation ("make the synagogue of Satan"). Use "Studying the Bible" to explain possible meanings of "open door."

Fill in the chart for (5) warning or commendation ("I will keep . . . upon the earth"). Point out that Philadelphia is the only church that Christ does not warn. Use "Studying the Bible" to explain interpretations of "keep thee from . . . temptation."

DISCUSS: If Christ were writing our church, would He warn or condemn us? Why?

Although 3:11–13 are not part of the focal passage, quickly fill in the chart for (6) solemn refrain and (7) reward promised. Let members suggest (8) a title (church with opportunity).

Ask members to read silently 3:15–22. Fill in the chart for (1) church and (2) attribute (none).

Ask members to fill in (3) condition of the church ("neither cold nor hot" and "wretched . . . naked"). Ask: How does John indicate that Jesus knew the condition of the church? (Walks in their midst—1:13.) Fill in (4) exhortation (vv. 19–20). Point out that what makes 3:20 so sad is that it is a picture of Christ knocking, trying to get in His church, and they will not let Him in. Fill in (5) warning or commendation (v. 18). Use "Studying the Bible" to explain the background of Jesus' warning to the Laodiceans.

Fill in (6) solemn refrain, (7) reward promised ("grant to sit . . . in his throne"—3:21), and (8) title (consider: "complacent").

DISCUSS: What causes a church that was once strong and vibrant to become a complacent church? What does it take to change? What makes an individual complacent? What does it take to change?

Give the Truth a Personal Focus

IN ADVANCE, on a chalkboard or a large sheet of paper, draw two doors. Over one write *Open* and over the other write *Closed.* Ask: Which "door" would you use to describe our church? your spiritual life?

Point out that all churches and individuals have an open door of opportunity if they will take it. Let members suggest some opportunities they have as a church or as individuals. List these on the "open" door you have drawn. Ask members to choose one or more of these opportunities and plan how they can achieve it.

May

4

1997

The Redeeming Lamb

Basic Passage: Revelation 4–5

Focal Passage: Revelation 5:1–10

Following the letters to the seven churches in Revelation 2–3 is a twofold vision in Revelation 4–5. Revelation 4 pictures the throne of God and all beings praising God. Revelation 5 pictures the Lamb who alone is worthy to open a mysterious scroll and all beings praising Him.

Study Aim: *To describe what John heard, felt, and saw in Revelation 5:1–10*

STUDYING THE BIBLE

OUTLINE AND SUMMARY

I. Vision of the Holy God (Rev. 4:1–11)

1. The throne in heaven (4:1–3)

2. Beings around the throne (4:4–7)

3. Praises to the holy Creator (4:8–11)

II. Vision of the Lamb (Rev. 5:1–14)

1. The scroll with seven seals (5:1–4)

2. The Lion-Lamb (5:5–7)

3. Worshiping the Lamb (5:8–14)

Called up into heaven, John saw a vision of an awesome throne (4:1–3). Around the throne were twenty-four elders, four living beings, seven lamps of fire, and a sea of glass (4:4–7). After the four beings praised God's holiness, the elders fell down and worshiped Him (4:8–11). John saw the figure on a heavenly throne holding a scroll with seven seals, and John wept because no one was worthy to open the scroll (5:1–4). When an elder told John that the Lion of Judah was worthy to open the scroll, John saw a slain Lamb with seven horns and seven eyes (5:5–7). After the elders and beings praised the Lamb for giving His life to redeem people of every nation, angels joined all creation in declaring the worthiness of the Lamb to receive all glory (5:8–14).

I. Vision of the Holy God (Rev. 4:1–11)

1. The throne in heaven (4:1–3)

A door was opened in heaven, and John was called to come up and see things that shall take place (v. 1). As he was in the Spirit, John saw a throne and someone sitting on it (v. 2). The One on the throne looked like a jasper stone and a sardius, and an emerald rainbow encircled the throne (v. 3).

2. Beings around the throne (4:4–7)

Around the throne were twenty-four thrones on which sat twenty-four elders dressed in white with gold crowns (v. 4). Thunder and lightning came from the throne; and before it burned seven lamps, which are the seven Spirits of God (v. 5). In front of the throne was what looked like a sea of glass; and in the center around the throne were four living creatures (v. 6). The first was like a lion; the second, an ox; the third, a man; and the fourth, an eagle (v. 7).

3. Praises to the holy Creator (4:8–11)

The living creatures sang day and night, "Holy, holy, holy, Lord God Almighty, which was, and is, and is to come" (v. 8). The twenty-four elders fell down and worshiped by casting their crowns before the throne and praising God (vv. 9–11).

II. Vision of the Lamb (Rev. 5:1–14)

1. The scroll with seven seals (5:1–4)

1 And I saw in the right hand of him that sat on the throne a book written within and on the backside, sealed with seven seals.

2 And I saw a strong angel proclaiming with a loud voice, Who is worthy to open the book, and to loose the seals thereof?

3 And no man in heaven, nor in earth, neither under the earth, was able to open the book, neither to look thereon.

4 And I wept much, because no man was found worthy to open and to read the book, neither to look thereon.

North Syrian and Hittite stamp-type seals. Credit: Bill Stephens.

Most of the books of John's day were actually scrolls. The description of this "book" shows that it was a scroll with seven seals and written inside and outside. A Roman law required that seven witnesses affix their seals to a will, thus ensuring its validity. This scroll was not a will, but the seven seals attested to its validity. The writing inside and outside shows that it was full.

The scroll was held out in God's right hand, and the loud voice of a strong angel asked who was worthy to open the scroll by breaking the seals. Apparently at first no one stepped forward, for John reported that no one anywhere was found who was worthy to open the scroll and to reveal its contents. John was devastated by this news. He had come to see what was going to take place. The answer was in the scroll. It appeared that the scroll was going to remain sealed and a mystery.

2. The Lion-Lamb (5:5–7)

> 5 And one of the elders saith unto me, Weep not: behold, the Lion of the tribe of Juda, the Root of David, hath prevailed to open the book, and to loose the seals thereof.

A Torah (Genesis-Deuteronomy) scroll being held in its wooden case at a celebration in Jerusalem. Credit: Bill Stephens.

One of the twenty-four elders spoke to John in his sorrow and told him to stop weeping because One was found who could break the seals and open the scroll. He is called the Lion of the tribe of Judah. The lion was a symbol of power and royalty. In Jacob's final blessings to his sons, he called Judah "a lion's whelp" and foretold the coming of Shiloh (Gen. 49:9–10). The Lion was also called the Root of David. This reflects another messianic prophecy in Isaiah 11:1–10, which describes One who is the root of Jesse, David's father. These two prophecies were part of the promise of a Messiah who would fulfill God's promises to David and reign with royal power.

The elder told John that this King was worthy to open the scroll because he "hath prevailed." The word means to overcome or be victorious. It is the same word that the Lord used in challenging the seven churches to overcome in the face of persecution (2:7, 11, 17, 26; 3:5, 12, 21). More is revealed in verses 6–10 about the kind of victory He won.

> 6 And I beheld, and, lo, in the midst of the throne and of the four beasts, and in the midst of the elders, stood a Lamb as it had been slain, having seven horns and seven eyes, which are the seven Spirits of God sent forth into all the earth.

The elder had told John that a Lion was worthy to open the scroll; but when John looked, he saw a Lamb. The Lamb was alive and standing, but it showed evidence of having been slain. The Lamb was the Lamb of God who takes away the sin of the world (John 1:29). The Old Testament background included the Passover lamb that was killed to deliver the Israelites from the death angel (Exod. 12:1–16). Even more significant is the prophecy of the Suffering Servant in Isaiah 53. The Servant was "brought as a lamb to the slaughter" (Isa. 53:7), but He went voluntarily to offer Himself for the sins of others. Philip told the Ethiopian that this prophecy was fulfilled in Jesus (Acts 8:30–35).

These two strains of Old Testament prophecy—the coming King and the Suffering Servant—came together in Jesus Christ. During His earthly ministry, Jesus was cautious about accepting the title of King. He knew that many had a purely earthly image of what the Messiah was to do (John 6:15). Even His disciples did not understand Jesus' words about the necessity of suffering and dying (Matt. 16:21–23; Mark 9:32). When Jesus died, His followers thought of His death as a defeat. Only in light of His Resurrection did they see that the cross and Resurrection won the victory of the Lion-Lamb over sin, death, and Satan. Other kings seek to win victories by force of arms; this Lion-Lamb won the victory by giving Himself for others.

The slain Lamb had seven horns and seven eyes, which are the seven Spirits of God. Horns, like lions, were a symbol of royal power. Most Bible students believe that the seven Spirits signify the Holy Spirit. The seven spirits are the eyes of Christ in the world. The Gospel of John describes the Holy Spirit sent forth into the world to convict of sin and to exalt Christ (14:26; 15:26; 16:7–15). The Book of Acts describes Christ continuing His work in the world through the Holy Spirit (Acts 1:1–8).

During the Middle Ages, some painters sought to capture the scene by painting a slain lamb with seven horns and seven eyes. Christians readers of the first century knew that the vision signified Jesus Christ, the Lamb of God. The reality was not an actual lamb with seven horns and seven eyes. The reality was what that signified. Keep this in mind as you read other strange visions described by John. In other kinds of literature, the words describe the reality in straightforward terms. In prophetic visions, the reality is often not the sign itself, but something that the sign pointed to.

> 7 And he came and took the book out of the right hand of him that sat upon the throne.

In a dramatic move the slain Lamb went to the throne where God was holding the scroll in His right hand. The force of "took" is as if the wording were, "He went up and took it, and now He has it."

3. Worshiping the Lamb (5:8–14)

> 8 And when he had taken the book, the four beasts and four and twenty elders fell down before the Lamb, having every one of them harps, and golden vials full of odours, which are the prayers of saints.

Who were the twenty-four elders? Some Bible students think that they and the four living beings were angelic orders around God's throne. Many think that the elders represented the redeemed people of God, who are described in the song of verses 9–10. The new Jerusalem is described as having twelve gates named for the tribes of Israel and twelve foundations named for the apostles (Rev. 21:12, 14). Therefore, could the twenty-four elders be Old and New Testament believers? Some Bible students think that the twenty-four elders represent the church that had been raptured and that much of the rest of Revelation describes events of the Great Tribulation.

The twenty-four elders worshiped the Lamb by falling down before Him.

Each elder had a harp for praise in song, and golden vials which represented the prayers of the saints. Christians are sometimes tempted to believe that their prayers are not heard. First-century believers were being persecuted. They prayed for the Lord to come. However, their persecutors continued their evil work and the Lord continued to delay His coming. John's vision assured him and other persecuted believers that their prayers were like incense that goes up before God and Christ. Such prayers are heard and answered in God's way and in God's time.

> 9 And they sung a new song, saying, Thou art worthy to take the book, and to open the seals thereof: for thou wast slain, and hast redeemed us to God by thy blood out of every kindred, and tongue, and people, and nation;
>
> 10 And hast made us unto our God kings and priests: and we shall reign on the earth.

The redeemed of God sang a new song declaring that the Lamb was worthy because He had redeemed them and made them a kingdom of priests. Slaves could be set free by the payment of a redemption. By His death, Jesus set us free from sin and death by purchasing us with His own blood. The redeemed come from all nations, languages, and people groups, not just from the Jews.

As in Revelation 1:6, the word "kings" means "kingdom." The background is Exodus 19:6, where God promised to make Israel "a kingdom of priests, and an holy nation." The New Testament cites this verse as fulfilled in all God's people in Christ (see 1 Pet. 2:9). In a sense, God's kingdom has already come; and Christ and His people already reign. However, this is apparent only through eyes of faith. When the kingdom comes, Christ will reign; and He will share His reign with His people (Rev. 2:26–27; 3:21; 20:6).

Millions of angels around the throne and the four living beings joined with the twenty-four elders to praise the Lamb as worthy of all glory (vv. 11–12). They in turn were joined in praise to the Lamb by all creatures in heaven, and on earth, and under the earth (v. 13). The four living beings said, "Amen"; and the twenty-four elders fell down and worshiped Him that lives forever and ever.

APPLYING THE BIBLE

1. We can never know all about God. British author H. G. Wells (1866–1946), in his novel *The Soul of a Bishop*, tells about a conversation a bishop had with an angel. Discussing the greatness of God, the bishop said, "But the Truth; you can tell me the Truth." Smiling, the angel cupped his hands over the bishop's bald spot, stroked it affectionately, and said: "Truth! Yes, I could tell you the Truth, but could this hold it? Not this little box of brains. You haven't things to hold it with inside this."

Although John labors in 4:1–7 to describe God's glory and majesty, John barely touches the truth about God's nature, character, and glory. Jesus reveals the Father to us, but still we can never know all there is to know about God.

2. Praise spontaneous. An elderly woman dearly loved her Lord, and during her pastor's sermons she would frequently shout, "Praise the

Lord!" When she shouted he would lose his line of thought in his sermon. He spoke to her about it one day, and she promised to contain her emotions. For a while she did well, but one day a visiting preacher was preaching on the forgiveness of sin, and "Aunt Mary" cut loose with one of her "Praise the Lord" shouts. Later, she confided to her pastor, "promise or no promise, I just couldn't help but praise the Lord for He has forgiven all my sins."

Verse 8 shows the spontaneous praise to God of the heavenly being. Seeing His glory and majesty, they cry out day and night, "Holy, holy, holy, Lord God Almighty, which was, and is, and is to come."

God expects and commands us to praise Him for it is pleasing to Him (see the Psalms). It is a natural thing for the believer to praise his God, but we do all too little of it.

3. Who knows the future. There is a craze in the world today about psychics and astrologers. And almost every newspaper in the nation daily carries the astrology charts. This is an abomination to the Lord (Mic. 5:12). Our future is not to be found in the pagan study of the stars; it is found in Jesus Christ, the star of David, the Bright and Morning Star (Rev. 22:16; 2 Pet. 1:19). Only He can unlock for us the future (5:1–7).

4. Christ the key. Lewis Carroll is famous for his children's story *Alice in Wonderland.* In one of his other stories, Carroll tells about an animated padlock. Alive, then, with spindly legs and arms, the padlock is in great distress. When another character in the story asks the padlock what is wrong it replies, "I am seeking for the key to unlock myself!"

When the angel asked, "Who is worthy to open the book, and to loose the seals thereof?" Jesus stepped forward to open the book (5:7). Only Jesus knows the future.

5. He only said, "I love you." Several years ago the newspaper carried the sad story of five-year-old Jeffrey Lansdown, who was beaten to death by his father. His mangled body was found at the bottom of an embankment near a desert road. For three weeks before his murder, little Jeffrey had suffered unmercifully at the hands of his crazed father. The mother later said she did not intervene because she was afraid the father would hurt her and their other children.

After Jeffrey's body was discovered, the police asked his mother what Jeffrey said when his father had threatened to kill him. Sobbing, the mother replied, "Jeff only said, 'Daddy, I love you.'"

That's all Jesus said when they nailed Him to the cross. Jesus still bears the marks of His love for us in His risen, glorified body. John sees Jesus as "a Lamb as it had been slain" (5:6, 9). Our redemption is an eternal cost to Jesus. And all he said was "I love you!"

TEACHING THE BIBLE

- *Main Idea:* Jesus alone is worthy because He was crucified and resurrected.
- *Suggested Teaching Aim:* To lead adults to worship Jesus because of who He is and what He has done for us.

A TEACHING OUTLINE

1. Use a thought question and a hymn to introduce the Bible study.

2. Use Scripture search and group discussion to search for biblical truth.

3. Plan a brief time of worship to conclude the lesson and to honor Christ.

Introduce the Bible Study

Ask members if they remember the one symbol that tied both of the letters to Philadelphia and Laodicea together. (Door.) Ask them to look at 4:1. Ask: How is the door used in this verse? (The scene of revelation shifts from earth to heaven; John sees into heaven through the door.)

IN ADVANCE, enlist a member to read the hymn, "Holy, Holy, Holy." Then ask members to skim Revelation 4 and see how many references to the hymn they can find in this chapter. Point out that this sets the stage for the rest of the book.

Search for Biblical Truth

Ask members to read 5:1–4 silently. Ask: What did the angel ask? (For someone worthy to open the scroll.) What was John's reaction? (Wept because no one was found who could open the scroll.)

Ask members to read 5:5–7. Ask members to identify the terms used to describe Jesus. (Lion, Root, Lamb.) Using "Studying the Bible," lecture briefly on the following points: (1) the significance and background of each of the three names; (2) the relationship between the royalty of Jesus and the Suffering Servant; (3) the meaning and significance of the seven horns, eyes, and spirits; (4) the reality of the vision was not an actual lamb but what the lamb signified.

Ask members to read 5:8–10. Ask: Who were the twenty-four elders? (See "Studying the Bible" for options.) What message in verse 8 did these elders communicate to first-century Christians and hence to us? (Prayers were like incense that went to God; God heard and received all the prayers.) What did the elders announce? (Jesus was worthy to open the scroll.)

Ask volunteers to read: (1) Exodus 19:6 (point out that this verse is set in the context of God giving the Ten Commandments on Sinai—Exod. 20); (2) 1 Peter 2:9; (3) Revelation 1:6 (preferably in a translation that uses "kingdom" instead of "kings").

Ask: What does it mean to be a "kingdom of priests"? How do we demonstrate our priesthood toward ourselves? toward others? toward Christ?

DISCUSS: How important is the concept of the priesthood of the believer to you? Why?

Give the Truth a Personal Focus

Read the "Suggested Teaching Aim: To lead adults to worship Jesus because of who He is and what He has done for us." Ask: What has Jesus done for you? What have you done for Him? Suggest that one aspect of the Old Testament priesthood was to lead in worship. As New Testament priests, we, too, are to worship and praise Jesus. Read or sing the words to "Holy, Holy, Holy" as a concluding praise.

May

11

1997

Provision for the Redeemed

Basic Passage: Revelation 7:1–17

Focal Passage: Revelation 7:1–3, 9–10, 13–17

Revelation 7 records two visions. Revelation 7:1–8 pictures 144,000 servants of God who receive the seal of divine protection. Revelation 7:9–17 pictures a great multitude of the redeemed serving before the throne of God.

Study Aim: *To describe the two visions in Revelation 7*

STUDYING THE BIBLE

OUTLINE AND SUMMARY

I. Vision of 144,000 Sealed Servants of God (Rev. 7:1–8)
  1. Seal of the living God (vv. 1–3)
  2. The 144,000 (vv. 4–8)

II. Vision of a Multitude of the Redeemed (Rev. 7:9–17)
  1. A great multitude (vv. 9–12)
  2. Their identity (vv. 13–14)
  3. Their destiny (vv. 15–17)

John saw four angels holding back the four winds and another angel with the seal of the living God (vv. 1–3). He heard that 144,000 servants were sealed, 12,000 from each tribe of Israel (vv. 4–8). He saw a great multitude from all nations clothed in white and holding palms, and he heard their cry of praise for salvation to God and the Lamb (vv. 9–12). When John told one of the elders that he didn't know who they were, the elder told him that they were those out of great tribulation who had washed their robes in the blood of the Lamb (vv. 13–14). They serve before God's throne, enjoy His eternal presence, and are exempt from the blights of earthly life (vv. 15–17).

I. Vision of 144,000 Sealed Servants of God (Rev. 7:1–8)

1. Seal of the living God (vv. 1–3)

1 And after these things I saw four angels standing on the four corners of the earth, holding the four winds of the earth, that the wind should not blow on the earth, nor on the sea, nor on any tree.

2 And I saw another angel ascending from the east, having the seal of the living God: and he cried with a loud voice to the four angels, to whom it was given to hurt the earth and the sea,

3 Saying, Hurt not the earth, neither the sea, nor the trees, till we have sealed the servants of our God in their foreheads.

Revelation 6 provides the background for this vision. Six of the seven seals were opened. The opening of the sixth seal led to an outpouring of divine wrath. The rulers on earth said that "the great day of his wrath is come; and who shall be able to stand?" (v. 17). Revelation 7 answers that question.

The seventh seal of the scroll (Rev. 5) had not yet been broken. Thus the scroll still remained sealed. Before it was opened and God's final wrath was described, the two visions of Revelation 7 were presented as assurances to the people of God. Before God's wrath fell, four angels appeared. They were holding back the four winds so that the winds might not blow on the earth, the sea, or any tree.

Then another angel came from the east with the seal of the living God. He commanded the four angels not to hurt the earth, the sea, or any tree until God's servants could be sealed on their foreheads. This is a picture of restrained judgment and of divine protection for God's servants.

A seal in the ancient world referred to an impression made by a seal of a person's identity and authority. The seal was affixed to documents to show their authenticity and authority. Today we would use a notarized or guaranteed signature. Ancient kings often used a signet ring as their seal. Pharaoh gave Joseph such a ring (Gen. 41:42). The stone of the lion's den in Daniel 6:17 was sealed with the signet rings of the Persian king and nobles.

The Old Testament background to Revelation 7:1–3 was the blood of the lamb over the doors of the Israelites during the final plague on Egypt. The death angel passed over their homes when he visited death on the firstborn of each house without the blood (Exod. 12:23). In the same way, the sealing of God's servants in Revelation marked them as belonging to God and thus exempt from His judgments on the ungodly.

Another New Testament reference to sealing is the revelation that believers have been sealed with the Holy Spirit unto the day of redemption (Eph. 4:30). The Spirit is a divine pledge of our final redemption (Eph. 1:13; 2 Cor. 1:22).

2. The 144,000 (vv. 4–8)

The servants of God who were sealed numbered 144,000, with 12,000 from each of the twelve tribes of Israel.

II. Vision of a Multitude of the Redeemed (Rev. 7:9–17)

1. A great multitude (vv. 9–10)

> 9 After this I beheld, and, lo, a great multitude, which no man could number, of all nations, and kindreds, and people, and tongues, stood before the throne, and before the Lamb, clothed with white robes, and palms in their hands;
>
> 10 And cried with a loud voice, saying, Salvation to our God which sitteth upon the throne, and unto the Lamb.

In this vision, John saw a great multitude too numerous to count. They were from every language, nation, and people group. They were standing before the throne described in Revelation 4–5. They were clothed in white robes and held palms in their hands, and they praised God and the Lamb for divine salvation.

The white robes are explained in verse 14. The palms were signs of God's deliverance and care. The background was the Feast of Tabernacles, which celebrated God's deliverance of Israel from Egypt and His care of them in the wilderness (Exod. 12–18; Lev. 23:39–43; Neh. 8:14–17). Thus the great multitude stood before the throne of God and loudly declared the salvation of God and the Lamb.

In another link with the visions of chapters 4–5, the angels, elders, and living beings around the throne worshiped God with lavish words of praise (vv. 11–12).

2. Their identity (vv. 13–14)

> 13 And one of the elders answered, saying unto me, What are these which are arrayed in white robes? and whence came they?
>
> 14 And I said unto him, Sir, thou knowest. And he said to me, These are they which came out of great tribulation, and have washed their robes, and made them white in the blood of the Lamb.

As in Revelation 5:5, one of the twenty-four elders around the throne of God spoke to John. The elder asked him two questions: Who are these clothed in white robes? Where do they come from? The Book of Revelation has many similarities to the Book of Ezekiel. When the Lord showed Ezekiel the vision of dry bones, God asked the prophet, "Can these bones live?" to which the prophet replied, "Thou knowest" (Ezek. 37:3). John made the same humble reply to the elder. Neither Ezekiel nor John presumed to know the answer to the questions until it was revealed to him.

The elder identified the multitude clothed in white as those who had washed their robes white in the blood of the Lamb. The gospel song "Are You Washed in the Blood of the Lamb?" correctly interprets the meaning of Revelation 7:14. The blood of the Lamb provides salvation from sins. When sinners repent of their sins and trust Christ as Lord and Savior, their lives are cleansed and they are forgiven of their sins. Paul wrote of Jesus Christ, "We have redemption through his blood, the forgiveness of sins, according to the riches of his grace" (Eph. 1:7). In the introductory words of Revelation, John praised Christ who "loved us, and washed us from our sins in his own blood" (Rev. 1:5).

The elder also explained that the great multitude were "they which came out of great tribulation." In discussing a similar promise in Revelation 2:10, we differentiated between tribulation as punishment from God and tribulation as persecution of Christians by ungodly people. The comment was made that believers are exempt from the former, but not the latter. The coming of the white-robed throng "out of great tribulation" is understood by some Bible students to mean that they were delivered from the divine wrath to be visited on the ungodly. Others understand the meaning to be deliverance through persecution. In other words, these were those who overcame and won the victory through a perseverance that was rooted in preservation by the Lord.

3. Their destiny (vv. 15–17)

> 15 Therefore are they before the throne of God, and serve him day and night in his temple: and he that sitteth on the throne shall dwell among them.

16 They shall hunger no more, neither thirst any more; neither shall the sun light on them, nor any heat.

17 For the Lamb which is in the midst of the throne shall feed them, and shall lead them unto living fountains of waters: and God shall wipe away all tears from their eyes.

The multitude of the redeemed were standing before the throne of God, which was described in chapters 4–5. They are described as serving God day and night in His temple. This shows that the future life of the redeemed is not a dull, useless existence. Instead, the redeemed shall serve the Lord. The Bible does not describe all the forms that this service will take, just as it does not try to explain to earthbound minds all of the glories of the future. Knowing the redeemed will serve Him is enough for now.

The central reality of future blessedness is that God Himself shall dwell with His people. The heart of Christian hope focuses not on ourselves and our survival, but on God and His glorious purpose and presence. Believers in every generation seek God's presence through faith now and confidently hope for His full and eternal presence when God's kingdom comes.

Because God abides with His people, those things that have blighted earthly life will be no more. This is one way the Bible does seek to communicate to us the glory of heaven—by telling us the things that will not be there. The elder revealed to John that the white-robed multitude would not hunger or thirst any more. The burning sun and stifling heat will be no more. The Lamb, who shed His blood for redemption, was described as the Good Shepherd. He shall feed and lead the redeemed unto living springs of water. Like some other parts of verses 15–17, the final promise of verse 17 foreshadows the later description of the new heaven and new earth in Revelation 21:1–22:5.

As in other parts of the Book of Revelation, Bible students agree about some things in chapter 7, and disagree about others. The Book of Revelation was written in a prophetic style called apocalyptic (uh pahk uh LIP tik) literature. The meaning is not presented in the straightforward manner as in biblical narratives, letters, and laws. The symbols of apocalyptic literature are subject to a variety of interpretations.

Some Bible students identify everything after Revelation 4:1 as taking place after a secret rapture of the church. They see the 144,000 as Jews converted during a seven-year tribulation. They see the great multitude as Gentiles converted by the testimony of believing Jews. These tribulation saints then serve in a restored temple during the thousand-year reign (Rev. 20:1–10), called the millennium.

Other Bible students identify the 144,000 sealed servants of God as the same people described as a great multitude of redeemed people. The difference between the groups is not that one was Jewish and the other was Gentile. The difference is that verses 1–8 describe the redeemed on earth, and verses 9–17 describe them in heaven. The number 144,000 is a symbolic way of describing all God's people. According to this view, the sealing of the 144,000 servants shows that God will guard and preserve His people through earthly tribulations. The praises of the white-robed multitude signify the certainty of final salvation into eternal life for God's redeemed people.

In spite of these disagreements, nearly everyone agrees that both groups represent God's redeemed people who are saved by grace through faith. The two visions communicate assurance to people of faith that God protects them and that they shall share a future glory beyond human description.

APPLYING THE BIBLE

1. The judgment to come. The county sheriff was an honest, moral man but he was not a Christian. A pastor in the community was concerned about the sheriff's salvation and urged him to trust Christ as his Savior. The aggravated sheriff replied, "I am not afraid to die." He said he refused to be scared into "religion." But the pastor persisted, telling the sheriff that judgment and eternity lay beyond the grave. The pastor's words got through to the sheriff's heart; and he said that although he was not afraid to die, he trembled when he thought of the judgment to come.

Our lesson today speaks about the coming judgment of God against the wicked, but it also reveals that the believer shall be protected by the grace of God in that judgment day (vv. 1–3).

2. Marked by the blood. G. Campbell Morgan (1863–1945), the well-known British preacher, crossed the Atlantic fifty-four times in his evangelistic ministry. Once, when he was preaching to the "down-and-outs" in a mission, an old, gaunt rag picker came down the aisle and knelt at the altar. Campbell spoke to him about the blood of Jesus that cleanses us from all our sins. Next to the old beggar knelt the mayor of the city; and Morgan told him, too, about the cleansing blood. Campbell said he knew that sometime ago the mayor had sentenced the old rag picker to a month at hard labor and that the man had only recently gotten out of jail.

When the men arose from their knees, the mayor said, "Well, we didn't meet here last time," and the old beggar replied, "No, we will never meet again like we did the last time, praise God!"

As the Israelites were marked by the blood when the death angel passed over Egypt, so every believer in Christ is changed and marked by Christ's blood when he or she turns in faith to Christ (v. 3).

3. The conversion of B. H. Carroll. B. H. Carroll was the founder of Southwestern Baptist Theological Seminary, in Fort Worth, Texas. Although he had been baptized as a child, young Carroll said he wasn't a Christian. Wounded at the Battle of Mansfield, Louisiana, in the Civil War, Carroll returned home to Caldwell, Texas, avowing that he had turned himself "over to infidelity." At the age of twenty-two he vowed never to enter a church again. Carroll's mother, however, persuaded him to attend a Methodist camp meeting one morning in the fall of 1865. Returning to the meeting that evening with his brother, Carroll made a profession of his faith in Christ, and the infidel became a preacher. For almost fifty years Carroll served Christ faithfully and powerfully, and his influence continues to this day.

In his vision on Patmos, John saw "a great multitude" out of all nations who were "clothed in white robes" (v. 9). They were praising

God and saying, "Salvation to our God which sitteth upon the throne, and unto the Lamb" (v. 10).

Jesus saves and cleanses sinners without regard to standing, race, or sinfulness. As he saved Carroll, the infidel, so will he save all who come to him in faith.

4. Answering heaven's roll call. An anonymous poet wrote:

Traveler, what lies over the hill?
Traveler tell to me;
I am only a child—from the window sill
Over which I cannot see.

What lies over "the hill" for the believer? More than we can ever dream! British author William Thackeray tells about old Colonel Newcome, who was bedridden. Just before he died, Newcome heard the bells in the nearby school chapel tolling the hour. The old colonel's hands were outside the covers, and his feeble fingers beat the time as the bell rang. With the last ring, he said, barely above a whisper, "Adsum." That was the Latin word meaning "present" that they answered in the school of his boyhood days when the teacher called the roll.

One of these days Jesus will call the roll in heaven. What will heaven be like? We don't know a great deal about heaven, but John describes some of its glories in verses 15–17.

TEACHING THE BIBLE

- *Main Idea:* God's presence with His people assures them of protection and a future glory beyond human description.
- *Suggested Teaching Aim:* To lead adults to describe the assurance God offers to His people.

A TEACHING OUTLINE

1. *Use an open-ended sentence to introduce the Bible study.*
2. *Use a lesson poster to guide the Bible study.*
3. *Use lecture and questions to search for biblical truth.*
4. *Use summarizing to identify God's assurance.*

Introduce the Bible Study

On a chalkboard or a large sheet of paper write: *Heaven is a place where . . .* As members enter, ask them to write their response to the sentence on the board or a sheet of paper. Begin by reading their responses. Say: The lesson today will describe some of what heaven is like.

Search for Biblical Truth

Make a lesson poster by copying the outline on page 274. Cover all the points until you are ready to teach them.

Uncover the first main point and the first subpoint on the poster. Briefly set the context of this chapter by explaining the following from

"Studying the Bible": (1) Revelation 7 answers the question in 6:17; (2) the two visions in chapter 7 were presented as assurances to God's people before His final wrath fell; (3) how seals were used in the ancient world; (4) the Old Testament background (Exod. 12:23) of Revelation 7:1–3; (5) the purpose of the sealing of God's servants was to mark them as belonging to God and exempt them from His judgments on the ungodly.

Uncover the second subpoint on the outline and state that those sealed were 12,000 from each tribe, symbolizing all of the people on earth who were believers.

Uncover the second major outline point and the first subpoint under it. Ask members to find words in verse 9 that describe this multitude. (So many they could not be counted; from every nationality, race, and language; clothed in white and carried palm branches.) Ask: What were they doing? (Praising God for His salvation.) What do the palm branches remind you of? (Possibly Jesus' royal entry into Jerusalem; the Feast of the Tabernacles which celebrated God's deliverance of Israel from Egypt and His care of them in the wilderness (Exod. 12–18; Lev. 23:39–43; Neh. 8:14–17).

Uncover the second subpoint on the outline. Ask: What two questions did the elder ask John? (Who are these, and where do they come from?) What was the elder's response? (The multitude are those who had been cleansed by the blood of the Lamb and who had come out of the tribulation on earth.)

Use "Studying the Bible" to explain the two interpretations of "came out of great tribulation": (1) those who had escaped the tribulation because of God's deliverance or (2) those who had passed safely through it and had survived it.

Uncover the third subpoint on the outline. Ask: What do the redeemed do in heaven? (Serve God.) What will be the relationship of God to the redeemed? (God will dwell with His people.) What will heaven be like because of God's presence? (No hunger, thirst, burning heat; the Lamb will provide food and water for the redeemed; God will remove everything that causes sadness.)

Use "Studying the Bible" to explain two of the interpretations of this chapter: (1) events taking place after a secret rapture of the church or (2) events that depict the redeemed on earth and also in heaven. You may want to present both views as described in "Studying the Bible" so members can make up their minds.

Give the Truth a Personal Focus

Ask members to think about the chapter and to express in one word what the chapter says to believers of the first century and to us. (Their choice, but consider: assurance.) Ask members to identify statements from this chapter that give them assurance. Challenge all members to be certain they are a part of the redeemed so they can experience God's presence and all that involves.

The Victorious Christ

Basic Passage: Revelation 19–20
Focal Passage: Revelation 19:11–16; 20:11–15

Revelation 19–20 contain many powerful images of Christ as Victor. Volumes have been written about each of the various images, especially Revelation 20:1–10. This lesson will focus on two visions: Christ coming as Victor and Judge in Revelation 19:11–16 and the final judgment in Revelation 20:11–15.

Study Aim: *To describe the visions of Christ as Victor and the final judgment*

STUDYING THE BIBLE

OUTLINE AND SUMMARY

I. Visions of Christ's Victory (Rev. 19:1–21)

1. Victory over the harlot (19:1–5)

2. Announcement of the marriage of the Lamb (19:6–10)

3. King of kings and Lord of lords (19:11–16)

4. Victory over the beast and false prophet (19:17–21)

II. Final Victory (Revelation 20:1–15)

1. Binding Satan (20:1–3)

2. The thousand-year reign (20:4–6)

3. Final victory over Satan (20:7–10)

4. Final judgment (20:11–15)

Heaven celebrated the destruction of the harlot (19:1–5). Many voices announced the marriage of the Lamb (19:6–10). A vision of Christ showed Him as Victor and Judge (19:11–16). The beast and false prophet shall be cast into a lake of fire (19:17–21). An angel shall bind Satan and throw him into a bottomless pit for a thousand years (20:1–3). Christ and His people shall reign for a thousand years (20:4–6). Satan shall be loosed and gather an army only to be thrown into the lake of fire (20:7–10). At the final judgment, those whose names are not in the book of life will experience the second death in the lake of fire (20:11–15).

I. Visions of Christ's Victory (Rev. 19:1–21)

1. Victory over the harlot (19:1–5)

Revelation 17–18 describe a great harlot (Babylon the great), her destruction, and the mourning over her fall. Revelation 19:1–3 is a vision of a great multitude in heaven praising God for His judgment on the great harlot. The twenty-four elders and four living beings join in these hallelujahs (vv. 4–5).

2. Announcement of the marriage of the Lamb (19:6–10)

John heard the voice of a great multitude announce that the time for the marriage of the Lamb had come (v. 6). The bride was ready (vv. 7–8).

A blessing was pronounced on those invited to the marriage of the Lamb (vv. 9–10).

3. King of kings and Lord of lords (19:11–16)

> 11 And I saw heaven opened, and behold a white horse; and he that sat upon him was called Faithful and True, and in righteousness he doth judge and make war.

John was allowed another glimpse into heaven. He saw a white horse and rider. The titles for the One on the white horse and the descriptions of what He does leave no doubt that the rider is Jesus Christ. Earlier Jesus had identified Himself as "the faithful and true witness" (Rev. 3:14; see also 1:5; 3:7). His faithfulness inspires faithfulness in His people. Because He is faithful, He will never allow His people to suffer alone. Because He is true, we know that truth will eventually prevail.

He is coming as a righteous Judge who will make war on Satan and all his evil allies. These two themes run throughout the rest of chapters 19—20. Christ is and will be the Judge; He is and will be the Victor.

> 12 His eyes were as a flame of fire, and on his head were many crowns; and he had a name written, that no man knew, but he himself.

Eyes like flames of fire was one of the descriptions of Christ in the initial vision of the Book of Revelation (1:14; see also 2:18). His eyes like fire are part of His role as Judge. His knowledge of each person is penetrating and piercing.

The dragon of Revelation 12:3, identified as Satan in 12:9, had seven heads and ten horns with a crown on each head. The beast from the sea in Revelation 13:1 had seven heads and ten horns with a crown on each horn. This shows that Satan and his ally had a certain amount of sovereignty. Christ, however, had "many crowns." His many crowns show that He has unlimited sovereignty, including authority over Satan and the sea beast.

In the ancient world, a person's name represented the person. Knowing a person's name gave someone power over the person whose name he knew (Gen. 32:29; Judg. 13:18). Thus God revealed some of His names, but only in such a way as to show that humans can never fathom all the mysteries of God (Exod. 3:14; 33:18–34:7). This may be the meaning of the last part of verse 12. Christ has revealed many of His names, but His full glory remains beyond our ability to fathom.

> 13 And he was clothed with a vesture dipped in blood: and his name is called The Word of God.

Bible students discuss whether the blood on His clothes represents His own blood (7:14), blood of the faithful martyrs (6:10), or blood from the flesh of His enemies (19:18). Since all three are images in the Book of Revelation, arguments can be made for each of these possibilities.

Christ is the eternal Word of God, who shares the very nature of God and through whom all things were created (John 1:1–3). "And the Word was made flesh, and dwelt among us, (and we beheld his glory, the glory as of the only begotten of the Father,) full of grace and truth" (John 1:14). This same Word of God will appear as Judge and Victor over evil.

14 And the armies which were in heaven followed him upon white horses, clothed in fine linen, white and clean.

Were these angels, or were they the redeemed people of God? Angels are described as heavenly hosts who serve God in various ways (Pss. 103:21; 148:2; Luke 2:13). Also, angels will be associated with the coming of Christ (Matt. 13:41; 16:27; 24:30–31). However, two factors favor the view that the armies in verse 14 describe the redeemed people of God. For one thing, the saints will share in Christ's sovereign reign (Rev. 2:26–27; 5:10; 20:4, 6). Revelation 17:14 tells how the King of kings and Lord of lords will overcome the beast and his forces; those with Christ are "called, and chosen, and faithful." Second, the description of clean, white clothes is used elsewhere for those whose robes have been washed white in the blood of the Lamb (7:14).

15 And out of his mouth goeth a sharp sword, that with it he should smite the nations: and he shall rule them with a rod of iron: and he treadeth the winepress of the fierceness and wrath of Almighty God.

16 And he hath on his vesture and on his thigh a name written, KING OF KINGS, AND LORD OF LORDS.

Christ is pictured entering battle armed with a sword that goes out of His mouth. This image is part of the initial vision of the Book of Revelation (1:16). Christ, the living Word of God, wins victory armed with the sword of His Word. Christ and His people do battle armed with the Word. The specific meaning in verse 15 is His word as Judge and King.

Psalm 2:9 provides the background for this and other references about the reign of Christ with a rod of iron (Rev. 2:27; 12:5). Part of His work in the last days will be as an instrument of divine wrath. He alone is qualified to perform such judgment, for He is King of kings and Lord of lords. None of the titles of Christ better describes His complete sovereignty and authority.

4. Victory over the beast and false prophet (19:17–21)

John heard an angel's voice calling all birds to come to the supper of God, and to feast on the flesh of armies and horses (vv. 17–18). John saw the beast of 13:1 and the kings of the earth gather for war against Christ (v. 19). The beast, false prophet (13:11–17), and those who worshiped them were seized and thrown into a lake of fire (v. 20). Their followers were slain and the birds devoured their flesh (v. 21).

II. Final Victory (Rev. 20:1–15)

1. Binding Satan (20:1–3)

John saw a mighty angel with the key to the bottomless pit and a huge chain (v. 1). The angel seized Satan, bound him for a thousand years, cast him into the pit, and set a seal on him (vv. 2–3).

2. The thousand-year reign (20:4–6)

John saw thrones of the faithful ones who reigned with Christ for a thousand years (v. 4). John heard a blessing pronounced on these who have part in the first resurrection because the second death has no power over them and because they shall reign as kings and priests with Christ.

The rest of the dead shall not live again until the end of the thousand years (vv. 5–6).

3. Final victory over Satan (20:7–10)

After the thousand years, Satan shall be loosed from his prison (v. 7). He shall deceive the nations, gather a great army, and surround the camp of the saints and the holy city. Then fire from God shall devour them (vv. 8–9). Finally, the devil shall be cast into the lake of fire, where the beast and false prophet are; and they shall be tormented forever (v. 10).

4. Final judgment (20:11–15)

> 11 And I saw a great white throne, and him that sat on it, from whose face the earth and the heaven fled away; and there was found no place for them.

When John saw a great white throne and someone seated on it, he also saw earth and heaven flee from His presence. Insofar as earth and heaven include evildoers, none will succeed in escaping (Rev. 6:16–17). The main idea here seems to be that the old earth and heaven vanish to make way for the new heaven and new earth (Rev. 21:1). Peter described this heaven passing away with a great noise and elements melting with fervent heat (2 Pet. 3:10).

> 12 And I saw the dead, small and great, stand before God; and the books were opened: and another book was opened, which is the book of life: and the dead were judged out of those things which were written in the books, according to their works.
>
> 13 And the sea gave up the dead which were in it; and death and hell delivered up the dead which were in them: and they were judged every man according to their works.
>
> 14 And death and hell were cast into the lake of fire.
>
> This is the second death.
>
> 15 And whosoever was not found written in the book of life was cast into the lake of fire.

Verse 13 describes the dead, regardless of earthly position, standing before God for judgment. The dead were summoned there, regardless of the place of their death. The sea, for example, gave up its dead. Death and hell gave up their dead. "Hell" is the Greek *hades.* It referred to the place of departed dead. Jesus used this word in describing the fate of the rich man in Luke 16:23.

The dead shall be judged from the book of life and from books showing their deeds. Since the book of life contains the names of the redeemed, anyone whose name is not in it stands condemned. The other books serve to verify their destiny based also on how they lived. Being cast into the lake of fire is referred to as the second death. This place of eternal punishment will already hold Satan, the beast, and the false prophet (19:20; 20:10).

This passage says nothing specifically about the judgment of those whose names are written in the book of life. This shows that the redeemed people of God will never be condemned and experience the second death. This does not mean that believers will not be judged and rewarded according to their works. Paul wrote that each of us must give account to God (Rom. 14:12). Paul included himself when he wrote, "We must all appear before the judgment seat of Christ; that every one may receive the things done in his body, according to that he hath done, whether it be good or bad" (2 Cor. 5:10; see also 1 Cor. 3:11–15).

Some Bible students think that the great white throne judgment will take place at a different time from the judgment of believers before the judgment seat of Christ. Others think they may be simultaneous. In either case, unbelievers will be condemned to hell because they are not in the book of life; and although Christians will be judged by their Lord, this will not mean condemnation to eternal punishment.

APPLYING THE BIBLE

1. Justice at the judgment. When General Robert E. Lee was the president of Washington College, in Lexington, Virginia, a student was brought before him who had broken the rules. In an attempt to calm the rattled nerves of the boy, the compassionate general said, "You need not be afraid; you will get justice here."

"I know, General," replied the boy. "That's what I'm scared of!"

In 19:1–5 John sees the "great whore," which had shed the blood of the saints, being judged by God. The "great whore" was Rome (see ch. 17), and she was brought down to ruins. As we know from history, this, indeed, took place. God's judgment is always just.

2. The marriage supper. The Old Testament writer employed the metaphor of marriage to indicate the bond of love between God and Israel. But Jesus also used it to describe His love for all believers. This is how it is used here (19:7–10).

A wedding is a wonderful thing: the beautiful bride (vv. 7–8); the handsome groom (vv. 7, 9); and all the festivities that accompany a wedding (v. 9).

John writes to the persecuted saints in Asia Minor and encourages them to be faithful to Jesus for the day would soon come when they would be forever united with their Lord (vv. 7–10).

3. Eyes only for Jesus. There is an ancient legend that tells about a beautiful Christian girl who was condemned to death in a Roman arena where she would be torn to pieces for the amusement of her pagan persecutors. Among the spectators was a Roman prince who dearly loved the girl and pled for her release but to no avail. When the lion's cage was opened, much to the surprise of the spectators, the fierce lions didn't attack her. She appeared to be at perfect peace. Her persecutors declared that she "was charmed by the gods" and released her. When she was led out of the arena and reunited with her lover, he asked her the secret of her composure and she replied, "I had eyes only for you."

The saints in Asia Minor had suffered much for their faith, but John writes to encourage them to be faithful to Jesus and have eyes only for Him (vv. 11–16). The day was coming when suffering would be over, and they would meet their Lord, the King of kings and the Lord of lords, face to face (v. 16). It would be worth it all when they saw Jesus.

4. Doctor Faustus's bargain with Satan. In his play *The Tragical History of Doctor Faustus*, English author Christopher Marlowe tells how the legendary Faustus struck a bargain with the devil. In the bargain, the devil would be the servant of Faustus for twenty-four years. The devil would give Faustus everything he wanted, but at the end of the twenty-four years the devil would claim the soul of Faustus. At the end, Faustus sees what a terrible bargain he has made when Satan says to him:

> O Faustus,
> Now hast thou but one bare hour to live
> and then, thou must be damned perpetually.

Satan is powerful, but his power is limited by Christ. In 12:2 Satan has seven crowns upon his seven heads. In 13:1, Satan has ten crowns on his ten heads. He is powerful. But in 19:12, Jesus has "many crowns" on his head. The message for the saints in the first century, and for us today, is that Christ is more powerful than Satan and Christ will have the last word when Satan is cast into hell. The saints must be faithful to Christ even when they were being persecuted for His sake.

5. The hopelessness of hell. Over the huge doors of the prison de la Roquette, in Paris, are inscribed the words, "Abandon hope, all ye who enter here!" The prison, set apart for criminals who are condemned to die for their crimes, offers absolutely no hope.

Those who live without Jesus as their Savior have no hope for eternity (Eph. 2:12). Their hopeless condition is clearly seen in 20:15.

TEACHING THE BIBLE

- *Main Idea:* Jesus will ultimately be victorious over evil and be crowned King of kings and Lord of lords.
- *Suggested Teaching Aim:* To lead adults to crown Jesus as King of kings and Lord of lords.

A TEACHING OUTLINE

1. *Use a writing activity to introduce the Bible study.*
2. *Use a chart to identify the names of Jesus in these passages.*
3. *Use questions-answers to search for biblical truth.*
4. *Use questions to make the Bible study personal.*
5. *Use "How to Become a Christian" feature to acquaint members with how to commit their lives to Christ.*

Introduce the Bible Study

As members enter, ask them to go to a chalkboard or a large sheet of paper and write the most unusual name of a person they have ever heard. Read aloud some of the names and ask: What's in a name? Why are names important? Why do couples normally spend so much time picking the right name? Point out that our Scripture passage today mentions several names of Jesus; it also mentions that Jesus has one name that no human knows.

Search for Biblical Truth

Ask members to open their Bibles to Revelation 19:11–16 and skim those verse to identify all the names and titles of Jesus. Write these on a chalkboard or a large sheet of paper. (Faithful, True, Word of God, King of kings, Lord of lords.) After members have listed the names, use "Studying the Bible" and the following questions to explain each of the names: What effect does Jesus' faithfulness have on His people (v. 11)? As a righteous judge, on whom will Jesus make war (v. 11—Satan and his allies)? What description of Jesus from 1:14 is used in verse 12? What was significant about Jesus' "many crowns" (v. 12a)? What was significant about humans not knowing a name of Jesus (v. 12b)? Whose blood had Jesus' clothes been dipped in (v. 13)? Why is Jesus referred to as the "Word of God" in this passage (v. 13)? Who makes up the army (v. 14)? What description of Jesus from 1:16 is used in verse 15? How does the description of Jesus with a sharp sword coming out of His mouth relate to the title, "Word of God"? What does the title "Lord of lords and King of kings" mean to you?

Use "Studying the Bible" to summarize briefly 20:1–10. Ask members to look at 20:11–15. Use "Studying the Bible" and the following questions: Who was seated on the great white throne (v. 11)? What purpose did earth and heaven's fleeing serve (v. 11)? What is the purpose of the book of life (v. 12)? What happens to those whose names are not found in the book (v. 15)? What assurance does this give believers?

DISCUSS: Which name of Jesus means the most to you? Why? Which one comforts the most? Why? Which one is the most fearful? Why?

Give the Truth a Personal Focus

Ask: How do you feel about Christ's final victory and judgment? Are you ready for it? (If you have members in your class who are not Christians, pray that the Holy Spirit will use this class as an opportunity to lead them to Christ.

Close with a prayer that all members will have their names written in the Lamb's book of life.

May

25

1997

A New Heaven and Earth

Basic Passage: Revelation 21:1–22:5

Focal Passages: Revelation 21:1–7, 22–27

The final chapters in Revelation describe the completion of God's redemptive work and the blessed state of His people. God seeks to communicate the glory of heaven by describing what will be there and by naming things that will not be there.

Study Aim: *To describe the new heaven and new earth in terms of what will be there and what will not be there*

STUDYING THE BIBLE

OUTLINE AND SUMMARY

I. New Creation (Rev. 21:1–8)

1. Introduction (21:1–4)

2. Completion of salvation (21:5–6)

3. Challenge (21:7–8)

II. New City (Rev. 21:9—22:5)

1. Description of the city (21:9–21)

2. God's glory (21:22–27)

3. Paradise restored (22:1–5)

The new heaven and new earth will have a holy city in which God dwells with His people and takes away all that blights earthly life (21:1–4). God who began all things will bring His purposes to a consummation (21:5–6). Those who overcome will inherit all things, but those who reject God will be in the lake of fire (22:7–8). The holy city will be of gold and precious stones (21:9–21). The new earth will have no temple and no sun because of God's glorious presence (21:22–27). The holy city will have a river of water of life and a tree of life (22:1–5).

I. New Creation (Rev. 21:1–8)

1. Introduction (21:1–4)

1 And I saw a new heaven and a new earth: for the first heaven and the first earth were passed away; and there was no more sea.

John had seen earth and heaven flee away before the face of the One on the great white throne (Rev. 20:11). Beginning in Revelation 21:1, John saw a new heaven and a new earth. The words "no more sea" reflect the fears of the ancient world of the sea. Seas were wild stormy places of danger and death for many who ventured out on the seas. John also reflected his own circumstances as an exile on a small island, separated from fellow Christians by the sea.

2 And I John saw the holy city, new Jerusalem, coming down from God out of heaven, prepared as a bride adorned for her husband.

A central feature of the new heaven and new earth will be a holy city. It will be a new Jerusalem, in contrast to the earthly Jerusalem, which had desecrated its intended purpose by killing God's messengers and even God's Son (see Matt. 23:37). Notice that it is pictured as coming down from God out of heaven. It will be no earthly utopia erected by human initiative and efforts. This holy city will be a gift and creation of God.

The holy city will be adorned as a bride for her husband. Paul wrote of the church as the bride of Christ (Eph. 5:25–33). Revelation 19:7–9 describes an announcement of the marriage supper of the Lamb. In Revelation 21:2, John saw the bride come to be joined with the Lamb. Notice that the holy city describes both the people of God and their eternal abode. This double meaning was used in Revelation 17–18 to describe the antithesis of the new Jerusalem and the bride of Christ: the great harlot was described as an evil city, Babylon the great.

> 3 And I heard a great voice out of heaven saying, Behold, the tabernacle of God is with men, and he will dwell with them, and they shall be his people, and God himself shall be with them, and be their God.

Verse 3 describes the central feature of the new heaven and new earth: perfect fellowship with God. The word "tabernacle" reminds us of the tabernacle where God's presence rested among His people, but no one could see His face and live (Exod. 33:20). Only a few were allowed to approach Him and carry back His messages. When the living Word became flesh and dwelt among people, God was with those who recognized Christ as Immanuel, God with us (John 1:14; Matt. 1:23). Believers know God through faith in His Son, but believers throughout the ages have dreamed of a time when they would see and know God face to face (Matt. 5:8). John heard a great voice announcing that God's tabernacle or dwelling place would now be among His redeemed people.

> 4 And God shall wipe away all tears from their eyes; and there shall be no more death, neither sorrow, nor crying, neither shall there be any more pain: for the former things are passed away.

This is one of the most precious promises of the Bible. The Word of God seeks to communicate the glories of heaven by telling us some of the things that will not be there. Because God will be there, all that blights earthly existence will not be there. God Himself will be the Comforter who wipes away all tears from our eyes. Death, that dogged reminder of our sinful heritage, will have been conquered and cast into the lake of fire (1 Cor. 15:26; Rev. 20:14). Sorrow and crying will be no more because the causes of grief and tears—death and pain—will be no more. They are dreadful realities in this earthly existence; but when this earth and its order shall pass away, they will pass away with it.

If you were God and you wanted to communicate to earthbound minds what heaven will be like, how would you do it? One way that God did it was to remind us of some of the things that make earthly life a vale of tears. Then with a shout of victory we are told that none of these things will be in God's new creation. I don't believe God intended to limit the list just to what was named in verse 4. I believe that the message of verse 4 is that none of what blights earthly life will be in heaven. We can get some idea of the glory of heaven by considering it in this way: everything that makes earthly life painful and deadly will be no more; everything that makes earthly life joyful and fruitful will be magnified by the direct presence of God.

2. Completion of salvation (21:5–6)

> 5 And he that sat upon the throne said, Behold, I make all things new. And he said unto me, Write: for these words are true and faithful.
>
> 6 And he said unto me, It is done. I am Alpha [AL fuh] and Omega [oh MEG uh], the beginning and the end. I will give unto him that is athirst of the fountain of the water of life freely.

Paul wrote of each person in Christ as a new creation, in which "old things are passed away; behold, all things are become new" (2 Cor. 5:17). God used similar language to describe the new heaven and new earth. He commanded John to write because these words bear the stamp of divine truth and trustworthiness.

"It is done" means literally "they have come to pass." Jesus' words from the cross, "it is finished," signaled the victorious completion of His atoning work (John 19:30). God's words "it is done" declare the completion of God's redemptive purposes. All the redeemed will have been gathered home; and sin, death, and Satan will have been totally and forever vanquished.

As in Revelation 1:8, God spoke of Himself as Alpha and Omega, the first and last letters of the Greek alphabet. He is the beginning and the ending because He is the eternal Creator who created this universe and who will create for His children a new heaven and a new earth. God promised that in that new creation, all who are thirsty will drink of the fountain of living water freely (see Isa. 55:1; John 4:14; Rev. 22:17).

3. Challenge (21:7–8)

> 7 He that overcometh shall inherit all things; and I will be his God, and he shall be my son.

As we have seen, the challenge to overcome (literally, to gain the victory) is found over and over in Revelation (2:7, 11, 26; 3:5, 12, 21). These challenges to win the victory are accompanied by God's promises to those who overcome. God promised to be their God and to count them as children in the family of the new creation. As such they would receive their full inheritance from their Heavenly Father.

Verse 8 looks back to the scenes of judgment in Revelation 20:11–15 and reminds us that not all people are God's children. Verse 8 lists those groups that were not in the new creation.

II. New City (Rev. 21:9–22:5)

1. Description of the city (21:9–21)

An angel called John for a closer look at the bride of Christ (21:9). The Spirit took him up into a high mountain for a view of the holy Jerusalem (21:10). John saw the glory of God like precious stones (21:11). He saw the wall and gates with each gate named for a tribe of Israel (21:12–13). He saw the foundations named for the twelve apostles (21:14). The angel with a measuring rod described the dimensions of the city and its wall (21:15–17). The wall was of jasper and the city was pure gold (21:18). The foundations were garnished with precious stones, each gate was a pearl, and the streets were gold (21:19–21).

2. God's glory (21:22–27)

> 22 And I saw no temple therein: for the Lord God Almighty and the Lamb are the temple of it.
>
> 23 And the city had no need of the sun, neither of the moon, to shine in it: for the glory of God did lighten it, and the Lamb is the light thereof.

The temple was the center of old Jerusalem. Like the tabernacle before it, the temple represented the presence of God among the people. His glorious presence was promised as long as His people served Him. But it was a mediated presence and veiled glory, and the people so sinned that His glory left the temple (Ezek. 10:18; 11:23). The new Jerusalem will have no need for a temple, because God and the Lamb will dwell directly with the redeemed. The old earth is lighted and warmed by the sun, with the moon providing some light even at night. Since God Himself and the Lamb will be the light for the new creation, there will be no sun or moon.

> 24 And the nations of them which are saved shall walk in the light of it: and the kings of the earth do bring their glory and honour into it.
>
> 25 And the gates of it shall not be shut at all by day: for there shall be no night there.
>
> 26 And they shall bring the glory and honour of the nations into it.
>
> 27 And there shall in no wise enter into it any thing that defileth, neither whatsoever worketh abomination, or maketh a lie: but they which are written in the Lamb's book of life.

Previously in Revelation, "nations" and "kings" stood for people and leaders who gave their allegiance to Satan and his allies (11:18; 18:3, 23). Such nations and kings were defeated and made subject to Christ (19:15). The nations and kings of Revelation 21:24 describe people of the new earth who are redeemed people of God. We know little about how life will be organized in the new earth, but we know that all honor and glory will be given to God.

Gates were necessary in ancient cities. Since night was a time of danger from enemy attacks, gates were closed. The new Jerusalem will have a wall and gates, but the gates will never be closed because there will be neither enemies nor night. The open gates are a sign of total security and safety.

Verse 27, like verse 8, reminds us that nothing or no one who is evil will enter the city. Such people and things have no part in the new earth or the holy city. Only those whose names are written in the Lamb's book of life will abide there.

3. Paradise restored (22:1–5)

John saw a river of water of life proceeding out of the throne of God and of the Lamb (22:1). He saw a tree of life with leaves for the healing of the nations (22:2). The curse of sin will be no more because God's servants shall see His face and have His name on their foreheads (22:3–4). There will be no night, no candles, and no sun, for God will lighten them and reign forever (22:5).

APPLYING THE BIBLE

1. No fear in heaven. In January 1960, a smelly wretch named Grisha Sikalenko appeared before his neighbors in Tsirkuny in the Ukraine. His neighbors were shocked because they thought he had died a hero's death fighting the Germans. The truth was that on the night his company marched off to war, Grisha deserted and sneaked home. His mother made for him a hiding place under the manure pile at the back of the goat shed, and for eighteen years he existed in a living grave. In the winter he almost froze to death, and in the summer he nearly suffocated. But his fear of being found and prosecuted made him stay in his miserable hovel. When he finally emerged, he found that his fears were groundless for the statute of limitations had long since made him immune from prosecution.

The Jews were not sea-going people. When John says there is "no more sea" (v. 1) in heaven, he is telling his readers that our greatest fears on earth will be barred from heaven!

2. Heaven, pure and holy. When one walks down the streets of our largest cities, one observes how dirty and filthy they are. But the alleyways are even grimmer, filled with huge piles of garbage. Humankind dirties and ruins everything we touch. Even nature suffers, because of human sins. But John saw a new Jerusalem, coming down from God out of heaven, prepared as a bride adorned for her husband (v. 2). Nothing is purer or more beautiful than an innocent bride coming down the aisle to be united in marriage with her groom. This is a graphic picture of heaven's purity.

3. No disappointments in heaven. Over the great doorway of the cathedral at Milan, Italy, three inscriptions have been carved. On the first arch appear the words, "All that which pleases is but for a moment." Over the second arch are sculpted the words, "All that troubles is but for a moment." And on the great central arch are the words, "That only which is eternal is important."

The most important thing in life is to be sure we are going to heaven when we die. John says there are no disappointments or separations there (v. 4).

4. Does God know you are coming? A small boy visiting New York City was riding up the elevator of the Empire State Building. As they traveled higher and higher, the little fellow looked down, gulped, and asked his father, "Daddy, does God know we are coming?"

It's a good question. But more important is the question, "Do *you* know you are going to heaven when you die?" You can know. Fully trust in Christ's shed blood and you *will* know (John 14:6).

Main Idea: Heaven is a place for God and His people.

Suggested Teaching Aim: To lead adults to describe who will be in heaven.

Introduce the Bible Study

IN ADVANCE, arrange for enough hymnals for each member to have one. As members enter, ask them to find three of their favorite hymns about heaven. On a chalkboard or a large sheet of paper, list these hymns and rank them to find the three favorite hymns about heaven. Save this list to use at the conclusion of the lesson.

Search for Biblical Truth

NOTE: If you choose not to form two groups, you can do this as a class. Ask half the class to read Revelation 21:1–7 and the other half to read 21:22–27. Give the half of the class assigned 21:1–7 a copy of the following questions without answers and ask them to answer them. Allow six to eight minutes for study and then call for reports.

Group 1—The New Creation

Revelation 21:1–7

1. What was the most obvious absence in the new heaven and new earth (v. 1)? (No sea.)
2. Why do you think this was so? (Sea was fearful to nomads.)
3. What do you think is the significance of the New Jerusalem's coming down out of heaven? (No earthly utopia.)
4. What is the central feature of the new heaven and the new earth (v. 3)? (Fellowship with God; would see Him face to face.)
5. What act of tenderness will God perform (v. 4)? (Wipe away tears.)
6. Why will there not be any more sorrow and crying (v. 4)? (Death and pain—the causes of sorrow—will not be in heaven.)
7. What does the promise in verse 5 mean to you?
8. Verse 5 is the third time the phrase "Alpha and Omega" appears in Revelation (after 1:8, 11) and it will appear in 22:13. In 21:6 the reference is to God; in the other cases, it refers to Jesus. What can you draw from this? (They are one.)
9. What will God give His children (v. 6)? (Water of life.)
10. What benefit do we receive if we overcome? (God will be our God and we will be His children.)

Group 2—The New City

Revelation 21:22–27

1. What building will not be in the New Jerusalem (v. 22)? (Temple.)
2. Why will there be no temple in heaven (v. 22)? (Temple represented God on earth; He will dwell with us in heaven.)
3. Why will night not exist in heaven (v. 25)? (There is no sun or moon—v. 23.)

4. What will the nations of the earth give God (v. 24)? (Glory and honor.)
5. Why are the gates never closed in heaven (v. 25)? (Nothing evil to keep out.)
6. Who/what will not be in heaven (v. 27a)? (Anything or anyone who is evil.)
7. Who will be in heaven (v. 27b)? (Those whose names are written in the Lamb's book of life.)
8. What must we do to be certain our names are written in the Lamb's book of life?

DISCUSS: Which feature of heaven gives you the most comfort?

Give the Truth a Personal Focus

Refer to the list of favorite hymns. Ask: What about the hymns you chose makes them your favorites? Is it the words? music? where you learned them? Sing or read the words of the hymn that was ranked first. Close in a prayer that all members will know beyond any shadow of a doubt that they will experience heaven.

Guidance for Ministry

INTRODUCTION

This month's studies are a five-session course on the pastoral epistles. These three letters comprise the last group of Paul's letters. He wrote them after being released from the imprisonment described in the closing chapters of the Book of Acts. The pastoral letters to Timothy and Titus contain many personal references about Paul himself and his two faithful coworkers, but the letters are primarily pastoral in nature. These letters offered guidance and advice on problems faced by first-century churches. Encouragement was given to Timothy and Titus to remain faithful as they faced false teachings.

Throughout the course, the meaning of being a servant is considered. A servant of Christ must set a good example, teach godliness, endure suffering, teach faithfulness, and encourage community.

June

1

1997

Christ's Servant Sets an Example

Background Passage: 1 Timothy 4:6–16
Focal Passage: 1 Timothy 4:6–16

After Paul left Timothy, his son in the faith and his trusted coworker, in Ephesus, Paul wrote 1 Timothy to encourage Timothy to continue the work there (1 Tim. 1:3). Paul wrote instructions and admonitions about Timothy's life and work in Ephesus. First Timothy 4:6–16 is an example of what Paul wrote. One of the themes of the passage was Paul's challenge for Timothy to set a good example as a good servant of Jesus Christ.

Study Aim: *To explain what Paul said to Timothy about setting an example as a good servant of Jesus Christ*

STUDYING THE BIBLE

OUTLINE AND SUMMARY

I. A Good Servant of Jesus Christ (1 Tim. 4:6–10)
1. Good doctrine (v. 6)
2. Exercise to godliness (vv. 7–8)
3. Motivating power of hope (vv. 9–10)

II. Personal Words to Timothy (1 Tim. 4:11–16)
1. Practice what you preach (vv. 11–12)
2. Read, preach, teach (v. 13)
3. Don't neglect God's gift (v. 14)
4. Give yourself wholly (vv. 15–16)

A good servant of Jesus Christ finds nourishment in and teaches others good doctrine (v. 6). Physical exercise has some value, but moral and spiritual exercise have earthly and eternal value (vv. 7–8). Confident hope in God as Savior motivates believers to faithful and arduous efforts (vv. 9–10). Timothy should defuse any criticism of his relative youthfulness by being a good example of Christian words, deeds, and attitudes (vv. 11–12). As a leader, Timothy was to read the Scriptures publicly, preach, and teach (v. 13). He was not to neglect God's gift that had been recognized by elders of the church (v. 14). By giving himself totally, Timothy could be blessed and used by the Lord (vv. 15–16).

I. A Good Servant of Jesus Christ (1 Tim. 4:6–10)

1. Good doctrine (v. 6)

6 If thou put the brethren in remembrance of these things, thou shalt be a good minister of Jesus Christ, nourished up in the words of faith and of good doctrine, whereunto thou hast attained.

The word translated "minister" means "servant." In the New American Standard Bible, it is translated "servant" (Matt. 23:11), sometimes "minister," and sometimes "deacon" (1 Tim. 3:8). Thus the word "minister" often doesn't refer to what we call a "minister" or ordained church leader; instead it means simply one who serves. Jesus taught that true greatness is marked by humble service. He said, "Whoever will be great among you will be your minister" (Mark 10:23).

This word study reminds us that humble service should be the mark of all believers. All God's people have been called to the work of the ministry (Eph. 4:12). Church leaders like Timothy should set the example of humble service.

Verse 6 sets forth one of the marks of a good servant of Jesus Christ. Running through the pastoral letters are warnings against false teachings. Verses 1–5 contrasted false and true teachings. Verse 6 says that Timothy was to teach the truth to members of the family of faith. If he did this, he would be a good servant of Jesus Christ.

In order to teach good doctrine to others, Timothy himself had been nourished and fed in the words of faith and sound teaching. The word translated "attained" can mean "studied" or "followed." Actually Timothy had done both. He had studied the words of truth, and he had made them the standard for his life and faith.

2. Exercise to godliness (vv. 7–8)

> 7 But refuse profane and old wives' fables, and exercise thyself rather unto godliness.
>
> 8 For bodily exercise profiteth little: but godliness is profitable unto all things, having promise of the life that now is, and of that which is to come.

Paul described the false teachings as "profane." The people who set forth these teachings claimed their ways were moral and spiritual. Examples include their ban on marriage and their refusal to eat meat (v. 3). Paul considered such ideas as profane because they denied God's good creation (vv. 4–5). He also called their empty teachings "old wives' fables." In 1 Timothy 1:4, he called them "fables and endless genealogies." The false teachers filled the air with meaningless words like idle people with nothing to do but gossip.

Paul used a strong word to tell Timothy to refuse such profane and futile activities. Instead, he should exercise himself to godliness. Paul used the analogy of physical exercise to emphasize the priority of moral and spiritual exercise. Paul's writings contain several references to athletic sports of his day (see 1 Cor. 9:24–27; Eph. 6:12; Phil. 3:13–14; 2 Tim. 2:5). So he was aware of athletic events and physical exercise.

In verse 7, he acknowledged the value of physical exercise; but he quickly added that exercise to godliness is far more valuable. Physical exercise can improve physical health and well-being, but its value is limited to this life. By contrast, godliness has value in this life and in the world to come. Moral and spiritual characteristics are eternal. Our relation to God, our relation with others, and our character determine who and what we will be in God's eternal order.

The comparison to physical exercise can communicate to many people today. Many realize that their physical well-being depends on proper exercise. Muscles that are not used become flabby and useless.

Likewise, our moral and spiritual well-being depend on exercising our faith, hope, and love. Such exercise determines our effectiveness as servants of Jesus Christ.

3. Motivating power of hope (vv. 9–10)

9 This is a faithful saying and worthy of all acceptation.

10 For therefore we both labour and suffer reproach, because we trust in the living God, who is the Saviour of all men, specially of those that believe.

Verse 9 is a formula found several times in the pastoral letters (1 Tim. 1:15; 2 Tim. 2:11; Titus 3:8). It calls attention to an important saying that was probably well-known by Timothy and the believers in Ephesus. In looking at 1 Timothy 4:9, Bible students debate whether Paul had in mind the saying in verse 8 or the one in verse 10. The consensus is that it was verse 8; but a case also can be made for verse 10.

The word translated "trust" is literally "hope." Biblical hope differed in many ways from the common hopes of nonbelievers. One basic difference is the element of confidence in biblical hope. People of faith have confidence in God's promises for the future precisely because they are God's promises. God Himself is our hope. Our hope of salvation is based on the fact that God is the Savior of all people. This doesn't mean that He saves everyone, because He allows people to choose or reject His salvation. However, God is potentially the Savior of all people; and He is the actual Savior of believers.

Such confident hope has tremendous motivating power. We work, suffer, and strive to be good servants of Christ because we know that God is our Savior.

II. Personal Words to Timothy (1 Tim. 4:11–16)

1. Practice what you preach (vv. 11–12)

11 These things command and teach.

12 Let no man despise thy youth; but be thou an example of the believers, in word, in conversation, in charity, in spirit, in faith, in purity.

Paul challenged Timothy to command and teach the good teachings that he had been taught and about which Paul wrote. Paul also stressed the importance of Timothy being a good example to believers of the things he taught.

Verse 12 gives a hint about Timothy's age. We use the word "youth" for a child or adolescent. The word in verse 12, however, was used of young men up to the age of forty. A similar word was used of Paul in Acts 7:58, the first mention of him in the Bible. Considering how long Timothy had been helping Paul, most Bible students think that he was between thirty-five and forty.

Because of the respect given to older people in the first century, Timothy was still a young man compared to the wise elders in the church at Ephesus. Some people think they see hints in Paul's letters to Timothy that Timothy was especially timid, even fearful at times. However, this is probably reading too much into verses like verse 12. That verse may reflect only the fact that older people in the church considered Timothy too young for them to follow his instructions and admonitions. They looked on him with disdain because they thought they themselves were older and wiser.

Paul's advice to Timothy was to show them his maturity and commitment by how he spoke and lived. The word translated "conversation" means his way of living. Timothy was to be a good example of all those areas in which older people often criticize younger people. His words and deeds were to be above reproach. His love was to be genuine, in spite of their criticism. His faith was to be strong. His thoughts, words, and deeds were to be pure.

2. Read, preach, teach (v. 13)

> 13 Till I come, give attention to reading, to exhortation, to doctrine.

As a church leader, Timothy was to set the example for public meetings of believers. Three activities were highlighted. "Reading" referred to the public reading of the Scriptures. "Exhortation" referred to the preaching of the Word. "Doctrine" meant "teaching."

3. Don't neglect God's gift (v. 14)

> 14 Neglect not the gift that is in thee, which was given thee by prophecy, with the laying on of hands of the presbytery.

The word translated "gift" is *charisma.* We use the word to refer to something that a few people have that makes them attractive leaders. The original word meant "gift of grace." It referred to a gift of God's Spirit bestowed not because of a person's worth but because of God's grace. Paul reminded Timothy not to neglect God's gift to him. Such a gift brings with it great responsibility to glorify God and to meet the needs of others.

At some point, a prophetic word pointed to the gift of God in Timothy. The elders of the church laid their hands on him to signify his being set apart to practice God's gift. Second Timothy 1:6 shows that Paul also laid his hands on his beloved son in the faith.

4. Give yourself wholly (vv. 15–16)

> 15 Meditate upon these things; give thyself wholly to them; that thy profiting may appear to all.
>
> 16 Take heed unto thyself, and unto the doctrine; continue in them: for in doing this thou shalt both save thyself, and them that hear thee.

The word translated "meditate" can also mean "practice." A person should both meditate on God's truth and put it into practice. There was to be nothing halfhearted in Timothy's practice of the Christian faith. God's gift demanded total commitment from Timothy. The word translated "profiting" has a clearer meaning of "progress." In order for Timothy to be an example, his progress had to be apparent to others. Recall what Jesus said about letting our lights shine. People will see our good works and glorify God (Matt. 5:16).

Timothy was to watch himself carefully, knowing that others were looking carefully at his life. By watching his life and teachings, Timothy could be used by God to grow in grace and to lead others to salvation. In trying to understand the last line of verse 16, remember two things: (1) Only God saves anyone (Eph. 2:8–10). (2) Salvation is sometimes described as a process of being saved from the power of sin (Phil. 2:13). Thus Timothy's commitment and faithfulness would contribute to God's continuing work of grace in him and in others through him.

APPLYING THE BIBLE

1. The royal law. When Elizabeth II was crowned queen of Great Britain in June 1953, she wore on her head the crown of Saint George, encrusted with three thousand diamonds. Her gown was embroidered with the emblem of the Commonwealth, outlined in gold, silver and pearls. In her hand she held a globe of the world studded with precious jewels and a silver scepter, symbolic of her power as a ruling monarch. In the ceremony, her chaplain approached her and placed in her hand a small Bible. As he gave it to the new queen he said: "Herein is wisdom, earth's greatest treasure. Here is the Royal Law, here are the lively oracles of God."

Into Timothy's hands had been placed the Royal Law of God, the Holy Scriptures. He was told by Paul to feed on it and teach it to the believers at Ephesus (v. 6). The Word of God was needed then as it is needed today. It is always relevant to every situation we face.

2. Humble service. Dr. Albert Schweitzer caught the attention of the world when he forsook a brilliant career and went to Africa as a missionary/doctor. For his work in the hospital he established at Lambaréné, he was awarded the Nobel Peace Prize in 1952.

A brilliant organist, theologian, and medical doctor, Schweitzer determined early in life to give himself to the arts and sciences until he was thirty, hoping that by that age he would be financially secure to give himself unreservedly to the service of humanity. At thirty-eight, after having earned his medical degree, he moved to Lambaréné, where he established his first jungle hospital in a chicken coop. He later built a large hospital where thousands were treated. Schweitzer was a humble servant of God, loved and respected to this day.

When Paul encouraged Timothy (v. 6) to be a "good minister of Jesus Christ," he meant Timothy should serve humbly, lovingly and faithfully, qualities that always mark the true "servant" of Jesus.

3. Good exercise. Many Americans are exercise enthusiasts. We spend hundreds of millions of dollars a year on exercise facilities and machines and countless hours jogging and working out to keep our bodies in shape. A recent television program stated that we ought to get at least thirty minutes a day of "moderate to heavy" exercise. And all that is good and ought to be encouraged. But at the same time, these millions of people who exercise physically give little or no thought to spiritual exercise. Paul emphasized that exercising spiritually—unto "godliness"—is far more profitable because it has a "promise of the life that now is, and of that which is to come" (v. 8).

4. Is youth a problem to leadership? William Cullen Bryant was only about twenty-three when he wrote his immortal poem, "Thanatopsis." John Keats, the English poet, was only twenty-six when he died. Mozart was dead at thirty-five. When he was only twenty-six, Napoleon was proclaimed the hero of Paris, and at thirty-five he was crowned the emperor of France. And Jesus was only thirty-three when He died. Being young was no barrier to their being respected as leaders.

As our lesson writer points out, Timothy was probably between 35 and forty when Paul wrote to this young pastor: "Let no man despise thy youth." Timothy may have felt threatened by the older leaders in the Ephesian church. Paul told him to stop it, do the best he could, and trust the results to God.

5. The worth of a good example. David Brainerd was a pioneer missionary to the American Indians. After a life of hardship and suffering, Brainerd died at twenty-nine. But Brainerd's life so inspired Henry Martyn that he gave his life in missionary service in India. Brainerd's life was a prime factor in inspiring William Carey, the father of modern missions, to become a missionary to India. Carey's life inspired Ann and Adoniram Judson to go to India as missionaries—America's first foreign missionaries. It was the example of a shoe cobbler which led Carey to the Savior. "He could not answer my questions, but I could not answer his life," Carey wrote.

The worth of a good example cannot be overstated. Paul told Timothy that, in spite of his youth, he should be "an example of the believers, in word, in conversation, in charity, in spirit, in faith, [and] in purity" (v. 12).

What kind of example are we setting for others?

TEACHING THE BIBLE

- *Main Idea:* Christ's servants should set an example for others to follow.
- *Suggested Teaching Aim:* To identify ways we can set good examples as servants of Jesus Christ.

A TEACHING OUTLINE

1. Use a collage to create interest.

2. Use a unit poster to see the flow of the lesson.

3. Use Bible search to identify what a good servant of Jesus should be.

4. Use a "Word List" poster to identify difficult words.

5. Use a writing exercise to identify how members can be good servants.

Introduce the Bible Study

Cut pictures of exercise equipment and people exercising from magazines and papers and paste them on a large poster. Ask: How many of you get enough exercise? Why do you not get more? How would you compare your spiritual exercise with your physical exercise? Say: Today's lesson compares these two parts of our lives.

Search for Biblical Truth

Make a unit poster by placing the dates, titles, and Scriptures on a large sheet of paper. Place this on a wall and leave up for the month. Cut out a large colored arrow and place beside the lesson being studied each week.

On a chalkboard or a large sheet of paper write: *A good servant of Jesus . . .* Ask a volunteer to read aloud 1 Timothy 4:6–10. Use "Studying the Bible" to explain the meaning of "minister." Make a "Word List" poster for the unit that you can leave on the wall. Write *minister* and a definition beside it. Ask members to suggest what a good servant of Jesus will do according to these verses. Use members' suggestions, but you should have something like *teaches and obeys good doctrine* for verse 6. Ask: What in Timothy's background equipped him to teach good doctrine to others? (He had grown up on sound teaching.)

Ask: What will a good servant do according to verses 7–8? *(Ignore worthless teachings but grow spiritually.)* Use "Studying the Bible" to identify some of the "profane" teachings Paul had in mind. On a chalkboard or a large sheet of paper write at the top of one column: *Physical Exercise* and at the top of a second column: *Spiritual Exercise.* Ask: How does physical exercise benefit a person? Write responses under *Physical Exercise.* How does godliness profit the believer? (Has value in this life and the life to come.) Write this and other suggestions under *Spiritual Exercise.* Ask: What lessons can we draw from these verses about the need for spiritual exercise?

Ask: What will a good servant do, according to verses 9–10? *(Hope in the living God.)* Ask members what "saying" they think Paul referred to in verse 9. (Could be either the saying in verse 8 or the one in verse 10; see "Studying the Bible" for more information.)

Ask a volunteer to read aloud 4:11–16. Ask members to list what Paul commands, Timothy to teach (v. 11). Write these on a chalkboard or a large sheet of paper. (Use their responses but consider these: Don't let anyone make fun of you; set an example; keep reading the Bible; keep teaching and preaching; use the gift God gave you; commit yourself to doing these things; be careful about the way you live and teach.) Ask members to rank in importance these statements. Ask: Which of these suggestions do you practice now? Which ones of these would help you if you did practice them?

Give the Truth a Personal Focus

Ask members to write a definition of a good servant based on this study. Ask members to complete this sentence: *A good servant of Jesus Christ . . .*

Close in prayer that members will take more seriously the call to be servants this week.

Christ's Servant Teaches Godliness

June
8
1997

Background Passage: 1 Timothy 6:2b–12
Focal Passage: 1 Timothy 6:2b–12

"Godliness" is a key word in 1 Timothy (1 Tim. 2:2; 3:6). It occurred twice in the previous session (1 Tim. 4:7,8). It occurs four times in 1 Timothy 6:2b–12 (vv. 3, 5, 6, 11). The word pointed to a godly way of living motivated by reverence toward God.

Study Aim: *To contrast what Paul taught about godliness with the ungodliness against which he warned*

STUDYING THE BIBLE

OUTLINE AND SUMMARY

I. Warning Against False Teachers (1 Tim. 6:2b–5)
1. True versus false teachings (vv. 2b–3)
2. Characteristics of false teachers (vv. 4–5)
II. Contentment Versus Love of Money (1 Tim. 6:6–10)
1. Blessings of contentment (vv. 6–8)
2. Perils of love of money (vv. 9–10)
III. Charge to Timothy (1 Tim. 6:11–12)
1. Godly qualities to pursue (v. 11)
2. Remaining true to God's calling (v. 12)

False teachings are different from what Jesus and the apostles taught (vv. 2b–3). False teachers practice pride, greed, and other worldly sins (vv. 4–5). True godliness goes with true contentment (vv. 6–8). The love of money leads to temptations, snares, sins, and ultimately to self-destruction (vv. 9–10). Paul charged Timothy to flee such sins and to pursue godly living (v. 11). The apostle charged Timothy to strive faithfully, keeping his eyes on eternal life and remembering his profession (v. 12).

I. Warning Against False Teachers (1 Tim. 6:2b–5)

1. True versus false teachings (vv. 2b–3)

2 These things teach and exhort.

3 If any man teach otherwise, and consent not to wholesome words, even the words of our Lord Jesus Christ, and to the doctrine which is according to godliness;

The last part of verse 2 is a charge found elsewhere in 1 Timothy. For example, in 1 Timothy 4:11, Paul wrote, "These things command and teach." Verse 2 may refer to what Paul had just written in verses 1–2, to what he was about to write, or in general to all he said about sound teaching.

Verse 3 contrasts sound teachings with false teachings in three ways: (1) The words "teach otherwise" translate one Greek word that means to "teach a different doctrine." The teaching was different from the teaching of Paul and the other apostles, which had been passed along to Timothy. (2) The apostles, of course, got their doctrine from Jesus Christ. The word translated "consent" means to "attach oneself to" something. The false teachers had attached themselves to teachings that were different from "the words of our Lord Jesus Christ." Paul may have had in mind the teachings from Jesus, the gospel message about Jesus, or both. The Gospels contain both. (3) The false teachings were also different from the teachings that led to godliness. Their ungodliness is spelled out more completely in verses 4–5.

2. Characteristics of false teachers (vv. 4–5)

> 4 He is proud, knowing nothing, but doting about questions and strifes of words, whereof cometh envy, strife, railings, evil surmisings,
>
> 5 Perverse disputings of men of corrupt minds, and destitute of the truth, supposing that gain is godliness: from such withdraw thyself.

Verses 4–5 continue the sentence from verse 3. Verses 4–5 describe the kind of person who teaches a doctrine different from Jesus and the apostles.

The words translated "is proud" means literally "to wrap oneself in smoke." It suggests a person who lives in a cloud of conceit. Such people think they know everything, but actually they know nothing of truth and substance. The word translated "doting" suggests an unhealthiness that is the opposite of the healthy or "wholesome" (v. 3) words of divine truth. Their disease showed itself in preoccupation with irrelevant questions and wrangling about words (see 1 Tim. 1:4, 6). They manifested what Paul elsewhere called "works of the flesh" in contrast to "fruit of the Spirit" (Gal. 5:19–23). Envy and strife were among their leading sins. So were "slanders" (the meaning of "railings") and "evil suspicions" (the meaning of "evil surmisings").

These people of "corrupt" or depraved minds engaged in constant wrangling. What they taught and how they lived showed that they were totally "destitute of the truth." One evidence of their depravity was their view about the relation between religion and wealth. The last part of verse 5 states one of their basic presuppositions. They believed that "gain is godliness." The following verses make clear that they were thinking of financial gain. In other words, these first-century teachers claimed that religion should result in wealth. One of the problems in the first-century churches was traveling preachers, some of whom exploited generous and trusting Christians.

II. Contentment Versus Love of Money (1 Tim. 6:6–10)

1. Blessings of contentment (vv. 6–8)

> 6 But godliness with contentment is great gain.

Some readers might assume that Paul was denying that godlines results in gain. Therefore, he clarified the meaning of "gain." Paul di not agree with the false teachers that religion ought to make one finan cially wealthy. He did teach that godliness results in moral and spiritual wealth.

Another key word is "contentment." True godliness frees a person from the worldly preoccupation with getting more and more material things. It does this by creating a spirit of gratitude and contentment with what God has provided. The word translated "contentment" represented the ideal of the first-century Stoics. They prized a self-sufficiency that was not dependent on things. Although Paul used their word, he had a different source of contentment than the self-sufficiency sought by the Stoics. His classic testimony is in Philippians 4:10–13. Paul testified that he had learned to be content with little or much. He expressed his secret in Philippians 4:13, "I can do all things through Christ which strengtheneth me."

> 7 For we brought nothing into this world, and it is certain we can carry nothing out.
>
> 8 And having food and raiment let us be therewith content.

Verses 7–8 reinforce verse 6. These verses remind us of teachings of Jesus on the same subjects. The parable of the rich fool makes the same point as verse 7 (Luke 12:13–21). Jesus told the parable to warn against the same kind of love of money against which Paul warned in 1 Timothy 6:10. His story makes Paul's point in verse 7: No matter how rich we may be, we don't take any of it with us when we die.

Verse 8 reminds us of the familiar passage in Jesus' Sermon on the Mount about living in trust rather than anxiety (Matt. 6:19–34). Worldly people are forever discontent because there is always something else that they want. Jesus and Paul were grateful to God and content for what they had received.

2. Perils of love of money (vv. 9–10)

> 9 But they that will be rich fall into temptation and a snare, and into many foolish and hurtful lusts, which drown men in destruction and perdition.

Verse 9 refers to the deadly plight of people who desire to be rich. The word translated "will be" means to "want to be" or "desire to be." Their goal in life is to become rich. Many, of course, never become wealthy. As far as Paul was concerned, it was irrelevant whether a greedy person ever became rich. The dangers applied to anyone whose consuming passion was to accumulate money and possessions.

Paul traced three steps in the destruction of such people: (1) Their greed placed before them all kinds of temptations. (2) Their lustful greed took many foolish and harmful forms. (3) The final result of such greed was total destruction. They were pictured as drowning in an ocean of complete destruction.

> 10 For the love of money is the root of all evil: which while some coveted after, they have erred from the faith, and pierced themselves through with many sorrows.

Here is the most familiar verse in the entire passage. Some people misquote the verse by leaving out the words "the love of." However, Paul did not say that money itself is the root of all evil; he said that the

Roman coins. Credit: *Biblical Illustrator.*

love of money is. Luke 16:19–31 records Jesus' story of the rich man and Lazarus. The self-centered rich man ended up in hell because his wealth was his god. However, we must not overlook another rich man in the story. By the standards of his day, Abraham was a rich man; yet he was in heaven. Money can and should be used for God's glory by meeting human needs. Used in this way, money is good. However, selfishness and greed lead to many other sins as well.

Paul, of course, wasn't teaching that love of money is the source of all human evil. This infamous distinction goes to self-centered turning from God to live as one pleases. On the other hand, the love of money is a key sin that spawns a multitude of other evils. One father advised his son: "Son, make money. Make money honestly if you can, but make money." If becoming rich is one's consuming passion, how one gets rich becomes secondary.

The last part of verse 10 contains the chilling reminder that professing Christians are not immune from this danger. Paul knew of such people whose love of money resulted in them being led astray. By doing this, they brought great grief on themselves. They could not blame anyone but themselves, for "they pierced themselves through with many sorrows."

III. Charge to Timothy (1 Tim. 6:11–12)

1. Godly qualities to pursue (v. 11)

> 11 But thou, O man of God, flee these things; and follow after righteousness, godliness, faith, love, patience, meekness.

Scattered through 1 Timothy are a number of personal admonitions from Paul to his son in the faith. Here he reminded Timothy that he was a person who belonged to God. As such, he should flee certain things and pursue certain things. "Pursue" is the meaning of the word translated "follow after." This is the word Paul used when he wrote, "I press toward the mark for the prize of the high calling of God in Christ Jesus" (Phil. 3:14).

Timothy was to flee the sins Paul had just enumerated in verses 3–5, 9–10; instead he should pursue the qualities listed in verse 11. He was to do the right thing as God defined "right." He was to practice a godly life based on reverence for God. He was to live by faith in the Lord and show love for others in His name. He was to remain steadfast as he endured trouble. He was to display the kind of gentleness and self-giving that Jesus meant when He said, "Blessed are the meek: for they shall inherit the earth" (Matt. 5:5).

2. Remaining true to God's calling (v. 12)

> 12 Fight the good fight of faith, lay hold on eternal life, whereunto thou art also called, and hast professed a good profession before many witnesses.

The word translated "fight" was used of striving in athletic events and of struggling in battle. In the next session, we will study a passage in which Paul compared Christians to soldiers and to athletes (2 Tim. 2:3–6).

Paul did not use "lay hold on eternal life" to mean earn your own salvation. He had spent his entire ministry stressing that eternal life is the gift of God's grace, not a reward for personal righteousness. His point here is that Christians should keep their eyes fixed on eternal life as the goal toward which they are moving. This hope motivated faithfulness.

"Profession" may refer to Timothy's original profession of faith in his baptism, or it may refer to the special commitment that was made public when he was ordained. In either case, Paul challenged Timothy to look back and remember his commitment and to look ahead and see his goal. Both visions should motivate him to "fight the good fight of faith."

APPLYING THE BIBLE

1. Truth is costly. In an English cathedral there is buried the body of an early-day preacher. On the grave is the epitaph: "He was a painful preacher of the truth" (vv. 2–3).

Paul admonished Timothy to preach the truth. Later, Timothy was to learn that preaching the truth is often costly.

What has it cost you to teach, preach, and live the truth (John 14:6)?

2. Pride. The Bible has a great deal to say about pride. The word appears no fewer than forty-six times in the Bible. *Proud* and *proudly* appear about fifty-six times. Someone has said that the highest mountain to climb is the mountain of self. Pride is simply self exalting itself. Writer Elizabeth Fry said of herself: "You are a contemptible small lady, all outside and no inside."

Paul warned young Timothy about false teachers who are "proud, knowing nothing, but doting about questions and strifes of words" (v. 4). From them, Timothy was to withdraw himself (v. 5).

3. Contentment. A Persian poet by the name of Saadi said that he never complained about his lot in life except once, when he had no shoes and no money to buy them. But when he met a man without feet, he instantly became contented and thanked God for His mercies.

Henry Thornton was an American philanthropist. One day a minister called on Thornton and asked for a donation for missions. Immediately Thornton wrote out a check for $25. No sooner had he written the check than a telegram was delivered to him. Suddenly, he turned ashen and told the minister he must return the check. Handing the check back, the minister didn't know what to think. As Thornton wrote out a check for $250 he said to the minister: "I have just been told I have lost thousands of dollars in an investment that I made. God has told me I may not have my wealth much longer. I must use it well!"

Paul taught Timothy that godliness *with* contentment is much gain. It seems that it is much easier to make money than it is to find peace of heart. But peace of heart is the thing for which all of us are searching.

4. Shun the love of money. In one of his short stories, O. Henry tells about Jim and Della. They had little but were madly in love. At Christmas, when Della counted her money, she had only $1.87. But she had one glorious asset—golden hair that fell around her body like a robe. She sold her hair and, with the money, bought Jim a platinum fob for the gold watch his father had given him. Meanwhile, Jim was shopping for Della. Selling his precious watch, he bought Della two combs embossed with precious jewels. When they met that evening at home, Jim was shocked to see that Della had cut her hair, but she was so beautiful that he loved her more than ever. Then he handed Della her combs, which she couldn't use. And she handed Jim the watch fob, which he couldn't use. They still had nothing in the way of money, but they enjoyed Christmas all the more because they still had each other.

There is nothing wrong with having money, but the love of money ruins us (vv. 9–10). Having a lot of money can rob us of having anything!

TEACHING THE BIBLE

- *Main Idea:* Christ's true servants teach and live godly lives.
- *Suggested Teaching Aim:* To lead adults to identify ways they can avoid ungodliness and live godly lives.

A TEACHING OUTLINE

1. Use an illustration to introduce the Bible study.

2. Use two listening teams to identify godly and ungodly characteristics.

3. Use lecture and Scripture search to explore the Scripture passage.

4. Use listing and goal setting to give the truth a personal focus.

Introduce the Bible Study

Use "Truth is costly" from "Applying the Bible" to introduce the Bible study.

Search for Biblical Truth

IN ADVANCE, write the lesson poster on the following page on a large sheet of paper and place it on the focal wall:

Christ's Servant Teaches Godliness

1 Timothy 6:2b–12	
Words of Warning	*(6:2b–5)*
Words about Money	*(6:6–10)*
Words of Encouragement	*(6:11–12)*

On a chalkboard or a large sheet of paper write *Godliness* and *Ungodliness* at the top of two columns. Ask half the class to listen for ways Paul suggested that Timothy and we could be godly, and ask the other half to listen for characteristics of ungodly people. Distribute paper and pencils so members can make notes during your presentation. Ask a volunteer to read aloud 6:2b–5. Present a brief lecture in which you (1) contrast sound teachings with false teachings (see "Studying the Bible" for three contrasts), and (2) describe the characteristics of false teachers. Write characteristics of godliness and ungodliness on the poster.

Ask a volunteer to read aloud 6:6–10. Use "Studying the Bible" to explain "godliness" and "contentment." Write *contentment* and a definition on the Word List you began last week. Ask: Why did Paul suggest that we should be content? (We can't take anything with us; if we have enough to eat and enough to wear, that should be sufficient.) What three steps of destruction do those who have sold out to riches go through? (See "Studying the Bible.")

Write on a chalkboard or a large sheet of paper: *Money is the root of all evil.* Ask: What is wrong with this phrase? (It's the *love of money* that is the root of evil.)

DISCUSS: If becoming rich is one's consuming passion, how does that influence how one makes money? Do you have to have a lot of money to be selfish? What can believers do to keep from letting the love of money control their lives? Write characteristics of godliness and ungodliness on the poster.

Ask a volunteer to read aloud 6:11–12. Point to the third point on the outline. Ask: What did Paul tell Timothy to flee? (The things mentioned in vv. 9–10.) What did Paul tell Timothy to pursue? (See v. 11.) How does keeping our eyes on eternal life motivate us?

DISCUSS: How do the characteristics mentioned in verse 11 compare with the qualities the world says a successful person should have? Write characteristics of godliness and ungodliness on the poster.

Give the Truth a Personal Focus

Ask members to look at the listings of godly and ungodly characteristics. Ask: Which of the godly characteristics would you like to incorporate in your life? With which of the ungodly characteristics do you have problems? What specific steps can you take to eliminate the ungodly characteristics and incorporate the godly ones? Ask members to write two or three steps they will take this week to do this.

June

15

1997

Christ's Servant Endures Suffering

Background Passage: 2 Timothy 2:1–13
Focal Passage: 2 Timothy 2:1–13

When Paul wrote 2 Timothy, he was imprisoned and expecting soon to be executed (2 Tim. 1:8; 2:9; 4:6). Most likely, he was imprisoned and later executed during Nero's persecution in Rome during the middle 60s. Paul's final letter to his son in the faith is filled with emotion and challenge. One of the strong themes was Paul's challenge to Timothy to endure suffering faithfully.

Study Aim: *To identify various ways Paul challenged Timothy to endure suffering*

STUDYING THE BIBLE

OUTLINE AND SUMMARY

I. Be Strong in Grace (2 Tim. 2:1–2)
   1. Strong in Christ's grace (v. 1)
   2. Pass it on (v. 2)
II. Be Like a Soldier, Athlete, and Farmer (2 Tim. 2:3–7)
   1. Be a good soldier (vv. 3–4)
   2. Be a disciplined athlete (v. 5)
   3. Be a hardworking farmer (vv. 6–7)
III. Remember the Faithfulness of Christ (2 Tim. 2:8–13)
   1. Remember Jesus Christ (v. 8)
   2. Motivation for Paul's endurance (vv. 9–10)
   3. Christ's faithfulness (vv. 11–13)

Paul challenged Timothy to be strong in Christ's grace (v. 1) and to entrust the gospel message to faithful men who would teach others (v. 2). Christians are to be like obedient soldiers (vv. 3–4), disciplined athletes (v. 5), and hardworking farmers (vv. 6–7). They are to remember the risen Lord Jesus Christ (v. 8). Paul was suffering unjustly, but he endured for the sake of those yet to experience God's glorious salvation (vv. 9–10). Christ is faithful to His promises and warnings because these reflect who He is (vv. 11–13).

I. Be Strong in Grace (2 Tim. 2:1–2)

1. Strong in Christ's grace (v. 1)

1 Thou therefore, my son, be strong in the grace that is in Christ Jesus.

Paul felt that this was his last letter to Timothy, whom he called "my dearly beloved son" (1:2). Although he urged Timothy to come to him quickly (4:9), Paul knew that this letter might be his last opportunity to address his young friend. Running through the letter are challenges fo

Tim ageous (1:7). Paul knew that times of per-
seci ealized that every believer needed to be
arn rom Christ. Since Paul thought of Timothy
as turally wanted to do everything he could to
pre ul.

"F d "be strong" that he used in Ephesians 6:10,
P in the power of his might." In both passages,
H source of strength for Christians is the Lord.
le us to be courageous in the face of dangers.

s that thou hast heard of me among many wit-
commit thou to faithful men, who shall be able
so.

e gospel to Paul and the other apostles. They in
to others like Timothy. Paul's son in the faith had
d from Paul many times in the presence of many
that he was about to die. He believed that the
e because God's word was free and powerful (see
or spreading and preserving the gospel was for each
on to pass it along to the next. Thus he told Timothy
of God to faithful men, who in turn would teach oth-

a Soldier, Athlete, and Farmer (2 Tim. 2:3–7)

1. Be a good soldier (vv. 3–4)

3 Thou therefore endure hardness, as a good soldier of Jesus Christ.

4 No man that warreth entangleth himself with the affairs of this life; that he may please him who hath chosen him to be a soldier.

Paul often compared the Christian life to various aspects of military life (see 1 Cor. 9:7; Eph. 6:11–18). Paul mentioned three comparisons between Christians and soldiers. (1) The word translated "endure hardship" means "take your full share of suffering." Christians, like soldiers, must be willing to take their full share of suffering and hardships. (2) When soldiers are on duty, they must concentrate on being soldiers. They can't be distracted by other things. By the same token, Christians must concentrate on God and His kingdom and not become entangled in worldly things. (3) A good soldier obeys his or her military commander. Such obedience to orders is drilled into soldiers of every generation. Christians are to render absolute obedience to Christ our Lord. Pleasing Him is our goal.

2. Be a disciplined athlete (v. 5)

5 If a man also strive for masteries, yet is he not crowned, except he strive lawfully.

The word translated "strive for masteries" is a word from which we get our word "athlete." Just as Paul often compared Christians to soldiers, he also often compared them to athletes (see 1 Cor. 9:24–27; Phil. 3:13–14; 1 Tim. 4:8). In verse 5, he stressed that in order to win, an ath-

lete must "strive lawfully." This may mean that he or she must compete according to the rules; however, Paul probably meant that an athlete must discipline himself or herself by rigorous training. The Greeks used the word in this way. For them, the rules included the necessary discipline and training. Olympic athletes, for example, had to take an oath that they had trained for ten months. Christians must subject themselves to rigorous self-discipline if they are to fulfill God's expectations for them.

3. Be a hardworking farmer (vv. 6–7)

> 6 The husbandman that laboureth must be first partaker of the fruits.

"Husbandman" translates a word meaning "worker of the earth." Paul's point was that a hardworking farmer should be the first to eat of the crops he had grown. Paul used a similar comparison in 1 Corinthians 9:10–11 to argue that preachers should expect financial support. His point in verse 6 is that Christians are in some ways like farmers. He stressed the hard work that goes into farming in order to make a crop. Christians must also be willing to work long and hard for a spiritual harvest.

> 7 Consider what I say; and the Lord give thee understanding in all things.

Paul had used simple comparisons to make his point that Christians must faithfully endure hardships and sufferings for the sake of Christ. He knew that this was not an easy lesson to learn or to accept. Thus he paused to challenge Timothy to reflect on what he had said. Paul promised that if Timothy paid heed to the message, the Lord would give him understanding.

III. Remember Christ's Faithfulness (2 Tim. 2:8–13)

1. Remember Jesus Christ (v. 8)

> 8 Remember that Jesus Christ of the seed of David was raised from the dead according to my gospel:

Paul had been using human comparisons to make his point. Now the apostle made clear that Jesus Christ is the ultimate One to whom believers should look for all things. Paul called Timothy to remember the heart of the good news that Paul preached. Jesus was the Christ or Messiah who came to fulfill God's promises about David having a descendant who would reign forever. The certainty of this divine visitation in human history was the resurrection of Jesus Christ from the dead (see Rom. 1:3–4).

2. Motivation for Paul's endurance (vv. 9–10)

> 9 Wherein I suffer trouble, as an evil doer, even unto bonds; but the word of God is not bound.

As Paul challenged Timothy to endure suffering for Christ's sake, the apostle testified of his own endurance in suffering. Verse 9 is one of several verses that show Paul wrote 2 Timothy from prison. He was suffering trouble and he was in bonds or chains. He wrote that he suffered as an "evil doer." The only other use of this word in the New Testament is of the common criminals crucified with Jesus (Luke 23:32, 39). Paul was no evil doer or criminal, but he was imprisoned as a common criminal.

This probably reflects the false charges made against Christians by Nero to justify his persecution of them.

Confinement, suffering, and slanders were not easy for Paul to take. However, he endured because although he was bound, the Word of God was not bound. Paul believed that God's Word would continue to go forth. Persecution might seem to destroy the church and its leaders, but God's Spirit would raise up others to continue the work. Paul counted on people like Timothy to continue to declare the gospel.

> 10 Therefore I endure all things for the elect's sakes, that they may also obtain the salvation which is in Christ Jesus with eternal glory.

Verse 10 explains one source of Paul's motivation for enduring suffering. He did it for the sake of others. "Elect" means "chosen." It was one of the words Paul used to describe believers. The word reminds Christians that they were chosen by God before they chose God. It stresses that salvation is by God's grace. He took the initiative in seeking sinners, even sending His Son to die for us while we were yet sinners.

Paul used the word here to describe all those whom God had chosen who had not yet experienced his salvation. Thus Paul saw his faithful endurance as contributing to the salvation of people yet unsaved. Because of this, he was willing to endure suffering. Salvation was the guiding purpose and hope of Paul's life. He could endure suffering because it would be used by God in the fulfillment of His glorious salvation.

3. Christ's faithfulness (vv. 11–13)

> 11 It is a faithful saying: For if we be dead with him, we shall also live with him:
>
> 12 If we suffer, we shall also reign with him: if we deny him, he also will deny us:
>
> 13 If we believe not, yet he abideth faithful: he cannot deny himself.

Paul quoted another "faithful saying" (1 Tim. 1:15; 4:9; Titus 3:8). Many Bible students think that verses 11–13 may have been words of an early Christian hymn. The words are surely in a poetic form of four couplets. Verse 11 calls to mind Romans 6:1–11. Baptism into Christ means sharing Christ's death and resurrection. This means death to the sinful life and resurrection to new life. It also points to the Christian hope of victory over death. The first part of verse 12 also points to the bright future for the faithful. Those who suffer faithfully for Christ shall share in His victorious reign. Both of these couplets challenge Christians to faithful endurance by pointing to the end result of such steadfastness.

The last part of verse 12 calls to faithful endurance by warning of the judgment on those who deny the Lord. Paul no doubt had in mind the saying of Jesus about denying those who deny Him (Matt. 10:33). During times of trial, some professing believers show by their actions that they never knew the Lord (Matt. 7:21–23).

The theme of verse 13 is the faithfulness of Christ, but Bible students disagree about the application of such faithfulness in verse 13. Some believe that verse 13 reinforces verse 12b. In other words, Christ shows His faithfulness to His own character by denying those who deny Him. Other Bible students interpret Christ's faithfulness as His faithful love for His people. The choice is not easy because both teachings are found elsewhere in the Bible. If the latter is the point here, Paul was stressing that although true faith leads to faithfulness, our faithfulness is only a reflection of His perfect faithfulness.

APPLYING THE BIBLE

1. Last words. The last words of friends and loved ones mean much to us. Among John Wesley's last words were these: "The best of all is, God is with us." George Washington's last words were: "Doctor, I am dying, but I am not afraid to die." On his deathbed, Sir Walter Scott, the great Scottish novelist, begged Lockhart, his son-in-law, to read to him. When Lockhart asked what he should read, Scott replied: "Can you ask? There is only one Book."

Today we are studying Paul's last words, and of what did he speak? "Remember that Jesus Christ of the seed of David was raised from the dead, according to my gospel."

For the living or the dying, these are the most important last words.

2. Pass it on! One day Billy Sunday, then a hard-drinking professional player for the Chicago White-stockings, was leaning half-drunk against a Chicago city wall. A small group from the Salvation Army came to where Sunday was standing and began to sing. The preacher brought a brief sermon. Sunday followed them to the local Pacific Garden Mission, sat in on the service that followed, and was saved. Sunday later confessed, "I fell half-drunk into the arms of Jesus!" For a while he worked with the YMCA; and then, when evangelist Wilbur Chapman, whom Sunday had been assisting, left evangelism, Sunday began to hold revival meetings. In New York City alone, between May and June of 1907, Sunday preached 120 times to masses of people with thousands being saved. During his ministry he "passed it on" (the gospel) to at least 100 million people with, it is said, more than 1 million converts.

Paul instructed Timothy to pass the good news on to others "who shall be able to teach others also." This task was given not only to Timothy, Billy Sunday, and Billy Graham, but also to each of us who is a believer (v. 2).

4. A soldier's faithfulness. Paul compares the Christian life to that of a soldier, an athlete, and a farmer. Each must be faithful to his respective task (vv. 3–6).

In A.D. 79, Mount Vesuvius erupted and buried the city of Pompeii, Italy under tons of lava and ashes. Many were buried alive. Modern archaeologists have excavated the city and found the remains of people in deep vaults where they had gone for security. Others were frozen in the lava in the activity in which they were engaged when the holocaust befell them.

The lava preserved the remains of one Roman sentinel. He stayed at his post, spear in hand, doing his duty as the earth shook around him.

Paul encouraged Timothy, the young pastor, to work hard like the farmer, run faithfully like the athlete, and stay at his assigned task of declaring the good news like a good soldier.

TEACHING THE BIBLE

➧ *Main Idea:* Christians are to be faithful servants even if they have to suffer.

➧ *Suggested Teaching Aim:* To lead adults to commit themselves to serve Christ even if it causes suffering.

A TEACHING OUTLINE

1. *Use an illustration to introduce the Bible study.*
2. *Use a lesson outline poster to guide the Bible study.*
3. *Use Scripture Search and discussion to study the text.*
4. *Use a commitment card to make the Bible study personal.*

Introduce the Bible Study

Use "Last words" from "Applying the Bible" to introduce the Bible study. Point out the lesson on the unit poster you made for June 1.

Search for Biblical Truth

IN ADVANCE, make the following lesson outline poster:

Christ's Servant Endures Suffering

1. Be Strong in Grace (2 Tim. 2:1–1)
2. Be like a Soldier, Athlete, and Farmer (2 Tim. 2:3–7)
3. Remember the Faithfulness of Christ (2 Tim. 2:8–13)

Cover each point until you are ready to teach it.

On a chalkboard or a large sheet of paper write the following without the italicized phrases:

Question	Answer
Who?	*Timothy, Paul's "son"*
What?	*Endure suffering*
Why?	*Paul was imprisoned and felt this might be his last chance to instruct Timothy to be strong in the Lord*
When?	*Possibly around* A.D. *64*
Where?	*Rome*

IN ADVANCE, enlist a reader to read aloud all the Scripture. You might want to use a modern translation.

Uncover the first point on the lesson outline poster. Call for the reader to read aloud 2 Timothy 2:1–2. Lecture briefly covering these points: (1) Paul and Timothy's relationship; (2) Paul's fear that he might be put to death in Rome (possibly A.D. 64) before he could see Timothy; (3) Paul's challenge to Timothy to be strong in the Lord; (4) God's method of spreading the gospel was one person telling another. Fill in the above chart with members' answers.

Uncover the second point on the lesson outline poster. Ask members to listen for the three types of persons Paul used to make his point. Call for the reader to read aloud 2:3–7. Write the specific verse on the lesson outline poster above each type. Ask: What characteristics does a soldier have that a Christian should practice? (Use "Studying the Bible" to point out the three comparisons between Christians and soldiers.) athletes? farmers?

DISCUSS: What three modern occupations could Paul use if he were writing today? Why?

Uncover the third point on the lesson outline poster. Call for the reader to read aloud 2:8–10. Ask: What is the heart of the good news described by Paul in verse 8? (Jesus is the Messiah who came to fulfill God's promise about David having a descendant who would reign forever.) What kind of suffering was Paul experiencing, according to verse 9? Why was Paul willing to suffer (v. 10)?

Ask members to follow in their Bibles as the reader reads 2:11–13. On a large sheet of paper write:

If we do this . . .	Christ will do this . . .
Die with Him	We will live with Him
Suffer with Him	We will reign with Him
Deny Him	He will deny us
Are faithless (believe not)	He will still be faithful

Use "Studying the Bible" to explain verse 13.

Give the Truth a Personal Focus

Distribute paper and pencils and ask members to write: "I am so grateful to Christ for what He has done for me that I will strive to live for Him regardless of what it may cost me." Have a time of silent prayer and ask members to determine if they can sign this statement. Ask them to slip quietly from the class when they have decided either way.

Christ's Servant Teaches Faithfulness

June
22
1997

Basic Passage: 2 Timothy 4:1–18
Focal Passage: 2 Timothy 4:1–18

When Paul wrote 2 Timothy, he realized that the time of his death was drawing near. Faithfulness is a strong theme of the closing chapter. Second Timothy 4 contains Paul's final charge for Timothy to be faithful. It also contains Paul's powerful testimony of faith and faithfulness as he faced death.

Study Aim: *To describe Paul's final call for Timothy to be faithful and Paul's testimony of his own faithfulness*

STUDYING THE BIBLE

OUTLINE AND SUMMARY

I. Charge to Be Faithful (2 Tim. 4:1–5)
- **1. Paul's charge to Timothy (vv. 1–2)**
- **2. A warning against false teachers (vv. 3–4)**
- **3. A challenge (v. 5)**

II. Testimony of Faith and Faithfulness (2 Tim. 4:6–8)
- **1. Facing death (v. 6)**
- **2. Found faithful (v. 7)**
- **3. Crown of righteousness (v. 8)**

III. Final Words (2 Tim. 4:9–18)
- **1. Instructions to Timothy (vv. 9–15)**
- **2. Personal testimony (vv. 16–18)**

Paul solemnly charged Timothy to be faithful in preaching the word (vv. 1–2). He warned that selfish hearers would turn from the truth to teachers who would tell them what they wanted to hear (vv. 3–4). Paul challenged Timothy to watch, endure, work, and finish his ministry (v. 5). Paul's life was an offering, and his time of departure was near (v. 6). He had faithfully finished what God had called him to do (v. 7). He looked forward to the gift and eternal reward for faithfulness (v. 8). Paul shared some final information and instructions with Timothy (vv. 9–15). He testified that the Lord, who had always stood with him, would deliver him into His heavenly kingdom (vv. 16–18).

I. Charge to Be Faithful (2 Tim. 4:1–5)

1. Paul's charge to Timothy (vv. 1–2)

1 I charge thee therefore before God, and the Lord Jesus Christ, who shall judge the quick and the dead at his appearing and his kingdom;

Paul reminded Timothy that the two of them lived in the presence of God and the Lord Jesus Christ. Standing in the divine presence, Paul delivered a solemn charge to Timothy. The word "appearing" sometimes was used of Christ's appearance during His earthly life and ministry (2 Tim. 1:10). At other times, the word was used of Christ's coming appearance (1 Tim. 6:4). Here it is used of Christ's future appearance when He will judge the living (meaning of "quick") and the dead. The living will be those alive when He comes, and the dead will be those raised to stand before the Judge (1 Thess. 4:16–18). Unbelievers will be condemned when they stand before the Judge (Rev. 20:11–15). Believers will not be condemned, but they will be judged according to their faithfulness (2 Cor. 5:9–10).

> 2 Preach the word; be instant in season, out of season; reprove, rebuke, exhort with all longsuffering and doctrine.

Paul charged Timothy that his main task was to be a herald of the good news. "Be instant" stresses the need to stay at his post. Timothy was not only to preach when he felt good and conditions were good; he was to preach the word at all times and in all seasons. This task was further defined by three words. "Reprove" means "convince" and appeals to the reason. "Rebuke" carries a note of moral censure and appeals to the conscience. "Exhort" appeals to the human will. It can mean either to urge or to encourage. Preaching must do some of both.

The final words of verse 2 point to the spirit of the preacher and the preaching. Some rebuking is part of preaching the truth; but preachers must avoid a harsh, vindictive spirit. Instead they must fulfill their task with the same kind of longsuffering that Jesus perfectly exemplified. The word "doctrine" or "teaching" is a reminder of Paul's words in 2 Timothy 2:24: "The servant of the Lord must not strive; but be gentle unto all men, apt to teach."

2. A warning against false teachers (vv. 3–4)

> 3 For the time will come when they will not endure sound doctrine; but after their own lusts shall they heap to themselves teachers, having itching ears.
>
> 4 And they shall turn away their ears from the truth, and shall be turned unto fables.

Paul predicted a time when false teachers would be even more popular than they were in his own time. Verses 3–4 focus on the sins of the people who make false teachers popular. He made two serious charges against the people who turn to false teachers. For one thing, they turn from the truth of sound doctrine. Their other sin is that they replace loyalty to the truth with determination to satisfy their own desires. Thus they seek out teachers who say what their itching ears want to hear. The sin of the false teachers is that they are willing to say whatever their hearers want to hear. However, such self-serving scoundrels could never deceive anyone unless selfish, gullible people rewarded these tellers of fables.

3. A challenge (v. 5)

> 5 But watch thou in all things, endure afflictions, do the work of an evangelist, make full proof of thy ministry.

Paul called Timothy to remain alert as he sought to fulfill his ministry. Those who are committed to preach the truth need to beware the shallow hearers and self-serving preachers. Those who stand for the truth in such a time need to be prepared to endure afflictions and hardships.

Paul told Timothy to do the work of an evangelist. Some in the church were called and gifted as evangelists (Eph. 4:11). They majored on telling the good news to lost and unbelieving people. At the same time, the work of evangelism was not confined to a special group of people bearing that name. The risen Lord called all His people to be witnesses of Him (Acts 1:8).

"Make full proof of" literally means to "accomplish," "complete," or "fulfill." Because Paul was facing death, he no doubt had given much thought to the meaning of fulfilling one's ministry. Nothing is so important for a person whose goal in life is to do God's will. In verses 6–8, Paul testified that he had fulfilled his ministry. To the best of his ability, he had done what Christ had commissioned him to do. He wanted Timothy to reach the end of his days and to be able to know that he had fulfilled his ministry.

II. Testimony of Faith and Faithfulness (2 Tim. 4:6–8)

1. Facing death (v. 6)

> 6 For I am now ready to be offered, and the time of my departure is at hand.

Paul obviously felt that the time of his death was at hand. He was in prison awaiting what he expected to be his final hearing. Ancient tradition says that he was in a Roman prison during the persecution of Roman Christians by Nero. Tradition also says that Paul was beheaded during that persecution.

Paul used two pictures to show that he was facing death. The first line literally says, "I am already being offered." Paul pictured his life as a sacrificial offering. During his first imprisonment, he had used the same analogy in Philippians 2:17: "If I be offered upon the sacrifice and service of your faith, I joy, and rejoice with you all." In a sense, Paul's whole life in Christ was lived as a sacrifice unto God. Now he was in the process of that sacrifice leading to his death.

The word translated "departure" was sometimes used of the loosing of a ship from its moorings in preparation for setting sail. It was also sometimes used of soldiers breaking camp as they prepared to depart. In other words, it was used of leaving one place in preparation for moving to another. Paul was ready to leave this earthly life and depart to be with the Lord.

In fact, Paul had used the verbal form of the noun "departure" during his first imprisonment. He testified to his readiness to die or to live for Christ in Philippians 1:23–24: "I am in a strait betwixt two, having a desire to depart, and to be with Christ; which is far better: Nevertheless to abide in the flesh is more needful for you." At that time, Paul was ready to depart; he even preferred to go to be with the Lord. However, he believed that the Lord still had work for him on earth. In 2 Timothy 4:6, Paul was ready to depart and expected soon to do so.

2. Found faithful (v. 7)

7 I have fought a good fight, I have finished my course, I have kept the faith:

Paul's highest objective in life was to do God's will for his life. Verse 7 shows that he felt that he had finished what God had commissioned him to do. He used three pictures to testify to that fact. The first picture was the good fight Paul had fought. Many Bible students think that this was a picture of an athlete. Others feel that Paul pictured himself as a military veteran who had done his best in battle. As we saw in our study of 2 Timothy 2:3–5, Paul challenged Timothy to be as a good soldier and a disciplined athlete.

The second picture is definitely taken from a race. Paul pictured himself as a runner who had finished the race course. Again it is interesting to compare what Paul wrote during his first imprisonment about life as a race. Paul pictured himself as a runner straining with all his might toward the finish line: "Forgetting those things which are behind, and reaching forth unto those things which are before, I press toward the mark for the prize of the high calling of God in Christ Jesus" (Phil. 3:13–14). Paul testified in verse 7 that he had finished that race.

The third picture is of a steward who had been entrusted with a valuable deposit. Paul may have had in mind the treasure of the gospel, or he may have been thinking of God's precious call to him, or he may have had both in mind. In any case, he testified that he had faithfully kept the faith God had entrusted to him.

3. Crown of righteousness (v. 8)

8 Henceforth there is laid up for me a crown of righteousness, which the Lord, the righteous judge, shall give me at that day: and not to me only, but unto all them also that love his appearing.

In his writings, Paul expressed his hope of life beyond death in many ways. Here he pictured a crown of righteousness to be given to him and to others by the righteous Judge. This picture doesn't contradict Paul's teaching of salvation by grace. God accepts sinners as righteous through their faith in Christ (Rom. 3:21—5:10). However, Christ's Spirit within believers produces righteous living (Rom. 6—8).

In either case, the righteousness is a gift of God, not a human achievement. Christ calls His people to be faithful and rewards us according to our faithfulness. Jesus taught the importance of faithfulness (Matt. 25:14–30). So did Paul (1 Cor. 3:11–15; 4:2). Although all God's rewards are ultimately gifts of His grace, God nonetheless rewards faithfulness. Paul testified that he would receive a reward for faithfulness; but he made two things clear: (1) His crown of righteousness was ultimately a gift of the Lord. (2) All those who love the Lord's appearing will be given crowns.

III. Final Words (2 Tim. 4:9–18)

1. Information and instructions (vv. 9–15)

Paul urged Timothy to come to him quickly (v. 9). Of his fellow workers, only Luke was with him at the time of his writing (v. 11a). Some like Demas (DEE muhs) had forsaken him; and others like

Crescens (KRES uhnz), Titus, and Tychicus (TIK ih kuhs) had been sent on missions (vv. 10,1 2). Paul asked Timothy to bring Mark with him (v. 11b). Paul also asked for his cloak, scrolls, and parchments (v. 13). He warned Timothy against Alexander, who had done Paul much harm (vv. 14–15).

2. Personal testimony (vv. 16–18)

Paul said that he had no one to stand with him at an earlier hearing, but he testified that the Lord stood with him (vv. 16–17a). The Lord who strengthened him on that occasion would deliver him into His heavenly kingdom (vv. 17b–18).

APPLYING THE BIBLE

1. Then what? Charles G. Finney (1792–1875) was one of America's greatest evangelists and pastors. Before he entered the ministry, Finney was a lawyer.

One day young Finney was talking to an old lawyer who asked, "Finney, what are you going to do when you become a lawyer?" Finney replied, "Put out my shingle and get rich."

"And what then?" asked the lawyer. And Finney replied, "Retire."

"And what then?" the lawyer asked. "Die," Finney replied.

"And what then?" his friend asked. With a tremble in his voice, Finney answered, "The judgment."

Finney's answer startled him. Leaving the office, he went to the nearby woods and determined not to leave until he had made peace with God. When he emerged later in the evening, he was a new man with the peace of Christ in his heart.

Paul told Timothy in verse 1 that each of us shall stand before God on the Day of Judgment and give account of ourselves. This was the message Timothy was to preach.

2. Faithful to his call. John Wesley, the founder of Methodism, was faithful to his call. He set a worthy example for every preacher to emulate.

On Tuesday, March 1, 1791, the day before he died at nearly eighty-eight years of age, Wesley said weakly, "The best part of all is, God is with us."

For fifty-six years Wesley traveled across England and Scotland, again and again, preaching the gospel in taverns and churches, but mostly out-of-doors. He rode his horse, or walked, five thousand to eight thousand miles a year—more than a quarter of a million miles in his lifetime. He preached fifteen times or more a week. In addition, he witnessed to people daily as he traveled. His exhausting ministry has been called "the most amazing record of human exertion."

Above all, Wesley's ministry was characterized by faithfulness to his holy calling. To that faithfulness in preaching, Paul called young Timothy (v. 2).

3. Get to the heart of things. A man was filling out an application for a job in a factory when he came to the question, "In case of an accident, whom should we notify?" Pausing a moment to ponder the question, the man wrote, "Anybody in sight!"

That wasn't the answer that was expected, but at least the man got to the heart of the thing: in a crisis call out to the first person one sees!

Paul told Timothy that in his preaching he should get to the heart of the gospel message by "reproving," "rebuking," and "exhorting" (v. 2) his listeners to flee quickly to Christ for salvation. That's good advice.

4. Preaching that strikes home. English author G. K. Chesterton (1874–1936) said that the church stands in danger that the time will come when it can pick up a microphone and address the world only to discover it has nothing to say! He also pointed out that many thinkers who try to explain Christianity only explain it away.

Paul warns Timothy about false teachers who would come with high-sounding but empty words. They would have something to say, but it would not be true to the Word of God (vv. 3–4).

Church members need to weigh carefully what their pastors preach and ask themselves, "Is what I am hearing sound doctrine?"

5. The work of evangelism. The late R. G. Lee emphasized the importance of winning just one person to Christ, but winning that one can be many: Andrew brought Peter to Jesus, but that one was many for Peter preached at Pentecost when 3,000 were saved. Joel Stratton, who was a restaurant waiter, won one—John Gough. But that one was many because Gough won many more to Christ. Sunday School teacher Ezra Kimball won one to Jesus, Dwight L. Moody. But that one was many because Moody led tens of thousands to Christ. Evangelist Mordecai Ham won Billy Graham to Christ, but that one was many because Graham has preached to more people than anyone else in history.

Paul instructed Timothy to "do the work of an evangelist" (v. 5). Telling the good news, winning people to Christ, is every Christian's responsibility. As someone has aptly put it, it is one beggar telling another beggar where to find bread.

TEACHING THE BIBLE

- *Main Idea:* God's servants will be faithful to Christ regardless of what it may cost.
- *Suggested Teaching Aim:* To encourage adults to be faithful in their daily lives.

A TEACHING OUTLINE

1. Use an illustration to introduce the Bible study.
2. Use an acrostic to search for biblical truth.
3. Use questions and group discussion to examine the Bible passage.
4. Use goal setting to give the truth a personal focus.

Introduce the Bible Study

Use "Faithful to his call" from "Applying the Bible" to introduce the Bible study.

Search for Biblical Truth

Point out the lesson on the unit poster (See June 1). Ask members to describe Paul's situation at this point. (He is in jail, probably in Rome, awaiting execution.) Make an acrostic by writing the word **FAITHFUL** horizontally across a chalkboard or a large sheet of paper. You will add to this as you study the lesson. Your finished acrostic should look something like this:

```
      b
      e   f f
      w   o i
      a   u n
      r   g i
      e   h s
      f   t h c
      a w g e r
  P   l a o d o
b r b s t o c w
e e e e c d o n
F A I T H F U L
a c n e a i r a
i h s a n g s i
t t t c d h e d
h h a h w t   u
f e n e o     p
u w t r r
l o   s k
  r
  d
```

Call for a volunteer to read aloud 2 Timothy 4:1–2. Ask: What did Paul challenge Timothy to do in verse 1? (Be **F**aithful—Write this phrase so the *F's* in Faithful match up.) What were the first two commands Paul gave Timothy in verse 2? (Pre**A**ch the Word; Be **I**nstant—Write these on the acrostic.) What other commands did Paul give? (If possible have verse 2 read aloud in a modern translation.) Use "Studying the Bible" to explain each of these commands.

Call for a volunteer to read aloud 4:3–5. What did Paul warn against in these verses? (Beware false **T**eachers.) Use "Studying the Bible" to point out the two charges against the people who turn to false teachers. Ask: What command did Paul give? (Watc**H** and work.)

Call for a volunteer to read aloud 4:6–8. Ask: What did Paul say he had done in verse 7? (Fought good **F**ight.) Use "Studying the Bible" to explain the images in verse 6. After you have explained *departure*, add it to your Word List (see June 1 lesson). Use "Studying the Bible" to explain the three pictures Paul used to show he had finished what God had given him to do. (Write Finished Co**U**rse.) Ask: What did Paul say was waiting him? (Crown **L**aid up.) Use "Studying the Bible" to explain this crown.

June

22

1997

Give the Truth a Personal Focus

Ask members to look at the completed acrostic. Ask: How many of these apply to you today? (All of them can—the last three will depend on them.) Challenge them to choose one of these and list steps they will take to accomplish this goal this week.

Christ's Servant Encourages Community

June

29

1997

Basic Passage: Titus 3:1–11

Focal Passage: Titus 3:1–11

Although Titus comes after 2 Timothy in our Bibles, Titus was actually written before 2 Timothy, which was Paul's final letter. When Paul wrote Titus, he had not yet been arrested for the final time. Paul had left Timothy to serve in Ephesus (1 Tim. 1:3); he had left Titus in Crete (Titus 1:5). Both younger associates were to work with local churches and church leaders. Both faced difficult situations, but Crete seemed to have been an especially hard field of service (Titus 1:12–13). This lesson is based on Paul's final exhortations to Titus, which dealt with appropriate behavior for Christians in light of God's saving mercy.

Study Aim: *To identify Christian behavior resulting from being saved by God's mercy*

STUDYING THE BIBLE

OUTLINE AND SUMMARY

I. Citizenship and Community (Titus 3:1–2)

II. Saved and Transformed (Titus 3:3–7)

1. The old life (v. 3)

2. Saved by God's mercy (vv. 4–7)

III. Doing Good and Avoiding Controversies (Titus 3:8–11)

1. Doing good (v. 8)

2. Avoiding controversies (vv. 9–11)

Christians are to be law-abiding citizens and to be a force for good in the community (vv. 1–2). The old sinful life was what they once lived (v. 3). God saved them by His mercy, not by deeds of righteousness they had done: cleansing, regenerating, making them new, and justifying them (vv. 4–7). Believers are to do good works (v. 8). They are to avoid meaningless arguments and seek to confront troublemakers in a redemptive way (vv. 9–11).

I. Citizenship and Community (Titus 3:1–2)

1 **Put them in mind to be subject to principalities and powers, to obey magistrates, to be ready to every good work,**

2 To speak evil of no man, to be no brawlers, but gentle, shewing all meekness unto all men.

Earlier exhortations in Titus focused on responsibilities in the Christian community. Titus 3:1–2 focuses on Christian responsibility to the community as a whole. This is apparent in the words describing government officials in verse 1 and the words "unto all men" in verse 2.

Submission to government authority and obedience to government officials is a familiar theme in the New Testament. The classic biblical treatment is in Romans 13:1–7; but the same theme is in 1 Timothy 2:1; Titus 3:1; 1 Peter 2:13–14. Jesus had taught His followers to render to Caesar what is his and to God what is His (Matt. 22:21; Mark 12:17; Luke 20:25). Except when the government preempted supreme allegiance to God—as in Acts 5:29—the general rule was for Christians to be law-abiding citizens.

The last part of verse 1 and verse 2 refers to Christians' responsibilities to the community of which they are part. Believers have responsibilities beyond the family of faith. They are always to be ready to participate in good work on behalf of others. They certainly are not to be slanderers or gossips who speak evil of others. Nor are they to be quick to take offense and to get involved in some argument or fight. Instead, like our Lord, they are to be gentle people who practice what He taught and exemplify the meekness of those who live by the standards of God's kingdom (Matt. 5:5). Such meekness is not weakness but strength to live by the higher demands of God's way of relating to other people, including difficult people.

II. Saved and Transformed (Titus 3:3–7)

1. The old life (v. 3)

> 3 For we ourselves were sometimes foolish, disobedient, deceived, serving divers lusts and pleasures, living in malice and envy, hateful, and hating one another.

Verse 3 is a dark picture of the kind of life lived by Christians before they met Christ. A number of Paul's letters contain similar descriptions of the old sinful life (1 Cor. 6:9–11; Eph. 4:17–24). Paul included himself among those who were once guilty of such sins.

They were foolish in choosing the irrational destruction of sin. Although like Eve they were deceived, they were responsible for their disobedience to God. As a result, they became slaves (the meaning of "serving") of sinful desires and practices. Their sins against God were apparent in their sins against one another. They lived in malice and envy. They were themselves hateful, and they hated one another.

2. Saved by God's mercy (vv. 4–7)

> 4 But after that the kindness and love of God our Saviour toward man appeared,
>
> 5 Not by works of righteousness which we have done, but according to his mercy he saved us, by the washing of regeneration, and renewing of the Holy Ghost;
>
> 6 Which he shed on us abundantly through Jesus Christ our Saviour;
>
> 7 That being justified by his grace, we should be made heirs according to the hope of eternal life.

Titus 3:4–7 is one of the most powerful Bible passages about divine salvation. Based on the words "This is a faithful saying" in verse 8, many Bible scholars think that Paul was referring to the words of an early

Christian hymn. We cannot be sure about that, but we can be sure that Paul covered the main aspects of salvation in a beautiful and powerful way.

Verse 4 echoes the central message of the Bible so clearly stated also in verses like John 3:16. The word "appeared" shows that Paul had in mind the historical appearing of God's salvation in the life, death, and resurrection of Jesus Christ. Notice that the title "Saviour" is used of God in verse 4 and of Jesus in verse 6. The Father and Son were together in this great work of salvation from sin.

Back of the whole enterprise stands the kindness and love of God. Paul used a word emphasizing God's goodness and kindness along with a word stressing God's love for sinful humanity. God's motivation for our salvation grew not out of what humanity deserved. In fact, sinful humanity deserved only judgment. God loved us in spite of our sins and showed this love when Christ died for us while we were yet sinners (Rom. 5:6–8).

The first part of verse 5 stresses salvation by grace, not by human efforts. People are not saved by their own righteousness, but by the mercy and grace of God. Paul spent much of his life preaching this gospel of grace and refuting persistent human efforts to base salvation on human righteousness. One of Paul's points was that when our self-righteousness is compared with God's glory, all our righteousness becomes like filthy rags (Isa. 64:6; Rom. 3:1–23). Paul forced people to realize that God's love and Christ's sacrificial death were not necessary if people could save themselves by their own goodness (Gal. 2:21). Thus the death of Christ is the ultimate proof that people are sinners who need saving, not righteous people who need rewarding.

The last part of verse 5 and verse 6 focus on the work of God's Holy Spirit in salvation. The Spirit cleanses, regenerates, and makes sinners new. God is not stingy in pouring out His Spirit; instead, He pours out His Spirit abundantly through Jesus Christ.

Notice the variety of word-pictures used in verses 4–7 to portray the wonders of divine salvation. The word "saved" itself is an ordinary word that the Bible uses to describe deliverance from sin and death. Verse 5 adds the pictures of washing, being born anew, and being made a new creation.

Verse 7 adds another familiar New Testament picture of salvation: "justified." The word means to be put right. It is a word from the courtroom that describes what happened when an accused person was acquitted. Paul seized on this term and used it to describe the miracle of God acquitting guilty sinners (Rom. 4:5). Because of Christ's death for sinners, God accepts sinners as acquitted from sin and put right with Him when sinners repent of sin and trust Christ.

Paul used another descriptive word in verse 7: "heirs." He elsewhere described Christians as sons of God who await the full inheritance that God has promised. We are "heirs according to the hope of eternal life." Some Bible passages speak of eternal life as something we already have (John 3:16); other passages speak of it as a hope. Both are right. We already know the life that comes with the presence of God's Spirit; we await the full inheritance that this entails. As Paul wrote in Ephesians 1:14, we know that we shall have the full inheritance because we already have the earnest of our inheritance.

III. Doing Good and Avoiding Controversies (Titus 3:8–11)

1. Doing good (v. 8)

> 8 This is a faithful saying, and these things I will that thou affirm constantly, that they which have believed in God might be careful to maintain good works. These things are good and profitable unto men.

The reference to a "faithful saying" occurs also in 1 Timothy 1:15; 4:9; 2 Timothy 2:11. Most Bible students think Paul used it in verse 8 to refer back to what he had just written about salvation rather than to what he was about to write.

Paul's concern in verse 8 was the behavior of those who believed in God. The evidence of their salvation was to be their transformed lives. Verse 3 described the kind of sinful, selfish, and hateful people many of them had once been. Now they were to be a totally different kind of people. They were to be diligent to apply themselves to good deeds. This kind of living is pleasing to God and good and profitable to others.

Compare verses 8 and 5. Some of Paul's critics could never understand how the same person could make both statements. Many critics accused Paul of fostering sinful living by insisting that people are not saved by works of righteousness that they have done. The critics said that if people got the idea that they could be saved without good works, they would live sinful lives and never do good works.

Paul's answer was that if they truly had been saved, all their motivations would be toward pleasing the Lord with a new life (Rom. 6:1–4). Thus the apostle could insist that believers do good works, although the good works were not essential for their salvation. Paul saw good works as the *fruit,* not the *root* of salvation.

2. Avoiding controversies (vv. 9–11)

> 9 But avoid foolish questions, and genealogies, and contentions, and strivings about the law; for they are unprofitable and vain.

Both Timothy and Titus were plagued by people who considered themselves experts on what Paul considered religious trivia. These self-appointed experts loved to argue about these issues (1 Tim. 1:4; 6:4; 2 Tim. 2:23; Titus 1:10–16). Paul told Titus to avoid getting involved in useless arguments about such things. The word translated "avoid" literally means to turn oneself about so as to face the other way.

> 10 A man that is an heretick after the first and second admonition reject;
>
> 11 Knowing that he that is such is subverted, and sinneth, being condemned of himself.

The word translated "heretick" is the Greek word from which we get our word "heretic." The original meaning of the Greek word was an opinionated and argumentative person. Only later did the word come to refer to a person of unorthodox views. Paul was writing about people who definitely were argumentative, but some of their views were dangerously close to heresy.

Paul set forth a way of dealing with such people that is similar to what Jesus taught in Matthew 18:15–17. The apostle told Titus to try to confront the troublemakers in a redemptive way. If they resisted such efforts at Christian discipline, they stood self-condemned.

APPLYING THE BIBLE

1. "Don't forget whose son or daughter you are." A boy was leaving home to go to college. His mother was busy preparing and packing his clothes. When she kissed him goodbye, she handed him a box of freshly baked cookies but was too choked up to say anything. His father took the boy to the train station, and as he was boarding the train, the father gave the boy this advice: "Son, don't forget whose son you are." Enough said!

Paul told Titus to remind the believers on Crete whose sons or daughters they were. They would demonstrate to others that they were followers of Jesus by obeying the civil laws (v. 1) and by being humble and kind toward others (v. 2).

2. Burning bridges. G. Campbell Morgan (1863–1945) was one of Britain's greatest preachers. When Morgan was pastor in London, a young man came to see Morgan, saying, "I want to become a Christian and join your church." He was received into the church and for months attended faithfully. Then he dropped out. Concerned about him, Morgan went to the young man's room, where the preacher was welcomed coldly. When Morgan told the young man that he was being missed at church, he growled: "I tried your Christianity, and it doesn't work."

Seeing a number of lewd pictures on the mantel, Morgan gathered them up, threw them in the fire, and said sternly: "How can you expect to live a genuine Christian life when you feed on this garbage? You will never be a genuine follower of Jesus until you burn all your bridges behind you!"

In verse 3, Titus was reminded of the kind of life many Christians lived (including Titus and Paul) before they came to Christ. But both men had burned the bridges behind them when they came to Christ. Titus was to instruct those to whom he preached to do the same thing.

3. The gift of grace. When Queen Victoria was ruling England (1837–1901), she and an attendant went one day to visit a paper mill near Windsor. The foreman who was showing them around did not know who she was until after they left. Her last stop in the mill was the rag room. Huge piles of filthy rags were piled high in the room, and the queen asked how they were used. The foreman told her they would be sorted out and then used to make the finest white paper. Some days after her visit, she received a package that contained the most delicate white paper. The watermark on the paper was a likeness of the queen.

God has chosen us in Christ. When he called us we were poor, unworthy sinners; but He has washed us in His blood, made us clean, and put on us the impression of Himself. That's grace, and that is what Paul wrote about in verses 4–7.

4. Avoid strife. In my college days, I was pastor of a country church in which a number of people quarreled over trifles. One particular point of contention was where the piano should be set. Some wanted it on the right, while others wanted it on the left. Whichever group got to church first rolled the piano across the auditorium to where they wanted it. The next Sunday it would be on the other side. How foolish! What did it matter where the piano was placed?

A few churches split over important doctrinal issues, but not many. Most church divisions come over something that doesn't amount to a "hill of beans." Selfishness divides more churches than doctrinal issues ever did!

Paul instructed Titus to refrain from getting involved in foolish issues (v. 9). It's good advice for any pastor or church to follow.

TEACHING THE BIBLE

- *Main Idea:* Christ's servants should build and encourage community.
- *Suggested Teaching Aim:* To lead adults to identify behavior they will adopt because they have been saved by God's mercy.

A TEACHING OUTLINE

1. Use the unit poster to introduce the lesson and review the unit.

2. Use listening teams and a chart to examine actions of believers before and after they come to Christ.

3. Use a writing assignment (paraphrase or hymn writing) to examine the salvation Christ offers.

4. Use a chart to help members identify behavior they will strive to follow.

Introduce the Bible Study

Place the unit poster on the wall and point out that today's lesson is the last in the unit. Read aloud the titles of the lessons of this unit. Point out that the last lesson describes the way Christ's servant can encourage community.

Search for Biblical Truth

IN ADVANCE, write in two columns on a chalkboard or a large sheet of paper: **Before Christ** and **After Christ.** Assign half the class to look for ways people behave *before* they come to know Christ and the other half to look for ways people should behave *after* they come to know Christ. Ask members to search Titus 3:1–3. Write members' suggestions under the appropriate heading. Ask: are you surprised that Paul listed any of these? Why?

DISCUSS: Does a Christian ever have a right not to obey civil law? How do we know when this might be justified?

Distribute paper and pencils to all members. Ask them either singly or in pairs to paraphrase 3:4–7. If you have people capable of writing a hymn based on a familiar hymn tune, suggest that some may want to do that. Call for several to read aloud their paraphrases or sing their hymn.

Use "Studying the Bible" to lecture briefly covering these points: (1) this may have been an early Christian hymn; (2) Jesus "appeared" in His life, death, and resurrection; (3) back of our salvation stands God's kindness and love; (4) salvation (v. 5) is by grace; (5) the Holy Spirit's role in salvation; (6) the many words in verses 4–7 that describe deliverance from sin; (7) the meaning of "justified." (To the "Word List" you have been making during this unit, add "justified.")

Ask members to read verses 8–10. Ask the same two groups to list behavior *Before* or *After* Christ. How could Paul write both verse 5 and verse 8? Is he contradicting himself? Why? (See "Studying the Bible.") After your discussion, write on a chalkboard: "Paul saw good works as the *fruit,* not the *root* of salvation." Ask members if they would agree with this statement.

DISCUSS: What principles can we develop from this passage about how to deal with an opinionated and argumentative person?

Give the Truth a Personal Focus

Ask: What difference will this lesson make in the way you live this coming week? Why?

Ask members to look at the *Before* and *After* chart. Ask them silently to study the *Before* side to see if any of these characteristics describe their lives now. Ask them to consider what changes they need to make in their lives so that none of their behavior will fit on that side of the chart.

If you have members present who are not Christians, suggest that they can respond to Christ's love and kindness by asking Christ to save them. Offer to be available after class to talk with anyone who wishes. Be careful not to embarrass anyone or put anyone on the spot.

Close in prayer that all will live this coming week in such a way that they truly honor Christ.

A Call to Faithfulness

INTRODUCTION

"A Call to Faithfulness" is a two-unit study of nine sessions based on passages from the Book of Hebrews. This challenging book consists of great doctrinal truths about Jesus Christ with interspersed exhortations about how to be faithful to Him.

Unit I, "The Greatness of Christ," consists of four sessions about the excellence of Jesus Christ. He is presented as Son of God, our Savior, our great High Priest, and the once-for-all, all-sufficient sacrifice for sins.

Unit II, "Be Faithful Followers of Christ," focuses on five exhortations about being faithful to the Lord Jesus. Readers are encouraged to grow in faithfulness, to remain near to God, to remember the past, to renew commitment, and to accept responsibilities.

July

6

1997

Jesus Is God's Son

Background Passages: Hebrews 1; 3:1–6
Focal Passages: Hebrews 1:1–5; 3:1–6

The average Christian probably knows less about the Book of Hebrews than any book of its length in the New Testament. Most people are familiar with a few memorable verses and with the famous chapter 11. The rest is largely unknown territory. One reason is that much of Hebrews deals with ancient rituals that are not part of our lives. The difficult passages, however, contain divine truths that apply in every generation.

Study Aim: *To describe how Christ is superior to the prophets, angels, and Moses*

STUDYING THE BIBLE

OUTLINE AND SUMMARY

I. Superior to the Prophets (Heb. 1:1–3)
- **1. God spoke (1:1–2a)**
- **2. The exalted Son of God (1:2b–3)**

II. Superior to Angels (Heb. 1:4–5)
- **1. Better than the angels (1:4)**
- **2. Scriptural support (1:5–14)**

III. Superior to Moses (Heb. 3:1–6)
- **1. Builder and house (3:1–4)**
- **2. Son and servant (3:5–6)**

The divine revelations of the old covenant were from God, but His supreme revelation was in His Son (1:1–2a). Christ is exalted as divine Son of God (1:2b–3). Christ is superior to the angels because He is the divine Son whom they worship, the sovereign Creator whom they serve, and the Son seated at God's right hand (1:4–14). Christ is superior to Moses because although both were faithful, Christ was Creator of God's people and Moses was one of the people (3:1–4). Also, Christ is the divine Son while Moses was a servant who pointed to Christ's coming (3:5–6).

I. Superior to the Prophets (Heb. 1:1–3)

1. God spoke (1:1–2a)

> 1 God, who at sundry times and in divers manners spake in time past unto the fathers by the prophets.

Skeptics maintain that God is silent—either because He doesn't exist or He doesn't care. Hebrews begins with the assertion that God spoke. Verse 1 focuses on God's revelation in Old Testament times. The same God spoke in Old and New Testament times. This is the unifying factor that binds both Testaments into what Christians call the Holy Scriptures. Significant differences exist between the two stages of revelation, but each stage represents divine revelation.

In Old Testament times, God spoke and acted at many different times and in a variety of ways. The "fathers" are the generations of Old Testament people to whom God spoke. "Prophets" refers to persons through whom God spoke in Old Testament times, whether they were prophets, priest, kings, or wise men.

> 2 Hath in these last days spoken unto us by his Son.

Verse 2 emphasizes that the fulfillment of earlier revelations was in Christ and that He is the supreme revelation of God. God spoke in many different ways through the prophets, but He has spoken His ultimate revelation in His Son.

By comparing verse 1 and verse 2a, we can see three contrasts between the two stages of revelation. Note the contrast between the words "in time past" and "in these last days." Jesus divided history. His coming, life, death, and resurrection marked the end of the age of promise and inaugurated the age of fulfillment. The second contrast is between the recipients of the two stages of revelation: "fathers" and "us." Today people are privileged to live in the age of fulfillment. The third contrast is between the sources of revelation: "prophets" and "Son."

What does the New Testament mean when it describes Jesus as God's Son? To some people the word "son" suggests one to whom his parents gave life. When this understanding is applied to Jesus as God's Son, it leads to the false conclusion that Jesus is a created being. Verses 2b–3 and many New Testament passages exalt Jesus as sovereign Lord over all things. This use of the word "Son" matched the first-century Jewish concept of sonship. A son was to be like his father. He looked like his father. He followed his father's trade. In other words, when people met a man's son, in a real sense they had met his father.

2. The exalted Son of God (1:2b–3)

> 2*b* whom he hath appointed heir of all things, by whom also he made the worlds.

The author of Hebrews reinforced verses 1–2a with a sevenfold exaltation of Christ in verses 2b–3. Two of these appear in the last part of verse 2.

God appointed His Son as heir of all things. As eternal Son of God, Christ shared the divine sovereignty over everything. This eternal reality was declared with power through the resurrection and ascension of Christ. Someday every knee will bow and every tongue confess that Jesus is Lord; meanwhile, this reality is seen only through the eyes of faith (Phil. 2:9–11).

The Son shared in the creation of the universe. Genesis 1 declares how God spoke the universe into being through His word. John 1:3 reveals that Christ is that divine Word.

> 3 Who being the brightness of his glory, and the express image of his person, and upholding all things by the word of his power, when he had by himself purged our sins, sat down on the right hand of the Majesty on high.

In Greek, verses 1–4 are one sentence, but in verse 3 the subject changes from God to Christ. Christ radiates God's glory.

The word "glory" refers to the full splendor of God's presence.

He bears the full likeness of God. The "express image" was often used of an image on a coin. The word is similar in meaning to the word "Son," who bears the exact likeness of God's image.

Christ not only created all things, but He also upholds all things by His power. The word "upholding" means not only sustaining the universe but also moving it toward God's purpose.

Christ came to save sinners. He dealt with sin through His death for our sins. Thus He made purification for our sins.

The position at a king's right hand was a place of authority and honor. Psalm 110:1 promised this place to the Messiah, a promise fulfilled in Jesus Christ.

II. Superior to Angels (Heb. 1:4–5)

1. Better than the Angels (1:4)

> 4 Being made so much better than the angels, as he hath by inheritance obtained a more excellent name than they.

Hebrews 1:1–3 presents the theme of the book: the revelation in Christ is superior to the revelation of the old covenant. Verses 4–14 add another illustration to that theme by showing that Christ is superior to the angels.

Why was the author concerned so deeply about angels? Some Bible students have suggested that angel worship may have been a problem. More likely, however, the author had in mind the view that the old covenant was mediated through angels. The Old Testament writers often mentioned angels as messengers through whom God spoke to human beings. Thus verses 4–14 give another example of how God's revelation in His Son was superior to the methods of revelation in the old covenant.

2. Scriptural support (1:5–14)

> 5 For unto which of the angels said he at any time, Thou art my son, this day have I begotten thee? And again, I will be to him a Father, and he shall be to me a Son?

Verse 5 introduces a series of Old Testament quotations designed to support the point in verse 4. The first quotation is from Psalm 2:7. This verse supports the New Testament claim that Jesus is God's Son. This verse is reflected in the divine voice at Jesus' baptism (Matt. 3:17; Mark 1:11; Luke 3:22) and at His transfiguration (Matt. 17:5; Mark 9:7; Luke 9:35). Paul quoted Psalm 2:7 in preaching the resurrection of Christ (Acts 13:33).

The second quotation in verse 5 comes from 2 Samuel 7:14. These words were spoken by God when he promised David that one of his descendants would establish an eternal kingdom. Verse 5 shows that Christ is superior to the angels because He alone is the divine Son of God.

Verses 4–14 make three main points to show that Christ is superior to angels: (1) God referred to Christ as His Son and called the angels to worship Him (vv. 5–6). (2) Angels were only servants of the Lord, who is the sovereign, eternal Creator (vv. 7–12). (3) The Son was seated at God's right hand, but the angels were only sent forth to serve (vv. 13–14).

III. Superior to Moses (Heb. 3:1–6)

1. Builder and house (3:1–4)

1 Wherefore, holy brethren, partakers of the heavenly calling, consider the Apostle and High Priest of our profession, Christ Jesus;

Although the author of Hebrews had many hard things to write to his readers, he called them "holy brethren"; and he considered them "partakers of the heavenly calling."

One of the great values of the Book of Hebrews is that it keeps focusing our attention on Jesus Christ. Verse 1 uses two titles for Jesus. This is the only New Testament reference to Jesus as Apostle. The word means "one who is sent on a mission." Jesus used the word to describe His special witnesses whom He sent forth; however, Jesus Himself was the first Apostle. Because He completed His mission, His apostles had a message to tell.

Jesus is the High Priest. The sacrificial services of the old covenant had high priests, but their work only foreshadowed the One who would be both High Priest and once-for-all, all-sufficient sacrifice for sins. This theme runs throughout the Book of Hebrews.

2 Who was faithful to him that appointed him, as also Moses was faithful in all his house.

3 For this man was counted worthy of more glory than Moses, inasmuch as he who hath builded the house hath more honour than the house.

4 For every house is builded by some man; but he that built all things is God.

Just as Hebrews 1:1–3 showed Christ's superiority over prophets who spoke for God during the old covenant, and Hebrews 1:4–14 showed His superiority over angels, so does Hebrews 3:1–6 show His superiority over Moses. Moses was the most important figure in first-century Jewish religion.

Verse 2 affirms the faithfulness of Christ to God, but it also affirms the faithfulness of Moses. Nothing is said about Moses' imperfections and failures. Tribute is paid to Moses' faithfulness. The superiority of Christ was shown not by minimizing Moses, but by exalting Christ.

Verses 3–4 use the analogy of a builder and the house he builds. A builder is superior to the house because he created and built it. In this case, verse 6 reveals that the house was the people of God. Verse 4 states that the builder is the divine Creator. Hebrews 1:2 and John 1:3 show that Christ shared in the creation. By contrast, although Moses was a responsible leader of God's people, he was not the Creator of God's people. He in fact was part of God's people.

2. Son and servant (3:5–6)

5 And Moses verily was faithful in all his house, as a servant, for a testimony of those things which were to be spoken after;

6 But Christ as a son over his own house; whose house are we, if we hold fast the confidence and the rejoicing of the hope firm unto the end.

Moses was a servant in his house. That is, he was a servant-leader of God's people. By contrast, Christ is the divine Son over His people. Of course, the New Testament shows that Christ fulfilled His mission by becoming the Suffering Servant; but He was still the divine Son.

The last part of verse 6 is similar to many challenges in the Book of Hebrews. Some people interpret such "if" clauses as calling in question the security of believers. Many of us see them as examples of the Bible's doctrine of perseverance. The Bible teaches both assurance and perseverance. Understood correctly, they complement rather than contradict each other. We show ourselves to be God's people by holding fast.

APPLYING THE BIBLE

1. Not a mechanical god. In the city of Copenhagen, Denmark, an unusual clock was put on display in the Town Hall. The men who built it worked on it for thirty years at a cost of a million dollars. It has ten faces and 15,000 working parts. It is a perpetual calendar and computes the days of the week, the month, and the year for thousands of years into the future. It also charts the movement of the planets and calculates the course of the stars for the next 25,000 years. It is so accurate in telling time that, in the course of 750 years, it is not expected to be off schedule more than one second.

Some people see God like this—some kind of robot who goes through the motions of sustaining the universe with no thought of or compassion for humankind. But our lesson today (v. 1) declares that He speaks to us, cares for us, and guides us through His Son, Jesus Christ. He is neither unmoved by our cares nor inadequate to meet our needs.

2. Jesus, the Word of God. John introduced his Gospel with the statement, "In the beginning was the Word, and the Word was with God, and the Word was God." Verse 2 of our lesson today states that God "hath in these last days spoken unto us by His Son"—that is, Jesus is the Word of God.

To those of us who have been confused by describing Jesus as the "Word of God," William Barclay offers a helpful word: Jesus is a means of communication to us; Jesus, as the Word, is the expression of a thought; to express my thoughts to others, I have to find a word; Jesus is the full expression of God's thoughts; and Jesus, as the Word of God, is the mind of God. He interprets life to us so that it makes sense. Therefore, verse 2 declares that in these last days God has given the full revelation of Himself through Jesus, the Word of God.

3. Christ, the center of all life. When Raphael's great picture of the Sistine Madonna was first brought to Dresden, Germany, for display, it was placed in the throne room. But the most prominent place in the throne room was occupied by the throne itself. The king, upon seeing that, pushed the throne aside, saying, "Make room for the immortal Raphael!"

Christ is the center, the Lord of all things. Our Scripture lesson today says that He is the "heir of all things, by whom he has made the worlds."

4. What is God like? Marie Antoinette (1755–1793) was the beautiful queen of France who died on the guillotine. Her husband, King Louis XVI, had been beheaded nine months earlier.

Once during the early days of the French Revolution, a girl was trampled by a mob and seriously injured. Queen Marie saw what had happened, rushed to the girl's side, and began to wipe the blood from her face. When the girl regained consciousness, she recognized the queen and exclaimed, "Oh! I did not know you were like that."

What is God like? Jesus said, "No man hath seen God at any time; the only begotten Son, which is in the bosom of the Father, he hath declared him" (John 1:18). Verse 3 of our lesson today declares that Jesus is the "express image of his person."

What is God like? He is compassionate, tenderhearted, full of grace and mercy. He is perfectly and exactly revealed in Jesus Christ. What a great comfort this is.

5. Jesus, God's Son. Daniel Webster (1782–1852), an able lawyer and the best-known orator of his day, was once asked, "Can you understand Jesus Christ?" Webster replied to the question like this: "No! I would be ashamed to acknowledge Him as my Savior if I could understand Him. I need a superhuman Savior—one so great and glorious that I cannot comprehend him!"

Verse 5 shows us this superhuman Savior we can only understand by faith. God says He is "my Son." We accept Jesus as just that by faith or not at all.

TEACHING THE BIBLE

- *Main Idea:* Christ is superior to the prophets, angels, and Moses.
- *Suggested Teaching Aim:* To lead adults to list ways Christ is superior to the prophets, angels, and Moses.

A TEACHING OUTLINE

1. Use an illustration to introduce the Bible study.
2. Use a poster to see the relationship of each lesson to the others.
3. Use small groups or work as a whole class to search for biblical truth.
4. Use unfinished sentences to make the Bible study personal.

Introduce the Bible Study

Use "Christ, the center of all life" from "Applying the Bible" to introduce the lesson. **IN ADVANCE,** make a poster on which you list the lesson titles, Scriptures to be studied, and the dates for the next nine lessons on Hebrews. Make a colored arrow and position it beside the title each week. Briefly share the information in INTRODUCTION on page 333 to introduce the study of Hebrews.

Search for Biblical Truth

Determine in advance if you want to organize members into three groups or if you will do this as a whole class. Working in three groups will save some time. Place three large sheets of paper on the focal wall. Write on the first, *Jesus—Superior to Prophets (Heb. 1:1–3).* On the second write, *Jesus—Superior to Angels (Heb. 1:4–5).* On the third write, *Jesus—Superior to Moses (Heb. 3:1–6).* If you decide to organize three groups, assign each group one of these sheets to study the passage and list on the sheet how Jesus is superior. Call for reports after about six to eight minutes of study. Use **"DISCUSS"** following each report.

If you choose to do this as a whole class, ask a volunteer to read aloud 1:1–3. Ask members to search the passage to find how Jesus is superior to the prophets. As members suggest ways, list these on the poster.

DISCUSS: One modern cult describes Jesus as another "prophet" in a long line of prophets that culminates with their prophet. How would you respond to someone who made this claim?

Call for a volunteer to read aloud 1:4–5. Ask members to search their Bibles to find how Jesus is superior to angels. List these on the poster.

DISCUSS: What implications would this passage have for today's society and its great interest in angels? Which do you think the average person on the street would come nearer responding to, Jesus or an angel? Why?

Call for a volunteer to read aloud 3:1–6. Ask members to search their Bibles to find how Jesus is superior to Moses. List these on the poster.

DISCUSS: What is the relationship between Jesus' superiority as our great High Priest and our belief that Jesus holds safely for all eternity those who trust Him for salvation?

Give the Truth a Personal Focus

Ask members to review the three posters. Ask if they can think of others ways Jesus is superior to the prophets, angels, and Moses. If they can, list these on the posters.

Use the same three groups (if you used groups originally) or ask members to complete these three sentences: *Because Jesus is superior to prophets . . .*; *Because Jesus is superior to angels . . .*; *Because Jesus is superior to Moses. . . .* Ask members to suggest their reasons. Urge them to see that Christ's superiority should influence the ways they think and live.

Close in prayer.

Jesus Is Savior

Basic Passage: Hebrews 2

Focal Passage: Hebrews 2:5–11, 14–18

As we saw in the preceding lesson, the Book of Hebrews exalts Jesus Christ. The book contains some passages that are hard to understand, but the central message is clear. Hebrews 2 presents the Son of God becoming fully human in order to save humanity from temptation, sin, and death.

Study Aim: *To give reasons why the Son of God became human*

STUDYING THE BIBLE

OUTLINE AND SUMMARY

I. Hear and Heed God's Word (Heb. 2:1–4)

II. Why God's Son Became Human (Heb. 2:5–18)

1. **To fulfill God's promise to humanity (vv. 5–9)**
2. **To lead many sons to glory (vv. 10–13)**
3. **To defeat death and the devil (vv. 14–15)**
4. **To deal with sin and temptation (vv. 16–18)**

Because God's supreme revelation is in Christ, we should heed what we have heard (vv. 1–4). God's promise of dominion to humanity has not yet been fulfilled, but Christ has been crowned with glory and honor (vv. 5–9). Christ became the Pioneer of salvation to lead many sons to glory (vv. 10–13). He became human to defeat death and the devil (vv. 14–15). He is our High Priest, who reconciles us to God and helps us in temptation (vv. 16–18).

I. Hear and Heed God's Word (Heb. 2:1–4)

Hebrews is basically an exhortation (13:22). Great doctrinal truths about Jesus Christ are interspersed with practical challenges to faithfulness. Hebrews 2:1–4 is the first such exhortation. It calls for a proper response to the truth of Hebrews 1—that Jesus Christ is God's supreme revelation. Readers of Hebrews were challenged to hear and heed this supreme Word of God. Hearing in the biblical sense always involves obedience.

II. Why God's Son Became Human (Heb. 2:5–18)

1. To fulfill God's promise to humanity (vv. 5–9)

> 5 For unto the angels hath he not put into subjection the world to come, whereof we speak.

Hebrews 2:5–18 connects with Hebrews 1:4–14. The theme of Christ's superiority to the angels continues. Verse 5 makes the point that God did not promise the angels to subject the world to come unto them. Verses 6–9 show that God made this promise to humanity and that the promise will be fulfilled in the Son of God who became a human being.

6 But one in a certain place testified, saying, What is man, that thou art mindful of him? or the son of man, that thou visitest him?

7 Thou madest him a little lower than the angels; thou crownedst him with glory and honour, and didst set him over the works of thy hands:

8 Thou hast put all things in subjection under his feet.

Hebrews 2:6–8a is a quotation from Psalm 8:4–6. Genesis 1:26–28 seems to have been the ultimate background for both passages. The psalmist was praising God for His creation of man and woman in His own image. Part of their assigned role was to exercise dominion on God's behalf over the rest of His creation.

Thus in Genesis 1 and in Psalm 8 the first meaning of "son of man" is humanity made in God's image. The context of Hebrews, however, shows that the divine assignment to humanity was not achieved. Genesis 3 shows how the purpose of God was marred by those made in His image. The ultimate fulfillment of the promise to humanity, therefore, will be achieved in the unique Son of God and Son of Man, Jesus Christ.

8*b* For in that he put all in subjection under him, he left nothing that is not put under him. But now we see not yet all things put under him.

9 But we see Jesus, who was made a little lower than the angels for the suffering of death, crowned with glory and honour; that he by the grace of God should taste death for every man.

The promise of divine subjection of all things has not yet been fully realized for humanity, but the fulfillment is certain. Like the rest of the New Testament, the Book of Hebrews stresses that the divine Son of God became fully human. Otherwise, He could not have become the Savior of sinful humanity. Verse 9 stresses His humanity in the words "made a little lower than the angels." As John wrote, "The Word was made flesh" (John 1:14). The One who was Prince of Heaven and superior to the angels in every way became for a while a human being. He did this in order to suffer and die so that he could taste death for every person.

Many saw His suffering and death as a hopeless defeat. In fact, His followers did until He appeared to them alive and victorious over death. Thus people of faith see Jesus already crowned with glory and honor. Although the world has not yet been subjected to Him, we believe that when He returns every knee shall bow and every tongue shall confess that He is Lord (Phil. 2:9–11).

2. To lead many sons to glory (vv. 10–13)

10 For it became him, for whom are all things, and by whom are all things, in bringing many sons unto glory, to make the captain of their salvation perfect through sufferings.

Verses 9–10 are the Book of Hebrews' version of the doctrine of the second Adam (compare Rom. 5:12–21; 1 Cor. 15:22). Jesus shared the humanity of Adam, but He didn't share Adam's sin. He fulfilled what God intended for humanity and opened the way of salvation for the descendants of Adam.

God's purpose was to bring many sons to glory. God fulfilled that purpose in Christ, who is called the Captain of salvation. The word translated "captain" means "leader." "Pioneer" communicates the meaning to those of us schooled in the history of pioneers, who led the way for others to follow. Jesus has blazed a trail for us to follow, and He has come back to lead us in the pilgrimage of faith as we move toward God's purpose for us. We shall never find ourselves in a tangled wilderness through which He has not passed before us. We see His blaze marks along the way, and we sense His presence with us.

In what sense did God make Christ "perfect through suffering"? Jesus is and has always been morally perfect (Heb. 4:15). The word "perfect" can mean "complete." The meaning of verse 10 is that Jesus' suffering was essential for completing His mission.

> 11 For both he that sanctifieth and they who are sanctified are all of one: for which cause he is not ashamed to call them brethren.

Verses 11–13 stress the oneness between the unique Son and the many sons whom He leads to glory. Although the Son is the sanctifier and they are the ones who are sanctified, He and they have one thing in common. Although Jesus is the unique Son of God, the one Son and the many sons share a common humanity.

Because of this common experience, Jesus "is not ashamed to call them brethren." He was not ashamed of the sacrificial role whereby the Son became Brother to the many sons whom He led to glory. Verses 12–13 quote Psalm 22:22 and Isaiah 8:17–18 to show that the Old Testament taught the concept of Jesus as Brother. The Gospels also relate how Jesus referred to His followers as "brethren" (Matt. 28:10; John 20:17).

3. To defeat death and the devil (vv. 14–15)

> 14 Forasmuch then as the children are partakers of flesh and blood, he also himself took part of the same; that through death he might destroy him that had the power of death, that is, the devil;
>
> 15 And deliver them who through fear of death were all their lifetime subject to bondage.

Another reason why God's Son became human was in order to defeat death and the devil. Notice how verse 14 again emphasizes the humanity of Jesus. He partook of the same flesh and blood as the rest of humanity. Incarnation, atonement, and resurrection are all tied together. If incarnation is a sham, so is Christ's victory over temptation, sin, and death. Because He became truly human, the victory is real.

Verses 14–15 are one of several New Testament passages that describe what Jesus did as a victory over the devil (see John 12:31; 16:11; Col. 2:15; 1 John 3:8). This particular aspect of His victory was the defeat of death, one of Satan's domains. By defeating sin and death, Christ delivered a death blow to the devil. He still goes about "as a roaring lion . . . seeking whom he may devour" (1 Pet. 5:8), but his days are numbered because he has received a mortal blow.

Notice the method of Christ's victory over death. From the world's point of view, the method of His victory was ironic. He destroyed death by dying. Of course, the way He died and what happened later are crucial. He died for our sins, and He was raised victorious over death.

Notice the practical result of His victory over death. He delivered humanity from slavery growing out of the fear of death. The certainty of death hangs like a heavy cloud over humanity. Satan uses this fear to control and enslave us. Christ removes the sting of sin and death (1 Cor. 15:55–57). He frees believers from the tyranny of fear of death. Because He lives, we shall live also. Thus Christians can live with confidence and hope, peace and joy—even in the face of the dread specter of death.

4. To deal with sin and temptation (vv. 16–18)

> 16 For verily he took not on him the nature of angels; but he took on him the seed of Abraham.
>
> 17 Wherefore in all things it behoved him to be made like unto his brethren, that he might be a merciful and faithful high priest in things pertaining to God, to make reconciliation for the sins of the people.
>
> 18 For in that he himself hath suffered being tempted, he is able to succour them that are tempted.

Christ was not made with the nature of angels. Instead He became human like the seed of Abraham. Verse 17 adds that He was made like His brothers. Christ as Brother shared the humanity of His brothers. He did it in order to become our great High Priest. A priest represented humanity before God and God to humanity. Our High Priest is divine and human. His humanity ensures His empathy and help for human problems.

Verse 17 introduces one of the distinctive themes of the Book of Hebrews. Jesus is presented as our great High Priest. The theme is focal in the Bible passages for next week's lesson. Further explanations will be given in looking at those passages. However, the central points of the doctrine are summarized in verses 17–18. Christ's humanity enabled Him to so enter into human experience that His mercy and understanding are expressed for all to see. We see the love of God revealed in Christ's merciful way of dealing with human problems.

Specifically, our High Priest made reconciliation for our sins. Sin is humanity's basic problem. Through His sacrificial death, the High Priest provides forgiveness and reconciliation. The Book of Hebrews stresses that our great High Priest also offered Himself as the once-for-all, all-sufficient sacrifice for human sin (see Heb. 9:1–10:18 in the lesson for July 27).

Christ also provides help when we are tempted. This is because He Himself was "tempted like as we are, yet without sin" (see comments on Heb. 4:15 in the lesson for July 20). Because His temptations were real, He is able to empathize with us when we are tempted. But He is able to do more than offer understanding. Because He overcame temptation, He is able to help us overcome.

APPLYING THE BIBLE

1. The incomparable Christ. In infancy He startled a king. In boyhood He puzzled the teachers of the law. In manhood He commanded the sea to be still. He healed the sick without medicine and charged nothing for His services. He never wrote a book, but all the libraries could not hold what has been written about Him. He never wrote a song, but He is the theme of our sweetest hymns. He never founded a university, but His students outnumber all the university students of the last two thousand years. Death could not destroy Him, and the grave could not hold Him. He still lives, and His influence is greater than ever. Indeed, He is the incomparable Christ (vv. 5–8).[1]

2. The sufferings of Jesus. Verse 10 speaks of "The captain of their [our] salvation . . . [and His] sufferings." Of what did these sufferings consist? This is a direct reference to Christ's crucifixion.

No Roman citizen could be crucified, only Roman subjects—members of a conquered nation, such as Jesus was. The upright pole was placed in the ground, and the cross beam was placed on the ground. Stripped naked, Jesus was laid on the ground; his hands were nailed to the beam. His legs were jerked out of joint to render Him helpless; then the cross beam was nailed to the upright beam. His feet were crossed and, probably to keep them from tearing, they were nailed to a small platform on the upright beam. For six hours—from 9 A.M. until 3 P.M.—He suffered excruciating pain. His body was so stretched that the ribs could be counted. The heart and stomach arteries were surcharged with blood, producing a throbbing headache. Every nerve, muscle, and tendon of His body ached as the blood dripped from His wounds. The inflamed wounds produced fever throughout His body. Every ray of the sun became a leech, sucking the life-giving fluids from his body. As His body dehydrated, His mouth became dry as a desert, His lips parched, and His tongue became swollen. Add to this physical agony the spiritual agony as He died with the sins of the world upon Him. His greatest suffering came as, though difficult it is to understand, God turned His back on Jesus, and the Son wept aloud, "My God, my God, why hast Thou forsaken Me?" All of this—and much more—is described in verse 10 as "sufferings."

Lest we forget, His sufferings were for you and me!

3. The death of death. For the believer, death is only an incident, not a finality!

Dr. George W. Truett, who served the First Baptist Church of Dallas just a short fifty years, told about the wife of a prominent judge, both of whom were members of Truett's church. Although devout, the woman had an uncommon fear of death. More than once she sought consolation from her pastor; and he assured her that when that hour came, God would give her dying grace. But all was in vain, and her fear persisted.

On the night she died, she looked up at her doctor and asked, "Doctor, is this death?" and he replied, "Yes, this is death."

"Oh, it cannot be, for it is so pleasant," she replied. Shortly thereafter she closed her eyes and fell asleep in Jesus.

For the believer, and only for the believer, the sting of death has been removed. For us, the death, burial, and resurrection of Jesus are the death of death (vv. 14–15). God gives dying grace to His children when death stands at the door. The suffering that often precedes death may, indeed, be extremely painful, but not death itself. Jesus' favorite word for death, as it was with Paul, was "sleep." To die is to fall asleep in the arms of Jesus as a weary child would fall asleep in his or her mother's soft arms. Thanks be to God!

TEACHING THE BIBLE

- *Main Idea:* God's Son became human to help us.
- *Suggested Teaching Aim:* To express thanks to Jesus for what He has done for them.

A TEACHING OUTLINE

1. *Use an illustration to introduce the Bible Study.*
2. *Use strip posters to guide the search for biblical truth.*
3. *Use questions and group discussion to explain the Scripture.*
4. *Use review to give the truth a personal focus.*

Introduce the Bible Study

Use "The incomparable Christ" from "Applying the Bible" to introduce the Bible study. Identify the lesson on the Hebrews Poster you made last week.

Search for Biblical Truth

IN ADVANCE, make the following heading and four strip posters. Tape the four posters to the backs of four chairs and tape the heading to the focal wall.

	Why God's Son Became Human
1.	To fulfill God's promise to humanity (Heb. 2:5–9)
2.	To lead many sons to glory (Heb. 2:10–13)
3.	To defeat death and the devil (Heb. 2:14–15)
4.	To deal with sin and temptation (Heb. 2:16–18)

Briefly summarize the information under "I. Hear and Heed God's Word."

Ask for the person who has the first strip poster to place it on the focal wall under the heading. Call for a volunteer to read aloud 2:5–9. Ask: How did Jesus fulfill God's promise to humanity? Use the following to help members understand the answer to this question: (1) To whom did God *not* promise He would subject the world? (Angels.) (2) What is the double meaning of "son of man" in verse 6? (Human beings in the Psalms and Jesus in Hebrews.) (3) Why did Jesus suffer and die? (To taste death for every person.) (4) If Jesus has not subjected the world to Himself, when will this happen? (When Jesus returns.)

Ask for the person who has the second strip poster to place it on the focal wall under the heading. Call for a volunteer to read aloud 2:10–13. Ask: How did Jesus lead many sons to glory? Ask: What title is applied to Jesus in these verses? (Captain or Pioneer [NRSV].) (Use "Studying the Bible" to explain the meaning of this term.) In what sense did God make Christ "perfect through suffering"? (See "Studying the Bible" for an explanation of "perfect.") How is Jesus like the many "sons" He leads to glory? How is He different?

Ask for the person who has the third strip poster to place it on the focal wall under the heading. Call for a volunteer to read aloud 2:14–15. Ask: How did Jesus defeat death and the devil? How does verse 14 emphasize Jesus' humanity? (Took of the same flesh and blood as the rest of humanity.) What did Jesus do to the devil's power? (Destroyed it.) How did Jesus defeat death? (Died.) What was the result of His death? (Delivered humanity from slavery to sin.)

Ask for the person who has the fourth strip poster to place it on the focal wall under the heading. Call for a volunteer to read aloud 2:16–18. Ask: How did Jesus deal with sin and temptation? Why did Jesus become human? (To become our great High Priest.) How did His becoming human help Him? (He could put Himself in our place.) How does He help in our temptations? (Understands and helps us overcome temptation.)

Give the Truth a Personal Focus

Read aloud from the poster the four reasons God's Son became human. Ask: Which of these reasons speaks the most to you? Why?

Close in a prayer of gratitude for what Jesus has done. Let each person express silently his or her gratitude to Jesus, and then close with a verbal prayer.

---

1. Walter B. Knight, *Master Book of New Illustrations* (Grand Rapids: William B. Eerdmans Publishing Co., 1956), 336.

July

20

1997

Jesus Is High Priest

Basic Passages: Hebrews 4:14–5:10; 7

Focal Passage: Hebrews 4:14–5:10

The most distinctive contribution of the Book of Hebrews is its doctrine of Christ as High Priest. The priestly work of the Lord is implied and the sacrificial death of Jesus is emphasized in other books, but Hebrews elaborates on the picture of Jesus as High Priest.

Study Aim: *To testify what blessings have come because Christ is our High Priest*

STUDYING THE BIBLE

OUTLINE AND SUMMARY

I. A Challenge and an Invitation (Heb. 4:14–16)
- **1. A sympathetic High Priest (4:14–15)**
- **2. Invitation to the throne of grace (4:16)**

II. Qualified to Be High Priest (Heb. 5:1–10)
- **1. Qualifications for high priest (5:1–4)**
- **2. Appointed by God (5:5–6)**
- **3. A sympathetic High Priest (5:7–10)**

III. The Kind of Priest People Need (Heb. 7:1–28)
- **1. After the order of Melchizedek (7:1–14)**
- **2. A Priest forever (7:11–28)**

Our High Priest is able to help with temptations because He was tempted yet without sin (4:14–15). Therefore, we are invited to come boldly to God's throne of grace to receive mercy and help (4:16). Human high priests must be compassionate, and they must be appointed by God (5:1–4). Jesus was divinely appointed (5:5–6). He experienced suffering as He obeyed God's will (5:7–10). Jesus, like Melchizedek (mel KIZ uh dek), is superior to the Levitical priests (7:1–10). He is an eternal High Priest who continues His intercessory ministry (7:11–28).

I. A Challenge and an Invitation (Heb. 4:14–16)

1. A sympathetic High Priest (4:14–15)

> 14 Seeing then that we have a great high priest, that is passed into the heavens, Jesus the Son of God, let us hold fast our profession.
>
> 15 For we have not an high priest which cannot be touched with the feelings of our infirmities; but was in all points tempted like as we are, yet without sin.

These verses show the careful balance between the divine and human in Christ. On the one hand, He is the Son of God who already has been exalted into the heavens. On the other hand, the power of His sympathetic ministry is rooted in His earthly experience.

The reality of His human experience is stated nowhere so strongly as in verse 15. His temptations were real. In that sense, they are like ou temptations. Of course, none of us can be tempted to use divine power to turn stones into bread; but Jesus—like each of us—was tempted to compromise God's will for His life. The good news is that whereas each of us has given in at some point to temptation, Jesus resisted its full fury and overcame it.

His twofold experience explains why He is able to sympathize and help us when we are tempted. On one hand, He knows from experience what temptation is. On the other hand, He overcame. Thus He is better equipped to help than someone who once gave in to the same temptation as ours. Such a person can sympathize and point us to sources of help, but Jesus Himself offers both understanding and help.

2. Invitation to the throne of grace (4:16)

> 16 Let us therefore come boldly unto the throne of grace, that we may obtain mercy, and find grace to help in time of need.

Hebrews is filled with passages that are hard to understand, but verse 16 is not one of them. Everyone can understand this invitation based on the High Priest's sympathetic ministry. Most of us have memorized this great Bible promise.

People can come boldly because God in Christ has opened a way for sinners to come to God. He has shown that His throne is indeed a throne of grace. Although people are unworthy, God invites them to come. In this sense, Hebrews 4:16 stands with other great Bible invitations (Matt. 11:28–30; Rev. 3:20; 22:17).

The invitation offers mercy in spite of our sins and failures. It also promises timely help to meet our needs. The grace that God gives is not always what one asks or expects, but it always is what one needs (2 Cor. 12:9).

II. Qualified to Be High Priest (Heb. 5:1–10)

1. Qualifications for high priest (5:1–4)

> 1 For every high priest taken from among men is ordained for men in things pertaining to God, that he may offer both gifts and sacrifices for sins:
>
> 2 Who can have compassion on the ignorant, and on them that are out of the way; for that he himself also is compassed with infirmity.
>
> 3 And by reason hereof he ought, as for the people, so also for himself, to offer for sins.

A high priest was chosen from among men to represent them in things relating to God. Specifically, the high priest offered gifts and sacrifices to atone for human sins. Many priests served in the tabernacle and later in the temple, but only the high priest went once a year into the holy of holies on the Day of Atonement (Lev. 16:16–28). Not just any human being could fulfill such a responsibility. He must be the kind of person who deals gently and compassionately with ignorant and wayward people. Obviously no other high priest so perfectly fulfilled this quality as Jesus Himself (Matt. 9:36; Luke 7:13).

Other high priests were not only human but also sinful. Thus when they offered sacrifices for the sins of others, they also had to make atonement for their own sins. Hebrews 4:15 makes plain that our High Priest had no sins for which to offer atonement. Jesus our sinless High Priest offered Himself as the once-for-all, all-sufficient sacrifice for human sins (Heb. 9).

> 4 And no man taketh this honour unto himself, but he that is called of God, as was Aaron.

People did not volunteer to become high priests in the biblical sense. Nor were they chosen or elected by others. Biblical high priests were appointed by God. Exodus 28 describes how Aaron was appointed by God to serve as the first high priest.

2. Appointed by God (5:5–6)

> 5 So also Christ glorified not himself to be made an high priest; but he that said unto him, Thou art my Son, to day have I begotten thee.

Jesus did not appoint Himself to be High Priest. God appointed Him. The author of Hebrews quoted Psalm 2:7 to prove this point. The same verse was quoted in Hebrews 1:5 to show that Jesus Christ is superior to angels because He is the divine Son of God. As we noted in commenting on that verse, this appointment was confirmed in the life of Jesus at His baptism (Matt. 3:17; Mark 1:11; Luke 3:33) and at His transfiguration (Matt. 17:5; Mark 9:7; Luke 9:35). Paul said that the ultimate declaration of Jesus as Son of God was when God raised Him from the dead (Rom. 1:4; Acts 13:33).

> 6 As he saith also in another place, Thou art a priest for ever after the order of Melchisedec.

Two messianic psalms are often quoted in the New Testament as fulfilled in Jesus Christ. They are Psalms 2 and 110. Verse 6 quotes Psalm 110:5 as fulfilled in Jesus Christ. The same quotation is used in verse 10. However, the explanation of this identification is not given until Hebrews 7, which is one of our basic passages. However, since the quotation appears twice in the focal verses, some summary of its meaning seems appropriate at this point in our comments.

Melchizedek was "king of Salem" and "priest of the most high God" (Gen. 14:18), whom Abraham met when he returned from rescuing Lo (Gen. 14:1–17). Melchizedek blessed Abraham and praised God fo giving him victory. Abraham, in turn, gave tithes to Melchizedek (Gen 14:19–20). Psalm 110:4 recorded God's promise to make His anointe King a priest like Melchizedek.

In what sense was Jesus a priest after the order of Melchizedek? Th Book of Hebrews stresses two parallels. For one thing, Melchizedek wa a unique priest. Not only was he also a king, but he stood alone in the Ol Testament record. He lived centuries before God appointed Aaron a high priest or named the tribe of Levi to serve as priests. Jesus was lik Melchizedek in that he was prior to and superior to the Levitical priests

Second, Jesus is an eternal priest. The Old Testament contains n record of the ancestry of Melchizedek. Some Bible students think he wa an Old Testament manifestation of the second person of the Trinity. Another possibility is that genealogy was not mentioned because it was not the basis for his priestly calling. In either case, Melchizedek is seen as a sign of a kind of priest that "ever liveth to make intercession" for our sins (Heb. 7:25).

3. A sympathetic High Priest (5:7–10)

> 7 Who in the days of his flesh, when he had offered up prayers and supplications with strong crying and tears unto him that was able to save him from death, and was heard in that he feared.

This vivid description of the anguish and faith of Jesus' prayers fits the agony of His prayer in Gethsemane only hours before His death (Mark 14:33–34; Luke 22:44). He prayed to be spared from rejection and crucifixion, if that were possible, but He committed Himself to God's will, which included the cross. Thus, in one sense, He was not spared from death by crucifixion; however, in a larger sense, God did save Him from death through raising Him from the dead.

> 8 Though he were a Son, yet learned he obedience by the things which he suffered;
>
> 9 And being made perfect, he became the author of eternal salvation unto all them that obey him;
>
> 10 Called of God an high priest after the order of Melchisedec.

In what sense did Jesus learn obedience through suffering? If this were said of anyone except Jesus, we might assume that the person's stubborn self-will was broken as he learned obedience through suffering. However, this is not the meaning of verses 8–9. Jesus was always obedient to God's will. He was always morally perfect. The meaning of this passage, like the parallel in Hebrews 2:10, is that the human experience of Jesus confirmed the reality that suffering inevitably accompanies obedience.

The point of verses 7–9 in the total context of Hebrews 4:14–5:10 is that the human experience of Jesus magnifies His role as sympathetic High Priest. He knows what it is to be tempted, and He knows what it is to suffer. Therefore, He is touched by the feelings of our infirmities because He knows them firsthand (4:15). He can have compassion on the ignorant and straying (5:2). We, therefore, can boldly come to God's throne of grace through Him, and receive mercy and grace to help in time of trouble (4:16).

III. The Kind of Priest People Need (Heb. 7:1–28)

1. After the order of Melchizedek (7:1–14)

The basic facts about Melchizedek from Genesis 14:18 are summarized. Jesus was like Melchizedek in that He was a King-Priest who was different from and superior to the Levitical priests.

2. A priest forever (7:15–22)

In a sense, Melchizedek signified a priest made "after the power of an endless life" (v. 16). Interpretations differ about how this applies to Melchizedek, but it clearly describes Jesus as our great High Priest. The Levitical priests were mortal. Jesus is eternal King-Priest, who continues

His intercessory ministry even now. "Wherefore he is able also to save them to the uttermost that come unto God by him, seeing he ever liveth to make intercession for them" (v. 25).

APPLYING THE BIBLE

1. Our eternal High Priest. In Washington, D.C., there is a small room on Tenth Street, across the street from Ford's Theater, where Abraham Lincoln, the sixteenth president of the United States, died. Throughout the night a small band of family members and other mourners stood over the president's bed. At 7:22 A.M., on April 15, 1865, Lincoln died from the bullet of John Wilkes Booth. When Lincoln was pronounced dead, Secretary of War Edwin Stanton rose from the bedside where he had been kneeling, pulled down the blind to shut out the rising sun, and then turning to look at the dead president said, "Now he belongs to the ages."

That, of course, is only partially true; but it is fully true of Jesus Christ our High Priest. He has died for our sin, been raised for our justification, and ascended for our intercession. He belongs to everyone in every age who will call Him Savior and Lord (7:11–28).

2. Jesus is my brother. When English preacher Charles Haddon Spurgeon was at the height of his fame in London, a poor fisherman went to hear Spurgeon. But the church auditorium was filling rapidly, and the members were being seated first.

An usher asked the old fisherman if he were a member. "No," the old man replied, "I am not a member here. But do you know Jesus? I am his brother!" At once the old man was ushered in.

Jesus is our High Priest, as our lesson points out. But remember, He is also our elder Brother.

3. Christ the Comforter. A small English boy was asked one day by a gentleman who knocked at the door, "Is your father home?"

"No, he isn't," answered the boy.

"Can you tell me where I can find him?" the caller asked.

"No, I do not know where he has gone. But look among the sick and the hurting people of our town. There you will find him."

If one had been seeking Jesus in Galilee, where would they have found Him? He would have been among the needy—the sick and the hurting. And that's where He is today—in the sick room, or beside the deathbed, or anywhere His people are hurting (4:15).

4. Christ's offering for our sins. William Barclay quotes W. D. Davies when he writes that in the temple at Jerusalem every year there were sacrificed 1,093 lambs, 113 bulls, 37 rams, and 32 goats. These were the official sacrifices and do not count the private ones. Each of these was a type, a foreshadowing of Christ the "Lamb of God" who would take away the sins of the world.

The writer of Hebrews puts a heavy emphasis on the blood sacrifice of Jesus. Commenting on the importance of Christ's blood, English writer Guy H. King says that the red stain is to be seen all through Scripture. From Genesis through Revelation typically and prophetically the blood of God's Lamb is clearly seen. Cain's sacrifice, King comments was rejected because there was no blood in it. Although it, no doubt, was an excellent sacrifice in its own way; it was not God's way. The blood is the only way to God (5:1–4).

5. Life through the blood. Several years ago, a dying woman was told she must have a transfusion to live. Her husband said he had the same type. He was tested to be sure; and since there was no time to waste, he was told to lie down. A tube was connected to one arm of each. Soon the life and color began to return to her face. In like manner, through the shed blood of Christ we who receive Him receive His life (5:7–10).

TEACHING THE BIBLE

- *Main Idea:* Jesus is our High Priest who has made the eternal sacrifice for us.
- *Suggested Teaching Aim:* To lead adults to testify to what blessings have come because Christ is our High Priest.

A TEACHING OUTLINE

1. Use questions to introduce the Bible study and relate it to members' lives.

2. Use Scripture search to help members search for biblical truth.

3. Use a brief lecture to compare and contrast Jesus and Melchizedek.

4. Use a chart to compare Jesus/Melchizedek and the Levitical priesthood.

5. Use discussion and listing to make the truth personal.

6. Use sentence completion to identify blessings they have because Christ is our High Priest.

Introduce the Bible Study

Ask: What do you think of when you hear the word *priest?* What qualities should a priest have? What do you think when you apply that term to Jesus? Is this a difficult term for you to apply to Jesus? Why? Point out that today's lesson will help us understand the importance of this aspect of Jesus' role. Identify the lesson on the Hebrews poster you made for July 6.

Search for Biblical Truth

Ask members to turn in their Bibles to Hebrews 4:14–15. On a chalkboard or a large sheet of paper write, "A Challenge and an Invitation." Ask: What do these two verses tell us about Jesus' role as High Priest? (He's in heaven; He's God's Son; understands our weaknesses; was tempted in every way we are tempted; sinless.) Because of who Jesus is, what is our responsibility? (Hold faith firmly; come boldly to the throne of grace.)

DISCUSS: How does Jesus' being tempted influence the way He deals with us when we sin?

Ask members to turn in their Bibles to 5:1–10. On the chalkboard or large sheet of paper write, "Qualified to Be High Priest." Ask members to search these verses for characteristics that qualify Jesus for being our great High Priest. (Called by God; like human priests, He is gentle; unlike them, Jesus is sinless; eternal; sympathetic.)

Use "Studying the Bible" to explain the comparison to Melchizedek. In a brief lecture point out: (1) who Melchizedek was; (2) why Jesus is said to be like Melchizedek; (3) how Melchizedek illustrated Jesus' eternal priesthood; (4) what the phrase "learned he obedience" means.

On a chalkboard or large sheet of paper write *Jesus/Melchizedek* in one column and *Levitical Priest* in another. Ask members to compare and contrast these two so they can see how Jesus differs from the Levitical priest.

DISCUSS: What aspect of Jesus' priesthood means the most to you? Why? Because you have received God's mercy and grace, how does this help you live?

Give the Truth a Personal Focus

Ask members to turn to a person near them and discuss for two minutes, *What blessings have come to me because Christ is my High Priest?*

After discussion, let members suggest the blessings they have mentioned. List all of these on the chalkboard or large sheet of paper.

Distribute paper and pencils and ask members to complete the following sentence: *Because Christ is my High Priest, I. . . .* Allow as many members as possible to read aloud their responses.

Close in a circle of prayer. Suggest that members express their gratitude for the aspect of Jesus' High Priesthood that means the most to them personally.

Jesus Is the Sacrifice

Basic Passage: Hebrews 9:11–10:18

Focal Passage: Hebrews 10:1–14

The ordinary Jewish high priests offered animal sacrifices for themselves and for the people. Jesus Christ, our sinless High Priest, offered Himself as the sacrifice for human sin. This theme runs through the Book of Hebrews, but it is spelled out in Hebrews 9:11–10:18.

➧ **Study Aim:** *To testify to the way in which Jesus offered Himself as the sacrifice for human sin*

STUDYING THE BIBLE

OUTLINE AND SUMMARY

I. Blood of the Covenant (Heb. 9:11–28)

1. **Christ shed His own blood (9:11–14)**
2. **His death ratified God's testament (9:15–22)**
3. **Three appearances (9:23–28)**

II. Christ's Sacrifice for Human Sins (Heb. 10:1–18)

1. **Futility of animal sacrifices (10:1–4)**
2. **Christ offered Himself (10:5–9)**
3. **Once-for-all, all-sufficient sacrifice (10:10–14)**
4. **Fulfilled the new covenant (10:15–18)**

The old covenant provided the blood of animals, but Christ shed His own blood (9:11–14). Since a death is necessary to make a will effective, Christ died to ratify God's testament (9:15–22). He appears now in heaven for us because He appeared as incarnate Savior to die for our sins, and He will appear at His future coming (9:23–28). The very repetition of animal sacrifices shows they are unable to deal with sin (10:1–4). Christ voluntarily offered His life according to the will of God (10:5–9). His death was the once-for-all, all-sufficient sacrifice for human sins (10:10–14). His sacrifice fulfilled the new covenant provision for forgiveness of sins (10:15–18).

I. Blood of the Covenant (Heb. 9:11–22)

1. Christ shed His own blood (9:11–14)

Christ entered a heavenly tabernacle (v. 11). He offered not the blood of goats and calves, but His own blood (v. 12). Whatever value animal sacrifices had, Christ's shedding of His own blood was a perfect sacrifice for sin (vv. 13–14).

2. His death ratified God's testament (9:15–22)

For a will or testament to become effective, someone must die (v. 16). It is not in force while the person is alive (v. 17). Through His death, Jesus Christ became Mediator of God's will or testament (v. 15). The people and all things pertaining to the old covenant were sprinkled with the blood of animals (vv. 18–21). This established the principle of forgiveness through shed blood (v. 22).

3. Three appearances (9:23–28)

Christ now appears in heaven on our behalf (vv. 23–24; see also 7:25). He does not need to offer Himself over and over as the Jewish high priests offered animal sacrifices over and over (v. 25). Instead Christ offered Himself once when He "appeared to put away sins by the sacrifice of himself" (v. 26). Each person dies once and faces judgment (v. 27). Christ appeared once to bear human sin, and "unto them that look for him shall he appear the second time without sin unto salvation" (v. 28).

II. Christ's Sacrifice for Human Sins (Heb. 10:1–18)

1. Futility of animal sacrifices (10:1–4)

> 1 For the law having a shadow of good things to come, and not the very image of the things, can never with those sacrifices which they offered year by year continually make the comers thereunto perfect.

Compare this verse with Hebrews 1:1. Both verses affirm the divine purpose in Old Testament revelation, but both make clear that the purpose of these things was to point to God's ultimate revelation and Savior. The things of the law foreshadowed the good things to come; however, they were not the very image of the fulfilled realities. Some readers of Hebrews apparently were clinging to the shadows as if they were the realities. The Book of Hebrews challenged them to see the fulfillment in Christ, in this case in His sacrifice.

> 2 For then would they not have ceased to be offered? because that the worshippers once purged should have had no more conscience of sins.

The old covenant sacrifices had been offered year by year for centuries. The purpose of sacrifices was to enable sinners to seek to worship the holy God by removing sin as a barrier. At best, the animal sacrifices only foreshadowed the adequate sacrifice. Otherwise, animal sacrifices would have ceased to be offered. If people's guilty consciences had been cleansed and they had been perfected for fellowship with God, the sacrifices would have achieved a permanent effect. The very fact that the sacrifices continued year by year shows that they were ineffective in cleansing from sin.

> 3 But in those sacrifices there is a remembrance again made of sins every year.

The animal sacrifices of the law had a positive purpose in foreshadowing the true sacrifice of Christ, but they also served a negative purpose in continually reminding people of their sins. In a sense, this is the same point Paul made when he wrote that the Law does not save, but shows us our sins and thus points us to Christ (Gal. 3:21–25).

> 4 For it is not possible that the blood of bulls and of goats should take away sins.

Hebrews 9:12 says that the animal sacrifices had some value in purification of the flesh. Their main values were in foreshadowing the coming of God's once-for-all, all-sufficient sacrifice in Christ and in convicting people of their need for the Savior. Verse 4 flatly denies that the blood of animals could take away human sins.

2. Christ offered Himself (10:5–9)

> 5 Wherefore when he cometh into the world, he saith, Sacrifice and offering thou wouldest not, but a body hast thou prepared me:
>
> 6 In burnt offerings and sacrifices for sin thou hast had no pleasure.

The speaker at the beginning of verse 5 is the incarnate Jesus. Verses 5–6 quote Psalm 40:6, one of many Old Testament passages that expressed the ineffectiveness of animal sacrifices. David expressed in Psalm 40 the insight that truly worshiping and serving God is not achieved through offering burnt offerings and sin offerings. Jesus the Son of God and descendant of David used David's inspired words to affirm this truth.

> 7 Then said I, Lo, I come (in the volume of the book it is written of me,) to do thy will, O God.

Verse 7 is a part of the quotation of Psalm 40 by the incarnate Christ. He quoted Psalm 40:7–8. David had recognized that God was not looking for animal sacrifices, but for total commitment of the worshiper. Thus he had declared his commitment to do God's will. The author of Hebrews pictures the incarnate Son of God using David's words to express His voluntary and total commitment to do God's will. David was a frail, sinful man offering himself to do God's will. Although he was a man after God's own heart, the Bible clearly shows his failures and sins. By contrast, David's descendant Jesus offered Himself totally to God.

> 8 Above when he said, Sacrifice and offering and burnt offerings and offering for sin thou wouldest not, neither hadst pleasure therein; which are offered by the law;
>
> 9 Then said he, Lo, I come to do thy will, O God. He taketh away the first, that he may establish the second.

Verses 8–9 explain the author's purpose in using these quotations from Psalm 40. The law's sacrifices did not fulfill the requirements of God for real atonement for sins. Christ's voluntary offering of Himself for the sins of the world ended the first (the old sacrificial system) and established the second (the new covenant of forgiveness based on the sacrifice of Christ).

The overall point of verses 5–9 is the contrast between the involuntary and ineffective animal sacrifices and the voluntary and effective sacrifice of Christ. The animals had no choice in being offered; however, Jesus had a choice in whether to offer Himself. His life was not taken; it was given of His own free will. The Gospels make plain that He took this drastic step because He was convinced it was God's will (John 10:14–18). This was not an easy commitment for Jesus to make; nonetheless, He made it (Luke 22:42–44; Heb. 5:7–9).

3. Once-for-all, all-sufficient sacrifice (10:10–14)

10 By the which will we are sanctified through the offering of the body of Jesus Christ once for all.

Verse 10 reminds us that His death was an offering He freely made. It was made "once for all," and it was sufficient to sanctify sinners. The word "sanctify" means to set apart by God and for God. It stresses that God not only has forgiven our sins but also has set us apart to live a holy life. Being sanctified does not mean that we have already become all that God will make of us. It does mean that we have been accepted as children and worshipers of God based on the death of Jesus for us. We are able to come boldly to God's throne of grace because the Son of God died for our sins and made us acceptable in Him.

> 11 And every priest standing daily ministering and offering oftentimes the same sacrifices. which can never take away sins:

Generation after generation of priests lived and died. Each generation offered daily sacrifices for sins. Still the sense of guilt remained for those who brought their sacrifices to the tabernacle or temple. As Hebrews 10:1–4 stresses, the very repetition of the sacrifices showed that the animal sacrifices never took away sins.

> 12 But this man, after he had offered one sacrifice for sins for ever, sat down on the right hand of God;
>
> 13 From henceforth expecting till his enemies be made his footstool.
>
> 14 For by one offering he hath perfected for ever them that are sanctified.

By contrast to the daily sacrifices, Christ offered one sacrifice that was effective forever. The divine assurance of this fact was revealed in the exaltation of Jesus Christ to the right hand of God. At the time, the death of Jesus was considered a defeat even by His closest followers. Only when God raised Jesus from the dead did believers see the victory in the self-giving sacrifice of Christ. At His ascension He was exalted to the right hand of God, the place of highest honor and authority.

Verse 13 repeats the New Testament emphasis on the universal sovereignty of the exalted Lord. Although such sovereignty is not yet fully realized, Christians already claim Jesus as Lord and Savior. We confidently expect His rule eventually to be manifest over all things (see Phil 2:6–11; Heb. 2:8–9).

Verse 14 sums up verses 10–14. Christ's one offering sanctified or perfected worshipers to come to God. No one ever need offer another sacrifice for sins. Christ's sacrifice is once for all, and it is all sufficient He put an end to the sacrificial system. Never doubt that His death avails to forgive our sins, no matter what they are.

4. Fulfilled the new covenant (10:15–18)

The new covenant is characterized by forgiveness of sins. The sacrificial death of Christ made such forgiveness possible.

APPLYING THE BIBLE

1. Who was the one crucified? Zechariah 12:10 declares: " and the shall look upon me whom they have pierced." John quotes this passage in John 19:37 after describing how the soldier had pierced the heart of

Jesus (John 19:34). It is a prophecy of the sacrifice of Jesus written six hundred years before the Cross.

One Hebrew scholar writes that the "whom" of Zechariah 12:10 (KJV) is simply the first and last letters—*aleph* and *tav*—of the Hebrew alphabet. This corresponds exactly to Revelation 1:8 where Jesus calls Himself the "Alpha and Omega, the beginning and the ending." "Alpha" is the first letter of the Greek alphabet and "Omega" is the last letter.

Who was the One crucified? He was none other than Jesus, God in the flesh! God, in Christ, shed His own blood for our redemption (9:12). What holy ground is this!

2. Cash or credit? Someone has observed that those before the Cross were saved on credit, and those after the Cross were saved on cash payment. Certainly, no irreverence is intended by this analogy. The daily sacrifices in the temple were intended to point the repentant toward the day when that blood sacrifice would be ratified and fulfilled by Jesus, who would shed His own blood. Those in ancient days who repented from their sin and accepted God by faith were saved exactly as we are saved—by faith in God, who would ratify His "divine will" through the death of His Son, the once-for-all sacrifice for our sin (9:15–22). We are saved through the blood of Jesus Christ, for there is no other way.

3. The fountain filled with blood. The hymn "There Is a Fountain Filled With Blood" was written by the English poet William Cowper (KOO per). This is one of the favorite hymns of the English language.

Cowper at periodic times during his life fought a terrible battle with depression. At least five times he tried to commit suicide. But at other times, when the darkness lifted and his faith revived, he wrote some of the best-loved hymns of Christendom. Among them is this one: "There is a fountain filled with blood/Drawn from Immanuel's veins/And sinners plunged beneath that flood/Lose all their guilty stains" (see Heb. 9:22, 23–24; 10:10).[1]

4. How can God forgive sins? Socrates, one of the wisest of the Greek philosophers, said one day to Plato, another Greek philosopher: "O Plato, Plato, God can forgive sins, but I cannot tell how!"

A pastor once asked an inquisitive young boy if he knew anything God cannot do. Quickly, the boy answered, "Oh, yes, I know something God cannot do. He cannot see my sins through the blood of Jesus."

The little boy was wiser than Socrates. God can only forgive sins through the shedding of Christ's blood (9:12, 14, 22; 10:12).

5. The costliest bridge. It cost $7 million to disassemble London Bridge and reassemble it in Lake Havasu City, Arizona. Stone by stone, into 10,246 numbered pieces, it was torn down and reassembled across the Atlantic Ocean.

The Golden Gate Bridge, which spans the entrance to San Francisco Bay, is 6,450 feet in length and cost $35 million to build. It was completed in May 1937.

The San Francisco-Oakland Bay Bridge, also called the Transfar Bridge, is eight and one-fourth miles long—the world's longest bridge. It cost $77.2 million.

The George Washington Memorial Bridge is the third-longest suspension bridge in the world. Spanning the Hudson River between Fort Lee, New Jersey, and New York City, it was opened in 1931 at a cost of $60 million.

But the costliest bridge in history is of flesh and blood—the blood of Jesus Christ—which spans the awful chasm between sinful man and a holy God. It cost God His only begotten Son (John 3:16; Heb. 10:10).[2]

TEACHING THE BIBLE

- *Main Idea:* Jesus offered Himself as a sacrifice for sin.
- *Suggested Teaching Aim:* To lead adults to describe how Jesus offered Himself as a sacrifice for sin.

A TEACHING OUTLINE

1. *Use an illustration to introduce the Bible study.*
2. *Use an assignment to involve a member in the class.*
3. *Use a chart to search for biblical truth.*
4. *Use paraphrasing to help members understand the Scripture.*
5. *Use review and a writing exercise to give the truth a personal focus.*

Introduce the Bible Study

Use "Cash or credit?" in "Applying the Bible" to introduce the Bible study. Point out the lesson on the Hebrews poster you made for July 6.

Search for Biblical Truth

IN ADVANCE, enlist a member to give a two- to three-minute overview of the material in "Studying the Bible" on "I. The Blood of the Covenant (Heb. 9:11–22)." Give the member a copy of the material to summarize. Call on the member to present the overview at this point.

On a chalkboard or a large sheet of paper write *Jesus' Sacrifice* and *Animal Sacrifice*. Ask members to open their Bibles to Hebrews 10:1. Ask a volunteer to read aloud 10:1–4 as members follow in their Bibles. If members have various translations, let several read them to help understand the Scripture. Ask members to compare and contrast animal sacrifices with Jesus' sacrifice. Use members' suggestions, but under *Animal Sacrifice* you might have: shadow of good things; offered year after year; cannot free people from sin; reminds people of their sins. Under *Jesus' Sacrifice* you might have: the real sacrifice; offered once; can free people from sin; removes sin.

Distribute paper and pencils and ask members to turn to someone near them and paraphrase these verses. Let several read aloud their paraphrases.

Ask volunteers to read aloud 10:5–9 in various translations and follow the above procedure. *Animal Sacrifice:* God doesn't want sacrifices; God not pleased with burnt offerings; animals involuntarily sacri ficed. *Jesus' Sacrifice:* God wants obedience; God pleased with Jesus' commitment to do His will; Jesus voluntarily offered His life.

Use "Studying the Bible" to show how the writer of Hebrews used quotations from the Psalms. Distribute paper and pencils and ask members to turn to someone near them and paraphrase these verses. Let several read their paraphrases.

Ask volunteers to read 10:5–9 in various translations and follow the above procedure. *Animal Sacrifice:* can't make us holy; sacrificed by priests daily; can't remove guilt. *Jesus' Sacrifice:* makes us holy; offered Himself only once; removes guilt; sits at God's right hand; will defeat His enemies.

Distribute paper and pencils and ask members to turn to someone near them and paraphrase these verses. Let several read their paraphrases.

Give the Truth a Personal Focus

Ask members to review the statements under *Jesus' Sacrifice.* Ask: Which of these statements means the most to you? Why?

Ask members to turn their paraphrase sheets over and to work with a person near them to write an explanation based on this lesson about why Jesus offered Himself as the sacrifice for human sin. Ask them to write this as though the person knew nothing about Jesus. Let all who will, read their statements aloud.

Close in prayer.

---

1. James B. Fowler, Jr., *Illustrated Sermon Outlines* (Nashville: Broadman Press, 1987), 38–39.

2. Adapted from Walter B. Knight, *Knight's Up-to-the-Minute Illustrations* (Chicago: Moody Press, 1974), 59.

August

3

1997

Grow in Faithfulness

Basic Passage: Hebrews 5:11–6:12

Focal Passage: Hebrews 5:11–6:10

During the previous four lessons, we have looked at four great doctrinal truths about Jesus Christ. For the five lessons in August, we will look at some of the exhortations in the Book of Hebrews. The focal passage in today's lesson is one of the most famous and certainly the most controversial in the Book of Hebrews.

Study Aim: *To summarize the main points in the challenge to grow in faithfulness*

STUDYING THE BIBLE

OUTLINE AND SUMMARY

I. Moving Beyond Spiritual Immaturity (Heb. 5:11–6:3)

1. Marks of spiritual immaturity (5:11–14)

2. Leaving spiritual kindergarten (6:1–3)

II. Call to Perseverance (Heb. 6:4–12)

1. A strong warning (6:4–6)

2. Bearing bad fruit (6:7–8)

3. Words of affirmation (6:9–10)

4. Need to mature in faith (6:11–12)

The readers of Hebrews showed too many marks of spiritual immaturity (5:11–14). They were challenged to move beyond the elementary teachings of new converts (6:1–3). They received a strong warning of a sin for which there was no repentance (6:4–6). A plant bearing bad fruit is good for nothing but burning (6:7–8). The author of Hebrews expected better things of his readers (6:9–10). However, he warned of slothfulness and called them to faith and patience (6:11–12).

I. Moving Beyond Spiritual Immaturity (Heb. 5:11–6:3)

1. Marks of spiritual immaturity (5:11–14)

11 Of whom we have many things to say, and hard to be uttered, seeing ye are dull of hearing.

The author of Hebrews had just introduced the idea that Jesus was a Priest after the order of Melchizedek (5:6, 10). The author had more to say on the subject, but he noted that his readers lacked the spiritual maturity to understand what he needed to write about Christ's priestly role. These things were hard to explain not because the author couldn't explain them but because his readers were "dull of hearing." They were not hard of hearing in the physical sense, but they were spiritually sluggish and immature.

12 For when for the time ye ought to be teachers, ye have need that one teach you again which be the first principles of the ora-

cles of God; and are become such as have need of milk, and not of strong meat.

The readers of Hebrews were not new converts. They had been disciples long enough to have moved beyond spiritual milk to solid food. Milk is appropriate for new believers (1 Pet. 2:2); however, growth in Christ requires more than milk (1 Cor. 3:1–3a).

As Christians grow, they become better able to minister to others. The New Testament stresses the ministry of teaching. Some Christians are called to exercise a special gift of teaching (Rom. 12:7; 1 Cor. 12:28–29), but all are called to the more informal ministry of teaching and admonishing one another (Col. 3:16). Christians who remain spiritually immature are unable to do either kind of teaching. Instead of helping teach others, immature believers must themselves continually be retaught the basics of the faith.

13 For everyone who uses milk is unskilful in the word of righteousness: for he is a babe.

14 But strong meat belongeth to them that are of full age, even those who by reason of use have their senses exercised to discern both good and evil.

Spiritual immaturity produces moral immaturity. Those who remain babes in Christ lack moral sensitivity and discernment. The Bible pronounces a woe on those "that call evil good, and good evil" (Isa. 5:20). By contrast, spiritually mature believers "have their senses exercised to discern both good and evil." We get our word "gymnasium" from the Greek word translated "exercised." Mature Christians develop their consciences through enlightenment from the Scriptures and by daily practice of godly living.

2. Leaving spiritual kindergarten (6:1–3)

1 Therefore leaving the principles of the doctrine of Christ, let us go on unto perfection; not laying again the foundation of repentance from dead works, and of faith toward God,

2 Of the doctrine of baptisms, and of laying on of hands, and of resurrection of the dead, and of eternal judgment.

3 And this will we do, if God permit.

"The principles of the doctrine of Christ" are the same as "the first principles of the oracles of God" (5:12). These are foundational things that are appropriate for the beginning of the Christian life, but mature believers build on them and move forward. The word "leaving" does not mean "forsaking." Instead, they were to leave these things in the same way a builder leaves the foundation once it is securely laid.

The author named six foundational doctrines in three pairs: (1) repentance and faith, (2) baptism and laying on of hands, and (3) resurrection and judgment. Repentance and faith describe two sides of a sinner's initial response to the gospel (Mark 1:15; Acts 20:21–22). Baptisms and laying on of hands also had to do with the early stages of a life of faith. Future resurrection and judgment are basic doctrines in the instruction of new believers. All of these were crucial doctrines, but all were part of a foundation that should be laid early in one's experience with the Lord. Then believers need to build on these as they grow in the Lord.

II. Call to Perseverance (Heb. 6:4–12)

1. A strong warning (6:4–6)

4 For it is impossible for those who were once enlightened, and have tasted of the heavenly gift, and were made partakers of the Holy Ghost,

5 And have tasted the good word of God, and the powers of the world to come,

6 If they shall fall away, to renew them again to repentance; seeing they crucify to themselves the Son of God afresh, and put him to an open shame.

If this is not the most difficult passage in the New Testament, it is surely one of the most difficult. It has perplexed interpreters and disturbed rank-and-file believers. A variety of interpretations have been suggested, and the passage has often been the focal point of sharp differences of opinions. When dealing with such a controversial passage, we are wise to approach it with humility and tolerance for others.

Some feel that the passage teaches that true believers can turn from Christ and become lost. Such apostasy is different from the view that one can be in and out of a state of grace, because this verse refers to the plight of the apostate as beyond repentance. This view is rejected by those who believe in the perseverance of the saints.

Another view is that the people described in verses 4–6 were unsaved people who were exposed to the good news of salvation, but who hardened their hearts and thus eventually become hopelessly lost. They experienced all the God-given opportunities for repentance, but they hardened their hearts. Those who continue to refuse to repent finally become hardened in their impenitence.

Some interpreters take their cue from verses 9–10. They feel that this is a hypothetical warning, not an actual possibility. That is, if believers were to do what is described, they would indeed be hopeless; however, verses 9–10 assured the readers that they had not actually done these things.

Another view is that these verses were written to immature believers in order to challenge them to move ahead in the Christian life. This fits the context of Hebrews 5:11–6:3. In other words, the warning was not o eternal condemnation but of loss of privileges that come only to mature believers.

Closely related is the view that stresses the doctrine of perseveranc of the saints. This interpretation assumes that the purpose of this stron warning was to challenge professing Christians to be sure that their rela tionship with the Lord is genuine. Like many other New Testament pas sages, this one asserts that true faith perseveres.

The New Testament teaches both assurance and perseverance. Ou salvation is rooted in the grace of God, but faithfulness is a mark of tru faith. Presumption is a distortion of assurance. Professing believer ought not presume that their profession by itself assures salvation (Matt. 7:21). Thus the strongly worded warning of verses 4–6 may have been designed to warn some slackers in the church that they needed to look to their relationship with the Lord.

2. Bearing bad fruit (6:7–8)

> 7 For the earth which drinketh in the rain that cometh oft upon it, and bringeth forth herbs meet for them by whom it is dressed, receiveth blessing from God:
>
> 8 But that which beareth thorns and briers is rejected, and is nigh unto cursing; whose end is to be burned.

The Bible often uses the analogies of plants that bear good or bad fruit. Isaiah's song of the vineyard described Israel and Judah as a vineyard that had been properly tended, but that brought forth only wild grapes. As a result, it was left untended and grew up in briers and thorns (Isa. 5:1–7). Jesus warned of false teachers whose lives brought forth evil fruit (Matt. 7:15–19). He stated the principle, "By their fruits ye shall know them" (Matt. 7:20). This analogy is consistent with the doctrine of perseverance.

3. Words of affirmation (6:9–10)

> 9 But, beloved, we are persuaded better things of you, and things that accompany salvation, though we thus speak.
>
> 10 For God is not unrighteous to forget your work and labour of love, which ye have shewed toward his name, in that ye have ministered to the saints, and do minister.

Turning from the mild warning of Hebrews 5:11–6:3 and the strong warning of 6:4–8, the author of Hebrews wrote words of comfort and assurance in 6:9–10. This interspersing of warnings and assurances runs throughout the book.

Earlier, the author called his readers "holy brethren" (3:1); in 6:9 he used the more affectionate term "beloved." The only use of this word in Hebrews comes right after the book's sternest warning. The author thus assured his readers that he did not believe that any of them had committed the terrible sin described in 6:4–6. Although he wanted them to take the warning seriously, he expected better things of them.

The author felt accountable for warning them of the worst that might happen, but he hoped and prayed for better things. He also knew that just as words of warning have their place, so do words of love and assurance. People who are in danger of committing evil can sometimes be deterred by strong warnings; at other times, they can be led in a better way by words of affirmation. The Book of Hebrews contains both.

The author of Hebrews expected of his readers the "things that accompany salvation." In the verses that follow, he mentioned some of these "better things": love (6:10), faith (6:12), and hope (6:11, 18, 19). These three Christian qualities were often linked by Paul (1 Cor. 13:13; Col. 1:4–5; 1 Thess. 1:3; 5:8), and they are also found in Hebrews 6:9–20 and 10:22–24.

The author commended his readers for their acts of Christian love toward the saints (6:10). In 10:32–34, he gave more details of what they had done. These acts of love were not deeds of merit that deserved salvation but evidences of their salvation.

4. Need to mature in faith (6:11–12)

Although the author was reassured by their acts of love, he still felt that some of them needed to show more evidence of perseverance. He warned against being slothful and challenged them to claim the promises through their faith and patience.

APPLYING THE BIBLE

1. Spiritual immaturity. It is told that in the Kuhura Gardens in Tokyo there is a tree that is only twenty inches high and thirty-six inches across the top. It was planted four hundred years ago by a Japanese gardener. The gardener carefully trimmed the little pine tree every year. When he died his son took up the task: and his son after him and so on through nineteen generations. Today the tree is not much taller than it was when it was planted.

Our lesson today points out that many believers are like that dwarfed tree. They haven't grown in grace and in the knowledge of our Lord Jesus Christ because they have not obeyed Him (5:11–14).

2. Go deeper. A farmer was having a water well dug. He had agreed with the driller to dig just so many feet at so much per foot. The farmer was determined to keep the cost as low as possible.

At 125 feet, they struck a fair flow of water that tasted pretty good. But the farmer remembered the drought years, and wondered if the well would be strong enough to sustain his family and cattle through a drought. He remembered his neighbor's well that had gone dry one hot summer, and water had to be hauled in from ten miles away.

He talked to the well digger about the sufficiency of the well when the hot, dry weather came. The well digger told the farmer that his well was inadequate, that they would have to drill deeper where the fresh springs of water flowed in the earth. "But it is going to cost you more," the well digger said.

The farmer later said that day he learned an important lesson: one must go deeper and pay the price if he is to have the divine resources that will not fail in the hour of crisis.[1]

Some of these believers to whom the author of Hebrews wrote had not yet learned this lesson. In relationship to Jesus they had to go deeper (6:1–3).

3. Time to put our toys away. H. G. Wells (1866–1946) was a popular British author. As he grew older, knowing that time was running out for him, he felt as he used to feel when his nurse would say at nap time: "Master George, it's time to put your toys away."

That warning ought to ring soundly in our hearts. We ought to set straight our priorities and major on things of major importance because time is running out!

This is the warning Hebrews gave to its first readers. They had spent too much time in their spiritual kindergarten. It was time to move on to spiritual maturity (5:12; 6:1–3).

4. The athlete who failed. The greatest, most famous runner in modern track history was a Canadian Indian named Tom Longboat. Early in this century his name was a household word. For almost a quarter of a century he performed amazing feats, running from the mile to the twenty-six mile marathon. He rarely lost.

People from around the world followed his accomplishments,;schoolboys imitated him; mothers named their sons after him. Up until the end of his career, he earned more than any professional runner in history.

Then the races were over and his end was tragic. He wound up a beggar, sick, forgotten, and forsaken. He died at sixty-one and was buried in the obscurity of an Indian reservation in Ontario.

In 6:4–6 the writer of Hebrews gives a stern warning to us. It isn't that we can lose our salvation, for he assures his readers in 6:9–10 that this will not happen. But through spiritual carelessness we can lose our testimony and usefulness.

5. Time to search our heart. This lesson today is not intended to make us doubt our salvation, but to give us comfort and assurance that believers will persevere unto the end. But it certainly ought to make us search our hearts and renew our commitment to our Savior.

Alexander Whyte (White; 1836–1921) was one of the most outstanding preachers of Scotland. One day a friend visited Dr. Whyte and told him that an evangelist who was preaching in Edinburg (Edinborough) was lashing out against the local ministers.

"Why, Dr. Whyte, he even said you were not converted."

Walking over to his chair in absolute silence, he sat down and put his head in his hands.

"Please, dear friend, go and leave me with my Lord to search my heart."

Often each of us ought humbly to get alone with our Lord and search our hearts.

TEACHING THE BIBLE

- *Main Idea:* Believers should grow in faithfulness and maturity.
- *Suggested Teaching Aim:* To lead adults to identify steps they will take to grow in faithfulness and maturity.

A TEACHING OUTLINE

1. Use an illustration to introduce the Bible study.

2. Make a lesson outline poster to guide the Bible study.

3. Enlist a reader to read the Bible passage.

4. Use lecture and discussion to examine the Scripture.

5. Use a line chart to help members identify their spiritual maturity.

Introduce the Bible Study

Use "Go deeper" from "Applying the Bible" to introduce the lesson. Point out the lesson on the Hebrews poster you made for July 6.

Search for Biblical Truth

Make a lesson outline poster by copying the outline in the "Outline and Summary." Cover each point.

IN ADVANCE, enlist a reader to read the Scripture. If you prefer, you might suggest the reader use a modern translation because of the difficulty of the passage. Uncover "I. Moving Beyond Spiritual Immaturity (Heb. 5:11–6:3)" and "1. Marks of spiritual immaturity." On a chalkboard or a large sheet of paper write the following chart (omit italicized phrases):

Hebrews 5:6, 10–14	
1. The Issue:	*Melchizedek (5:6, 10)*
2. The Problem:	*Their inability to understand (v. 11)*
3. The Reason:	*Spiritual immaturity (v. 12)*
4. The Comparison:	*Baby drinking milk (vv. 13–14)*

Call for the reader to read Hebrews 5:11–14. Explain that "The Issue" or topic is *Melchizedek,* mentioned by the writer in 5:6, 10. Write this on your chart. Ask: Why could the author not tell them more about the comparison between Melchizedek and Christ? (Their inability to understand.) Why could they not understand? (Their spiritual immaturity.) To what did the author compare their spiritual immaturity? (A baby that had to drink milk and was not able to eat solid food.)

Uncover "2. Leaving spiritual kindergarten (6:1–3)." Call for the reader to read aloud 6:1–3. Use "Studying the Lesson" to explain (1) the "principles of the doctrine of Christ"; (2) the meaning of "leaving"; (3) the six principles; (4) the need to build on these principles.

Uncover "II. Call to Perseverance (Heb. 6:4–12)" and "1. A strong warning (6:4–6)." Using "Studying the Bible," prepare a lecture in which you explain the five possible interpretations of this passage. Be sure to read aloud the following statement: "When dealing with such a controversial passage, we are wise to approach it with humility and tolerance for others." Summarize your lecture by stating: "Professing believers ought not presume that their profession by itself assures salvation (Matt. 7:21). Thus the strongly worded warning of verses 4–6 may have been designed to warn some slackers in the church that they needed to look to their relationship with the Lord."

Uncover "2. Bearing bad fruit (6:7–8)." Call for the reader to read aloud 6:7–8. Ask: How does bearing fruit relate to the doctrine of perseverance?

Uncover "3. Words of affirmation (6:9–10)." Ask the reader to read aloud 6:9–10. Using "Studying the Bible," lecture briefly on: (1) the use of affectionate terms; (2) why the warning; (3) what are "things that accompany salvation."

Uncover "4. Need to mature in faith (6:11–12)." Briefly summarize the material in "Studying the Bible."

Give the Truth a Personal Focus

Draw a horizontal line on a chalkboard or a large sheet of paper. Number the left end of the line *1;* number the middle *5;* number the right end *10.* Above the line write *Spiritual Maturity.* Ask: Where on this line would you place the Hebrews? Where would you place yourself? Let them suggest steps to grow in faithfulness and maturity.

---

1. Adapted from Bejamin P. Browne, *Illustrations for Preaching* (Nashville: Broadman Press, 1977), 115–16.

August

10

1997

Remain Near to God

Basic Passage: Hebrews 10:19–39

Focal Passages: Hebrews 10:19–25, 32–39

We have noted how words of challenge, warning, and encouragement are interspersed through the Book of Hebrews. Hebrews 10:19–39 is another example of this fact. The basic appeal is to remain close to God with a faith that endures.

Study Aim: *To state how believers should respond to their access to God made possible through Jesus Christ*

STUDYING THE BIBLE

OUTLINE AND SUMMARY

I. Challenge (Heb. 10:19–25)

1. Therefore, brethren (vv. 19–21)

2. Call to faith, hope, and love (vv. 22–25)

II. Warning (Heb. 10:26–31)

1. Willful, persistent sin (vv. 26–27)

2. Divine judgment (vv. 28–31)

III. Encouragement (Heb. 10:32–39)

1. Remembering past faithfulness (vv. 32–34)

2. Challenge to continued faithfulness (vv. 35–39)

Because Christ has opened access to God (vv. 19–21), believers should practice faith, hope, and love (vv. 22–25). Willful, persistent sin is deadly serious (vv. 26–27). If God judged sinners under the law, how much more will He punish those who reject His Son (vv. 28–31)? The readers of Hebrews had been faithful in persecution (vv. 32–34). They were challenged to continued faithfulness as a mark of true faith (vv. 35–39).

I. Challenge (Heb. 10:19–25)

1. Therefore, brethren (vv. 19–21)

19 Having, therefore, brethren, boldness to enter into the holiest by the blood of Jesus,

20 By a new and living way, which he hath consecrated for us, through the veil, that is to say, his flesh;

21 And having an high priest over the house of God;

The word "therefore" shows that the author was preparing to draw practical lessons from the great truths set forth in Hebrews 7:1–10:18 The word translated "boldness" is the word translated "boldly" in Hebrews 4:16. The word describes the boldness with which believers should draw near to God. The author of Hebrews stressed that our confidence to approach God is based on what God has done through Christ The purpose of God's Son becoming flesh was that He might open this new and living way to God.

God is no less holy and majestic than He ever was; but He has shown Himself to be a merciful Savior and gracious Father who calls people to Himself. Under the old covenant, the holy of holies represented God's mystery and holiness. When Jesus died, the veil that separated the holy of holies was torn from top to bottom (Matt. 27:51). Under the old covenant, the veil guarded the holy of holies so that no one but the high priest could enter and he only once a year with proper sacrifices. Through Jesus' death, God opened the way through the veil for all believers.

2. Call to faith, hope, and love (vv. 22–25)

> 22 Let us draw near with a true heart in full assurance of faith, having our hearts sprinkled from an evil conscience, and our bodies washed with pure water.

Notice the structure of Hebrews 10:19–25. Based on the access to God described in verses 19–21, believers are called to three actions. Each action is introduced by the words "let us" (vv. 22–24).

Verse 22 calls on believers to exercise their faith. Chapter 11 defines and illustrates the broad scope of faith. Verse 22 focuses on faith that is exercised by drawing near to God. What good is access to God if people do not avail themselves of it? Through Christ the way is open for sinners to be forgiven and to have new life; but unless sinners turn to God in faith, they will miss what God offers them. When we exercise faith, believers' hearts are cleansed of guilt; and they can worship and pray to the Father. The reference to believers' bodies being washed with water probably points to baptism as the sign of inward cleansing.

> 23 Let us hold fast the profession of our faith without wavering; (for he is faithful that promised;)

The oldest copies of Hebrews have the word *hope* in verse 23. Even when the word *faith* is used in Hebrews, it generally includes the future dimension of faith. For example, Hebrews 11:1 says that "faith is the substance of things hoped for."

Verse 23 stresses that believers are to hold fast their profession of faith and hope because God is faithful to His promises. As noted earlier, the Book of Hebrews complements the doctrine of assurance with the doctrine of perseverance. At times, the Bible stresses the assurance that we are held fast in God's strong hand (John 10:27–29); but at other times, the Bible stresses the need for us to hold fast (Heb. 3:6).

> 24 And let us consider one another to provoke unto love and to good works:

Like many Bible passages, Hebrews 10:22–24 links faith, hope, and love (1 Cor. 13:13; Col. 1:4–5; 1 Thess. 1:3; 5:8; Heb. 6:9–20). Hebrews 10:24 is one of many New Testament passages that uses "one another" to stress various Christian responses to fellow believers (see, for example, John 13:34–35; Eph. 4:23; Gal. 6:2; Heb. 10:24–25, James 5:16).

The word translated *provoke* means "to sharpen, incite, or stir up." Paul wrote, for example, that love "is not easily provoked" (1 Cor. 13:5). The author of Hebrews used this word in a positive sense. Believers are to stir up or provoke one another to love and good works.

25 Not forsaking the assembling of ourselves together as the manner of some is; but exhorting one another: and so much the more, as ye see the day approaching.

Verse 25 is one of the more familiar verses in Hebrews. It reveals that some early believers has quit meeting with other believers. They may have simply grown indifferent, or they may have been afraid to be associated publicly with a persecuted group. The use of the work *forsaking* strengthens the latter view. The work conveys the idea of not simply leaving, as no longer part of the assembly, but of abandoning, leaving the assembly because it was exposed to peril.

Passages like Hebrews 10:32–34 show that the Christians had already gone through some persecution. Hebrews 12:4 shows that no one had yet been put to death, but Hebrews 13:12–13 strongly implies that the persecution would become more severe. Believers in some lands today can identify with the pressure that comes from persecution. In the United States we know little about such persecution except what we read. Most professing Christians who quit coming to church do so for reasons other than fear of persecution. They often grow lazy and indifferent and drift away from faithful meeting with their church. If it is a serious sin for believers to forsake the assembly because of fear, how much worse is it to forsake the assembly because of indifference?

II. Warning (Heb. 10:26–31)

1. Willful, persistent sin (vv. 26–27)

Hebrews 10:26–31 is a warning that ranks in seriousness with Hebrews 6:4–8. Many of the comments about 6:4–8 apply also to 10:26–31. Verses 26–27 describe willful, persistent sinning in spite of God's clear call through Christ. The serious plight of willful, persistent sinners refers to something other than the occasional lapses described in Galatians 6:1. In essence, such people reject the sacrifice of Jesus Christ.

2. Divine judgment (vv. 28–31)

Under the law, sinners received appropriate punishments. How much worse will be the judgment that comes to them who reject the sacrifice of Christ? Such sinners stand under the sure judgment of God's vengeance.

III. Encouragement (Heb. 10:32–39)

1. Remembering past faithfulness (vv. 32–34)

32 But call to remembrance the former days, in which, after ye were illuminated, ye endured a great fight of afflictions;

33 Partly, whilst ye were made a gazingstock both by reproaches and afflictions; and partly, whilst ye became companions of them that were so used.

34 For ye had compassion of me in my bonds, and took joyfully the spoiling of your goods, knowing in yourselves that ye have in heaven a better and an enduring substance.

Several New Testament books reflect times of persecution. Portions of the Gospels, Acts, Paul's Letters, Hebrews, 1 Peter, and Revelation reflect first-century persecution. Verses 32–34 reflect some of the kinds of persecution that stopped short of death itself: suffering, exposure to abuse and ridicule, imprisonment, and loss of property. The loss of property may have been by official confiscation or by looting.

The author of Hebrews commended them for their endurance, for their fellowship with and compassion for those who were suffering, and for their joy. The word translated "had compassion," like the English word *sympathy,* literally means to "suffer with." During times of persecution, showing compassion on prisoners is an act of courage and great compassion.

The word translated "companions" is the Greek word *koinonia,* used in the New Testament to describe the oneness of those who know the Lord Jesus. Those who were not so directly hit by persecution voluntarily chose to share the afflictions and to risk being persecuted themselves. They did this because they were members of the same family of faith and love.

The word "joyfully" shows that their joy was increased, not diminished, by sharing the afflictions. Jesus taught that His followers should rejoice in persecution (Matt. 5:10–12). Paul, James, and Peter echoed this teaching and extended its application to suffering of all kinds (Rom. 5:3; James 1:2–3; 1 Pet. 1:6–7). Hebrews 10:32–34 illustrates the practice of such joy by believers whose property was lost during persecution. They could rejoice in the loss of goods because they knew that they had lasting treasures in heaven (Matt. 6:19–21).

2. Challenge to continued faithfulness (vv. 35–39)

> 35 Cast not away therefore your confidence, which hath great recompense of reward.
>
> 36 For ye have need of patience, that after ye have done the will of God, ye might receive the promise.
>
> 37 For yet a little while, and he that shall come will come, and will not tarry.

The word translated "confidence" is the same word translated "boldness" in verse 19. In Hebrews 4:16 and 10:19, it means the boldness with which believers draw near to God. In Hebrews 10:35, it refers to the boldness with which believers maintain their Christian faith and witness (Acts 4:29, 31).

The word translated "patience" means "to continue steadfast in the face of trials and persecution." This kind of endurance is a mark of true faith. Those who do the will of God can endure because they believe that God keeps His promises. His great promise is that Christ is coming again.

> 38 Now the just shall live by faith: but if any man draw back, my soul shall have no pleasure in him.
>
> 39 But we are not of them who draw back unto perdition; but of them that believe unto the saving of the soul.

The author of Hebrews quoted Habakkuk 2:3–4. Paul used the same quote to undergird the teaching of salvation by faith. As used in Habakkuk, the emphasis is on faith that shows itself faithful. This is also the emphasis in Hebrews 10:38. God is not pleased by those who profess faith but who are not faithful.

Notice how words of encouragement are interspersed with warnings and challenges in verses 35–39. After commending his readers for past faithfulness, the author challenged them to remain faithful. He warned that some were in danger of drawing back. However, in verse 39, he reassured them in much the same way as he did in Hebrews 6:9–10. He was convinced that theirs was true saving faith.

APPLYING THE BIBLE

1. Cleansed by the blood. Reformer Martin Luther once dreamed that the Day of Judgment had come and he was standing before God. Satan was there accusing Luther of all kinds of sins. Indeed, when the books were opened, Satan pointed to transgression after transgression and Luther's heart sank in despair.

Luther then remembered the cross of Christ. Turning to Satan, Luther remarked, "There is one entry which you have not made."

"And what is that?" Satan asked.

Triumphantly, Luther said, "The blood of Jesus Christ his Son cleanseth us from all sin" (1 John 1:7).

Jesus is our high priest, and we believers have the unspeakable privilege of coming into the presence of God the Father cleansed by the blood of Jesus (vv. 19–21).

2. The pipes weren't connected. The story is told of a certain city that spent large sums of money laying water lines to the houses in a poor community. Sinks were installed by the homeowners, and they eagerly anticipated having fresh, running water.

But months and months went by after the lines were laid, and still the people had no running water because the pipes had not been connected to their homes.

In the discussion of verses 22–25, our lesson writer asks: "What good is access to God if people do not avail themselves of it?"

The application is simple: The water lines must be connected to get the fresh water. Our faith must be placed in Christ or we will miss the blessings He offers freely to all.

3. Sir Walter Raleigh's hope. Sir Walter Raleigh (1552–1618) served Queen Elizabeth I of Great Britain and her successor King James I. James I feared Raleigh and had him confined twelve years in the tower of London, where he lived comfortably with his family and servants. Released in 1616, Raleigh was sent to search for gold in South America, but ordered not to invade Spanish territory. When Raleigh's men attacked the Spaniards, Raleigh had to abandon the project. He returned home to England and was sentenced to be beheaded for disobeying orders. He faced death calmly, even giving the signal for the ax to fall.

Found in Raleigh's Bible after his death were these striking lines of hope, resurrection, and eternal life, written by Raleigh on the night before he died:

> Even such is time, that takes in trust
> Our youth, our joys, our all we have,
> And pays us but with age and dust;
> Who in the dark and silent grave,
> When we have wandered all our ways,
> Shuts up the story of our days.
> But from this earth, this grave, this dust,
> My God shall raise me up, I trust.

As Raleigh held on to his faith in life's greatest crisis, so we are encouraged to hold on to ours (v. 23).

4. Encouraging others. On the day Nathaniel Hawthorne (1804–1864) was discharged from his job at the Salem, Massachusetts, customs house, he dragged home, a discouraged, whipped man. When he told his wife the bad news, she replied, "Now you can write your book." She placed a pen and paper before him, and Hawthorne began writing his first novel, *The Scarlet Letter.* It was the making of Hawthorne, who became the first great American novelist and is recognized as one of America's greatest writers. Of his wife, Hawthorne later wrote: "That flower lent from heaven to show the possibilities of a human soul."

As Hawthorne's wife stirred him up to write ("to provoke"—v. 24), so we are "to stir up or provoke one another to love and good works," as our lesson writer today puts it.

5. Christian compassion. In the July 1980 issue of *Proclaim* there appeared a moving story of an American soldier in World War II (author unknown to me). He became separated from his company and took cover in a bombed-out building. Frightened by a noise nearby, the soldier looked around and saw the sagging body of a wounded German soldier. The American soldier said his first impulse was to drive his bayonet into the German. But, looking into the eyes of the wounded man, the American saw fear, pain, and heartache. The wounded soldier pulled a wrinkled picture of a woman and three children from his pocket, and when asked by the American, "Is this your family?" the German soldier nodded yes. The American gave the German a drink of water and sat with him until he died. "I wept for a German widow and three children," the American soldier later said.

The writer of Hebrews says that Christian compassion is a mark of genuine faith (v. 34).

TEACHING THE BIBLE

- *Main Idea:* Believers should use their access to God to live faithfully and to encourage others.
- *Suggested Teaching Aim:* To lead adults to identify ways they can use their access to God through Jesus to encourage others.

A TEACHING OUTLINE

1. *Use an illustration to introduce the Bible study.*
2. *Use a word list to explain some of the difficult words in the focal passage.*
3. *Use brief lectures to explain the focal passage.*
4. *Use brainstorming to give the truth a personal focus.*

Introduce the Bible Study

Use "Cleansed by the blood" from "Applying the Bible" to introduce the Bible study. Point out the lesson on the Hebrews poster you made for July 6.

Search for Biblical Truth

Write each of the following references on a separate sheet of paper and place them around the room: Hebrews 10:19–25; Hebrews 10:26–31; Hebrews 10:32–39. Make a word list for each member. List the following words and leave room for members to make notes or write definitions: "therefore" (v. 19); "boldness" (v. 19); "veil" (v. 20); "faith, hope, and love" (vv. 22–25); "forsaking" (v. 25); "companions" (v. 33); "compassion" (v. 34); "joyfully" (v. 34); "confidence" (v. 35); "patience" (v. 36); "live by faith" (v. 36).

Point to the poster with the reference to 10:19–25. Ask members to read these verses silently and come up with one word that would describe them. (Consider *Challenge* but let members suggest their own word.) Write the word on the poster.

Using "Studying the Bible," briefly summarize the material on 10:19–25. Then go back and explain the words on the word list that are in these verses. (This information is in "Studying the Bible.")

DISCUSS: Which is more important: to hold fast to God or for God to hold us? Why? For what reasons do we have a right to forsake "the assembling of ourselves" with other believers?

Point to the poster with the reference to 10:26–31. Ask members to read these verses silently and come up with one word that would describe them. (Consider *Warning* but let members suggest their own word.) Write the word on the poster.

Using "Studying the Bible," briefly summarize the material on 10:26–31. This is not a part of the focal passage, so do not spend a lot of time on it.

Point to the poster with the reference to 10:32–39. Ask members to read these verses silently and come up with one word that would describe them. (Consider *Encouragement* but use members' word.) Write the word on the poster.

Using "Studying the Bible," briefly summarize the material on 10:32–39. Then go back and explain the words on the word list that are in these verses. (This information is in "Studying the Bible.")

DISCUSS: How do we show our oneness with those who are suffering persecution for Jesus? How can we possibly be joyful in the midst of affliction and loss of goods? How do we know when to be patient in the face of tribulation and suffering and when to rise up with righteous indignation and do something about it? How much evidence could someone find if they were trying to convict you of living faithfully?

Give the Truth a Personal Focus

Share "Encouraging others" from "Applying the Bible." Ask members to turn to two or three people around them and discuss ways they can become encouragers. Ask members to share ideas. List these on a chalkboard or a large sheet of paper.

Ask members to identify at least one way they will encourage someone this week who is having a difficult time.

As a followup on this lesson, you might want to write a thank-you note to each member, thanking him or her for participating in class.

Remember the Past

Background Passage: Hebrews 11:1–40
Focal Passages: Hebrews 11:1–2, 6–10, 13–16, 39–40

Chapter 11 is the most familiar part of the Book of Hebrews. More sermons have been preached and more Sunday School lessons taught from Hebrews 11 than from any other part of the book. This is due partly to the difficulty of much of Hebrews, and is due partly to the beauty and power of chapter 11. The entire book is a call to faith. Chapter 11 focuses that call by giving examples of people of faith.

Study Aim: *To show how certain people of faith exemplify the definition of faith in Hebrews 11:1*

STUDYING THE BIBLE

OUTLINE AND SUMMARY

I. Faith Defined and Illustrated (Heb. 11:1–3)
II. Roll Call of Faith (Heb. 11:4–38)
 1. Early People of faith (vv. 4–7)
 2. Abraham and Sarah (vv. (8–12)
 3. Pilgrim faith (vv. 13–16)
 4. Abraham and the other patriarchs (vv. 17–22)
 5. Moses, the exodus, and the conquest (vv. 23–31)
 6. Panorama of faith (vv. 32–38)
III. Part of a Great Fellowship (Heb. 11:39–40)

Faith opens our eyes to unseen realities, like faith that God created all things (vv. 1–3). The early people of faith showed their faith by diligently seeking the God in whom they believed (vv. 4–7). Abraham and Sarah believed God's promises and obeyed His commands (vv. 8–12). They were pilgrims on earth with their faith fixed on the eternal city of God (vv. 13–16). Abraham showed faith in his willingness to sacrifice Isaac; the other patriarchs showed faith in what they did as they died (vv. 17–22). Moses' parents, Moses, the Israelites, and Rahab showed faith during the deliverance from Egypt and entry into Canaan (vv. 23–31). Later heroes of faith sometimes experienced dramatic deliverances and sometimes faithfully endured persecution and death (vv. 32–38). Old Testament and New Testament people of faith are part of the same great fellowship (vv. 39–40).

I. Faith Defined and Illustrated (Heb. 11:1–3)

1 Now faith is the substance of things hoped for, the evidence of things not seen.

Many people's view of faith is expressed in the proverb, "Seeing is believing." In other words, they will believe something only if it can be proved by undeniable physical evidence. Seeing is not believing. Rather, seeing is only recognizing what everyone knows to be true. Faith opens two realms of reality that can only be perceived through eyes of faith:

"things hoped for" and "things not seen." For these realities, an appropriate proverb would be "believing is seeing." The reality of God, the certainty of His promises, and the priority of eternal values are realities about which only faith can provide assurance and conviction.

2 For by it the elders obtained a good report.

The priority of "things hoped for" and "things not seen" cannot be proved in a laboratory, but among the objective evidences for faith are the transformed lives of a host of people throughout history. Verse 2 sets the stage for a roll call of Old Testament people of faith, which begins in verse 4. In various ways, God showed His approval of these people; thus, He bore witness to their faith and to the reality of what they believed.

Before he began the roll call of faith, the author of Hebrews mentioned one basic belief that all believers have in common—faith in God as Creator (v. 3).

II. Roll Call of Faith (Heb. 11:4–38)

1. Early people of faith (vv. 4–7)

The first three examples of people of faith are from the early chapters of Genesis: Abel (v. 4), Enoch (v. 5), and Noah (v. 7). The Old Testament describes how God showed His approval of each of these men of faith.

> 6 But without faith it is impossible to please him: for he that cometh to God must believe that he is, and that he is a rewarder of them that diligently seek him.

Verse 6 states a general principle about faith. The principle grows out of what Genesis 5:21–24 says about Enoch; but it also applies to Abel, Noah, and all people of faith. The point is that real faith goes far beyond belief in God's existence. Those with true faith respond to God by diligently seeking Him.

> 7 By faith Noah, being warned of God of things not seen as yet, moved with fear, prepared an ark to the saving of his house; by the which he condemned the world, and became heir of the righteousness which is by faith.

Noah began to build the ark long before there were any physical signs of the coming of a great flood. He acted only because through faith he felt that this was what God wanted him to do. Through faith, Noah thus saw the reality of "things not seen as yet." If he had waited to build the ark until the rain began, he could not have finished it in time to deliver his family.

2. Abraham and Sarah (vv. 8–12)

> 8 By faith Abraham when he was called to go out into a place which he would after receive for an inheritance, obeyed; and he went out, not knowing whither he went.

The New Testament writers often presented Abraham as an example of faith (Acts 7:2–8; Rom. 4; Gal. 6:6–9; James 2:21–23). The author of Hebrews devoted more space to Abraham than to any other Old Testament hero of faith. Verse 8 stresses three marks of Abraham's faith: (1) He had obedient faith. (2) He obeyed as soon as God's call came. (3) He obeyed although he had no idea where this would lead him. True faith always involves risk and adventure. God's call rarely reveals many details about the future. Therefore, faith involves relying on God's strength and guidance.

> 9 By faith he sojourned in the land of promise, as in a strange country, dwelling in tabernacles with Isaac and Jacob, the heirs with him of the same promise:
>
> 10 For he looked for a city which hath foundations, whose builder and maker is God.

In a sense, Abraham faced even more of a test when he arrived in the promised land. The land of promise was a foreign land in which he was only a sojourner or resident alien (Acts 7:6). Abraham was in Canaan, but Canaan belonged to the Canaanites. He was only a wanderer who lived in tents. Although God had promised Canaan to Abraham, nothing in Abraham's circumstances seemed to justify such a hope.

Thus another characteristic of faith is that believers must live with unfulfilled promises. They look ahead by faith and lay claim to realities that are only hoped for. Of course, the hope is based on the promises of God. Thus the ultimate goal of Abraham's faith was more than Canaan. The earthly promised land was a sign of the heavenly city that God is preparing for His people. This is spelled out in verses 13–16.

Verses 11–12 cite the faith of Abraham and Sarah in believing God's promise that they would have a son in their old age.

3. Pilgrim faith (vv. 13–16)

> 13 These all died in faith, not having received the promises, but having seen them afar off, and were persuaded of them, and embraced them, and confessed that they were strangers and pilgrims on the earth.
>
> 14 For they that say such things declare plainly that they seek a country.
>
> 15 And truly, if they had been mindful of that country from whence they came out, they might have had opportunity to have returned.
>
> 16 But now they desire a better country, that is, an heavenly: wherefore God is not ashamed to be called their God: for he hath prepared for them a city.

Verses 13–16 seem to relate most clearly to Abraham's experiences. Throughout his years in Canaan, Abraham was like an exile living in a foreign land. When Sarah died, he contracted to buy the cave of Machpelah (mak PEE luh) as a burial place for her. In addressing those from whom he purchased the cave, he said, "I am a stranger and a sojourner with you: give me a possession of a buryingplace with you, that I may bury my dead out of my sight" (Gen. 23:4). Later when Abraham died, Isaac buried him in the cave of Machpelah (Gen. 25:9). So far as is known, the only part of Canaan that Abraham ever owned was his tomb.

People who speak of themselves as pilgrims "declare plainly that they seek a country" (v. 14). What country was Abraham seeking? It surely was not his native city of Ur, or he would have returned to it (v. 15). No,

Abraham's eyes of faith were focused on "a better country, that is, an heavenly" (v. 16).

Faith is a pilgrimage through earthly life to the heavenly city. Pilgrims are on their way but not yet there. The theme of pilgrim faith is strong throughout Hebrews 11–13, but it is strongest in 11:13–16; 12:22; and 13:13–14. The ultimate goal of pilgrim faith is nothing in our earthly life, but is "the city of the living God, the heavenly Jerusalem" (Heb. 12:22). When the children of Israel neared Canaan and even after they entered and conquered the promised land, the people of faith among them realized that the promised rest of Canaan was only a shadow of the ultimate heavenly rest (Heb. 4:1–10).

4. Abraham and the other patriarchs (vv. 17–22)

The ultimate test of Abraham's faith was his willingness to offer Isaac as a sacrifice (v. 17). He was prepared to do this because he believed that God could raise Isaac from the dead (vv. 18–19). Isaac and Jacob showed their faith by bestowing a dying blessing on their children (vv. 20–21). When Joseph died, he gave instructions to return his body to Canaan when God led His people to the land (v. 22).

5. Moses, the exodus, and the conquest (vv. 23–31)

Moses' parents showed faith in hiding him as an infant (v. 23). Several examples of Moses' faith are cited. He showed courageous faith by forsaking the treasures of Egypt and casting his lot with his own people (vv. 24–27). He showed faith in keeping the Passover (v. 28). He and the people showed faith at the Red Sea (v. 29). They showed faith at Jericho (v. 30). Rahab showed faith in hiding the Israelite spies (v. 31).

6. Panorama of faith (vv. 32–38)

Four of the judges are listed as examples of faith: Gideon, Barak (BAY rak), Jephthah (JEF thuh), and Samson. In addition, mention is made of the faith of David, of Samuel, and of the prophets (v. 32). Their faith and the faith of others who followed them led at times to amazing deliverances (vv. 33–35a). At other times, believers showed faith by enduring faithfully although they were persecuted and even killed (vv. 35b–38).

III. Part of a Great Fellowship (Heb. 11:39–40)

39 And these all, having obtained a good report through faith, received not the promise;

40 God having provided some better thing for us, that they without us should not be made perfect.

With one significant difference, Old Testament people of faith and New Testament believers are all part of a great fellowship. The difference is that they lived in the age of promise and we live in the age of fulfillment. The Old Testament saints did not live to see what has been fulfilled in Christ. This makes their faith all the more remarkable.

In spite of this difference, Old Testament and New Testament believers are part of the same great family of faith. God's plan is that "they without us should not be made perfect." By the same token, we shall not reach the end of our pilgrimage apart from believers of other generations. Although Christians live on this side of God's full revelation in Christ we have not entered the heavenly city. Therefore, Christians, too, must live in the light of God's unseen reality and the certain fulfillment of all His promises.

APPLYING THE BIBLE

1. Operating by faith. It is not uncommon for someone to remark, "I will not believe in what I cannot see." Therein lies the problem most people have with God. They cannot see Him; therefore, they will not believe in Him.

But there is a great fallacy in this reasoning. Every day we believe in things we cannot see and respect those things and utilize them.

For example, we cannot see electricity, but we believe in it and use it. Some of you can remember the days when your home was lighted by kerosene lamps, and all labor was done by hand. But now electricity, invisible though it is, has revolutionized our lives. We come into our dark houses at night, flip a switch, and the whole house is bathed in light. Switches are thrown in our large cities, and dark streets are illuminated and skyscrapers are lighted. We do believe in what we cannot see (v. 1).

So it is with God. Although we do not see Him, we believe in Him as He has revealed Himself in Jesus Christ (John 20:29).

2. The best evidence that faith works. The best evidence that faith works is seen in changed lives.

Years ago, I had Commander Mitsuo Fuchida speak in a church where I was pastor. It was he who dropped the first bomb on Pearl Harbor on Dec. 7, 1941, plunging the United States into World War II. It was Fuchida who radioed back to the Japanese fleet the words, "Tora, Tora, Tora," indicating the attack was on.

After the war, Fuchida was handed a gospel tract at a Tokyo train station that resulted in Fuchida's conversion. Jacob DeShazar, a former Japanese prisoner of war, had been saved as a P.O.W. and had returned to Japan as a missionary. It was he who gave Fuchida the tract.

After reading the tract, Fuchida was saved and became a Presbyterian preacher working out of Seattle, Washington. His faith in Christ radically transformed his life.

It has ever been so as sinners have received Jesus into their hearts. Our lesson today cites numerous examples of lives transformed by faith. It is faith's "Hall of Fame" (Hebrews 11:1–40).

3. The man who forgot God. In 1879, a baby was born in Georgia, a province in southern Russia, to a humble shoemaker and his wife. As a young man he decided to become a priest and entered Tillis Theological Seminary. A year later he joined the Russian Social-Democratic Party, and a year later he was expelled from the seminary. Eventually, he became the Premier of Russia, and led Russia during the Second World War.

His name was Joseph Stalin, and, I have read, he was responsible for the deaths of 30 million people.

How could a man who started out so well end up being so evil? There is but one answer: he left God out of his life.

Verse 6 of our lesson shows us that it is impossible to please God without faith. It follows that it is impossible to build the right kind of life when faith in God is omitted.

4. Abraham, the man who looked for a better city. Our lesson writer says that "believers must live with unfulfilled promises. They look ahead by faith and lay claim to realities that are only hoped for."

It was so with Abraham, the father of the faithful. "The ultimate goal of Abraham's faith was more than Canaan. . . . [He knew it] was only a sign of the heavenly city," our writer today tells us.

I have traveled a good bit, but I have never been to Paris. I have a friend who was there recently, and he told me about the Eiffel Tower that rises majestically 984 feet over the city. He told me about the Louvre, the largest art museum in the world. He described other beautiful things about Paris, and I believe him because I trust him.

I have never been to heaven, and can tell you very little about it. But I have a Friend who lives there, and in the Revelation He has written to me about it, and I believe my Friend Jesus because I trust Him.

So, like Abraham, you and I look "for a city . . . whose builder and maker is God" (vv. 9–10).

TEACHING THE BIBLE

- *Main Idea:* Faith is something lived, not something believed.
- *Suggested Teaching Aim:* To lead adults to risk being people of faith.

A TEACHING OUTLINE

1. Use an illustration to introduce the Bible study.

2. Use posters to identify the themes of the focal passage.

3. Use questions to guide the search for biblical truth.

4. Use a paraphrase and questions to help members to give the truth a personal focus.

Introduce the Bible Study

Use "Operating by faith" from "Applying the Bible" to introduce the Bible study. Point out the lesson on the Hebrews poster you made for July 6.

Search for Biblical Truth

Make the following three strip posters:

Strip Posters	
I.	Faith Defined and Illustrated (Heb. 11:1–3)
II.	Roll Call of Faith (Heb. 11:4–38)
III.	Part of a Great Fellowship (Heb. 11:39–40)

Cut each strip, separating the Scripture reference and the heading. Tape these at random around the room.

Ask members to open their Bibles to Hebrews 11 and skim the chapter to determine which Scripture goes with which heading. Place these together on the focal wall.

Ask a volunteer to read aloud 11:1–2. Write "Seeing Is Believing" on a large strip and cut the words apart. Tape it to the focal wall. Ask: What is wrong with this statement? After members have responded, swap the first and last words so that the sentence reads "Believing Is Seeing." Point out that this would reflect Christian faith more accurately. If members have various translations, ask them to read aloud verse 1 in as many different translations as possible. Distribute paper and pencils and ask members to paraphrase this verse. (You will use these paraphrases in giving the truth a personal focus.)

Ask a volunteer to read aloud 11:6–10. Ask: Can you identify a faith principle in these verses? (Cannot please God without faith.) What does this say about our faith? (Faith is not just believing in God but living for Him.)

Ask: How did Noah's actions demonstrate faith? (Built an ark.) What does the author cite as examples of Abraham's faith? (Followed God to Canaan; dwelled in tents without owning any land.) What characteristics of faith can you identify from these two men's actions?

Ask a volunteer to read aloud 11:13–16. Ask: What characteristics of a pilgrim faith can you identify in these verses? (See "Studying the Bible.")

DISCUSS: Would you agree that the term "pilgrim" is a good one to describe believers? Why? In what ways are you like a pilgrim? In what ways are you unlike one?

Use the material in "Studying the Bible" to summarize verses 17–38.

Ask a volunteer to read aloud 11:39–40. Ask: What is the difference between Old Testament people of faith and New Testament believers? (They lived in the age of promise; we live in the age of fulfillment.) What difference does this make in eternity? (None. All shall be in Christ's presence.)

Give the Truth a Personal Focus

Ask several volunteers to read aloud their definitions of faith. Ask: What made the people listed in this chapter believe enough in God to risk even their lives for Him? How can we develop that same depth of faith? What steps do you need to take to accomplish this? What would you like to accomplish if you had enough faith?

Remind members that a deep faith is not a guarantee for safe passage through life; it may be just the opposite. Ask: Why do you think these heroes of faith did what they did? What would it take for you to follow in their footsteps?

Close in prayer that all will be willing to risk more for God.

Renew Commitment

Basic Passage: Hebrews 12:1–11
Focal Passage: Hebrews 12:1–11

Throughout our study of Hebrews, we have seen how doctrinal sections are followed with exhortations to practical actions. The great roll call of faith in chapter 11 thus leads to the exhortations of chapter 12. The examples of faith of Old Testament believers lead to a call for Christians to renew their own commitment to the Lord.

Study Aim: *To describe the kind of renewed commitment called for as a result of reviewing the Old Testament heroes of faith*

STUDYING THE BIBLE

OUTLINE AND SUMMARY

I. The Christian Marathon (Heb. 12:1–4)
- **1. Run with perseverance (v. 1)**
- **2. Fix your attention on Jesus (vv. 2–4)**

II. Enduring Opposition and Suffering (Heb. 12:5–11)
- **1. Suffering and sonship (vv. 5–8)**
- **2. Suffering and God's purpose (vv. 9–11)**

The Christian life is like a long-distance race for which believers need perseverance (v. 1). Jesus is Christians' example and helper in this race as He helps us follow Him in the way of the cross (vv. 2–4). When we are tempted to let troubles discourage us, we should remember that suffering is a sign of sonship (vv. 5–8). Although trouble is painful, God sometimes uses it to fulfill His good purpose in and among His people (vv. 9–11).

I. The Christian Marathon (Heb. 12:1–4)

1. Run with perseverance (v. 1)

1 Wherefore seeing we also are compassed about with so great a cloud of witnesses, let us lay aside every weight, and the sin which doth so easily beset us, and let us run with patience the race that is set before us,

Often the Bible compares the Christian life to an athletic contest. Paul was especially fond of this analogy. He referred to wrestling (Eph. 6:12) and boxing (1 Cor. 9:26–27), but his favorite athletic comparison was racing (1 Cor. 9:24–25; Gal. 2:2; Phil. 3:13–14). As Paul faced death, he wrote: "I have fought a good fight, I have finished my course, I have kept the faith" (2 Tim. 4:7).

The comparison of life to a race was developed in a powerful way in Hebrews 12:1–2. The word "wherefore" shows that the truths of chapter 11 are now to be applied. The author challenged his readers to picture themselves as athletes competing in a race. In the stands were the heroes of faith described in chapter 11. When this picture is applied to the present, we must picture the stands enlarged to include the generations of people of faith who have lived and died during and since New Testament times.

The heroes of faith are more than spectators to our race. They are called a "great cloud of witnesses." They are witnesses to the reality of spiritual and eternal things. They themselves successfully completed the race in their day. They persevered in the face of many obstacles because they believed in God and His promises. Their purpose is to encourage and challenge us to do the same in our own day.

Verse 1 describes some preparations that are necessary for successfully running the race. For example, runners get rid of excess weight and any equipment that may trip them up or slow them down. In the Christian race, we must "lay aside every weight, and the sin which doth so easily beset us." The "weight" represents anything that hinders believers' faithfulness to Christ. This may be something good in its proper place; but if it diverts from life's true priorities, it should be laid aside.

Sin in a Christian's life is the worst hindrance to running the race. People in the first century wore long robes. When they prepared to run, they had to remove or tie up the robes; otherwise, the robes would entangle their legs and feet. The words "which doth so easily beset us" may have been comparing sin to the entangling effect of long robes on a runner. Or the author may have had in mind a specific sin that each person considers "a besetting sin," to which that person was specially vulnerable. Believers in the race of life cannot be burdened down with sin and guilt. Sin must be confessed and forsaken.

The key word in verse 1 is "patience." The Greek word is not the word that means patient waiting. Instead, it is the word meaning endurance or perseverance. This word, used throughout Hebrews, means to continue steadfast in the face of trials and temptations. Thus the Christian life is like a long-distance run, not a short dash to a finish line. Success in a short dash depends on exerting every effort in a tremendous burst of speed. However, speed is not the primary component in a long-distance run. Success instead depends on the proper balance of speed and endurance. Hebrews stresses the kind of dogged "stick-to-it-ive-ness" needed to keep going in spite of any obstacle.

2. Fix your attention on Jesus (vv. 2–4)

> 2 Looking unto Jesus the author and finisher of our faith; who for the joy that was set before him endured the cross, despising the shame, and is set down at the right hand of the throne of God.

Although the heroes of faith are in the stands cheering us on, our eyes are not turned toward them. Instead, our eyes are fixed on Jesus. We must turn our eyes from all distractions and fix our attention on Him.

The word "author" can be translated "pioneer" (see comments on Heb. 2:10 in the lesson for July 13). He is the trailblazer who ventured into unknown territory on our behalf and then returned to lead us along the trail He has blazed. The human examples of faith in chapter 11 inspire later believers by their examples, but Jesus surpasses them in two important respects. On one hand, Jesus is the only perfect example of faith. His entire earthly life testifies to His perfect trust in the Father. In addition, Jesus is much more than a good example. He saves, sustains, and strengthens believers in the life of faith.

The best commentary on the word "joy" in verse 2 is Jesus' use of the word in the closing chapters of John's Gospel. Jesus said, "These things have I spoken unto you, that my joy might remain in you, and that your joy might be full" (John 15:11; see also John 16:20–24; 17:3). His joy came from fulfilling God's mission so that believers might share the life and joy that God offers.

3 For consider him that endured such contradiction of sinners against himself, lest ye be wearied and faint in your minds.

4 Ye have not yet resisted unto blood, striving against sin.

In verses 3–4, the author of Hebrews helped his readers contrast their suffering with what Jesus had suffered. Although many of them had successfully endured an earlier period of persecution (10:32–34), verse 3 implies that some of them were faltering in the face of the growing hostility of an unbelieving world. The author of Hebrews reminded his readers that Jesus had endured far greater hostility than they had faced. Their resistance against sin had not yet resulted in loss of life, but Jesus had given His life. The words "not yet" in verse 4 imply that they eventually might be faced with a persecution that would result in death.

The author's purpose was not to shame his readers but to challenge them. He wanted to force them back to the basic nature of a commitment to Christ. Jesus' invitation was to take up our cross and follow Him (Luke 9:23).

II. Enduring Opposition and Suffering (Heb. 12:5–11)

In the face of unexplained suffering, people ask: "Why?" People who ask this question are in good company. The Bible is filled with examples of people who asked similar questions: Job, Asaph (Ps. 73), Habakkuk, Jeremiah, John the Baptist, Paul, and even Jesus (Mark 15:34). The biblical answers to the questions do not provide a point-by-point explanation of God's purposes in suffering. Instead, the Bible challenges believers to trust God's grace even when they cannot understand. Hebrews 12:5–11 is such a challenge.

1. Suffering and sonship (vv. 5–8)

5 And ye have forgotten the exhortation that speaketh unto you as unto children, My son, despise not thou the chastening of the Lord, nor faint when thou art rebuked of him:

6 For whom the Lord loveth he chasteneth, and scourgeth every son whom he receiveth.

7 If ye endure chastening, God dealeth with you as with sons; for what son is he whom the father chasteneth not?

8 But if ye be without chastisement, whereof all are partakers, then are ye bastards, and not sons.

The author quoted Proverbs 3:11–12 to point out that suffering should assure believers that they are God's children (vv. 5–6). Just as earthly fathers discipline their children, so does the Heavenly Father discipline His (vv. 7–8). The author used this comparison to earthly fathers to make the point that God has a good and loving purpose in allowing His children to suffer.

Since human beings do not understand God's ways (Isa. 55:8–9), they cannot fathom His purposes. Therefore, they either can choose to trust Him or not to trust Him. No more basic statement of faith has been framed than the child's prayer, "God is great; God is good." When people ask us why some terrible thing happened to them, we cannot explain what we ourselves do not understand. However, we can assure them that whatever the cause of the suffering, God is at work to bring good out of it (Rom. 8:28).

2. Suffering and God's purpose (vv. 9–11)

> 9 Furthermore we have had fathers of our flesh which corrected us, and we gave them reverence: shall we not much rather be in subjection unto the Father of spirits and live?
>
> 10 For they verily for a few days chastened us after their own pleasure; but he for our profit, that we might be partakers of his holiness.
>
> 11 Now no chastening for the present seemeth to be joyous, but grievous: nevertheless afterward it yieldeth the peaceable fruit of righteousness unto them which are exercised thereby.

Verses 9–11 probe further into the Father's purpose in suffering. Earthly fathers discipline their children for a short time according to their limited understandings, but God disciplines us "for our profit, that we might be partakers of his holiness" (v. 10). The best earthly fathers seek to discipline their children to prepare them for life's opportunities and responsibilities. The Heavenly Father disciplines His children for life and eternity.

The point is that suffering sometimes becomes a learning and growing experience out of which people become better persons. This insight about suffering is affirmed at many points in the Scriptures (Rom. 5:3–5; James 1:2–3; 1 Pet. 1:3–7). However, it is presented differently from the commonplace wisdom that suffering automatically makes better people of us. One difference is that the Bible magnifies God's role in transforming people. A person may become a worse person in the face of suffering. Only by God's grace can people be refined by the fires of suffering.

Another difference between commonplace wisdom and biblical teachings is that God is transforming people for more than earthly life; He is taking the long look from the perspective of eternity. Thus the Bible contrasts the pain and frustration of present sufferings with the future glory for which believers are being prepared. This contrast is implied in verse 11. (See also Rom. 8:18; 2 Cor. 4:17–18.)

This positive explanation of suffering is much easier to affirm when people are not suffering than when they are. "Now no chasteneth for the present seemeth to be joyous, but grievous" (v. 11). Character is learned in the school of suffering, but none of us is standing in line to enroll.

APPLYING THE BIBLE

1. "Go about your business." A large, magnificent building was being built in London, and a place was prepared for a large clock. For some time the man responsible for inscribing a motto on the face of the clock had waited for instructions. When he had waited as long as he could, he began to ask the superintendent daily, "What do you want on the face of the clock?" Exasperated, the superintendent shouted back at the workman, "Go about your business!"

Mistaking the superintendent's angry words for the answer the workman needed, he inscribed those words on the clock in bold print. But the response of the people was so favorable that the words were allowed to remain.

In verse 1 of our lesson, the writer told his readers in the first century, and us in our day, to go about our business of serving Christ. To do so, he writes, we must lay aside "every weight" that hinders us, that we might serve our Lord to the very best.

2. Eyes only for Jesus. The late Norman Vincent Peale told about visiting Breendonk, an infamous Nazi prison midway between Antwerp and Brussels, Belgium. During the Nazi occupation of Belgium in World War II, the Nazis took loyal Belgium citizens who opposed the Nazi tyranny and kept them in cages like animals.

As the guide led Peale and his friends down the long tunnel with cages on either side, Peale asked, "How could people live in conditions so miserable?"

"I will show you the answer," the guide replied. Taking Peale to one of the darkest cells, he pointed out on the wall of the cell a crudely scratched outline of the face of Jesus.

"When things were the hardest for those men, when let out of their cells briefly, they would come in here and one by one put their hands on His face. Among them was my father. It was their way of remembering they were not alone."

Alone? No, we are not alone, however difficult our days may be (vv. 2–3). We must keep looking unto Jesus.

3. The Father's discipline. I can still hear the sound of my father's belt clearing all the loops on his trousers with a buzzing noise as I bent over as a boy to take my "licking." I can hear him even today saying to a ten-year-old boy, "Son, this hurts me more than it hurts you!" I didn't understand it then, but I do now.

The New International Version better translates verse 7: "Endure hardship as discipline; God is treating you as sons. For what son is not disciplined by his father?"

Divine discipline is a mark of sonship, the writer is saying. When our sons were growing up, their mother and I would discipline them when they were wrong. That might include a spanking, or the taking of certain privileges away from them. More than once I wanted to "whale" my neighbors' children, but I never did because they did not belong to me. They were not my sons.

Even so, God disciplines His sons and daughters when they sin and will not repent. He does it because they belong to Him and He loves them. The object of God's discipline is to develop character, trust, and obedience in His children.

4. Chastening brings us back. Harold John Ockenga says that "just as soon as we are out of touch with the Lord we become harsh in our judgment, censorious, irritable, provocative and incapable of participating in the joy of Christian living. Such a state is evident to those who are spiritual.[1]

How true this is. God won't let us go on and on that way because He loves us too much. He will step in with His discipline, which at the time may puzzle and hurt us, but not for long. Verse 11 explains how it works: "No chastening at the time seemeth to be joyous . . . nevertheless afterward it yieldeth the peaceable fruit of righteousness."

Most of us, as we look back across our Christian lives, can give a hearty "amen" to that.

TEACHING THE BIBLE

- *Main Idea:* Believers are called constantly to renew their commitment to the Lord.
- *Suggested Teaching Aim:* To lead adults to identify steps they will take to renew their commitment to the Lord.

A TEACHING OUTLINE

1. Use an illustration to introduce the Bible study.
2. Use a poster as a silent teacher.
3. Use Bible search, lecture, and group discussion to search for biblical truth.
4. Use thought questions and writing a commitment to give the truth a personal focus.

Introduce the Bible Study

Use "Eyes only for Jesus" in "Applying the Bible" to introduce the Bible study. Point out the lesson on the Hebrews poster you made for July 6.

Search for Biblical Truth

IN ADVANCE, prepare a poster with the words, "Character is learned in the school of suffering, but none of us is standing in line to enroll." Place this on the wall.

Ask members to open their Bibles to Hebrews 12:1–4. Use the information in "Studying the Bible" to set the context, especially the material on "wherefore." Ask: What two actions described in verse 1 does the believer need to do to get ready for the race? (Lay aside weights; run with patience.) Let members suggest what these weights may be. Ask: According to verse 2, how are we to run? (Eyes on Jesus.) What instruction does 12:3 give? (Consider Jesus.)

Use "Studying the Bible" to relate the author's description of Jesus: (1) the meaning of "author"; (2) Jesus as an example; (3) the "joy" Jesus received from the cross.

DISCUSS: What weights hold you back? What do you need to lay aside? Does thinking about the way Jesus was treated by sinners help you? How? Why?

Ask a volunteer to read aloud Proverbs 3:11–12. Ask members to find verses in Hebrews that sound like these verses from Proverbs (Heb. 12:5–6). Ask members to share table blessings that they or their children used when small. When someone mentions "God is great, God is good" (or you can mention it), ask members if they really believe that God is good. Point out that God's goodness is the most basic element of our belief about God; when we do not understand why we suffer, we can know that in some way God can use it for His glory and our good—even though we cannot explain how.

Call for a volunteer to read aloud verses 9–11. Ask: According to these verses, why does God punish us? (v. 10b.) Using "Studying the Bible," lecture briefly, describing the two differences between commonplace understanding of suffering and the biblical understanding of suffering: (1) the Bible magnifies God's role in transforming people; (2) God is transforming people for more than earthly life.

Affirm that we do not understand suffering and why God allows it; at times we can only rest on the knowledge that God is good even though we cannot see it at the moment. Point to the silent teacher poster you displayed.

DISCUSS: Why would you agree or disagree with this statement: "Questioning God in the face of suffering indicates that we believe He has an answer to our pain"?

Give the Truth a Personal Focus

Ask: What makes it most difficult to trust God in the midst of suffering and pain? Allow members to respond; do not condemn anyone because of a response.

Distribute paper and pencils. On a chalkboard or a large sheet of paper write, "God is Good." Ask: What steps do you need to take to affirm that statement?

Allow time for thinking about this statement. Ask members to write one or two steps they can take to help them deepen their commitment to God's will even though they may not be able to understand it.

Close by having a time of prayer where members can voice their desire for a deeper commitment to Christ.

---

1. Harold John Ockenga, *Preaching for Today* (Grand Rapids: William B. Eerdmans Publishing Co., 1959), 94.

Accept Responsibilities

Basic Passage: Hebrews 13
Focal Passage: Hebrews 13:1–16

Hebrews begins like a sermon and ends like a letter. The final chapter contains a number of exhortations about various aspects of Christian living in addition to some personal words from the author. The emphasis in this lesson is on the responsibilities that we are called to accept as followers of Christ.

Study Aim: *To identify responsibilities of those who faithfully follow Christ*

STUDYING THE BIBLE

OUTLINE AND SUMMARY

I. Demands of Love (Heb. 13:1–6)
  1. Brothers, strangers, and prisoners (vv. 1–3)
  2. Faithfulness in marriage (v. 4)
  3. Love of money (vv. 5–6)
II. Following Christ (Heb. 13:7–16)
  1. Leaders and the Leader (vv. 7–8)
  2. The danger of being led astray (vv. 9–11)
  3. Way of the cross (vv. 12–14)
  4. Priesthood of believers (vv. 15–16)
III. Personal Words (Heb. 13:17–25)

Believers should love their brothers in Christ, strangers in need of hospitality, and prisoners in need of help (vv. 1–3). Faithful love in marriage is essential (v. 4). Replace covetousness with contentment (vv. 5–6). Imitate leaders' faith in the unchanging Christ (vv. 7–8). True religion is an inward experience of God's grace, not such externals as what a person eats (vv. 9–11). In order to save people, Jesus endured rejection, abuse, and death; and those who follow Him must follow Him in the way of the cross (vv. 12–14). Christians' lives are sacrifices of praise to God and service to others (vv. 15–16). Believers should pray for others and let God work in and through their lives (vv. 17–25).

I. Demands of Love (Heb. 13:1–6)

1. Brothers, strangers, and prisoners (vv. 1–3)

1 Let brotherly love continue.

2 Be not forgetful to entertain strangers, for thereby some have entertained angels unawares.

3 Remember them that are in bonds, as bound with them; and them which suffer adversity, as being yourselves also in the body.

The Greek word translated "brotherly love" is not the usual word for Christian love, *agape.* Instead, the author used a word that emphasized the warmth of a family relationship.

Not only were Christians to love their local family of faith, but also they were to show love toward fellow Christians who were strangers. In the ancient world, travelers were dependent on hospitality. Few inns existed, and most were dangerous and expensive places to stay; therefore, Christians were dependent on the hospitality of fellow believers. Traveling evangelists and missionaries were especially dependent on Christian hospitality. By showing hospitality to travelers, some people (like Abraham and Sarah) had "entertained angels unawares" (v. 2; see Gen. 18).

Earlier, the author had commended his readers for showing compassion to fellow Christians who suffered ridicule and imprisonment (10:32–34). Believers who tried to aid prisoners ran the risk of being imprisoned themselves. Believers were to help fellow believers in prison because they themselves were "also in the body" (v. 3). The point is that they should recognize their oneness with those in prison.

2. Faithfulness in marriage (v. 4)

4 Marriage is honorable in all, and the bed undefiled: but whoremongers and adulterers God will judge.

The family is crucial to God's purpose, and marriage is the foundation of the home. Love and marriage go together. The sex act is the way in which one person makes a total commitment to another person in an atmosphere of responsible love. Marriage is the relationship in which a man and a woman express this kind of love. Therefore, the Bible sanctifies sex in marriage and condemns the misuse of sex for other purposes.

3. Love of money (vv. 5–6)

5 Let your conversation be without covetousness; and be content with such things as ye have: for he hath said, I will never leave thee, nor forsake thee.

6 So that we may boldly say, The Lord is my helper, and I will not fear what man shall do unto me.

The word translated "conversation" means way of life. Our way of life is not to be determined by covetousness or love of material things. Instead we are to be content with what we have. Jesus warned against anxiety about material things (Matt. 6:19–34). Paul exemplified gratitude and contentment with what God provides (Phil. 3:6–13).

The author of Hebrews reinforced his warning against covetousness with two quotations. The quotation in verse 5 recalls the Lord's promise to Israel and Joshua before they entered Canaan (Deut. 31:6; Josh. 1:5). The quotation in verse 6 is from Psalm 118:6. In times of trouble, persons who love money may be tempted to compromise. Christ has promised to help us in such times; therefore, we need not fear what may happen.

II. Following Christ (Heb. 13:7–16)

1. Leaders and the Leader (vv. 7–8)

7 Remember them which have the rule over you, who have spoken unto you the word of God: whose faith follow, considering the end of their conversation.

8 Jesus Christ the same yesterday, and to day, and forever.

The author of Hebrews challenged his readers to imitate the faith of past leaders. "The end of their conversation" referred to how they lived and died. Just as chapter 11 challenged them to imitate the faith of Old Testament believers, so verse 7 challenged them to imitate the faith of dedicated Christians they had known, especially those who spoke God's word to them.

Dedicated Christian leaders do not exalt themselves; they exalt Christ. Human leaders come and go, but Christ remains sufficient in every generation. Christ was totally adequate for people of faith in earlier generations. He is totally adequate today. No matter what the future brings, He will remain the same.

2. The danger of being led astray (vv. 9–11)

9 Be not carried about with divers and strange doctrines. For it is a good thing that the heart be established with grace; not with meats, which have not profited them that have been occupied therein.

10 We have an altar, whereof they have no right to eat which serve the tabernacle.

11 For the bodies of those beasts, whose blood is brought into the sanctuary by the high priest for sin, are burned without the camp.

The author of Hebrews feared his readers might be led astray from the complete adequacy of Christ by "divers and strange doctrines." He warned about teachings that emphasized what people ate rather than the grace they experienced in their hearts. Whatever the exact background to verse 9, the author's main point is clear: True religion is an inward and personal experience with the God of grace, not such externals as what a person eats.

This point is reinforced in verses 10–12. Unfortunately, the argument is hard to follow for later generations who are unfamiliar with the Jewish sacrificial system. The key seems to be the author's contrast between two kinds of sacrifices. One kind was eaten by the people; the other was not. After most animals were sacrificed, parts of the animals were eaten by priests and people (Exod. 12:8; Lev. 22:29–30). By contrast, no part of the sacrifices on the Day of Atonement was eaten (Heb. 13:11; Lev. 16:27).

Building on the Old Testament foundation concerning sacrifices, keep in mind three emphases in Hebrews: (1) Jesus fulfilled what happened on the Day of Atonement (9:25–26; 13:12). (2) Some readers of Hebrews were attracted to the old covenant's rituals. (3) The entire letter is an appeal to follow Christ totally and not to be held back by adherence to the old system.

3. Way of the cross (vv. 12–14)

12 Wherefore Jesus also, that he might sanctify the people with his own blood, suffered without the gate.

13 Let us go forth therefore unto him without the camp, bearing his reproach.

14 For here have we no continuing city, but we seek one to come.

In many ways, verses 12–14 provide the climax of the Book of Hebrews. The author made the same two points that Jesus made in His call to discipleship: (1) Jesus stressed the absolute necessity of His suffering, rejection, death, and resurrection (Mark 8:31). (2) Jesus also insisted that anyone who wanted to follow Him had to deny himself, take up his cross, and follow Christ (Mark 8:34).

Notice how the same two themes are brought together in Hebrews 13:12–13. During the wilderness period of the Old Testament, the camp represented holy ground. Criminals were punished outside the camp (Lev. 24:14, 23). Sin offerings were burned outside the camp (Heb. 13:11). In New Testament times, Jerusalem (the holy city) and the temple (the holy place) replaced the camp. When Jesus was crucified, He was led outside the gates of the holy city and crucified with criminals.

Jesus died in an unholy place and in an unholy way, but God used Him to make believers holy ("sanctify the people with his own blood," v. 12). Not only did Jesus die outside the gate, but He is still outside the gate. Verse 13 calls us to "go forth to him without the camp, bearing his reproach." Some readers of Hebrews were tempted to cling to the supposed security of the holy city and holy temple. The author of Hebrews challenged them to follow Christ and to risk sharing His reproach. After all, on this earth "we have no continuing city, but we seek one to come" (v. 14). This sounds the call to believers in every generation—to follow Jesus in the way of the cross.

4. Priesthood of believers (vv. 15–16)

15 By him let us offer the sacrifice of praise to him continually, that is, the fruit of our lips giving thanks to his name.

16 But to do good and to communicate forget not: for with such sacrifices God is well pleased.

The Book of Hebrews is a primary source for the doctrine of priesthood of all believers. The most familiar aspect of this doctrine is that believers do not need any other human priest to stand between them and God. Jesus Christ is our High Priest who has opened the way for each believer to come boldly to God's throne of grace (Heb. 4:16).

Hebrews 13:15–16 focuses on an equally crucial aspect of the priesthood of believers. Priests are expected to offer sacrifices with which God is well pleased. Paul described the basic sacrifice in Romans 12:1. We are to present ourselves as living sacrifices to God. Verses 15–16 describe two kinds of sacrifices that every believer is to offer to God. Verse 15 describes the sacrifice of praise that Christians are to offer to God in worship through prayers and songs. Verse 16 focuses on another category of sacrifices that Christians are prone to neglect even more—service to others, especially the generous sharing of material blessings.

III. Personal Words (Heb. 13:17–25)

The readers were challenged to obey their leaders (v. 17). They were to pray for the author, who himself was apparently one of the leaders, that he might soon be restored to them (vv. 18–19). The author pronounced on his readers the blessing of the God of peace (vv. 20–21). He challenged them to heed the exhortation they had received (v. 22). Timothy had been set free and would come to them shortly (v. 23). Greetings and a final blessing were sent to all (vv. 24–25).

APPLYING THE BIBLE

1. If you really cared. I once picked up an old man and took him to a mall in which there was a large cafeteria. I had been told about the old man. Years earlier, he had been won to Christ as he took shelter one cold night in the doorway of a building in Detroit. "He walks our town," my friend said, "carrying an old Bible and witnessing to everyone he meets."

I let the old man out and offered him a few dollars. To my surprise he walked off indignantly. Surprised that I had offended him, I got out of my car and walked over to him.

"If you had *really* cared for me, you would not have offered me money. You would have gone into the cafeteria, bought my meal, and sat with me."

I had been soundly rebuked. That evening I bought Jesus a cup of coffee, a boiled egg, and a piece of apricot pie! (See Matt. 25:40; Heb. 13:2–3)

2. The sanctity of sex. Pastor Nelson Price presents these interesting statements from some of the world's greatest psychologists:

- Dr. Francis J. Braceland, former president of the American Psychiatric Association said, "Premarital sex relations resulting from the so-called new morality have greatly increased the number of young people in mental hospitals."
- Dr. Eric Fromm, internationally known psychoanalyst, said that the current sexual freedoms in no way contribute to a true sense of aliveness or richness of experience. There is a frustrating emptiness that follows.
- New York psychiatrist Franz Winkler related that his case studies belie the statement that premarital sex is advisable preparation for marriage. He concluded that the more satisfactory the premarital sex relation the more unsatisfactory the marital sex relation. He identified psychological mental blocks growing out of guilt and suspicion as the cause.

Can this guilt over premarital sex be laid at the feet of the church and Christian teachings? No! Guilt comes because the sin violates both the character and word of God (v. 4)[1]

3. The curse of covetousness (vv. 5–6). What does "covet" mean? According to the dictionary, it is "to desire inordinately; to long for that which is unlawful to obtain or possess." According to Ephesians 5:5–6 it is idolatry. Idolatry is putting someone or something in the place of God. According to the verses just cited, a covetous person is an idolater and no such person "hath any inheritance in the kingdom of Christ and of God."

4. Christ is adequate. British theologian H. Wheeler Robinson (1872–1945) once slipped into a Paris cathedral and stood at the back of the church. The choir was singing "Lamb of God, who takes away the sin of the world, have mercy on us." Robinson noticed a poorly dressed old man standing beside him. As the choir sang, the man nervously twisted an old hat he held in his hand. Then the man suddenly muttered, "Oh God! Oh God, what a dream! If only He could. If only He could!" With that, the man turned and ran from the church.

Is it only a dream? Can Jesus take away the sin of the world? Has he taken away your sin?

The writer to the Hebrews confidently affirms that Jesus can and does (vv. 8–11). We need no other sacrifice for our sin.

TEACHING THE BIBLE

- *Main Idea:* Christians have responsibilities toward Christ and toward fellow believers.
- *Suggested Teaching Aim:* To lead adults to identify responsibilities toward Christ and others they will accept.

A TEACHING OUTLINE

1. Use an illustration to introduce the Bible study.
2. Use a poster/chart to guide the search for biblical truth.
3. Use a lecture to explain difficult concepts.
4. Use a review to challenge members to accept responsibilities of the Christian life.
5. Use an illustration to give a brief invitation if you have unsaved members present.

Introduce the Bible Study

Use "If you really cared" from "Applying the Bible" to introduce the Bible study. Point out the lesson on the Hebrews poster you made for July 6.

Search for Biblical Truth

On a large sheet of paper or a chalkboard write: *Believers should accept the responsibility of. . . .* Leave room under the heading to write eight phrases. Ask members to open their Bibles to Hebrews 13:1–6. Ask a volunteer to read aloud these verses. Ask: What responsibility does the author of Hebrews suggest in verse 1 that believers should accept? (In all of these responses, use members' suggestions, but the responses here should be similar to "Caring about other believers.") What responsibility in verse 2? (Hospitality.) What responsibility in verse 3? (Helping prisoners.)

DISCUSS: What thread do you see running through all three of these responsibilities? How well do you think Christians as a whole fulfill these?

Ask a volunteer to read aloud verses 4–7. Ask: What responsibility does the author suggest in verse 4? (Faithfulness in marriage.) In verses 5–6? (Generosity.) In verse 7? (Support of church staff.)

DISCUSS: How difficult are these responsibilities to fulfill? Why are they so hard? Which responsibility in verses 1–6 is most important? Why? Which is the hardest to fulfill? Why?

Ask a volunteer to read aloud 13:7–14, preferably in a modern translation. Prepare a lecture to explain the difficult concepts in these verses. Cover the following points: (1) Jesus is sufficient, so don't be led astray (vv. 8–9); (2) true religion is an inward and personal experience with God (see "Studying the Bible" for explanation of the two contrasting sacrifices); (3) point out the three emphases in Hebrews mentioned in "Studying the Bible"; (4) explain the relationship between sacrificing outside the camp and Jesus' sacrifice on the cross. On the poster write, *Trusting only in Jesus.*

Ask a volunteer to read aloud 13:15–16. Ask: What does the priesthood of the believer mean to you? After several members have responded, point out the two aspects of the doctrine in these verses: (1) offering praise to God (as priests), and (2) ministering to others. On the poster write, *Practicing the priesthood of the believer.*

DISCUSS: How good a job do you do of practicing the priesthood of the believer?

Give the Truth a Personal Focus

Briefly review the lesson by reading the statements from the poster. Ask members which statements they need to apply to their lives.

If you have unsaved members present, you might want to use "Christ is adequate" in "Applying the Bible." If you can do so under the Holy Spirit's leadership, urge them to accept the responsibility of trusting only in Christ for their salvation.

---

1. Nelson Price, *Shadows We Run From* (Nashville: Broadman Press, 1976) 91–94.

Respect for Human Life

Basic Passages: Genesis 1:27; Matthew 5:13–16,2 1–22, 27–28, 43–45a

Focal Passages: Genesis 1:27; Matthew 5:13–16, 21–22, 27–28, 43–45a

This is a special lesson for those who want such a lesson on Sanctity of Human Life Sunday. Many Bible passages support sanctity of human life. This lesson builds on the foundational teaching about the source of life in Genesis 1:27 and then examines passages from the Sermon on the Mount about respect for human life.

Study Aim: *To oppose abortion and all practices that show a lack of respect and appreciation for human life*

STUDYING THE BIBLE

OUTLINE AND SUMMARY

I. Source of Life (Gen. 1:27)

II. Respect for Life (Matt. 5:13–16, 21–22, 27–28, 43–45a)

1. **Role in society (Matt. 5:13–16)**
2. **Value of human life (Matt. 5:21–22)**
3. **Purity in relationships (Matt. 5:27–28)**
4. **Respect in action (Matt. 5:43–45a)**

God created male and female human beings in His own image (Gen. 1:27). Believers are so to live that their lives serve as an example that leads others to lifestyles that are wholesome and beneficial to all (Matt. 5:13–16). Followers of Jesus are neither to take human life nor to indulge emotions that lead to hostile acts (Matt. 5:21–22). Christians are not to commit adultery or even to lust after others (Matt. 5:27–28). Believers are to show their respect for all people by loving them, blessing them, doing good to them, and praying for them (Matt. 5:43–45a).

I. Source of Life (Gen. 1:27)

27 So God created man in his own image, in the image of God created he him; male and female created he them.

The early chapters of Genesis contain foundational teachings for all basic biblical teachings. None is so foundational as that God is the Creator of His good creation, and that human beings were created in God's own image. God breathed the breath of life into all living creatures, but only humans were created in His own image.

Humans are like the rest of creation in many ways, but we are also different in this important respect. We share the image of the God who made us. None of us understands all that this means, but it surely means that we were made with a unique capacity for relating to the God who made us. We are capable of loving and worshiping God.

All life is valuable for the purpose God made it, but human life is supremely valuable because of this capacity for knowing and serving God. After the flood, when God made His covenant with humanity, He based the prohibition of murder on the fact that humans are in the image of God (Gen. 9:6).

II. Respect for Life (Matt. 5:13–16, 21–22, 27–28, 43–45a)

1. Role in society (Matt. 5:13–16)

> 13 Ye are the salt of the earth: but if the salt have lost his savour, wherewith shall it be salted? it is thenceforth good for nothing, but to be cast out, and to be trodden under foot of men.
>
> 14 Ye are the light of the world. A city that is set on an hill cannot be hid.
>
> 15 Neither do men light a candle and put it under a bushel, but on a candlestick; and it giveth light unto all that are in the house.
>
> 16 Let your light so shine before men, that they may see your good works, and glorify your Father which is in heaven.

Salt was especially valuable in ancient society. It had many uses, but its primary value was as a preservative. As salt was used to preserve food from spoiling and ruin, so were followers of Jesus to be a preserving force in a corrupting society. Disciples of Jesus who fail in this crucial role are judged to be like salt without savor, "good for nothing."

The purpose of light is to shine and enlighten. As Jesus noted, no one lights a candle and then hides its light. Instead, the candle is used so that people might see. A city on a hill cannot be hid if even one candle is shining.

Jesus used these two simple analogies to commission His followers to a crucial role in the world. He called us the "salt of the earth" and the "light of the world." He has given us a crucial task and invested us with a great trust. We are to be a preserving force in the moral decay of a sinful world. We are to shine the light of God's judgment and salvation into the dark corners of life. Examples of moral decay abound: pornography, injustice, exploitation, violence, taking of helpless human life, and a multitude of other evils. Beginning with our own children, other youth, and peers, Christian adults can be salt and light.

Our goal is not to call attention to ourselves, either as reformers or deliverers. Our goal is to be instruments of the God of light in salvation and grace. After all, Jesus said that when they see our good works, they are not to praise us, but to "glorify your Father which is in heaven."

2. Value of human life (Matt. 5:21–22)

> 21 Ye have heard that it was said by them of old time, Thou shalt not kill; and whosoever shall kill shall be in danger of the judgment:
>
> 22 But I say unto you, That whosoever is angry with his brother without a cause shall be in danger of the judgment: but whosoever shall say to his brother, Raca, shall be in danger of the council: and whosoever shall say, Thou fool, shall be in danger of hell fire.

Jesus cited a number of examples of the demands of the kingdom of heaven that exceeded the traditional morality of the Pharisees (Matt.

5:20). All recognized the prohibition of murder in the Sixth Commandment (Exod. 20:13). Jesus went behind the act of murder to the attitudes that sometimes lead to murder. He condemned harboring wrath in one's heart toward another person. There is such a thing as righteous indignation, but most human anger is selfish and destructive.

Jesus condemned the kind of hatred that results in abusive speech to others. The words translated "raca" and "thou fool" were insulting terms of contempt. Jesus said that those whose hatred was so great courted the judgment of hell just as did those who actually were guilty of murder.

Jesus was not saying that hatred causes the same tragic result as actual murder. He was saying that hatred can lead to murder and that it is sinful even when it doesn't. For example, God warned Cain of murderous thoughts that he needed to control (Gen. 4:6–7). Those thoughts were sinful; but presumably if Cain had heeded God's warning, Abel's life might have been spared. Unfortunately, Cain kept feeding those evil thoughts; and this led him to murder his brother.

Verses 21–22 not only warn against murder and hatred but also affirm that all human beings should be treated with dignity and respect. Human life is taken and people are abused when such respect is missing from people's attitudes and beliefs. Every person—including the pre-born—deserves to be treated with dignity and respect. Such respect begins with every person's right to life, but it also includes the right to a life free from abuse and exploitation.

3. Purity in relationships (Matt. 5:27–28)

> 27 Ye have heard that it was said by them of old time, Thou shalt not commit adultery:
>
> 28 But I say unto you, That whosoever looketh upon a woman to lust after her hath committed adultery with her already in his heart.

Jesus referred to another of the Ten Commandments, the Seventh Commandment (Exod. 20:14). Jesus affirmed the prohibition against adultery. The family is the foundation of society and the basic arena for human relations. Marriage is the foundation for the home. No family can exist without the faithfulness and trust of husband and wife within the one-flesh union of marriage (Gen. 2:24). Thus adultery destroys the fabric of the most sacred of human relations.

As in the case with murder, Jesus went behind the actual act to the attitude and motive. He condemned not only adultery but also looking on another person with lust. Again, Jesus was not saying that lust does the same harm as the actual act of adultery. If that were His point, a man might say, "I am already guilty of lusting after her; I may as well go ahead and commit adultery." Jesus' point was that lust is what feeds sexual immorality; and even when lust doesn't lead to adultery, lust itself is sinful because it reduces another person to a sex object.

Our society pays little attention to what Jesus taught. Several years ago, the press made fun of a presidential candidate who referred to his efforts to honor this particular teaching of Jesus. The prevailing mood of our culture is sexual indulgence and unrestrained sexual activity—before marriage and outside of marriage. As a result, we live in a world where sexually transmitted diseases flourish and where abortions on demand are used as a method of birth control.

At the root of many of these problems is the prevailing view of many people that everyone should be completely free to have sex with any other person. Our culture promotes and popularizes this deadly view by all kinds of attractive propaganda. The sexual promiscuity and outrageous behavior of media figures are proudly displayed for the young to follow. Those who believe the Bible are facing a tremendous challenge in trying to buck this tide, but some progress is being made. Dedicated adults and youth can set an example and present an alternative to the destructive cycle of sexual immorality and all that spawns it.

4. Respect in action (Matt. 5:43–45a)

> **43 Ye have heard that it hath been said, Thou shalt love thy neighbour, and hate thine enemy.**
>
> **44 But I say unto you, Love your enemies, bless them that curse you, do good to them that hate you, and pray for them which despitefully use you, and persecute you;**
>
> **45 That ye may be children of your Father which is in heaven:**

Jesus' teachings in the Sermon on the Mount were revolutionary, none more so than His words about loving enemies. Polite society defines love primarily as an emotion and limits the scope of such love to people we like and people who like us. Jesus challenged both the definition and the scope of this view of love. For one thing, Jesus defined love not as something we feel so much as something we do. Christian love, or *agape,* is doing good to others no matter how we may feel about them or how they may feel about us (Luke 6:27–28).

This revolutionary definition of love enables us to enlarge the scope of love to include not only neighbors and friends but also enemies. By definition, our enemies don't like us. They often do things to hurt us. Yet Jesus said that in spite of how they hurt us and make us feel, we still can do good for them. This act of good is Christian love. Jesus pointed out that this is God's kind of love. The Heavenly Father does not love people because they are worthy or because they love Him. Instead He loves us while we are yet sinners (Rom. 5:6–8).

Luke 10:25–37 illustrates Jesus' teaching. The lawyer's question, "Who is my neighbour?" (v. 29) shows that he was trying to limit those to whom he should show love. The Samaritan in Jesus' parable acted in love. He may have felt a mixture of emotions—including fear and revulsion. What counted, however, was what he did. He stopped, helped the injured man, carried him to safety, and paid for his care. He did this for someone he didn't know, but someone who was probably a Jew—an enemy of his people the Samaritans.

Any generation would be revolutionized with Christian love if followers of Jesus practiced Matthew 5:43–45a. As applied to the current turmoil in society about abortion, this passage forces each follower of Christ to face questions about how we should act toward people who hold different views and have taken different actions than we have. How can we act redemptively toward proponents, practitioners, and prospects for abortion?

APPLYING THE BIBLE

1. Someone special. We are special because we were created in God's image (Gen. 1:27). William Gladstone (1809–1898), a devout Christian who served as British Prime Minister, said about man: "Man himself is the crowning wonder of creation; the study of his nature the noblest study the world affords."

Dr. H. H. Hobbs writes: "At the end of the first five stages in creation God saw that it was 'good.' But having made man, he saw that it was 'very good.' This suggests that man is someone special in God's creative act and purpose."[1]

The question, "Where did man come from?" has been raised repeatedly through the ages. The evolutionist answers that man evolved from a lower species of life. But, Hobbs says, "The theory of evolution will never become fact until the so-called 'missing link' between ape and man is found beyond question of doubt. . . . But there is no evidence that a lower species ever climbed to a higher level."[2]

The Christian answer is that God created man in His image—"an exact duplicate," Hobbs states. Therein lies our uniqueness, our "specialness."

2. The destructive power of hate. American lawyer Clarence Darrow (1857–1938) said, "I've never murdered a man, but I have read many an obituary with pleasure."

That's what Jesus is talking about here (vv. 21–22). He is not just condemning the act of murder but also hatred in the heart that produces it. The kingdom of God exceeds traditional morality and demands more. We are to shun even evil thoughts that produce evil deeds!

British novelist Thomas Hardy (1840–1928) wrote: "Sometimes more bitterness is sown in five minutes than can be gotten rid of in a whole lifetime." That's the idea behind Jesus' words. To these thoughts, let me add the remark of the African-American educator Booker T. Washington: "No man can drag me down so low that I will hate him."

The sanctity of human life must not only keep the Christian from taking a life but also from hatred that produces murder.

3. Love of neighbors. A man named Greene was thinking about moving his family to a town named Smithdale. Stopping at a gas station, he asked the elderly attendant, "What kind of people live here? Are they nice and friendly?"

The old gentleman scratched his unshaven chin and asked, "What kind of people live in your town?"

"Oh," said the stranger, "they are the nicest and kindest people you could find anywhere."

"Well," the attendant replied, "you know, that's just the kind of people who live in Smithdale."

Another stranger stopped at the station about a week later and asked the same question. And the attendant asked, "What kind of people live in your town?"

"Oh, they are miserable people, just miserable. They are the most unfriendly, stuck-up folks we ever met. We have been miserable the whole time we have lived there."

"Well," said the old-timer, "I would like to be more encouraging, but that is exactly the kind of people you will find here!"

Our attitude toward others very often determines their attitude toward us (vv. 43–45; Luke 10:25–37).

TEACHING THE BIBLE

- *Main Idea:* To show respect for human life.
- *Suggested Teaching Aim:* To lead adults to commit themselves to respect for human life.

A TEACHING OUTLINE

1. Use a graffiti wall to introduce the Bible study.
2. Use Scripture search and discussion questions to search for biblical truth.
3. Use a chart to explore the Scripture.
4. Use thought questions to give the truth a personal focus.

Introduce the Bible Study

Place two large sheets of paper on opposite walls. On one write *What is God like?* and on the other write *What are humans like?* As members enter, ask half of them to go to one of the walls and write a brief description to answer the question. Ask the other half to go to the other wall. Begin by reading some of the descriptions. Ask: If we are created in God's image, how should we live? Suggest that today's lesson will help us discover respect for human life.

Search for Biblical Truth

Read aloud Genesis 1:27. Ask: What does the fact that God made "male" and "female" in His image indicate? (Among other things, that the verse does not refer to physical characteristics of God.) How are we like God? How are we like the rest of creation?

DISCUSS: Since humans are made in God's image, what principle or principles can you draw from that fact?

Read aloud Matthew 5:13–16. Ask: What do you think Jesus meant by calling His followers the salt of the earth and the light of the world?

DISCUSS: What can you do in your family to fulfill your role as "salt of the earth" and "light of the world"? What can you do in the world?

Read aloud Matthew 5:21–22. On a chalkboard or a large sheet of paper write, *You have heard . . . but I say to you.* Under the first phrase write *Do not murder.* Point out that this is what the Sixth Commandment said (Exod. 20:13). Ask: What did Jesus say to do? (Don't be angry with anyone.) Write this under the last part of the heading.

DISCUSS: What principle can we draw from these verses about how we should relate to people?

Read aloud Matthew 5:27–28. On the chalkboard or large sheet of paper write, *Do not commit adultery.* Point out that this is the Seventh Commandment (Exod. 20:14). Ask: But what did Jesus say to do? (Don't be lustful.) Write this under the last part of the heading. Ask: Why is adultery wrong?

DISCUSS: What principle can we draw from these verses about how we should relate to people? What do they say about abortion?

Read aloud Matthew 5:43–45a. On the chalkboard or large sheet of paper write, *Love your neighbors; hate your enemies.* Ask: What did Jesus say to do? (Love your enemies.) Write this under the last part of the heading.

DISCUSS: What would it do in even one of your relationships if you obeyed this command? What should we do about people who have violated God's laws and showed disrespect for His people? Are we to love them, too?

Give the Truth a Personal Focus

Ask: What can we do to recover the image of God in our lives? How can you show more respect for human life? What should be our response toward those who hold different views and have taken different actions than we have?

Ask members to think of the person they are most angry with. Challenge them to show respect for that person by doing something to heal the anger. Point out that although we cannot change the world, we can change one relationship.

---

1. H. H. Hobbs, *The Origin of All Things* (Waco, Tex.: Word Books, 1975), 25.
2. Ibid., 27.

INDEX

The following index gives the lesson date on which a particular passage of Scripture has been treated in Broadman Comments from September 1991 through August 1997. Since the International Bible Lessons, Uniform Series, are planned in six-year cycles, the lessons during any six consecutive years include the better-known books and passages on central teachings. Thus, anyone who has access to the 1990–96 volumes of *Comments* can use this index to find a discussion of almost any part of the Bible he or she may be interested in studying.

* Denotes alternative lesson for 3rd week January.

Ruth

I Samuel

2 Samuel

I Kings

2 Kings

2 Chronicles

Psalms

Song of Solomon

Isaiah

Jeremiah

Ezekiel

Lamentations

Hosea

Amos

Obadiah

Jonah

Micah

Nahum

Habakkuk

Zephaniah

Matthew

Mark

Luke

John

Acts

Romans

1 Corinthians

2 Corinthians

Galatians

Ephesians

Philippians

Colossians

1 Thessalonians

2 Thessalonians

1 Timothy

2 Timothy

Titus

Philemon

Hebrews

James

1 Peter

2 Peter

Revelation